NEW
BUILDING
WORD POWER

Joseph R. Orgel, Ph.D.

Author of: Enriching Your Vocabulary,
Comprehensive English in Review

**SADLIER
OXFORD**

OXFORD BOOK COMPANY

A Division of William H. Sadlier, Inc.
NEW YORK   CHICAGO   LOS ANGELES

PREFACE

"Americans have never been willing to leave the English language alone," declared a writer in *Life* magazine recently, "and the 1960's bequest of new words to the 70's is a fairly large one. But the most striking linguistic phenomenon of the 60's is old words that have acquired vivid new meanings."

One has only to note the altered face of familiar current words and phrases like *bag, camp, hawk, dialogue, drop-out, moratorium,* and *turn on* to conclude that words, like people, have a life cycle — are born, evolve, change, and die. There is hardly a modern dictionary that has failed to make radical revisions recently in order to face up to the language challenges the fast-changing world has demanded.

BUILDING WORD POWER, long popular with teachers and students as an instrument for building vocabulary and honing verbal sense, now appears in modern dress, a thoroughgoing revision to fit the language needs of the 1970's.

NEW BUILDING WORD POWER retains those features of the original version that are still valid under present-day conditions, but it has added new features in a program designed to provide a fresher, more dynamic approach to a program of vocabulary building. Many of the older Basic Words have been retired to a secondary position or have been treated in a more up-to-date fashion; many new words have been added to the core list, expanding it to 450 words. Each key word is defined simply and analyzed pointedly, with etymology, pronunciation, related forms, relevant idiomatic phrases, and significant synonyms and antonyms, with their differences, often subtle, explicitly indicated. The student is thus introduced to an overall working vocabulary of several thousand words. To insure a clear understanding of the tone and climate of a Basic Word, and the way it is used idiomatically, the word is presented in the natural context of an illustrative sentence or paragraph. This realistic treatment of word study reflects the philosophy of two eminent linguists, A. K. Ogden and I. A. Richards:

"Words mean nothing by themselves . . . it is only when a thinker makes use of them that they stand for anything, or, in one sense, have meaning. They are instruments."

The new features also include guidance in the use of handy vocabulary aids such as the thesaurus, the dictionary (especially the under-utilized but often important sections of the entries), library reference materials, and the mass media. The student is encouraged to keep a personal notebook of the *Roget's Thesaurus* type in order to record new words and phrases he may come across in his reading. The study of core words in the text is enlivened by telling quotations ranging in scope from the Bible to contemporary journalists.

Recognizing that no effective vocabulary program would be complete without a study of the family resemblances among words, recalling the evolutionary development of the language and the social organization that it reflects, the author has included in each lesson a section entitled "Word Analysis and Development." The etymology and "Fun With Words" sections highlight international verbal kinships, vogue words, blends, loan words, and adoptions from all parts of the globe, including the too often neglected civilizations of Africa.

NEW BUILDING WORD POWER is intended primarily for students in the upper two years of secondary school and in junior colleges. At either the secondary school or college level, special provision is made for students at both ends of the ability spectrum — those who by wide reading and language maturity have acquired a working vocabulary above average and seek a more advanced curriculum, and those whose word range is limited and whose expression resources are eroded by clichés or befogged by imprecision.

This is a testing age. College-bound students, in particular, are required to take scholastic aptitude tests designed to measure reading comprehension and related verbal skills. To prepare students for this challenge, the key exercises in the book have been drawn up in a realistic framework that closely resembles in form, content, and difficulty the tests set by the Educational Testing Service and similar agencies. Candidates for college admission, as well as students taking college courses, will be helped particularly by the skills gained in working the objective tests dealing with analogies, one-word and two-word omissions, and reading comprehension passages.

The words that make up the Basic Word List have been chosen from word-frequency studies like the Lorge-Thorndike Semantic Count and other reputable measurement scales, as well as vocabulary criteria set by representative secondary school curricula. A prime reason for selection is the currency of the basic words and their ability to meet the student's expression needs, to stimulate his curiosity about words, and to broaden his verbal power. Some of the words are necessarily difficult for the average student, but they are considered all but indispensable to anyone seeking effective functional vocabulary equipment. None of the words is esoteric.

A number of standard dictionaries, such as the Random House Dictionary (unabridged), the American College Dictionary, Webster's New International Dictionary, the Winston Senior Dictionary, and the American Heritage Dictionary, have been used as authorities for definitions, etymologies, and pronunciation. The ultimate responsibility for judgment, however, lies in all cases with the author.

Aristophanes said it well: "By words the mind is excited and the spirit elated." Besides yielding pegs to hang ideas on and promoting academic success, a book about words can be great fun. With this view in mind the author has included a wide variety of exercises that will be found novel, intellectually stimulating, and it is hoped genuinely entertaining.

On the basis of many years of experience with the original version of this text, the author has every confidence that the program presented in NEW BUILDING WORD POWER will add significantly to the student's active vocabulary in writing, reading, and oral communication. Beyond this, it is hoped that the text will stimulate a wholesome interest in words and language, and a greater respect for verbal precision and clear thinking.

J.R.O.

CONTENTS

VII

VIII

LESSON ONE

1. abate
2. abet
3. abhor
4. abject
5. abstemious

6. abstruse
7. accessory
8. accord
9. acquit
10. acrimonious

1. **a-bate** ȧ-bāt′ [*abatre, abattre* (Old French); from *a*, "to" + *battre*, "to beat"] — To lessen in intensity, violence, amount.

The storm, which had been raging for hours, *abated* in time for us to set out on our hike.

Related Form: abatement

Synonyms: subside, slacken, ebb, wane, diminish (*noun:* diminution), moderate, recede (*noun:* recession; *adjective:* recessive), mitigate, alleviate

Antonyms: increase, intensify, heighten, augment, aggravate

Note 1: In law, to <u>abate</u> means "to put an end to, or annul, an action or a writ." To <u>abate</u> a nuisance is to suppress it.

Note 2: A <u>rebate</u> is "a partial refund." To <u>rebate</u> is to deduct or return part of the original or total amount; to give a discount.

2. **a-bet** ȧ-bĕt′ [*a*, "to" + *beter* (Scand.); "to bait or incite (as a bear)"] — To assist or encourage, especially in wrongdoing.

One way to *abet* juvenile delinquency, the speaker declared, is to fail to provide adequate recreational facilities in the community.

Related Form: abettor

Synonyms: instigate, incite, egg on, goad, spur, foment, connive at (meaning "to encourage secretly what one should openly oppose")

1

Antonyms: hinder, curb, restrain, dissuade, thwart, frustrate, discourage

Phrases: aid and abet an enemy

The Puritan hated bear-baiting, not because it gave pain to the bear, but because it gave pleasure to the spectators.
— MACAULAY, *History of England*

---

3. **ab-hor** ăb-hôr′ [*ab* "from" + *horrere* (Latin), "to shrink back" "to tremble at"] — To regard with horror or detestation.

"*Abhor* that which is evil; cleave to that which is good."

Related Forms: abhorrent, abhorrence

Synonyms: (*verbs*) abominate, detest, despise; (*nouns*) odium, aversion, repugnance, loathing, execration; (*adjectives*) odious, repugnant, execrable

Antonyms: (*verbs*) love, relish, cherish; (*nouns*) affection, regard, fondness

4. **ab-ject** ab′jekt ab-jekt′ [*ab*, "down" "from" + *jacere* (Latin), "to throw"]

1. Degrading; cast down in spirit or hope; wretched.

The family of the tenant farmer lived in such *abject* poverty that the children could not go to school because they lacked proper clothing.

Synonyms: disheartening, humiliating, debasing

Antonyms: proud, exalted, self-assertive

2. Mean-spirited; despicable.

Only an *abject* coward would stand by and see a defenseless woman beaten without going to her rescue.

Synonyms: mean, base, base-spirited, ignoble, disreputable

Antonyms: noble, estimable

2

3. Shamelessly servile; groveling (*verb:* grovel — "to humble oneself, as in fear or utter servility").

At the sound of thunder my dog dives under the bed in a state of utter and *abject* terror.

Synonyms: obsequious, cringing, fawning, humble, meek

Antonyms: arrogant, haughty, contemptuous, patronizing, condescending

Phrases: cap-in-hand, boot-licking
an *abject* (servile) flatterer
an *abject* (beggarly) posture

Supple knees
Feed arrogance and are the proud man's fees.
— SHAKESPEARE

---

5. ab-ste-mi-ous ăb-stē'-mĭ-ŭs [*abstemius* (Latin); from *abs*, "from" + *temetum*, "strong drink"] — Moderate, especially in the consumption of food and strong drink.

The eighty-year-old man attributes his good health to the fact that he has always been *abstemious* in his habits.

Related Forms: abstemiousness, abstemiously

Synonyms: temperate (moderate in opinion, food habits, drinking, indulgence of appetite), sparing, abstinent, moderate, ascetic; (*nouns*) forbearance (self restraint), sobriety, abstinence, abstention; (*verb*) abstain (used with *from*)

Antonyms: intemperate, gluttonous, self-indulgent; (*verb*) indulge (used with *in*)

Note 1: <u>To be abstemious</u> usually means to exercise self-restraint and moderation in the use of food as well as of drink. But to <u>abstain</u> (literally, "to hold oneself off") is often used in reference to strong drink alone, and then it means to refrain from drinking. For persons who do not drink alcoholic or intoxicating beverages we apply the term "total abstainers" or "teetotalers."

Note 2: To <u>abstain</u> in voting means to withhold one's vote.

Note 3: In a special sense, <u>temperance</u> is used to denote complete abstinence from the use of intoxicating liquors.

Phrases: an *abstemious* (sparing) diet
an *abstemious* (temperate) life
abstain *from*

6. **ab-struse** ăb-stro͞os′ [*abstrusus* (Latin), "to conceal"] — Difficult to understand or solve because the subject matter is too complicated or too abstract.

The scientist's report of his findings was full of *abstruse* formulas that only a few people could understand.

Related Forms: abstruseness, abstrusely

Synonyms: profound, obscure, recondite, occult, esoteric, erudite (scholarly)

Antonyms: clear, plain, manifest, obvious, easy, simple

Note: Observe the shades of difference in meaning of the following synonyms of <u>abstruse</u>.
<u>recondite</u> — characterized by profound scholarship; beyond ordinary understanding — a <u>recondite</u> treatise
<u>occult</u> — characterized by an air of secrecy or mystery — an <u>occult</u> science, like graphology, a study of handwriting as a clue to a person's character
<u>esoteric</u>: understood by only a few specially initiated persons — an essay full of <u>esoteric</u> references

Phrase: abstruse (difficult to understand) doctrines

7. **ac-ces-so-ry** ăk-sĕs′-ă-rĭ [*accedere* (Latin), "to yield"; from *ad* (Latin) "to" + *cedere* "to come forward"]

1. An accomplice; a person or thing playing a subordinate part or role.

If you aid and abet an illegal seller of narcotics, you are an *accessory* to his crime.

Synonyms: subsidiary, supplementary, adjunct, auxiliary; ally, confederate, colleague, collaborator

Antonyms: prime, principal, main

4

Phrases: a right-hand man, a fellow conspirator, an abettor, in league with

> **2.** Something added or attached that contributes attractiveness, convenience, garnishment, etc.
>
> The power tool had so many *accessories* that we felt that it would do everything but wash dishes.

Synonyms: ornamental, decorative

Note: In law, an <u>accessory</u> is one who aids or abets another in, or is privy to, the commission of a crime.

An <u>accessory before the fact</u> is guilty of assistance to the criminal without being present when the act is committed. An <u>accessory after the fact</u> deliberately conceals, and thereby assists another, in the commission of the crime.

8. ac-cord ă-kôrd′ [*ad*, "to" + *cor, cordis* (Latin), "heart"]

> **1.** (*noun*) Agreement of opinion or will.
>
> After days of discussion, an *accord* was finally reached and the strikers went back to work.
>
> **2.** (*verb*) To agree; to be in harmony with.
>
> Henry's version of how the accident took place *accorded* in every detail with the story several other witnesses recounted.
>
> **3.** (*verb*) To grant as suitable or proper.
>
> In honor of their achievements, the astronauts were *accorded* the honor of a parade through the city.

Related Forms: accordance, accordingly

Phrases: of his own accord (will), everyone supplied according to (in proportion to) his needs

Synonyms: (*nouns*) concurrence, harmony, congruence, consonance (*adjective:* consonant), concord, compatibility, conformity, consensus (general agreement); (*verbs*) concur, correspond, harmonize, conform

Antonyms: (*nouns*) dissent, discord (*adjective:* discordant), dissension, incompatibility

9. ac-quit ă-kwĭt′ [*ad* + *quite* (Latin), "free of," "released"] — To relieve from a charge of fault or crime.

Because of lack of evidence, the jury *acquitted* the defendant of the crime of which he was accused.

Synonyms: vindicate, exculpate, absolve, exonerate

Antonyms: inculpate, impugn, convict, incriminate

Related Form: acquittal

Phrase: acquit oneself, meaning "conduct oneself" (as, to *acquit* oneself well in one's mission)

10. ac-ri-mo-ni-ous ăk-rĭ-mō′-nĭ-ŭs [*acrimonieux* (French); from *acer* (Latin), "sharp"] — Harsh or bitter in speech or temper.

If debate becomes *acrimonious* rather than remaining reasonable, the trend of thought can be lost.

Related Forms: acrimony, acrimoniously, acrimoniousness

Synonyms: tart, acrid, caustic, sarcastic, stinging, mordant, biting, astringent

Antonyms: bland, gentle, mild

EXERCISES

I. Words Out of Context

In each group below, select the word or phrase that most clearly expresses the meaning of the word at the left:

1. **abstemious**   (*a*) self-indulgent   (*b*) temperate   (*c*) unsociable   (*d*) healthy

2. **abstruse**   (*a*) dull   (*b*) cunning   (*c*) larger than an acute angle   (*d*) hard to understand

3. **abhor**   (*a*) release   (*b*) detest   (*c*) disclaim   (*d*) reject vigorously

6

4. **acquit** (*a*) absolve (*b*) leave alone (*c*) give up (*d*) pay back

5. **abate** (*a*) tease (*b*) beat up (*c*) border on (*d*) lessen

II. Words in Context

A. One-Word Omissions

In each of the following sentences substitute for the blank an appropriate word selected from the Basic Vocabulary List for this lesson.

1. If you hide this man from the police you will aid and abet him in evading his just punishment.

2. In order to abate my mother's anger, I offered to wash the car.

3. Henry's reasoning became so abstruse that I had to ask him to explain what he meant.

4. As their discussion waxed more and more acrimonious, Bob and Tom began to hurl insults at each other.

5. My father, who is rather abstemious in regard to liquor, takes only an occasional glass of sherry.

6. Although our team lost, we felt that they had made a good showing against a much stronger team and had acquitted themselves nobly.

7. Paul so abhors any show of intolerance, that when faced with it he became incoherent with rage.

8. Since Mary Lou seems to feel that if one accessory is good two would be better, she frequently looks as decked out as a Christmas tree.

9. The abject appearance and obvious hunger of the stray dog forced me to bring it home to my mother.

10. Although at first I disagreed with you I now am in full accord with your views.

B. Words in Continuous Context

After reading the following passage, select the letter preceding the word which most nearly expresses the meaning of the underscored words as used in the selection.

The tremendous upsurge of interest in Dostoevsky in this country shows no signs of abating.[1] Recent years have seen the publication or reprinting of many studies devoted to the novelist. His complex characters have challenged the critic to explain their abstruse[2] motives and yet to this very day the problems they wrestled with still remain obscure[3] even to the average intelligent reader.

1. **abating**   (a) augmenting   (b) ebbing   (c) deferring   (d) perplexing

2. **abstruse**   (a) manifest   (b) astringent   (c) esoteric   (d) questionable

3. **obscure**   (a) abstinent   (b) conspicuous   (c) clear   (d) recondite

III. Synonyms and Antonyms

No two words in English ever really convey identical meanings; they may suggest close identification but they seldom are exact twins. Words denoting the same general meaning — synonyms — may often be employed interchangeably for a variety of reasons, not necessarily always valid.

Usage evolving over a long period of time has a way of fastening a special tone to a word, lending it a particular aura, shading, or tone, so that in addition to its core meaning the synonym carries an accessory meaning or climate. Saying that you *detest* spinach undoubtedly conveys your true reaction more forcefully than resorting to the comparatively mild "I *hate* spinach." Without these fine shades or difference in climate which synonyms — and antonyms too — convey, our language would be flat and dull, indeed.

To master a word fully one must be alert to its synonyms and antonyms. The three categories make an effective package. The dictionary, aware of its function to provide as much information as it can about a word, is not content merely to give a complete definition of the word, but adds a concise explanation of the fine distinctions in the meaning of its related words which the reader should know if he is to use the basic word accurately and effectively. The explanations of words commonly associated with the basic word are placed at the end of the vocabulary entry. Each synonym in the group is explained and differentiated from the principal meaning. Illustrative phrases or sentences are frequently added to point up the differences among the synonyms. A student who hopes to strengthen his word power cannot afford to overlook this special capsule discussion after a vocabulary entry.

A. Synonyms

For each word in Column A select a synonym in Column B.

(Observe that the words below are different from those you have studied in this lesson's Basic Vocabulary List. They are, however, included in the section designated as synonyms.)

A	B
1. absolve *k*	(a) subsidiary
2. mitigate *d*	(b) recondite
3. supplementary *a*	(c) instigate
4. esoteric *b*	(d) alleviate
5. grant *f*	(e) temperance
6. abominate *h*	(f) bestow
7. foment *c*	(g) base
8. mordant *l*	(h) loathe
9. self-restraint *e*	(i) deterrent
10. ignoble *g*	(j) castigation
	(k) exonerate
	(l) caustic

B. Antonyms

For each of the following words give three antonyms.

1. **recede,** *intensify, augment, increase*
2. **odium** *abhor affection, regard, fond*
3. **dissension,** *accord consent, agree, conform*
4. **manifest,** *abstruse profound, obscure recondite*
5. **egg on** *abet discourage, thwart, curb*
6. **adjunct,** *accessory main, principal, main*
7. **debasing** *abject noble, proud, arrogant*
8. **abstinent** *abstemious glutton, intemperate self-indulgent*
9. **consonance** *accord discord, discord, incomp't*
10. **absolve** *acquit convict, incriminate, in- culpate*

IV. Syllabication and Pronunciation

Syllabicate the following words correctly and place the major stress mark (') after the syllable which is accented when the word is pronounced.

Example: *mol' - li - fy*

1. abate,
2. abet
3. abject
4. abhor
5. abstemious
6. abstruse
7. accessory
8. accord
9. acquit
10. acrimonious

V. Analogies

Note the relationship of each of the following groups of four words:

sponge : water = blotter : ink
abstemious : gluttonous = poor : rich

Thus, *sponge* (which absorbs water) is related to *water* as a *blotter* (which absorbs ink) is related to *ink*. *Abstemious* is related to *gluttonous* (an antonym of *abstemious*) as poor is related to *rich* (an antonym of *poor*). Comparisons of this kind are called *analogies*.

In each of the following select the word in parentheses that completes the analogy correctly.

1. acrimonious: (bland, esoteric, mordant, obtuse) = intensify : slacken

2. solace : bland *mitigate gentil* = sarcasm : (despicable, caustic, discordant, abject)

3. drought : rainy weather = (abatement, connivance, fury, repugnance) : intensification

4. accessory : supplementary = (concurrence, discord, compatibility, abstention) : dissension

5. misfortune : (abject, exhilarated, abhorrent, abstemious) = triumph : jubilant

WORD BUILDING

In the Basic Vocabulary List words for every lesson you will find a section devoted to an analytical study of primary word components termed prefixes, suffixes and roots. These parts form the backbone of a substantial percentage of English words in current use. One way to expand your word power is to learn the meaning of derivative elements and to use them as keys to a wider understanding of new words that crop up in your reading and school studies.

I. PREFIXES

A. **a-, ab-, abs-** (Latin), "from" "off" "away from"

>   *abduct* — to lead away
>   *abstain* — to keep from participation
>   *abnormal* — away from the rule or normal

Other English words containing this prefix are *abhor, abrasion, absent, abrogate, abstract, absurd.*

B. **ad-** (Latin), "to" "toward" "about" When the prefix *ad* precedes a root beginning with a consonant, it sometimes drops its own final *d* and as a substitute for it doubles the following consonant letter which it precedes. Thus, *ad* may appear in the English word in the form of *ac-, af-, ag-, al-, an-, ap-, ar-, as-, at-*. This merging or fusion of the consonants is technically called *assimilation*.

>   *accumulate* — to gather into a mass
>   *affirm* — to state positively
>   *allude* — to refer to indirectly

11

II. ROOTS

A. bat-, batt-, from *battre* (French), "to beat"

    battery — an unlawful beating of another person; as in the phrase "assault and battery"

    batter — to beat violently

    abattoir — a slaughterhouse (literally, "a place where animals are beaten down")

Other words from this root are *bat, beat, battalion, battle, combat.*

B. ced-, from *cedere* (Latin), "to go" "to yield" "to approach" (This root appears as *ced* in some English words.)

    cede — to yield or assign

    recede — to withdraw or move back

    procedure — a step in a regular, definite order

Other words from this root are *recession, intercede, precedent, cession.*

C. The Latin root **acer** (Latin), "sharp" is found in the word *acrimonious* studied in this lesson.

    acrid — sharp to the taste

    exacerbate — to embitter

    acute — sharp, pointed, keen

    acerbity — sharpness of language

Other words derived from this root include *acute* and *acid.*

D. The Latin root **ject-** meaning "throw" is found in the word *abject* studied in this lesson.

    interject — to throw (a word or remark) in the midst of a flow of talk; to interrupt

    eject — to drive out or thrust out from within

    reject (literally, *ject* "to throw" + *re* "back") — repel

Other words derived from this root are *conjecture* "an inference arrived at on insufficient evidence or guesswork," *jetty, jet* (to spout forth, gush), *ejaculate, project, dejection* (cast down in spirit).

EXERCISES

I. Word Analysis and Word Building

1. The practice of setting dogs to fight a chained bear was a source of considerable amusement in the not too distant past. The sport was called *bear-baiting*. How do you account for the origin of the name of this sport using as basis the etymology of the word *bait*?

2. "The boys *baited* John about his fear of dogs." As used in the sentence, the *italicized* word means

   (a) criticized   (b) encouraged   (c) teased

3. What is the original root that is concealed in each of the following English words?

   jetty, cute, cease
   jet   *ced*

4. An *abject* liar is one who is

   (a) chronically untruthful   (b) despicable
   (c) aggressive   (d) incurable

5. *Accessories* of a costume are

   (a) essential and effective
   (b) unessential to the outfit but assisting to make it attractive
   (c) superfluous but basic
   (d) subsidiary, attractive, and expensive

6. From what root are *jetsam* and *jettison* derived? What does each word mean? What is the difference between *jetsam* and *flotsam*? The phrase "jetsam and flotsam" is sometimes used to describe derelicts. How do you account for the connection between the phrase and the underlined word?   *jactatio – throw*   *drifting goods   drifting vessel*   *pleave – abandonned*

7. To *abet* the commission of a crime means to

   (a) hamper it   (b) initiate it   (c) encourage it
   (d) deplore it

13

8. Pronounce aloud the words *pro'-ject* and *pro-ject'*.

   What is their difference in meaning between the two words when they are thus pronounced?

9. Which of the following sentences conveys the strongest sense of loathing? Defend your choice. *rebulsive*

   (*a*) I find his crude manners obnoxious. *repugnant detestable*

   (*b*) I *hate* his crude manners.

   (*c*) Henry's crude manners are *offensive!*

   (*d*) I *detest* manners of that kind.

10. What is the difference between an *abstemious* person and one who is *abstinent*? Fill each blank with the appropriate word.

    (*a*) Henry takes a drink once in a long while. He is *abstemious*

    (*b*) Smith never touches liquor. He is *abstains*

II. Fun With Words

A. Telling Phrases

1. Explain the meaning of the following phrases:

   "aid and abet the enemy"   "mere conjecture"

   "a teetotaler"   "a conspiracy of silence"
   doesn't drink   *a plan to do an evil act*

2. When one is told *to fish or cut bait*, he is being asked

   (*a*) to decide to join in a plan or scheme or be left out of consideration

   (*b*) to attach bait to his fishing hook

   (*c*) to make haste

3. A person who speaks with "bated breath" is

   (*a*) hurling insults at people

   (*b*) restrained in speech because of fear or excitement

   (*c*) stammering

4. In legal terminology, "to abate a nuisance" is to

   (*a*) suppress it   (*b*) encourage it

   (*c*) leave it undisturbed

14

Alice had not the slightest idea what latitude *was, or* longitude *either, but she thought that they were nice grand words to say.*

— LEWIS CARROLL, *Alice's Adventures in Wonderland*

B. It's the Law!

In this lesson we have referred to and defined a number of legal terms. The following questions may help you widen your legal knowledge.

1. Consult the dictionary for the meaning of the following words:

   shyster, barrister, writ, arbitrary

   Why would a respected lawyer object to being called "a shyster"? In which country is the term "barrister" used?

2. Match the legal term in Column **A** with the phrase that defines it in Column **B**.

A	**B**
1. **indictment** c	(a) a law passed by a duly authorized lawmaking body
2. **subpoena** e	(b) one who is guilty of a crime
3. **statute** a	(c) a formal written accusation of a crime
4. **culprit** b	(d) a temporary delay in carrying out a sentence
5. **reprieve** d	(e) a written order summoning one to court
6. **affidavit** h	(f) illegal
7. **plaintiff** j	(g) expel from the practice of law
8. **contraband** i	(h) a written statement under oath
9. **illicit** f	(i) smuggled goods
10. **disbar** g	(j) a complainant in a lawsuit

15

3. (*a*) What is a "quit claim"?

   (*b*) Show how the adjunct word *quit* in this phrase is related by origin to the word *acquit* in the Basic Vocabulary List.

   to accuse   *to prove*

4. What is the difference between *impeach* and *convict*? Which branch of Congress has the power to impeach a President of the United States? Which branch is authorized to judge him?   *House*   *Senate*

5. What is an "accessory after the fact"?

   acquited   absolve   vindicate   exonerate

6. Give three one-word synonyms for "to free of the charge" and three one-word synonyms for "to find a person guilty as charged."

   inculpate   impugn   convict

III. A Dictionary Project

The dictionary is the most important reference book and guide for the student who wishes both to increase his vocabulary and to gain the ability to use words with accuracy and effectiveness. An entry in an unabridged dictionary provides a wide range of information about the word being considered. The treatment is concise, and the information is authoritative. Each entry will usually provide the following information:

   (*a*) spelling and syllabication
   (*b*) pronunciation
   (*c*) identification of part of speech
   (*d*) inflections (tense, number, derivative forms, etc.)
   (*e*) etymology, or word origin
   (*f*) definition
   (*g*) illustrative and idiomatic phrases
   (*h*) special usages
   (*i*) synonyms and antonyms, with explanatory phrases or sentences to clarify the distinctions

Consider, as an illustration, the way *The Random House Dictionary of the English Language (Unabridged Edition)* treats the first word of this week's lesson, *abate*. Here is the entry:

Refer to the foregoing definition, and answer the following questions.

1. Define concisely the word "abate."

2. Illustrate its meaning in a phrase.

3. Give three special meanings of this word as it is used in law.

4. In law, what word is used to designate a person who annuls a writ? abotor

5. Several definitions of *abate* are given in the foregoing entry. Which meaning of the word is most common?

6. Give one synonym and two antonyms for *abate.*
   subside   increase intensify

IV. For the Ambitious Student

The words below are not on the regular Basic Vocabulary List and are suggested for study by students who want additional basic words for mastery.

Define each of the followings words, give its etymology, and use each in a short sentence.

1. abashed
2. abdicate
3. abjure
4. accolade
5. accretion
6. acquiesce
7. adage
8. addendum
9. ad hoc
10. adjudicate

17

LESSON TWO

11. acumen	16. aesthetic
12. adamant	17. affable
13. addiction	18. aggravate
14. admonish	19. aggressive
15. adulation	20. agnostic

11. **a-cu-men** ă-kū'-měn [*acuere* (Latin), "to sharpen"] — Superior mental acuteness; keen insight.

Because of his exceptional business *acumen*, Mr. Tolliver was able to manage the estate so that it yielded a greatly increased income to the heirs.

Synonyms: perspicacity (*adjective:* perspicacious), discernment, astuteness (*adjective:* astute), shrewdness

Antonyms: obtuseness, dullness

12. **ad-a-mant** ăd'-à-mănt [*adamas* (Latin), "the hardest metal." The Romans took this word to describe the hardest substance they knew, the diamond, from the Greek α, "not" + *daman*, "to conquer" or "to tame"] — Unyielding; firm in the face of opposition or plea.

Although a number of us pleaded with John to acknowledge his error, he remained *adamant* in his refusal to do so.

Related Form: adamantine

Synonyms: inflexible, inexorable, immovable (referring to a person's disposition or nature), obdurate (*noun:* obduracy), impervious, impenetrable, relentless, mulish

Antonyms: flexible, submissive, pliant, complaisant, relenting, plastic, malleable, amenable

Phrases: adamantine courage, *adamant* to a plea

Note: The English language is rich in adjectives that are synonyms or antonyms of words concerning the very human attitude of being unyielding in spite of all appeals. Such an attitude is occasionally referred to as "pig-headed." Here are a few suggested substitutes for adamant and its opposite pliable, not mentioned above.

Synonyms: headstrong, dogged, cross-grained

Antonyms: fawning, cringing, supple, compliant, deferential, docile, tractable, obsequious

13. **ad-dic-tion** ă-dĭk′-shŭn [*addictio* (Latin), "surrender to"; from *ad*, "to" + *dicere*, "to say" "to show" "to be dedicated"] — The state of being compulsive in the use of drugs; an unbreakable habit-forming practice or pursuit (usually morally evil or objectionable).

To Sophie coffee has become an *addiction*: she drinks at least ten cups of it a day.

Phrases: *addicted to* the drug; a coffee *addict*

Related Forms: (noun) an addict; (adjective) addicted (followed by *to*)

Synonyms: habituation, propensity (an irresistible longing for something objectionable); proclivity

Note 1: If one had an extraordinary leaning toward something good, we would say one has "a flair" for it.

Note 2: addicted to is used in a bad sense; devoted to, in a favorable sense.

"*To be wholly* devoted *to some intellectual exercise is to have suc-ceeded in life.*"

— R. L. STEVENSON

---

14. **ad·mon·ish** ăd-mŏn'-ĭsh [*ad,* "to" + *monere* (Latin), "to warn"] — To express disapproval, warning, in a gentle or friendly manner; to remind someone urgently about his obligation or duty; to give advice.

The teacher *admonished* Anne for her lack of effort in her studies, and threatened to fail her.

Related Forms: (noun) admonition, (*adjective)* admonitory

Synonyms: (*verbs*) reprove, caution, censure, rebuke, exhort, reprimand, reproach, chide (*past tense,* chid or chided), reprehend; (*nouns*) disapprobation, reproof, exhortation

Antonyms: praise, extol, laud, commend, eulogize

15. **ad·u·la·tion** ăd-û-lā'-shŭn [*ad,* "to" + *ulari* (Latin), "to fawn like a dog, to wag the tail"] — Servile flattery; excessive, abject admiration or devotion.

Even an older and more experienced performer might have had his head turned by the *adulation* of throngs of adoring fans.

Related Forms: (verb) adulate; (adjective) adulatory

Synonyms: eulogy (*adjective:* eulogistic) (to be distinguished from *elegy* (*adjective:* elegiac) "a mournful melancholy poem"), panegyric (*adjective:* panegyrical), encomium (*adjective:* encomiastic), commendation (*adjective:* commendatory), exaltation

20

Antonyms: (nouns) derision (adjective: derisive), scorn, depreciation (adjective: depreciative) — meaning a belittling, to be distinguished from *deprecation* meaning "strong disapproval or protest"; affront (insult), disparagement; (verbs) scorn, mock, gibe, jeer, hoot

16. **aes-thet-ic** ĕs-thĕt'-ĭk (sometimes spelled *esthetic*) [*aisthesis* (Greek), "perception by the senses"] — Pertaining to a sense of beauty; sensitive to the beautiful in nature or art.

From an *aesthetic* point of view the portrait did not appeal to me; however, it was a souvenir of the occasion, and therefore I decided to buy it.

Related Forms: **aesthetically, aesthetics** (a branch of philosophy dealing with the theories and principles of beauty in art and literature), **aesthete** (one who is sensitive to the beautiful. This term is more often used to mean "one who makes overmuch of his sensitivity to beauty.")

Note 1: The forms above deal with the idea of beauty. The same root (aisthesis) is also used in words that deal with the idea of feeling, in particular, pain. In this case, the root is used with the simplified spelling es (esthetics) rather than aes (aesthetics).

anesthesia — the absence of feeling or sensation

anesthetic — a drug, like chloroform or ether, that anesthetizes or, in other words, renders one insensible to pain.

anesthetist — one who administers an anesthetic
(The prefix an, in Greek, means "not.")

Note 2: Do not confuse aesthetic with a word that looks like it, ascetic. When used as a noun, an ascetic means one who leads an abstemious life, or practices a strict religious regimen. When used as an adjective, ascetic means severely abstinent or rigorously austere. (See page 73)

The abstract noun form of ascetic is asceticism.

17. **af-fa-ble** ăf'-à-b'l [*affabilis* (Latin), "easy to be spoken to;" from *affari*, "to speak to," from *ad*, "to" + *fari*, "to speak"] — Sociable, courteous, and agreeable in manner; easy to talk to or approach; friendly.

21

No matter how busy he is, our principal is never curt but always *affable*.

Related Forms: affably, affableness, affability

Synonyms: civil, benign, good-natured, complaisant (not to be confused with *complacent*, meaning "smug, self-satisfied with one's own merits or accomplishments, etc."), gracious, urbane (not to be confused with *urban*, meaning "relating to a city")

Antonyms: unsociable, surly, testy, ill-tempered, curt, rude, brusque

18. **ag-gra-vate** ăg'-rá-vāt [*aggravare, aggravatus* (Latin), "to make heavy"; from *ad* + *gravare*, from *gravis*, "heavy"] — To make worse or more severe.

Labor conditions in the country were improved by the new legislation, although it had been feared by some that the result would be merely to *aggravate* the tensions between labor and management.

Related Forms: aggravation, aggravating, aggravatingly

Synonyms: intensify, heighten, magnify, exacerbate, worsen

Antonyms: lessen, abate, alleviate, mitigate, assuage

Note: The use of aggravate in informal discourse to mean "to irritate" or "to annoy" has now received sanction as good usage.

19. **ag-gres-sive** ă-grĕs'-ĭv [*ad* (Latin), "toward," + *gradi, gressus*, "to step"] — Characterized by energy and vigor; participating in an action that violates by force the rights of another state.

Unlike his brother, who is mild-mannered and retiring, Tom is *aggressive* by nature.

Synonyms: (*adjectives*) energetic, combative, dynamic, self-assertive, pugnacious, vigorous, enterprising

(*nouns*) encroachment, infringement, intrusion

Antonyms: meek, inoffensive, diffident, retiring

22

Related Forms: aggressor, aggressiveness, aggression

An *aggression* is an unprovoked encroachment.

An *aggressor* nation is one that attempts offensive action against another to achieve its political or economic ends in disregard of, or in violation of, the victim's territorial rights.

The United Nations branded the nation that had encroached on its neighbor's territory as an *aggressor.*

Phrases: an aggressive act *against* another
an *aggressive* (forward and self-assertive) businessman; an *aggressive* policy; a war of *aggression*

In psychology, the term *aggression* is used to denote hostile action directed against someone or something stemming from frustrations.

"Most of the trouble in the world is caused by people wanting to be important."

— T. S. ELIOT, *The Cocktail Party*

---

20. **ag·nos·tic** ăg-nŏs'-tĭk [*a* (Greek), "not" + *gignosko* (Greek), "I know"] — A person who believes in the doctrine that existence and the nature of God are not known or knowable.

The scientist declared that he had not denied the existence of God; he wanted it clearly understood that he is an *agnostic,* not an atheist.

Related Form: agnosticism

Synonym: skeptic

Antonyms: devout, pious (*noun:* piety), pietistic

Phrase: a "doubting Thomas"

Note: Observe the difference in meaning between <u>agnostic</u> and each of the following words:

<u>freethinker</u> — one whose opinions are formed independently of traditional authority.

23

infidel — one who does not accept the tenets of the religion of the dominant group; thus, in Christian countries, a non-Christian; in Mohammedan countries, a non-Mohammedan.

atheist — one who denies the existence of a Supreme Being.

skeptic — one who is critical of all creeds and religious doctrine.

"It is wrong for a man to say that he is certain of the objective truth of any proposition unless he can produce evidence which logically justifies that certainty. This is what agnosticism* asserts."

— T. H. HUXLEY

---

* Thomas Huxley invented the term <u>agnostic</u>, as opposed to <u>gnostic</u>, "one who professes to believe a great deal."

EXERCISES

I. Words in Context

A. One-Word Omissions

In each of the following sentences substitute for the blank an appropriate word selected from Words 11-20.

1. The noise of a riveting machine in the street outside my window has *aggravated* my headache.

2. Our personnel manager is a very *affable* gentleman, who puts you at your ease by his friendly, informal manner.

3. The atheist denies the existence of God: the *agnostic* neither denies nor affirms His existence.

4. The governor was *adamant* in his refusal to grant a reprieve to the hardened criminal.

5. While Roman architects were essentially practical in their building design, Greek architects were more concerned with beauty and worked to produce buildings of a high *aesthetic* appeal.

6. Many crimes are committed by misguided young people who have developed an *addiction* to certain drugs and must have large sums of money to obtain their daily supplies.

7. Do you think that merely to *admonish* a person for driving a car without a license is strong enough punishment?

8. It will take great wisdom and much *acumen* to solve the problems of the world and bring about peace.

9. Their great courage and acumen gained for the astronauts the *adulation* of all the people of the country.

10. The *aggressive* measures which the military dictatorship resorted to in its attempt to further its territorial ambitions were condemned by outraged world opinion.

B. Two-Word Omissions

In each of the following selections, you will find two blanks indicating that a pair of words has been omitted. Following the selections are four choices lettered (a) to (d). Select the pair that will most satisfactorily complete the meaning of the selection.

1. A(n) *aggressive* war policy is necessarily *combative*

   (*a*) energetic — aggressive   (*b*) provocative — popular
   (*c*) legal — defensive   (*d*) aggressive — combative

2. Everyone who met the dramatist James Barrie was impressed by his *affability.* He was a man of quiet almost sly humor which he directed at himself, never at others. Benign of countenance, diminutive in stature, warm in his conversation, he did not at all look or act like a famous author. He hadn't an enemy in the world. *Gracious* is the best word to describe the author of *Peter Pan.*

   (*a*) irascibility — Benignity   (*b*) affability — Gracious
   (*c*) acrimony — Complacency   (*d*) acumen — Derision

3. *Aggressiveness* is an indispensable trait that a businessman must possess if he wishes to be successful. He cannot cultivate it; he either has it or does not have it. Consider the business structures erected by the tycoons of industry, and you will find that the keystone is *perspicacity*

25

(a) Perspicacity — acumen   (b) Cordiality — obtuseness
(c) Astuteness — fawning   (d) Aggressiveness — perspicacity

4. "I do not consider it an insult, but rather a compliment to be called a(n) ~~agnostic~~. I ~~do not claim~~ to know where many ignorant men are sure." — CLARENCE DARROW

(a) atheist — claim   (b) agnostic — only pretend
(c) skeptic — always made sure   (d) agnostic — do not pretend

II. Words Out of Context

In each group below select the word or expression that most clearly expresses the meaning of the word at the left.

1. **aggravate**   (a) make worse   (b) incite   (c) burden   (d) bait

2. **affable**   (a) imaginative   (b) civil   (c) talking in metaphors   (d) discourteous

3. **agnostic**   (a) atheistic   (b) referring to a diagnosis   (c) intolerant   (d) skeptical about religious creeds

4. **adamant**   (a) glittering   (b) virile   (c) obdurate   (d) frustrated

5. **aesthetic**   (a) rigorously self-denying   (b) sensitive to criticism   (c) concerned with beauty   (d) lacking consciousness

III. Synonyms and Antonyms

A. Synonyms

For each of the following words give three synonyms.

1. **addiction** aggressive   encroachment, combative vigorous
2. **reproach** reprimande, chide   4. **eulogistic** ondulate, praise compliment
3. **discernment** admonish   5. **aggressive**

addiction
habituation
propensity
proclivity

26

B. Antonyms

For each word in Column A select an antonym from Column B.

	A		B
1.	commend *k*	(α)	amenable
2.	chide *d*	(b)	denunciation
3.	astute *h*	(c)	complaisant
4.	inexorable *c*	(d)	laud
5.	encomium *b*	(e)	mitigate
6.	self-assertive *i*	(f)	self-assured
7.	surly *a*	(g)	indecisive
8.	intensify *e*	(h)	obtuse
9.	devout *j*	(i)	meek
10.	diffident *f*	(j)	impious
		(k)	reprehend
		(l)	ascetic

IV. Related Forms

encomiastic

1. *Give one adjectival form for each of the nouns below.*

   adulation   eulogize

   encomium   eulogy   admonition *tory*   adulation *tory*   panegyric *ical*
   commendation *tory*   depreciation *ative*   derision *derisive*

2. *Fill each blank with the proper form of the italicized word.*

   (a) He is *acute* in his judgments. He has *acumen / discernment*
   (b) He has *perspicacity*. He is *perspicacious*
   (c) He *discerns* quickly. He has *discernment*

V. Analogies

In the last lesson, you studied the structure and relationship of words in an analogy where you were given three terms and were required to choose a valid fourth. In this lesson, you will study another form in which an analogy appears. In this form you are required to select a pair of words which stand in the same relationship as the two words in a given pair. Here is a representative question:

chain: links = (1) paragraph : sentence (2) pages :
   book (3) sack : sugar (4) train : cars

The relationship of the words in italics may be expressed as
follows: A *chain* is made up of *several links*. The first choice
(1) is invalid because it mentions one sentence not several. If
the second term were sentences we might pause to examine
the relationship further. Choice (2) is incorrect because the
order of the terms is reversed: pages are not composed of a
book. Choice (3) is invalid because a sack contains sugar but
is not composed of it. Choice (4) provides a logical answer because a *train* is composed of several cars joined together.

In answering an analogy question given in the form above,
you are advised to follow these two steps.

Step 1. Determine the logical relationship between the terms
   A and **B**.

Step 2. Select the pair of words which are related to each other
   in the same way as **A** is related to **B**. The relationship
   in the four choices suggested must be expressed ex-
   actly like that given to the main pair of words. For
   example, one may not say that **A** is composed of **B**
   and then in analyzing an answer shift the order and
   say **B** is composed of **A**. In short, the terms of the
   answer must be directly proportional to those in the
   stated analogy.

The following commoner kinds of relationships appear frequently on aptitude tests and college entrance board examina-
tions. All verbal relationships are, of course, too numerous to
classify here.

Analogy 1. A is concerned with B

   A   **B**
   astronomer : stars = (1) archaeology : antiquities (2)
   aesthetics : sculpture (3) entomologist : insects (4)
   words : philologist

28

The correct answer is (3) entomologist : insects because an entomologist is concerned with insects in the same way as an astronomer is concerned with stars. Note the inverse order of (4), the wrong form of the term *archaeology* (1), the narrowness of the term *sculpture* (2), and with its wrong form.

Analogy 2. A causes B

A   B

failure : dismay = (1) explosion : debris   (2) danger : riot   (3) wealth : luxuries   (4) poverty : shame

The answer is (1): failure causes dismay; an explosion causes debris. Note that (2) danger does not necessarily cause a riot. The qualification *not necessarily* may likewise be applied to reject analogies (3) and (4).

Analogy 3. A is the state of being B

A   B

despondency : depressed = (1) exaltation : outlawed (2) exhilaration : gladdened   (3) precision : cautious (4) true : veracity

The answer is (2): despondency is the state of being depressed; exhilaration, the *opposite* of despondency, is the state of being gladdened, the *opposite* of depressed.

Analogy 4. A is approximately the same as B.

A   B

boisterous : rowdy = (1) gluttonous : hungry (2) urbane : suave   (3) doleful : elated   (4) sad : droll

The answer is (2): a *boisterous* person is *rowdy*, that is, disorderly and rough; an *urbane* person is *suave*, that is, calm and polite.

Analogy 5. A is the opposite of B.

A   B

desire : spurn = (1) beseech : implore   (2) caution : fearful   (3) equitable : arbitrary   (4) defer : refer

The correct answer is (3): desire, a verb meaning to crave or covet is the opposite of spurn, a verb meaning to reject; equitable, an adjective meaning fair or just, is the opposite of arbitrary, an adjective meaning unjust or biased. Answer (1) consists of two words that have the same meaning; in answer (2) caution is a noun and fearful is an adjective.

Analogy 6. A is an extreme of B.

A   B

minute : small = (1) cold : frigid   (2) tepid : lukewarm   (3) frugality : economy   (4) gargantuan : large

The correct answer is (4): minute means extremely small; gargantuan means extremely large. Note that (1) frigid is not the extreme. The order is inverse.

Analogy 7. A denotes the lack of B.

A   B

folly : sense = (1) aggressiveness : ideals   (2) circumspection : caution   (3) skepticism : faith   (4) deluge : water

The correct answer is (3): folly is the *lack* of sense; skepticism, being a philosophical attitude which demands proof of the validity of a doctrine or an assertion, is the *lack* of faith.

Analogy 8. A is similar in figure or appearance to B.

A   B

hoop : circle = (1) cylinder : ellipse   (2) polygon : pentagon   (3) orange : sphere   (4) pyramid : triangle

The correct answer is (3): a hoop is an example of the two-dimensional circle; in the same relationship of figure, an orange is an example of a three-dimensional figure, a sphere.

Complete the following analogies.

1. meek : arrogant = (*1*) plateau : peak (*2*) destitute : poor (*3*) hovel : palace (*4*) humility : crudeness

2. rung : ladder = (*1*) apartment : rooms (*2*) people : traffic (*3*) railing : escalator **(4)** step : stairway

3. duet : quintet = (*1*) double : quintuple (*2*) trilogy : quarto (*3*) rectangle : quadrangle (*4*) bisect : trisect

4. advertisement : purchaser = (*1*) acumen : business **(2)** bait : fish (*3*) bell : churchgoer (*4*) blurb : fame

5. mendacity : untrue = (*1*) pertinacity : rude **(2)** veracity : true (*3*) loquacity : diffident (*4*) versatility : hostile

6. ruby : emerald = (*1*) iron : mineral (*2*) carrot : grass (*3*) red : blue **(4)** color : stone

7. psychology : mind = (*1*) physiology : body (*2*) philately : coins (*3*) astrology : forecast (*4*) zoology : tissues

8. genesis : finale = (*1*) terminus : inception **(2)** birth : death (*3*) prologue : climax (*4*) registration : matriculation

9. admonish : delinquent = (*1*) censure : treason **(2)** chide : transgressor (*3*) laud : offender **(4)** chastise : misbehave

10. succumb : addiction = (*1*) resist : temptation (*2*) gratify : need (*3*) abide : decision (*4*) mitigate : injury

WORD BUILDING

I. PREFIX

The Latin prefix **ad**, meaning "to" "toward," which is found in many English words, is sometimes hidden when the letter *d* is dropped or assimilated to the succeeding consonant. For a discussion see the note on **ad** in Lesson 1, page 11. In this lesson the prefix **ad** appears in basic words *adulation, admonish, addiction, affable, aggravate* and *aggressive*.

II. ROOTS

A. The Latin root **fabula** meaning "a talk" "a story" is the source of the word *affable*, studied in this lesson. Other words derived from this root include:

fable — a short narrative teaching a moral and usually having as characters animals that talk and act like human beings; an improbable story

fabulous — like a fable; hence, astonishing or exaggerated

B. The Latin root **gravis** meaning "heavy" "severe" is the source of the word *aggravate* (ad + *gravis*), studied in this lesson. Other words derived from this root include:

> *grave* — serious
> *grave* — important
> *grievous* — grave, intense, severe

Still other words from this root are *aggrieved* (hurt by injustice, sorely troubled), *grief, grievance* (complaint), and *gravitate*.

C. The Greek root **gnosis**, meaning "knowledge" and derived from *gignosko* "I know" is the source of the word *agnostic* studied in this lesson. Other English words derived from *gnosis* include *diagnose* — to ascertain by study

prognosis (literally, "a knowing beforehand") — a forecast of the course of a disease or of an event

Additional words from this root are *cognoscenti* (specialists), *cognizant* (aware), *reconnoitre*.

D. The Greek root **theos** meaning "god" is the source of the word *atheist* studied in connection with the word *agnostic* in this lesson. Other words in English derived from this root include:

> *theist* — one who believes in one God as the creator of the universe

> *pantheist* — one who holds the doctrine that God is manifest in the material universe. The Greek root *pan* means "all."

> *theology* — *theos*, "god" + *logos*, "account of" — the nature and attributes of God

Other derivatives are *monotheism*, *theocracy*, *enthusiasm* (literally, "inspired by the gods," thus fervor), *polytheism* (poly, the Greek word meaning "many").

E. The Latin root **dic-dict-**, meaning "to say" "to give up" "to proclaim" is the source of the word *addiction*, studied in this lesson. Note the derivation of other English words from this root.

> *dictum* (literally, "a thing said") — authoritative statement

> *valedictory* (literally, "saying 'be well' ") — farewell

> *indict* (literally, "to declare against")— to charge with guilt

Other English words containing this root include *dictatorial*, *dictionary*, *edict*, *predicament*, *dedicate*, *indicate*.

F. The Latin root **gradi - gressus**, meaning "to walk" "to step," is the source of the word *aggressive* studied in this lesson.

degrade — to lower in status; to belittle
transgress — to go beyond the limits imposed by law
digress — to depart from a given course

Other English words containing this root include *ingredient*, *graduate*, *degree*, *gradual*.

EXERCISES

I. Etymology Mastery Test

1. *Show how a prefix can modify the core root* **gradi** *in each of the following words. Define each word in the light of the combination of the prefix and the root.*

   regress progress congress retrogress ingress egress

2. To get rid of the people who lingered at the exhibit and thus overcrowded his New York museum, P. T. Barnum rigged up a corridor toward the doorway to the street and displayed a prominent sign reading TO EGRESS. The ruse worked. Would you be deceived by this sign? What did the lingerers think the sign meant? What did the sign really mean?

3. What is a *fable*? Give the names of two authors who are famous for writing fables. How does a *fable* differ from an *allegory*? What meaning does the Latin root *fabula* contribute to the English word *fabulous*? What is the meaning of *fabulous* in the phrases "a man of *fabulous* wealth" "a *fabulous* adventure"?

4. What does *aggravate* mean in each of the following phrases: *aggravated* a grievance; caused me constant *aggravation*?

5. (*a*) What is a *ditty*? (*b*) If a *benediction* means "a blessing" what does *malediction* mean?

II. Word Analysis and Word Building

1. Give five words studied or referred to in this lesson which are derived from the Greek and five derived from the Latin.

2. What is meant by the phrase "snob appeal"?

3. The biblical prophet Zechariah thundered: "They made their hearts as adamant as stone." In the prophet's opinion, the people he was referring to were (a) fawning (b) docile (c) obdurate

4. An *aggressor* nation
   (a) is a progressive political unit
   (b) is one that is ruled by a despot
   (c) initiates an unprovoked hostile action

5. (a) What does *dogged in attitude* mean? (b) A bulldog is known to be tenacious or adamantine. What other animals are regarded as especially inflexible once they have made up their minds to something? (c) On the other hand, some animals are said to be easy-going, pliable. Name three. (d) Give some metaphorical expression that suggests firmness of mind. (Examples: *pig-headed, stiff-necked*)

6. Consult *Roget's Thesaurus* for: (a) five adjectives that are synonymous with headstrong or obstinate. (b) five adjectives that are antonyms to these words.

7. What is a *standpatter*? In what area of human activity is this term commonly used? Which of the following best describes a *standpatter*?
   (a) radical (b) conservative (c) progressive

8. *Analysis* means "a separation or breaking up into parts." What word ending in the syllable *sis* means "a unification or combination of the parts or elements into a whole"?

9. (a) Why are *agnostics* sometimes referred to as "unbelievers"? (b) Explain the meaning of the following words:
   diagnosis, prognosis, prognosticate

10. In a short paragraph relate briefly one of Aesop's fables. Tell why this narrative is called a *fable*.

III. Fun with Words

A. Thanks to the Greeks!

The word *aesthetic* studied in this lesson, is but one of numerous words in our language that have come down to us from the Greek. Though many contributions of our Greek progenitors deal with ideas and philosophy, a good percentage cover other areas of thought and activity. English words in the fields of science, religion, education, art, etc. are predominantly of Greek origin. The meaning of many of our words has been widened by using Greek prefixes and suffixes, as well as Greek roots.

1. *Define the following English words, derived from the Greek, and indicate what the original word or parts of the word meant in Greek. You may consult the dictionary.*

ethnic   archaic   telepathy   cryptogram   anachronism
decalogue   synopsis   astronomy   osteopathy   pentagon

2. The Greeks, regarding the diamond as the hardest substance then known to man, have given us our English word *adamant*, connoting "as hard as a diamond." Gems, in general, have lent color to our speech.

Identify each gem in Column A with its appropriate characteristic color in Column B.

A	B
1. ruby	(a) purple
2. sapphire	(b) of various colors
3. amethyst	(c) red
4. emerald	(d) yellow
5. topaz	(e) blue
6. opal	(f) green

B. Behaving Ourselves

The ability to describe precisely a person's behavior in a special situation or his general demeanor calls for an understanding of the basic meaning of certain words.

Complete each of the following sentences by choosing the correct word from the italicized list below.

affectation	sociability	snobbery	curt
bluster	affability	blasé	

1. Tina will associate only with those people who she feels are worthy of her attention. Tina offends people by her _snobbery_

2. Fred's speech is rude, abrupt, and brusque. I would describe his manner as _curt_.

3. Mary tries to give the impression that having had an excess of worldly pleasure, she is now bored with life. Mary would be flattered if you characterized her as _blasé_

4. Tony is easy to be with and talk to. His _affability_ causes him to be very well-liked.

5. Kurt's mode of behavior is not natural or genuine. He repels people by his _affectation_

6. Paula is loud, noisy, and boastful in speech and manner. Her _bluster_ is meant to hide a deep sense of inferiority.

IV. For the Ambitious Student

1. Many of our personal names are really Greek derivatives.

    As a library project trace the following names to their original meaning.

Peter	Eugene	Helen	Lily

2. *Theos* is a Greek word meaning "divine" "god."

    Define the following English words that are Greek in origin.

theology	theocracy	theosophy	pantheism

study of

3. *Logos* means "word" or "study" in Greek.

   With what subject or study does each of the following words concern itself?

   entomology   etymology   astrology
   anthropology   philology   ethnology

4. *Define the following words in the light of the Greek root.*

   eulogy   ecology   monologist   archeology
   genealogy   chronology   biology   mineralogy

V. A Dictionary Project

Religious Attitudes

   In Column **A** *you will find a list of words that crop up in a discussion of religion. In Column* **B** *are brief descriptive phrases which define the religious terms in Column* **A**. *Match each term with the appropriate definition. You will probably have to use the dictionary, since some of the terms are difficult.*

A	**B**
1. **pagan**	(a) a person who attacks cherished religious or traditional institutions
2. **secular**	
3. **bigot**	(b) a non-conformist
4. **iconoclast**	(c) a belief in the existence of one God
5. **dissenter**	(d) concerned with worldly matters, as contrasted with spiritual
6. **blaspheme**	(e) to speak irreverently of God or sacred things
7. **monotheism**	(f) one who believes in many gods
	(g) an utterly intolerant person

38

VI. Review

In each of the following sentences substitute for the blank an appropriate word selected from words 1-20 on the Basic Vocabulary List.

1. The utter lack of color in the room offended my _____ sensibilities. *aesthetic*

2. My father was *adamant* in his insistence that I get home every night by eleven o'clock.

3. If you had possessed greater *acumen* you would not have been deceived by the rather implausible statements of this swindler.

4. Mr. Smith was indicted for aiding and *abetting* the culprit in the commission of a felony.

5. Since we are of one mind on the subject, we may be said to be in *agreement - accord*

6. As time went on, tempers were frayed and words became increasingly *acrimonious*

7. When the rain had *abated* we ventured out to see how much damage had been done.

8. After long deliberation, the jury *acquitted* the defendant and he was immediately set free.

9. The old man attributed his remarkable health to his _____ habits. *abstemious*

10. Although we had worked on the problem for an hour, we gave it up as being too *abstruse* for our ordinary minds.

LESSON THREE

21. **a-grar-i-an** à-grâr'-ē-ăn (noun and adjective) [*ager* (Latin), "field"] — Relating to fields, their cultivation or, in general, interests of farmers.

The Industrial Revolution caused the change from an *agrarian* way of life to an urban one.

Related Form: agrarianism (the principle, theory, or practice of an equal or fair division of landed property)

Synonyms: rural, rustic, bucolic, pastoral, agricultural

Antonym: urban (pertaining to the city)

Phrase: agrarian laws

22. **a-lac-ri-ty** à-lăk'-rĭ-tĭ [*alacritas* (Latin), "liveliness"; from *alacer*, "lively"] — Briskness.

Laura was obviously pleased when I invited her to the Junior Prom, since she accepted my invitation with *alacrity*.

Related Form: alacritous

Synonyms: liveliness, sprightliness, promptness, eagerness

Antonyms: apathy, slowness, reluctance, unconcern, indifference, languor (*adj.* languid), dilatory

23. **al-le-vi-ate** ă-lē'-vĭ-āt [*alleviare, alleviatus* (Latin), "to lift up"; from *ad*, "to" + *levis*, "light"] — To lighten or lessen physical or mental pain or discomfort.

Henry's headache was so severe that only repeated doses of medicine could *alleviate* it.

Related Forms: alleviation, alleviative

Synonyms: assuage, allay, palliate, abate, mitigate, moderate, diminish, relieve

Antonyms: aggravate, intensify, increase, heighten

24. al-ter-ca-tion ôl-tĕr-kā'-shŭn [*altercatio* (Latin); from *alter*, "another"] — An angry, noisy dispute; a heated argument.

The discussion, which had begun with a friendly exchange of ideas, ended in an *altercation* of considerable bitterness.

Related Form: altercate

Synonyms: wrangle, brawl, quarrel, controversy, contention (*adj.* contentious)

Antonyms: amity (see Word 28), harmony, concord, agreement, accord, unison

25. al-tru-is-tic ăl-trōō-ĭs'-tĭk [*altruisme* (French), "altruism"; from *alter* (Latin), "another"] — Acting solely out of consideration for the welfare of others; unselfish.

"Most of us," Russell said, "are self-seeking; we believe that anyone who professes *altruistic* motives is either a liar or a fool."

Related Forms: altruism, altruist, altruistically

Synonym: charitable

Antonyms: egoistic, egocentric

And now abideth faith, hope, charity, these three; but the greatest of these is charity.

— *Bible*

---

26. a-mal-gam-ate ȧ-măl′-gȧ-māt [*amalgam* (Greek), "a softening agent"] — To combine into a uniform whole.

In order to reduce their operating expenses and consolidate their selling power, the two companies *amalgamated* into one large corporation.

Related Form: amalgamation

Synonyms: unite, unify, consolidate, merge (*noun:* merger), fuse (*noun:* fusion), confederation, alliance, blend, coalesce (*noun:* coalition)

Antonyms: disunite, sunder, sever (*noun:* severance), disunite, divide, diversify

Phrases: a *coalition* government, a *schism* (division) in the party.

In ethnology, an *amalgamation* of races is the biological fusion of diverse racial stocks. An *amalgam* is a mixture, union or combination of mercury plus some other metal; a mixture or combination.

27. am-biv-a-lent ăm-bĭv′-ȧ-lĕnt [*ambi* (Latin); "both" + *valens, valentis,* "worth"] — Wavering or uncertain because of an inability to make a choice between two conflicting courses of action.

My parents have *ambivalent* feelings about the college I have chosen: on the one hand, they are favorably impressed by its academic standards; on the other, they are unhappy about its great distance from home.

Phrase: an *ambivalent* emotion

Related Form: ambivalence

Note: Ambivalence, a term long common in psychology, has recently achieved the status of an everyday, vogue word. It denotes the coexistence within a person of contradictory viewpoints, conflicts in feelings about a person, a course of action, or of a thing. Since the conflicting feelings take place at the same time, the ambivalent feeling may result in indecisiveness or an emotional impasse.

42

28. am·i·ty ăm′-ĭ-tĭ [*amitié* (French); from *amicus* (Latin), "friend"] — Friendly relationship.

The treaty specified certain conditions under which *amity* between the two hitherto hostile nations might be attained.

Related Forms: amicable, amicably, amicability

Synonyms: accord, harmony, concord, friendliness, friendship, rapport

Antonyms: enmity, hostility, antipathy, discord, dissidence, friction

Phrases: to be en *rapport* (a relationship marked by harmony) *rapprochement* (establishment of state of cordial relations)

29. a·nach·ro·nism à-năk′-rŏ-nĭzm [*ana* (Greek), "backward" + *chronos,* "time"]

1. The misplacing of an event or object in a period (usually earlier) to which it cannot possibly belong; the event or object so placed.

   In *Julius Caesar,* Cassius' statement that "the clock has stricken three" is an *anachronism,* since mechanical clocks were not known in Roman times.

2. An occurrence which is incongruous with the present time or usage.

   Ten years ago a young man wearing long hair and a beard would have been considered an *anachronism;* today he is thought to be in fashion.

Related Forms: anachronistic, anachronous

Synonyms: obsolete, archaic

Antonyms: synchronize (*adj.* synchronous)

30. a·nal·o·gy à-năl′-ŏ-jĭ [*ana* (Greek), "upon," "according to," + *logos,* "ratio, proportion"]

1. A relation between two things that consists in the resemblance not of the things themselves but of their characteristics.

The poet drew an *analogy* between the laughter of children and the chirping of birds.

2. A proportion consisting of two pairs of things in which the relationship between the two things in each pair is the same.

man : house = bird : nest

Related Form: analogous

Synonyms: similarity, likeness, correspondence, congruence

Antonyms: dissimilarity, unlikeness, incompatibility, anomaly (deviation from the general rule, i.e. a fish that cannot swim)

An *anomaly* is a situation in which certain elements are self-contradictory; a paradox.

EXERCISES

I. Words Out of Context

In each of the following groups, select the word or phrase that most nearly expresses the meaning of the word at the left.

1. **ambivalent**   (a) equally divided   (b) skillful with both hands   (c) disquiet   (d) conflict of feelings

2. **alleviate**   (a) lighten   (b) intensify   (c) substantiate   (d) transpose

3. **anachronism**   (a) an ancient time   (b) a chronological error   (c) a contemporary occurrence   (d) a mistake in language

4. **analogy**   (a) transposition of the letters of a word   (b) correspondence   (c) separation of a material into its constituent elements   (d) a self-contradictory situation

5. **amalgamate**   (a) merge   (b) refine   (c) diversify   (d) subdue

II. Words in Context

A. Words in Phrases

Select the letter preceding the word or expression that best completes the meaning of the statement.

1. A spirit of *amity* is one that is (*a*) comic (*b*) enthusiastic (*c*) prompted by envy (*d*) friendly

2. An *anomalous* situation (*a*) is strangely inconsistent (*b*) conforms to a regular pattern (*c*) cannot easily be comprehended (*d*) is puzzling

3. I have *ambivalent* feelings toward Mary. My feelings are (*a*) deeply-rooted (*b*) hostile (*c*) decisive (*d*) mixed

4. The word "altruistic" might appropriately be applied to an action that is motivated primarily by (*a*) self-interest (*b*) consideration for others (*c*) vindictiveness (*d*) hostility

5. To *alleviate* a condition is to (*a*) make it easier to endure (*b*) to point out its less serious implications (*c*) render it more severe (*d*) criticize it bitterly

B. Words in Headlines

Select the letter preceding the word that expresses the meaning of the italicized word in each of the following newspaper headlines.

COURT BARS
PROPOSED *MERGER*

1. (*a*) disruption (*b*) amalgamation (*c*) dissidence (*d*) schism

JURY *ACQUITS*
ACCUSED OFFICIAL

2. (*a*) absolves (*b*) indicts (*c*) convicts (*d*) condemns

3. (*a*) congeniality (*b*) understanding (*c*) quarrel (*d*) accord

C. One-Word Omissions

In each of the following sentences substitute for the blank an appropriate word selected from words 21-30.

1. The two angry women engaged in an acrimonious *altercation*

2. Father Damien, the noble priest who exiled himself from France to live among lepers on the island of Molokai, was prompted by *altruistic* motives.

3. When Dad asked me to drive his new car to the station to meet our beautiful guest, you may be sure that I obeyed with undisguised *alacrity*

4. As the representative of a large agricultural state, Senator Wentworth was particularly interested in legislation which would bring about *agrarian* reforms.

5. Mutual interests and a compatibility of temperament have allowed Norway and Sweden to live side by side in *amity*

III. Synonyms and Antonyms

A. *Give three* **synonyms** *for each of the following words:*

1. **briskness** *alacrity*
2. **friendliness** *amity*
3. **self-centered** *selfish — egoistic*
4. **intensify** *aggravate — increase, heighten*
5. **accord** *harmony — concord, friendliness*
6. **ill-tempered** *surly, rude — curt*
7. **gracious** *amicable, urbane*
8. **mitigate** *abate — palliate, lessen*
9. **altercation** *quarrel — feud, contention, difference*
10. **sluggishness** *slowness — apathy*

B. *In each group below select the* **antonym** *of the word at the left:*

1. **alacrity**   (*a*) languor (*b*) sprightliness (*c*) irregularity (*d*) persecution

2. anachronism   (*a*) skepticism (*b*) antipathy (ⓒ) synchronism (*d*) enthusiasm

3. affable   (ⓐ) ill-tempered (*b*) unkind (*c*) merciful (*d*) untoward

4. aggravate   (*a*) arouse   (*b*) intensify   (*c*) diagnose (ⓓ) soften

5. alleviate   (*a*) render useful (ⓑ) aggravate (*c*) impeach (*d*) aggrandize

WORD BUILDING

I. PREFIXES

A. The Greek prefix **a-, an-** meaning "not," "without," "lacking," appears in many English words, including *anachronism*, which has been studied in this lesson. Note that the prefix takes the form **an** before a root beginning with a vowel and usually before the letter *h*. For example: *a* + *archy* becomes *anarchy*, meaning literally "without a ruler."

> *achromatic* — colorless

> *amoral* — without moral quality (that is, neither moral nor immoral)

B. The Greek prefix **an- ana-,** meaning "up," "upon," "back," "according to," "again," "excessively" is found in many English words, including *analogy*, studied in this lesson. You may recall that analogy is made up of two derivative parts *ana* "according to" + *logos*, "ratio," "proportion."

> *anagram* (literally, "letters *backward*") — the change of one word into another by altering the position of the letters

> *analysis* (literally, "a loosening *up*") — a separation or breaking up into parts

anatomy (literally "a cutting *up*") — the art of dissecting an animal or a plant; the structural makeup of the animal or plant

---

A DISTINCTION WITH A DIFFERENCE

A music critic once remarked that at a recent concert Madam Ferlendis, the great singer, sang dreadfully out of tune.

"Out of tune!" exclaimed one of her admirers. "No; she is not out of tune. She is singing in one key while the orchestra is playing in another."

C. The word **alleviate,** studied in this lesson, is derived from the Latin prefix *ad* (changed by assimilation to *al* before the consonant *l*) + *levis* "light."

levity — lightness of mind; frivolity

relieve — to free from a burden or lighten one's distress

Allied in meaning and form to the root *levis* "to lighten" is *levare,* "to raise" (oneself) "to lighten."

II. ROOTS

A. The Latin root **ager,** meaning "land," is used in a number of English words, including *agrarian,* studied in this lesson.

agriculture (*ager* "land" + *cultura* "cultivation") — the cultivation of land; farming

peregrination — traveling from one place to another; wandering about

B. The Latin root **alter,** meaning "other," is found in the word *altruistic* studied in this lesson.

alternative — a choice of one or another course of action, two courses proposed

48

alter ego — (literally "another") — a bosom companion, a very close friend

C. The Greek root **logy,** from *logos,* meaning "word," "study," "science," "ratio," "proportion," was studied in detail in the last lesson in connection with the word *analogy.* (See p. 43)

D. The Greek root **chrono, chronos** meaning "time," is found in many English words, among them *anachronism,* studied in this lesson.

chronic — continuing for a long time

chronicle — an account of facts or events in their proper order of time

synchronize — to coincide in point of date or time

EXERCISES

I. Word Analysis and Development

1. *Analysis* means "a separation or breaking up into parts." What word ending in the syllable *sis* means "a unification or combination of the parts or elements into a whole"? What is the adjective form of *analysis?*
analytical

2. How does an *egoist* differ from an *altruist?* What is *egoism?* What is the name of the great Viennese doctor who spent practically a lifetime exploring the workings of a man's ego? Consult an unabridged dictionary to determine the fine shade of difference between an *egoist* and an *egotist.* *Frued*
conserned with self   *selfist*

3. On one occasion a President of the United States, introducing his Secretary of State to a distinguished assembly, declared: "This gentleman is my *alter ego.*" What did he mean by this term?   *other self*

4. The Book of Exodus in the Bible tells of the *unleavened* bread made by the Israelites during the Passover. Explain the origin of this historic food. What is the name by which this *unleavened* food is commonly known? *Kosher*

5. In this lesson we studied the word *amity*, meaning "peace" "friendship."

   (a) Give one antonym for *amity*. *emmity*

   (b) What does "holding out an olive branch" mean? *peace*

   (c) Give the meaning of "They shall beat their swords into plowshares, and their spears into pruning hooks." Where does this quotation come from? *agrarian society from war people*

   (d) Which word in this group is out of place?
   controversy skirmish fray conciliation

   (e) What is Armageddon? *last days*

6. "Comparison" says the philosopher George Santayana, "is the expedient of those who cannot reach the heart of the thing compared." This is why we often refer to something not directly but something which suggests rather than denotes, our idea. For this purpose we often use figures of speech.

   Define each of the following common figures of speech.

   simile   metaphor   personification
   as

7. For each of the following definitions give a word with the Greek prefix *an, ana*:

   (a) the structural makeup of an animal *anatomy*

   (b) the change of one word into another by rearranging the letters *anagram*

   (c) the condition of a country without a ruler *anarchy*

8. Give the meaning of each of the following words in the light of its origin: *to lift - to lighten* (handwritten)
   (a) relevant (b) levitation (c) levy (d) lever

II. Quotations

(a) "The amity that wisdom knits not, folly
   May easily untie."

— Shakespeare

1. Give the meaning of this quotation in a short sentence.

2. Give a synonym for *amity* *friendship* (handwritten)

3. Give an antonym for *folly*.

4. Give an antonym for *untie*.

(b) "In the beginning," said a Persian poet, "Allah took a rose, a lily, a dove, a serpent, a little honey, a Dead Sea apple, and a handful of clay. When he looked at the *amalgam* — it was a woman." — William Sharp

5. What does the italicized word mean?

6. Give two synonyms for the italicized word.

(c) "As cold water to a faint soul,
   So is good news from a far country."

7. This proverb from the Bible is an example of a(n)
   (a) homily (b) parable (c) anachronism
   (d) analogy

(d) "There's *husbandry* in heaven;
   Their candles are all out."

— Shakespeare

8. Give a synonym for the italicized word.

9. What kind of night is described in Quotation (d)?

III. The Thesaurus: An Invaluable Vocabulary Aid

In the language family, no word is ever alone. It is dependent on relatives and friends — hosts of other words that contribute something of substance to its meaning. Occasionally a word stands out like a prodigy, like a comet in the sky, because it outshines all other words in shedding light on an idea: it says so much in its half dozen letters. The Latin has a word for this: *multum in parvo,* "much in little."

Every person, as he grows in ability to use his language, builds up a treasury of words and phrases, which are no more than interrelated words. One word suggests another, and the process goes on until you eventually are able to command a variety of words to convey concisely and interestingly what you wish to say. No word stands alone; neither does an idea stand alone. This interlocking of ideas is termed by psychologists "association of ideas."

A thesaurus is a special kind of dictionary in which basic words are classified according to ideas. It is a handy reference book for anyone who is hunting for a precise word.

A. Building Your Own Thesaurus

You might find it helpful to plan your own personal thesaurus as you proceed with the word studies in this book. Allot separate pages for general ideas suggested by the basic words. This arrangement will provide you with a reservoir of words to draw on for your writing. Let us plan a model page of your thesaurus using the concept of *time.* You may consult the dictionary as an auxiliary word builder.

TIME

1. Nouns

Give as many noun synonyms as you can for *time.*

Suggested Words: tenure, duration, infinity

Phrase Suggestion: ravages of time

2. **Verbs**

   Suggested Words: endure, abide, tarry

   Suggested Phrases: put in time, tide over

3. **Adjectives**

   Suggested Words: timeless, transient, brief, perpetual, ephemeral, prior, posterior

   Suggested Phrase: without end

B. Phrases Involving Time

1. A *time-server* is one who

   (*a*) chronicles great deeds (*b*) adjusts his conduct to his condition (*c*) repairs clocks

2. *Timely* advice is advice that is given

   (*a*) constantly (*b*) too late (*c*) at the right time

3. A *time-honored* tradition is one that

   (*a*) has been in effect a long time (*b*) is revered because it has continued long (*c*) requires time to attend to it

4. The opposite of *extinct* is

   (*a*) extraneous (*b*) extant (*c*) extrinsic (*d*) explicit

5. A *retroactive* clause in a contract is one that

   (*a*) cancels a previous clause (*b*) is made effective on a date prior to the enactment (*c*) becomes effective at a future date

6. *In good time* means

   (*a*) dilatorily (*b*) punctually (*c*) slowly

IV. Review

In each of the following sentences substitute for the blank an appropriate word selected from Words 1-30 on the Basic Vocabulary List.

1. I got into a very sharp _altercation_ with my sister over the question of whose turn it was to wash the dishes.

2. Even in the face of the most convincing arguments my stubborn neighbor remained _adamant_ in his point of view.

3. The picture in the gallery offended the _aesthetic_ sensibilities of the majority of people who saw it.

4. In his revision of his 1951 critical study of Marcel Proust, George Painter shows that he has lost none of his _adulation_ for the French novelist; in fact his admiration has assumed idolatrous proportions.

5. Although the medicine did not cure the patient's disease, it _abated_ his pain.

6. The author of this comic history filled his book with intentional _anachronisms_, such as having Mark Anthony's oration over Caesar's body broadcast by radio.

7. "You can catch more flies with sugar than with vinegar." That is what the diplomat means when he says that _amicability_ will make more conquests than hostility will.

8. The debate became increasingly _acrimonious_ as tempers rose and reason gave way to heated argument.

9. Ann's motives were frequently questioned, but I feel that her desire to help others is truly _altruistic_

10. The theory of relativity was so _abstruse_ that at one time only a few scientists could either understand it or explain it.

54

LESSON FOUR

31. a-nath-e-ma ȧ-năth'-ĕ-mȧ [*anathema* (Latin), "a curse"; from *anathema* (Greek), "a votive offering"]

1. Any object of intense dislike.

The word "capitalism" is *anathema* to the Communists.

Synonyms: detestation (*adjective:* detestable), abomination (*verb:* abominate), loathing, repugnance, abhorrence (*verb:* abhor), disgust

Antonyms: craving, covetousness

2. A curse; the person or thing cursed; denunciation.

Let us direct our *anathemas* not against individual evils, but rather against the society which allows such evils to exist.

Synonyms: malediction, execration, bane

Antonyms: eulogy, encomium

3. A formal ban or curse invoked by ecclesiastical (church) authority.

The Pope pronounced an *anathema* against the leader of the heretics who had openly defied his ecclesiastical authority.

Synonyms: excommunication, imprecation, execration, damnation, denunciation, proscription (*verb:* proscribe "outlaw")

Antonyms: blessing, benison, benediction

Related Forms: anathematize, anathematization

Note 1: An <u>anathema</u> is pronounced <u>against</u> a person or thing.

Note 2: In the New Testament, the word <u>anathema</u> was used to describe something accursed and therefore meriting condemnation and destruction. With the passing of time, the church authorities used the term <u>anathema</u> to designate a curse pronounced solemnly and formally whereby a thing or person was condemned as evil and consequently banned or excommunicated from the church. In general use today, an <u>anathema</u> is an object of utter repugnance.

Phrase: placed under a ban

32. an-i-mos-i-ty ăn-ĭ-mŏs'-ĭ-tĭ [*animus* (Latin), "courage," "spirit," "passion," "anger"] — Violent hatred, prejudice, or strong dislike, usually marked by outward expressions of hostility.

The *animosity* between the North and the South over the question of slavery was one cause of the Civil War.

Related Forms: animus (grudge, intense dislike). *Animus* is an English word derived from the Latin *animus,* meaning "soul" "spirit."

Synonyms: resentment, ill-will, enmity, antagonism, aversion

Antonyms: partiality for, proclivity, propensity, benevolence, cordiality, good-will

Phrases: a feeling of antagonism, felt animosity toward a person or thing

33. ap-a-thy ăp'-ȧ-thĭ [*a* (Greek) "without," + *pathos,* "suffering," "feeling"] — Lack of feeling, emotion, or interest.

Apathy is the enemy of freedom: concern will guard it.

Related Forms: apathetic, apathetically

Synonyms: lethargy, unconcern, indifference, aloofness, non-chalance

Antonyms: enthusiasm, interest, concern, zeal, eagerness, fervor, ardor

Note: A person is said to be "uninterested" when he takes no interest in a matter or is apathetic. A person is said to be "disinterested" when he has no self-interest in a matter, and is therefore unbiased or impartial.

34. a-pos-tate ȧ-pŏs'-tāt [*apo* (Greek), "away from" + *stasis*, "a standing"] — One who deserts his party, faith, or principles.

Although he knew that he would be condemned as an *apostate*, the statesman felt that he had to vote against his party's platform.

Related Forms: apostasy, apostatize, apostatism

Synonyms: (*nouns*) renegade, convert, deserter, turncoat; (*verbs*) forsake, abjure, repudiate

Note: An apostate turns <u>from</u> a cause or principles he professed; a convert turns <u>toward</u> a new cause or principles.

35. ap-pease ȧ-pēz' [*ad* "to" + *pax, pacis* (Latin), "peace"]

1. To satisfy by making concessions.

   Having submitted to Hitler's aggressive demands at Munich, Chamberlain learned to his regret that he failed to *appease* the dictator's lust for territorial aggrandisement.

2. Pacify, calm or soothe.

   There are times when only a hot dog and french fries will *appease* my hunger.

Related Forms: appeasement, appeaser

Synonyms: allay, assuage, placate, conciliate, propitiate (*adj.* propitiatory), mitigate

Antonyms: spurn, enrage, exacerbate, aggravate, defy

Phrase: a policy of appeasement

Note the use of the foregoing synonyms most of which can be used in clichés of everyday speech.

appease one's conscience   placate an enemy
allay thirst   assuage tension
mitigate an injury

36. **ap·pre·hen·sive** ăp-rĕ-hĕn′-sĭv [*ad* "to" + *prehendre, prehensus* (Latin), "to seize"] — Fearful of future danger or evil; anxious.

A black cat crossing my path lessened my already shaky self-confidence, and made me even more *apprehensive* of the test I was about to take.

Synonyms: uneasiness; presentiment (uneasy anticipation of danger), premonition, foreboding, qualm, misgiving (anticipation that unsettles one's self-confidence because of uncertainty)

Antonyms: self-confidence, composure, self-assurance, poise

Phrases: apprehensive *of* disaster; apprehensive *for* one's life

Note 1: Apprehension has two meanings, depending on the context. In the sentence, "Allan was filled with apprehension at the thought of going into a new business," the underlined word means "fear or anxiety as to the prospect." Apprehension may also mean "mental grasp," "intuitive understanding" or "perception," as in the sentence:
John Locke, the philosopher, was a man of keen apprehension.

Note 2: The verb apprehend may have a number of denotations:

1. To seize or take into custody:
The criminal was quickly apprehended.

2. To understand: I apprehended the meaning accurately.
(adj.: apprehensive; synonyms: perceptive, discerning)

3. To anticipate with anxiety:
To apprehend impending calamity may be more painful than to endure it when it comes.

58

37. ap-ti-tude ăp'-tǐ-tūd [*aptus* (Latin), "fitted"]

1. Natural or acquired ability.

   In order to become a professional pianist, one must possess both an *aptitude* for music and a willingness to practice for many hours each day.

2. Special fitness.

   Tom did very well in math and science, but he had no *aptitude* at all for languages.

Synonyms: talent, gift, capability, proclivity, bent, proneness (for)

Note the fine distinctions in the use of <u>apt, likely,</u> and <u>liable,</u> all of which have the general idea of "possessing a tendency in a certain direction."

<u>Apt</u> suggests the idea of habitual or inherent predisposition.
A careless driver is <u>apt</u> (i.e. prone or inclined) to be the cause of accidents to others as well as himself.

<u>Likely</u> suggests the idea of probable or expected.
It is <u>likely</u> to rain tomorrow.

<u>Liable</u> suggests an unpleasant eventuality.
The dog is <u>liable</u> to bite you if you keep teasing him.

<u>Apt</u> also means "appropriate," "relevant." <u>Adjectival synonyms:</u> germane, meet, fitting, pertinent.
an <u>apt</u> remark

38. ar-bi-tra-ry är'-bǐ-trǎ-rǐ [*arbitrare* (Latin), "to express an opinion as a witness"; from *arbiter*, "a witness," "a judge of any matter"] — Arrived at by the exercise of the will of an individual, not necessarily based on reason or justice, as an *arbitrary* decision, an *arbitrary* opinion.

The judge was accused of being *arbitrary* in meting out punishment: often he gave different sentences to two individuals guilty of like offenses.

Related Forms: arbitrarily, arbitrariness, arbiter (a judge), arbitrator, arbitration, arbitrable, arbitrament

Synonyms: (*adjectives*) autocratic, absolute, dictatorial, despotic, high-handed, overbearing, imperious, tyrannical; (*nouns*) moderator, referee

Antonyms: fair, just, equitable

Phrases: an *arbitrable* issue, *arbitrate* a dispute

Note: The verb <u>arbitrate</u> means "to submit or refer for decision to a referee or an arbiter."

39. ar·cha·ic är-kā′-ĭk [*archaios* (Greek), "old fashioned"] — Out-of-date; no longer used in ordinary speech or writing.

Such words as *oft* or *methinks* are archaic; no one would think of using these words in conversation today.

Related Forms: archaism (a rhetorical label denoting antiquated diction or style)

Synonyms: obsolete, antiquated

Antonyms: modern, recent, fashionable

40. ar·du·ous är′-dū-ŭs [*arduus* (Latin), "steep" + *ous* adjectival suffix meaning "characterized by"] — Requiring great exertion; severe.

It was an *arduous* task, but Cliff succeeded in overcoming the handicaps imposed by poverty and went on to become a respected lawyer.

Synonyms: strenuous, laborious, onerous, energetic, burdensome

Antonym: facile

Note: Do not confuse <u>arduous</u> (laborious — that is, difficult) with <u>ardent</u>, meaning "zealous," "fervid," as an <u>ardent</u> patriot (devoted, zealous). Synonyms of <u>ardent</u> include <u>fervid, eager, glowing.</u>

The noun form of <u>ardent</u> is <u>ardor.</u>

A related form of ardor is "ardency" — admired for the <u>ardency</u> (warmth) of his devotion.

EXERCISES

I. Words in Context

A. One-Word Omissions

In each of the following sentences substitute for the blank an appropriate word selected from the Basic Vocabulary List for this lesson.

1. The Emperor Julian was called Julian the _apostate_ because he had abandoned the Christian religion in which he had been brought up.

2. The idea of a totalitarian state is _anathema_ to every good American.

3. Although Mary has an analytical mind, she shows little _aptitude_ for mathematics.

4. Both the Democratic and the Republican leaders expressed concern over the _apathy_ of the voters: fewer than sixty per cent took the trouble to go to the polls.

5. I must admit that walking past a cemetery on a dark and windy night does make me feel _apprehensive_ though of what I don't know.

B. Words in Phrases

Each of the numbered phrases below contains an italicized word and is followed by four words or phrases lettered (a) to (d). Select the letter of the item that is closest in meaning to each italicized word, as used in the phrase.

1. *appeased* his indignation   (*a*) caused   (*b*) increased   (c) moderated   (*d*) eliminated

2. an *archaic* expression   (a) obsolete   (*b*) well expressed   (*c*) classic   (*d*) crude

3. an *arbitrary* judge (*a*) fair-minded (*b*) prejudiced (*c*) caustic (*d*) equitable

4. displayed *animosity toward* his rival (*a*) keen interest in (*b*) strong fear of (*c*) marked hostility to (*d*) magnanimity toward

5. an *arduous* campaign (*a*) tepid (*b*) tense (*c*) exciting (*d*) strenuous

C. Words in a Continuous Passage

In the passage below, certain words are underlined and numbered. Each numbered word is followed by four words or phrases lettered (a) to (d). Select the letter of the item that best completes the sentence.

"Hate is always tragic. It is as <u>injurious</u>[1] to the hater as it is to the hated. It distorts the personality and scars the soul. As a race we must work <u>passionately</u>[2] and <u>unrelentingly</u>[3] for first-class citizenship, but we must never use second-class methods to gain it. If this happens, unborn generations will be the recipients of a long and <u>desolate</u>[4] night of <u>bitterness</u>,[5] and our chief legacy to the future will be an endless reign of meaningless chaos."

— MARTIN LUTHER KING, JR.

1. A synonym for *injurious* is (*a*) acrimonious (*b*) noxious (*c*) sinister (*d*) apocryphal

2. *Passionately* means (*a*) apathetically (*b*) arduously (*c*) ardently (*d*) sincerely

3. *Unrelentingly* means (*a*) ceaselessly (*b*) sporadically (*c*) chronically (*d*) at once

4. *Desolate* means (*a*) tiring (*b*) uncompassionate (*c*) poverty-stricken (*d*) lonely

5. A synonym for *bitterness* is (*a*) discord (*b*) acrimony (*c*) pain (*d*) animosity

II. Words Out of Context

In each group below select the word or expression that most clearly expresses the meaning of the word at the left.

1. **arduous**   (a) warm-hearted (b) strenuous (c) devotional (d) keen

2. **aptitude**   (a) likelihood (b) gaucherie (c) ingenuity (d) natural ability

3. **arbitrary**   (a) in the nature of a referee (b) decisive (c) equitable (d) tyrannical

4. **apostate**   (a) renegade (b) missionary (c) adherent (d) evangelical

5. **apathy**   (a) calmness (b) lack of skill (c) indifference (d) concern

6. **animosity**   (a) liveliness (b) hostility (c) barbarism (d) nonchalance

7. **anathema**   (a) out of chronological order (b) grave concern (c) detestation (d) antipathy

8. **apprehensive**   (a) skilled (b) unaggressive (c) aggressive (d) anxious

9. **appease**   (a) divide (b) engage in belligerency (c) dissect (d) pacify

10. **archaic**   (a) chief (b) out-of-date (c) arrogant (d) domineering

III. Related Forms

1. *Give the noun form for the following words.*

appease   archaism   ardent   apathetic   apprehensive
apathy

2. In each of the following sentences, supply another form of the italicized word.

(a) A person who *appeases* is an _appeaser_

(b) An *apostate* is so-called because he has engaged in _apostasy_

(c) An *arbitrary* decision is characterized by _unfairness_

IV. Synonyms and Antonyms

A. For each group below select the synonym of the word at the left.

1. **palliate** _abate_   (a) incite   (b) abet   (c) egg on   (d) mitigate

2. **propitiate** _appease_   (a) alarm   (b) placate   (c) commiserate   (d) expropriate

3. **onerous** _arduous_   (a) burdensome   (b) unified   (c) uncivil   (d) noisy

4. **enmity** _amity (opp)_   (a) jealousy   (b) wrath   (c) antagonism   (d) cordiality

5. **malediction** _anathema_   (a) execration   (b) reluctance   (c) gossip   (d) despotism

B. For each word in Column A find an antonym in Column B.

A	B
1. obsolete _e_	(a) aggravate
2. exacerbate _d_	(b) anxiety
3. composure _b_	(c) authentic
4. overbearing _f_	(d) conciliate
5. assuage _a_	(e) fashionable
	(f) meek

64

WORD BUILDING

I. PREFIXES

A. The Greek prefix **a** (variant **an**) meaning "without" "not" appears in many English words, including *apathy, apostate,* studied in this lesson. For a detailed analysis and further discussion of this Greek prefix, see Lesson 3, p. 47. Other English words containing this prefix include *asymmetrical, atonal.*

B. The Latin prefix **ad,** "to" appears in many English words including *apprehensive, appease,* studied in this lesson. For a further discussion of this Latin prefix see Lesson 1, p. 11.

II. SUFFIXES

The Latin suffix **ous** (**osus**) "full of" "characterized by" "pertaining to" appears in numerous English words including *arduous,* studied in this lesson, *nervous* — affecting the nerves, *gracious* — characterized by grace or mercy.

III. ROOTS

A. The Greek root **pathos,** "suffering" has made an invaluable contribution to formation of many English words, particularly medical terms. The derivative *pathos* has been adopted without change into English and means "a quality that arouses sympathy or pity." The English stem *pathy* lends the meaning "feeling" "disease" "treatment" to the other parts with which it combines to form a complete word. Note the following words:

> *sympathy* (*sym* "with" + *pathy*) — feeling for, or identifying with, another's suffering
>
> *pathetic* — exciting pity or sorrow; sad, pitiable
>
> *psychopathy* (*psycho* "mind" + *pathy*) — mental disease

B. The Greek root **arch** (the *ch* is pronounced hard like *k*) takes a variety of related forms and meanings in Greek words.

> *archais* means "ancient"
>
> *arche* means "government, beginning"
>
> *archos* means "leader, commander"

The Greek root is found in the English word *archaic* studied in this lesson.

Other English derivatives include *archaeology* (variant spelling *archeology*), from *archais*, "ancient" + *logos*, "an account of," *anarchy* (see Lesson 3, p. 47 for a discussion of this word) *patriarch*, from *patria*, "clan" + *archos*, "ruler."

EXERCISES

I. Word Analysis and Word Development

Meederas is an arch bishop

1. The word *arch* is used in many phases in English and has various meanings. Compose three sentences, each of which uses *arch* to express a different (and correct) meaning. *Arohom is a patriarch*

2. Draw up a list of five English words that are derived from the Greek prefix *archaios, arche*. Show how the meaning of the word is derived from its Greek forbear.
archeology – study of the beginning

3. The words ardor and arson are related in meaning and origin to *arduous* studied in this week's lesson. What does ardor mean? Use it correctly in a sentence. What adjective is formed from this word? What is *arson*? Explain why this word should be used, to be precise, in only one kind of situation.

4. What is a prefix? What is a suffix? What does each of the following prefixes or suffixes mean: *ous, ad, ab, a, ana*? How does the prefix *ad* or *ab* change when added to roots

or stems beginning with a consonant? Give three words that are examples of such assimilation.

5. What does the phrase "bell, book and candle" signify? In what connection was this phrase used in the middle ages. Consult an unabridged dictionary for the interesting history behind this phrase. Explain the reference to the phrase in the sentence: "The heretic was not merely rebuked; he had bell, book and candle hurled at him."

II. Analogies

In each of the following select the word in parentheses that completes the analogy correctly.

1. planet : satellite = guru : (apostate, disciple, altruist, benison)

2. bees : apiary = birds : (allegory, alacrity, aviary, apathy)

3. authentic : counterfeit = chronological accuracy: (anachronism, agnosticism, asperity, punctuality)

4. assiduous : diligent = indolent : (inconsolable, lethargic, abstemious, charitable)

5. animosity : enemies = (aptitude, enmity, antagonism, congeniality) : friends

III. A Dictionary Project

Old-Fashioned or Modern

1. The following labels characterizing the nature of usage may be found at the end of certain entries in the dictionary.
   archaic   obsolete   vulgarism   colloquialism   slang
   vogue word

   Define each of these terms. Give two words for each of the above characterizations.

2. In your notebook, arrange the following words in lists under the following proper headings.

Archaic Slang	Accepted Current Usage Vogue Words	Provincialism	Colloquialisms
/ o'er	freak	hipped	hang-up
oddball	chunk	₂ exam	₂ confrontation
stench	brag	nutty	swinger
₂ monopoly	₂ methinks	tote	balled up
₂ pants	to crab	₂ extraordinary	₂ mystique

IV. Fun With Words

It Does Make a Difference!

1. Select the correct word in each group below:

   (*a*) What an (arduous, ardent) task we faced!

   (*b*) We achieved laudable results because we had (arduous, ardent) friends who were (sympathetic, antipathetic) to our cause.

   (*c*) The referee was condemned because his decision showed him to be obviously (disinterested, uninterested).

2. Explain how the misuse of a word in each sentence below conveys an erroneous and usually the opposite impression than was intended.

   (*a*) "Richardson, a life-long Republican, turned Democrat. He has been condemned by his former friends as an apostle." apostate

   (*b*) "Every one praised Judge Durant for his arbitrary decision. We need more judges like this fine jurist."

   (*c*) "Appeasement never works. Every time we try to appease a dictator we only make him more conciliatory." less

3. A story often is concealed behind a word in common use. Look up the names or stories from which each of the following words are derived. If possible tell the story. Define the word.

boycott   bedlam   *Pasteur* pasteurize   lynch   marionette
sandwich   academy   mesmerize   cantaloup   gospel
Karl

4. "I am the monarch of all I survey" — William Cowper

In which country listed under **B** would the titles (past and present) under **A** be correct.

A	B
1. **shogun**	(a) Venice
2. **doge**	(b) India
3. **sheik**	(c) Spain
4. **sachem**	(d) China
5. **shah**	(e) Germany
6. **maharani nabob**	(f) Japan
7. **mandarin**	(g) Arabia
8. **archon**	(h) Greece
9. **grandee**	(i) American Indian
10. **herr**	(j) Persia

CARRYING COALS TO NEWCASTLE

As Newcastle, England, is a big port from which coal is exported to all parts of the world, it would naturally be well stocked with coal. Hence, the expression "to carry coals to Newcastle" means to do what is superfluous or to take something to a place where it is already plentiful.

V. Word Building Activities

1. What is an *archdiocese*? What church official resides in an archdiocese? Give the adjective form of *archdiocese*.

2. If we said that Senator Burns is advocating *archaic* methods of dealing with a situation, we would be accusing him of proposing methods that are

   (*a*) highly effective (*b*) modern (*c*) antiquated
   (*d*) impractical

3. What is a *patriarch*? Who are three patriarchs mentioned in the Bible? Who is the *archfiend*, alluded to in the Bible, who rebelled against God?

4. In the phrase "an *arch* smile" the italicized word means
   (*a*) mischievous (*b*) cynical (*c*) lordly

5. The word *arch* in such phrases as "an arch enemy" "an arch rebel" means
   (*a*) very important (*b*) brave (*c*) dictatorial

6. An *archetype* is an original model or pattern. What is a *stereotype*? A *prototype*?

7. Which of the following church officials is *higher* in rank? *bishop, archbishop.* Explain.

8. Add *arch* to each of the following and show how the addition adds stature or dimension to the original word:
   angel   duke

9. What are *archives*? Explain this word in the light of its origin. You may consult the dictionary.

10. *Match the word in Column A with its meaning in Column B.*

A	B
1. **monarchy**	(*a*) government by the few
2. **hierarchy**	(*b*) rule by a sovereign
3. **oligarchy**	(*c*) a ruling body arranged into a series of grades

VI. For the Ambitious Student

1. The following are medical names of systems or methods of treating disease. With or without consulting the dictionary, tell what each of these terms means.

   1. hydropathy
   2. allopathy
   3. homeopathy
   4. osteopathy

2. John Ruskin coined the phrase *pathetic fallacy* to denote the fallacy of writers who under emotional stress endow inanimate objects with human feelings. For example: "the melancholy moon" "the angry sea."

   (*a*) Draw up a list of five other examples of the "pathetic fallacy."

   (*b*) What is the figure of speech which poets use in an attempt to make their imagery more vivid by ascribing human qualities to inanimate nature?

   (*c*) *Empathy* is a word that has recently become increasingly popular. What does this word mean? From what science was this word adopted? Describe a situation which illustrates a feeling of *empathy*.

3. What is mental tele*pathy*? Do you believe in such an occurrence? Defend your view.

4. "John is a psychopath," said Dr. Albert. This means that, in the doctor's view, John
   (*a*) is insane   (*b*) can easily read another's mind
   (*c*) is suffering from a mental disorder

5. To the viewer a *pathetic* sight is
   (*a*) horrifying   (*b*) touching   (*c*) exhilarating

6. A *pathological* liar is one who

   (*a*) lies occasionally and then only under emotional stress

   (*b*) tells "white" lies

   (*c*) lies continually and without self-restraint

VII. Review

A Backward Glance

Complete the following sentences by filling in each set of blanks with the appropriate pair of words or phrases.

1. One who is _adamant_ is _obdurate_.
   (*a*) adamant — obdurate (*b*) affable — imaginative
   (*c*) avid — dilatory

2. A person who is __b__ may be characterized as _____.
   (*a*) altruistic — egotistic (*b*) sparing in diet — abstemious (*c*) ascetic — agnostic (*d*) parsimonious — munificent

3. A(n) __c__ reply is usually _____.
   (*a*) ambiguous — decisive (*b*) chronic — timely
   (*c*) acrimonious — caustic (*d*) curt — banal

4. A treatise that is __b__ is _____.
   (*a*) abstruse — inane (*b*) recondite — esoteric
   (*c*) hackneyed — archaic (*d*) acute — pellucid

5. To __c__ a crime is to _____ it.
   (*a*) abate — solve (*b*) be an accessory to — abate
   (*c*) abet — encourage (*d*) prevent — alleviate

LESSON FIVE

41. aroma *fragrance*	46. assuage
42. ascetic	47. audacity
43. askew	48. augment
44. asperity	49. austere
45. assiduous	50. authentic

41. **a-ro-ma** à-rō'-mà [*aroma* (Greek), "spice"] — Fragrance usually from food, flowers or spices.

The *aroma* of freshly roasted coffee pervaded the room.

Synonyms: odor, scent, smell, redolence

Note: <u>Aroma</u> refers to a pungent, spicy odor; as, the <u>aroma</u> of pickles.

<u>Fragrance</u> describes a smell that is sweet and agreeable; as, the <u>fragrance</u> of honeysuckle.

<u>Odor</u> and <u>smell</u> refer to something that may be either pleasant or unpleasant, as, the <u>odor</u> of old leather, the <u>odor</u> of hydrogen sulphide.

<u>Scent</u> is less strong than <u>odor</u> or <u>smell</u>; as, the scent of lilac on a lady's handkerchief.

<u>Stench</u> is an offensive foul smell or odor; as the <u>stench</u> of burning rubber.

42. **as-cet-ic** ă-sĕt'-ĭk [*asketikos* (Greek), "an athlete," undergoing the training of an athlete. The term *ascetic* was given to the early Christian monks who gave up interest in worldly affairs to practice piety and religious devotion in solitude.]

1. (*noun*) One who devotes himself to a solitary, rigorously disciplined life, especially for religious reasons; one who practices extreme self-denial.

   Believing the world to be evil, the *ascetic* retired to a crude shelter in the woods and spent his time in contemplation and prayer.

2. (*adjective*) Rigidly self-denying, especially for religious or philosophical reasons.

   His room had an *ascetic* quality; it contained no personal possessions or ornaments of any kind.

Related Forms: asceticism, ascetical, ascetically

Synonyms: (*adjectives*) austere, rigid, severe, abstemious, unworldly; (*nouns*) puritan, recluse, hermit

Antonyms: (*adjectives*) self-indulgent, sensual, gluttonous; (*nouns*) hedonist, epicurean

Note 1: An <u>ascetic</u> exercises severe self-discipline for religious or philosophical reasons. A <u>stoic</u> aims to be calm, to be indifferent to pleasure or pain, to be independent of passion. A <u>hedonist</u> makes pleasure his principal aim.

Note 2: <u>Sensual</u> (noun: sensuality) refers to gratification of the appetites or to pleasures through the senses. The word is used in a disparaging sense.

The critics agreed that the much-advertised movie was merely extremely <u>sensual</u> and otherwise had nothing to recommend it.

<u>Sensuous</u> means "perceived by or affecting the senses."

He was attuned to the <u>sensuous</u> delights of the early morning: the high, sweet calls of the orioles, the smell of the salt marshes, the sparkle of the sun on the bay.

Phrase: the *sensuous* appeal of Keats' poem

Note 3: An <u>epicurean</u> is one who devotes himself to the pursuit of pleasure or luxury in any form. An <u>epicure</u> is one who gets special satisfaction and enjoyment primarily in eating and drinking.

THAT WORD
ASCETIC

The word ascetic *has an interesting history. In Greece the word meant hard-working and practicing self-discipline, and was applied to athletes who worked hard at gymnastics in order to win coveted prizes at Olympic Games. Among the early Christians to whom the term* ascetic *was applied were monks who practised not gymnastics but self-mortification — self-denial as a form of self-discipline. The ascetics, living apart from the world, were severely austere. Today, in a general sense, an* ascetic *is one who denies himself the normal pleasures of life which tend to accentuate material satisfaction.*

---

43. a-skew ȧ-skū′ [Derivation is uncertain; probably *skew* (English), "slanting"; from *eschever* (Old French), "eschew," "avoid"] — Out of position or line; turned to one side.

The drawers had been pulled out of the bureaus; the lamps had been knocked over; every picture on the wall was *askew*.

Synonyms: oblique, unsymmetrical, awry (pronounced à-rī'), distorted, crooked

Antonyms: straight, symmetrical, balanced, proportioned

Phrase: plans went *awry* (amiss, wrong)

Note: To look <u>askance</u> at a thing means to look sidewise or obliquely at it. The word <u>askance</u> (variant <u>askant</u>) carries the connotation of mistrust, suspicion, or disapproval.

44. **as-per-i-ty** ăs-pĕr'-ĭ-tĭ [*asper* (Latin), "rough"] — Severity of manner, temper, or language; sharpness or roughness of temper, tone, manner or language.

Michael apologized for the *asperity* of his speech, attributing the sharpness of his manner to a severe headache.

Synonyms: harshness, acerbity, acrimony, tartness, astringency, crabbedness, irascibility (*adj: irascible*), severity

Antonyms: gentleness, mildness, affability, cheerfulness

Phrases: the asperities (hardships, rigors) of life; an *astringent* (stern) remark

45. **as-sid-u-ous** ă-sĭd'-û-ŭs [*assiduus* (Latin), "sitting constantly in one place"; from *ad*, a prefix that intensifies the meaning of the verb *sedere*, "to sit"] — Performed with constant, energetic application; devoted.

By *assiduous* study and toil the immigrant students placed themselves on a par with their native-born classmates.

Related Forms: assiduously, assiduousness, assiduity

Synonyms: diligent, persevering, attentive, persistent, tenacious, unremitting, sedulous, industrious, unflagging

Antonyms: indolent, flagging, vacillating, dilatory, languid, slothful, torpid, inactive, inert, idle

Phrase: an *assiduous* worker

There is nothing truly valuable which can be purchased without pains and labour.

— JOSEPH ADDISON

---

46. as-suage ă-swāj′ [ad (Latin), "to" + suavis, "sweet"]
— To relieve or lessen, as grief or pain; to pacify or calm,
as passion; to put an end to by satisfying, as hunger or
thirst.

The minister did his best to *assauge* the grief of the distressed
parents.

Related Form: assuagement

Synonyms: alleviate (see page 40), mitigate, allay, palliate,
appease, abate (see page 1), mollify, moderate

Antonyms: aggravate (see page 22), increase, intensify, magnify, augment (see page 77), heighten

Note: Webster's New International Dictionary explains the difference in meaning of four of the above synonyms as follows: "Alleviate, mitigate, assuage, allay agree in expressing relief from some painful state. To alleviate is to lighten or render more tolerable. To mitigate is to soften or make
milder; as, to mitigate the severity of winter. To assuage is to quiet or
render less violent; as, to assuage resentment (anger). To allay is to abate
or bring down from a state of tumult or disturbance; as, to allay one's
fears or popular excitement."

A soft word turneth away wrath.

— The Bible

---

47. au-dac-i-ty ô-dăs′-ĭ-tĭ [audax (Latin), "bold"]

1. Daring disregard of danger.

Pioneering scientific exploration in the Arctic and the Ant-
arctic regions called for almost superhuman *audacity* on the
part of Admiral Byrd.

Synonyms: (*adjectives*) reckless, bold, venturesome, valiant,
adventurous

Antonyms: cowardly, craven, docile

76

2. Open, bold and arrogant disregard of propriety and law.

The *audacity* of the despot, who ignored all pleas for moderation and self-restraint, eventually incited the hopeless masses to rebellion.

Synonyms: boldness, brazenness, presumption (*adj:* presumptive, presumptuous)

Antonyms: meekness, timidity

3. Insolence.

Fred's *audacity* in heckling the invited speaker shocked even his friends in the audience.

Synonyms: effrontery (shameless, impudent audacity), temerity, impudence, gross indecorum

Antonyms: decorousness, decorum, propriety

Related Forms: audacious, audaciousness

Phrase: an *audacious* (bold, fearless — extremely original) exposé

---

48. aug-ment ôg-mĕnt′ [*augmentum* (Latin), "an increase"; from *augere*, "to increase"] — To increase in amount or intensity; to enlarge in size or extent.

If we are to contend with the population explosion, we must *augment* the world's food supply.

Related Forms: (noun) augmentation, (adjective) augmented

Synonyms: expand (adj. expansive), swell, extend, enhance (see page 233), distend, dilate

Antonyms: decrease, lessen, abate (see page 1), contract, shrink, shrivel, compress

Phrase: a *wizened* (shriveled) old woman

---

49. aus-tere ôs-tēr′ [*austerus* (Latin), "sour, harsh in taste," "severe"; from *austeros* (Greek), "dry, withered"]

1. Rigidly severe in character, manner, living conditions.

During World War II, living conditions for the people of England were extremely *austere* because of a shortage of food and fuel as well as all other forms of consumer goods.

Synonyms: stern, strict, rigorous (*noun:* rigor), ascetic, uncompromising, sober

Phrase: austerities (ascetic practices)

Antonyms: gentle, mild, affable, tolerant, indulgent, conciliatory

Phrase: a life of austerity (without luxuries, of limited means)

2. Severely simple; often said of a literary style or dress.

Religion as practiced by the Puritans was *austere* and without elaborate ceremonies and rituals.

Synonyms: severe, forbidding, stern, rigid

Antonyms: luxurious, ornate

Phrases: an *austere* (severely simple) regimen, a *forbidding* (stern, austere) manner

Related Forms: austerly, austerity, austereness

50. **au·then·tic** ô-thĕn'-tĭk [*authentique* (French); from *authentes* (Greek), literally "one who does something with his own hand"; from *autos*, "self" + *hentes*, doer] — Genuine in origin; trustworthy.

The dealer claimed that the newly-discovered painting was an *authentic* Rembrandt, but investigation proved it to be a forgery.

Related Forms: authentically, authenticate, authenticity

Synonyms: real, authorized, official, true, reliable

Antonyms: counterfeit, spurious, false, apocryphal

EXERCISES

I. Words in Context

A. One-Word Omissions

In each of the following sentences substitute for the blank an appropriate word selected from Words 41-50 on the Basic Vocabulary List.

1. The meeting house of the Puritans was a(n) *austere* structure, whose only outer architectural adornment was a tall white steeple.

2. Mr. Schultz glared at the fender of the car. Then turning and glaring at the driver of the other car, he said, with considerable *asperity,* "That is the fender I had put on just this morning!"

3. Kindness can do much to lessen hurt and *assuage* anger.

4. It took incredible *audacity* to serve for years as a spy in the innermost councils of the enemy's war headquarters.

5. St. Francis of Assisi, having taken the vows of poverty, chastity and humility, led a very *ascetic* life, providing his fellows with an exemplary model of self-denial.

B. Words in Phrases

Select the identifying letter of the word or phrase that is closest in meaning to the italicized word as used in each of the following phrases.

1. an *authentic* document (*a*) historical (*b*) certified (*c*) of doubtful authorship (*d*) signed

2. a policy of *appeasement* (*a*) terror (*b*) laissez-faire (*c*) despotism (*d*) conciliation

3. an *aesthetic* appeal pertaining to (*a*) beauty (*b*) self-denial (*c*) medicine (*d*) eloquence

79

4. *augmented* the malaise (*a*) allayed (*b*) aggravated
   (*c*) belittled (*d*) caused

5. noted for his *acumen* (*a*) keen insight (*b*) asperity
   (*c*) audacity (*d*) brusqueness

C. Two-Word Omissions

*Each selection below contains one or more blanks, indicating
the omission of material necessary to the sense. Following each
selection are four choices lettered (a) to (d). Select the letter
of the item that best completes the meaning of each selection.*

1. To propose such a radically drastic solution to a chronic
   problem required not only the _____ of a visionary but
   the _____ of a shrewd and practical statesman.

   (*a*) asperity — perspicacity   (*c*) alacrity — asceticism
   (*b*) acumen — authenticity   (*d*) audacity — acumen

2. "No great man is ever _____. It was his intellectual
   _____ and unconscious assumption of superiority that
   men like Chase and Sumner could never forgive." —

   JOHN HAY, *Lincoln*

   (*a*) audacious — meekness   (*c*) adamant — haughtiness
   (*b*) modest — arrogance   (*d*) acrimonious — affability

3. The students in the universities demanded a greater role
   in the policy-making decisions which they asserted affected them as much as they did the university adminis-
   tration. Having been denied this responsibility, they rose
   in noisy, often violent rebellion, insisting that the only way
   to _____ their discontent is to _____ their share in ad-
   ministering the universities.

   (*a*) mete out — increase   (*c*) ratify — amplify
   (*b*) augment — alleviate   (*d*) placate — augment

4. The marked contradictions in the leader of the poor people's protest puzzled many people, even those who knew him intimately. Personally he was _ᴀᴄ_, content with a few necessities and yet he wanted to see people get luxuries. Mild-mannered offstage, in his public utterances there was a bite to his language that amounted to _____.

    (*a*) ascetic — asperity   (*c*) altruistic — asceticism
    (*b*) stoic — affability   (*d*) abstemious — austerity

5. Vladimir Nabokov's early novels were published by emigrant Russian presses in Europe, and their potential readership must have been small and _ᴄ_ indeed. It is hard to guess what the other émigrés must have thought of him — this improbable monster of a writer who shared so little with his émigré associates beyond a common _____ of the regime which had driven them out of the Russia of their childhood.

    (*a*) prodigious — encomium   (*c*) confined — loathing
    (*b*) constricting — eulogy   (*d*) universal — anathema

D. Words in a Continuous Passage:

Read the following passage by the English poet Oliver Goldsmith in which he describes his father, the village parson. Then answer the questions below in relation to the numbered and underlined words in the passage.

> Thus to relieve[1] the wretched was his pride,
> And e'en his failings leaned to virtue's side;
> But in his duty, prompt at every call,
> He watched and wept, he prayed and felt for all.[2]
> And, as a bird each fond endearment tries
> To tempt its new-fledged offspring to the skies,
> He tried each art, reproved[3] each dull delay,
> Allured[4] to brighter worlds, and led the way.

1. A synonym for *relieve* is (*a*) exacerbate (*b*) condone (*c*) assuage (*d*) solace

2. A word which conveys the idea in the phrase *felt for all* is (*a*) empathy (*b*) pathos (*c*) omniscience (*d*) omnipresence

3. A synonym for *reproved* is (*a*) overlooked (*b*) justified (*c*) encouraged (*d*) disapproved

4. *Allured* as used in the context, means (*a*) enticed (*b*) urged on (*c*) deceived (*d*) accosted

II. Words Out of Context

In each group below, select the word or expression that most nearly expresses the meaning of the boldface word at the left.

1. **asperity** (*a*) hope (*b*) characteristic of an asp (*c*) astringency (*d*) hesitancy of speech

2. **assuage** (*a*) mitigate (*b*) sweeten (*c*) assault (*d*) intensify

3. **assiduous** (*a*) inert (*b*) attentive (*c*) sedative (*d*) treacherous

4. **augment** (*a*) enhance (*b*) diminish (*c*) beautify (*d*) solidify

5. **authentic** (*a*) spurious (*b*) apocryphal (*c*) authorized by law (*d*) genuine

6. **austere** (*a*) flexible (*b*) stern (*c*) sensitive to beauty (*d*) unpropitious

7. **askew** (*a*) puzzled (*b*) turned to one side (*c*) balanced (*d*) disorderly

8. **aroma** (*a*) false report (*b*) unpleasant noise (*c*) harsh sound (*d*) fragrance

9. **audacity** (*a*) insolence (*b*) sense of hearing (*c*) cowardice (*d*) brazenness

10. **ascetic** (*a*) beautiful (*b*) self-denying (*c*) gluttonous (*d*) bitter

III. Syllabication and Pronunciation

Syllabicate the following words correctly, and place the major stress mark (') after the syllable which is accented when the word is pronounced.

EXAMPLE: *in-volve'*

1. aro′ma
2. ascet′ic
3. askew′
4. asperity
5. assid′uous

6. assuage′
7. audacity,
8. augment′
9. austere′
10. authen′tic

IV. Related Forms

Give an adjectival form of the following nouns.

1. audacity *cious*
2. aromat *ic*
3. hedonism *nistic*
4. symmetry *tric*
5. languor *languid*

6. tenacity *tenuous*
7. palliation *ary*
8. presumption *ious*
9. expansion *tious*
10. rigor *ous*

V. Synonyms and Antonyms

A. *For each word in Column A select a synonym from Column B.*

A	B
1. timid *f*	(a) avoid
2. recluse	(b) arbitrary
3. awry	(c) asymmetrical
4. gourmand	(d) apt
5. eschew	(e) abstruse
	(f) retiring
	(g) hermit
	(h) glutton

B. *In each group of four words below select the two words that are either synonyms or antonyms.*

1. (a) stench (b) malignancy (c) maladroitness (d) aptitude

2. (a) epicurean (b) ascetic (c) aesthetic (d) acrid

3. (a) crooked (b) synchronous (c) obscene (d) awry

4. (a) resilient (b) abstruse (c) acrimonious (d) esoteric

5. (a) sedulous (b) flagging (c) sleepy (d) patriotic

WORD BUILDING

I. PREFIXES

The Latin prefix **ad,** meaning "to," intensifies the meaning of the verb *sedere,* "to sit" as seen in the meaning of *assiduous* "performed with *constant,* energetic application."

   adamant — very, or impenetrably, hard

Ad is often assimilated (merged) with another part of a word (usually a stem or root) and in the process takes on the first letter (consonant) of the root. Thus **ad** + **firm** becomes *affirm.*

II. ROOTS

A. The Latin root **sed (-sid), sess,** from *sedere, sessus,* "sit" is found in the word *assiduous,* studied in this lesson.

   obsession — continuous dwelling on one idea; also such an idea

   sedulous — untiring in application (sitting constantly) to one's work

   sedentary — characterized by much sitting

sediment — matter that settles to the bottom of a liquid

sedative — soothing, calming

Other words from this root are *seat* and *situation*.

B. The Greek root **auto(s)** meaning "self" or "same" appears in the word *authentic* studied in this lesson. Other words derived from this root are

autocrat — one who rules by himself

autonomy — self-government

autobiography — a biography written by the subject of the narrative himself

EXERCISES

I. Etymology Mastery Test

1. Ad is occasionally added to another Latin word to compose a phrase commonly used in English.

Define each of the following phrases and show the part the prefix **ad** *plays in the combination.*

ad libitum (short form: *ad lib*)   *to talk forever*

ad hoc *for this case only*   ad nauseam *to a sickening*

   ad infinitum

2. Give an English synonym for *monomania* which contains the Latin root **sed**.

3. Give a noun form for:

sedate

sedative   seditious   *obsessesion* obsessive   sedate

4. Show the part the Greek root **auto** plays in the meaning of *automatic, autogyro, autopsy*.

5. Define and use correctly in a sentence *sedate, preside, supersede*. *calm   live*

II. Word Analysis and Development

1. Explain the meaning of *austere* as used in each of the following sentences.

   (*a*) The classical essayist wrote in an *austere* style.

   (*b*) The *austere* clergyman opposed the frivolous amusements of his parishioners.

   (*c*) She wore the *austere* costume of a missionary nurse.

2. Why is a person who aims to undermine the authority of a government called *subversive*? What is meant by a "*seditious* speech"?

3. Explain the meaning of *authentic* in each of the following expressions: *authentic* news, an *authentic* signature, an *authentic* stage setting, an *authentic* portrait.

4. Here are several synonyms, each descriptive of a disagreeable manner, speech, or disposition: *tart, acidulous, astringent, acrid.*

   (*a*) Use each in a sentence.

   (*b*) How many other synonyms of these words can you give? (One suggestion: *vinegary*)

5. (*a*) What common root is found in the words *reside, preside, subside* and *residue*?

   (*b*) What personality traits would you associate with a person who is characterized as *sedate*?

   (*c*) What is a *sedentary* occupation?

   (*d*) Why is a bird that does not migrate with the change of seasons called *sedentary*?

6. Does this sentence, "Mary is said to have an obsession," mean that

   (*a*) Mary has a fixed idea on a subject that she cannot dispel?

   (*b*) Mary has a possession of great value?

   (*c*) Mary has a great fear?

7. "Whom the Lord loveth he chasteneth" — THE BIBLE. According to this statement
   (a) The Lord praises those whom He loves.
   (b) The Lord punishes those whom He loves in order to improve their conduct.
   (c) The Lord persecutes those whom He loves.

8. Which word is out of place in this series?
   gourmand   glutton   ~~ascetic~~   hedonist

III. Building Your Own Thesaurus

1. The word *askance* means "turned sideways or "with distrust," as in the sentence, "He looked at the signature *askance* (with distrust)." Here are ten synonyms for the general word "look."

glare	glance	leer	peep
ogle	peer	stare	gloat

   Each word of itself suggests the manner of looking. With or without the aid of a thesaurus (or a dictionary) compose a sentence in which each of these words is used so that its special meaning is clear.

2. With or without the aid of a thesaurus write as many synonyms as you can for "look" without duplicating any of those printed above.

IV. Review

Use each of the following Basic Vocabulary words in a sentence that clearly shows its meaning.

1. agrarian	6. arduous
2. analogous	7. acquit
3. accessory	8. abhor
4. accost	9. anathema
5. adulation	10. amity

V. Fun With Words

A. Manners Makyth Man

The word **asperity** studied in this lesson characterizes the tone, manner, or language of a person. Other aspects of manner and tone are described by the words under Column **A**. Match the type of person under **A** with the manner of his speech or conduct as described in **B**.

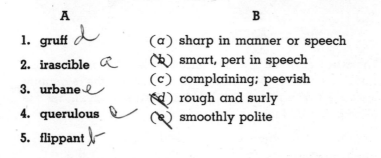

A	**B**
1. gruff	(a) sharp in manner or speech
2. irascible	(b) smart, pert in speech
3. urbane	(c) complaining; peevish
4. querulous	(d) rough and surly
5. flippant	(e) smoothly polite

B. One-Word Summaries:

The gist of the advice or idea in each of the following selections may be summarized in one word. Read each passage below carefully and then select one word of the four words lettered (a) to (d) that best describes the selections.

> Let liars fear, let cowards shrink
> Let traitors turn away,
> Whatever we dared to think
> That dare we also say.
>
> — JAMES RUSSELL LOWELL

1. (a) persistence (b) audacity (c) parsimony (d) asceticism

> Go to the ant, thou sluggard; consider her ways, and be wise.
>
> — Proverbs, THE BIBLE

2. In this proverb, Solomon preaches *against*
   (*a*) appeasement (*b*) indolence (*c*) cowardice
   (*d*) reconciliation

3. and in favor of
   (*a*) languor (*b*) procrastination (*c*) assiduity
   (*d*) prevarication

> I hold it truth, with him who sings
> To one clear harp in diverse tones,
> That man may rise on stepping stones
> Of their dead selves to higher things.
>
> — TENNYSON

4. The poet here said that he believed in
   (*a*) stoicism (*b*) Epicurianism (*c*) idealism (*d*) asceticism

> In the field of world policy I would dedicate this nation to the policy of the good neighbor.
>
> — F. D. ROOSEVELT, "First Inaugural Address,"
> March 3, 1933

5. President Roosevelt is here advocating a policy of
   (*a*) altruism (*b*) agnosticism (*c*) asceticism (*d*) altercation

> Ah, make the most of what we yet may spend,
> Before we too into the Dust descend;
>   Dust into Dust, and under Dust to lie,
> Sans Wine, sans Song, sans Singer, and sans End!
>
> — EDWARD FITZGERALD, *The Rubaiyat of Omar Khayyam*

6. The poet advises us to be
   (*a*) abstemious (*b*) hedonistic (*c*) altruistic
   (*d*) stoical

C. What's the Difference?

For each of the following pairs of words write two short sentences that clearly show the difference in meaning.

1. ascetic — aesthetic
2. odor — stench
3. sensual — sensuous
4. Epicurean — epicure
5. chew — eschew
6. luxuriant — luxurious

D. A Rose By Any Other Name

1. Answer each of the following questions with respect to the word *aroma*.

   (a) From what language is the word *aroma* derived?

   (b) What did the word in its original language mean?

   (c) Compose three short sentences that clearly bring out the differences in meaning between *aroma*, *odor*, and *stench*.

   (d) Label each of the following words according to whether it is a *spice*, a *color*, or an *aroma*.

   dill   clove   paprika   incense
   parsley   thyme   ebony   umber

2. The organ which is linked to the sense of smell is

   (a) tactile (b) gustatory (c) olfactory (d) auditory

3. Odor is used in connection with quality or fragrance. A cognate word is *odium*, meaning strong dislike or distaste. Indicate by a synonym or descriptive phrase the meaning of each of the following.

   (a) being in *ill* odor

   (b) a *rank* odor

   (c) a *fetid* odor

   (d) an *odious* miscarriage of justice

E. Names and Places

Each of the words in Column A has been derived from a name or a place. Consult the dictionary for the meaning and the derivation of each of the words in Column A. Then match each word with its origin in Column B.

A	B
1. academy	(a) the goddess of grains
2. atlas	(b) John Duns Scotus, a celebrated Oxford philosopher
3. bedlam	(c) Mausolus, King of Caria, for whom his wife built a great tomb
4. cereal	(d) a grove near Athens
5. damask	(e) an earl who, while at the gaming table, ate meat between slices of bread
6. dunce	
7. jovial	
8. mausoleum	(f) St. Mary's of Bethlehem, a lunatic asylum
9. sandwich	(g) Tantalus, whom Zeus punished by making him stand up to the chin in water which receded as he stooped to drink
10. tantalize	
	(h) Damascus
	(i) Jove (Jupiter), a planet which was believed by the ancients to effect good humor
	(j) a Titan who held on his shoulders the pillars of the universe

VI. For The Ambitious Student:

Define and use in a short sentence each of the following phrases.

1. alter ego
2. quid pro quo
3. ipse dixit
4. status quo
5. pièce de résistance

LESSON SIX

51. avarice	56. banal
52. averse	57. baneful
53. avid	58. bellicose
54. badger	59. benign
55. balk	60. bibliophile

51. **av-a-rice** ăv'-ȧ-rĭs [*avarus* (Latin), "greedy"] Excessive desire for wealth.

Because he knew that enormous profits were to be made, his *avarice* led him into the illegal sale of drugs.

Related Forms: avaricious, avariciously

Synonyms: cupidity, greed, covetousness (*verb:* covet), parsimony, niggardliness, miserliness

Antonyms: generosity, liberality, open-handedness, prodigality, magnanimity (*adj.* magnanimous)

Note: Do not confuse <u>covet</u>, "desire ardently," with <u>covert</u>, "hidden." a <u>covert</u> arrangement; <u>coveted</u> praise from his colleagues.

"The love of money is the root of all evil."

— New Testament

---

52. **a-verse** ȧ-vûrs' [*aversus* (Latin), "turned aside; "from *a*, "away" + *vertere*, "to turn"] — Disinclined; unwilling; opposed to; distasteful *towards.*

I am not *averse* to going on an outing, but I am reluctant to go to the same place year in and year out.

Related Form: aversion

Synonyms: reluctant (*noun:* reluctance *to*), loathe (*noun:* loathing) "strong dislike combining hatred and disgust," indisposed to, antipathetic (*noun:* antipathy), repugnant (*noun:* repugnance)

92

Antonyms: inclined, eager, have a *penchant* for (*nouns:* predilection, proclivity)

Phrases: have an aversion *to* or *towards; averse to* ice-skating; a loathing *toward* arithmetic

53. **av-id** ăv′-ĭd [*avidus* (Latin), "greedy"; "craving"]

    1. Greedy; keenly wanting.

       The child spent an hour each day looking with *avid* eyes at the toys displayed in the shop window.

    2. Extremely eager.

       Avid for knowledge, John was in the process of trying to read every book in the library.

Related Forms: avidity, avidly

Synonyms: covetous, rapacious "excessively grasping" (*noun:* rapacity), ravenous, desirous

Antonyms: 1. altruistic, bountiful, magnanimous, generous, munificent

       2. apathetic, indifferent

54. **badg-er** băj′-ẽr [source uncertain] — To tease (as the badger does in badger baiting); hence, to annoy by incessant petty attacks or torments.

    I listen while my parents try to *badger* me into cutting my hair, but I do not comply.

Synonyms: harass, torment, needle, pester, plague, bedevil, vex, bait, irritate, harrow, harry, distress

Antonyms: soothe, compose, pacify

Note: Farmers would appreciate the meaning of **harrow**, as a synonym for "irritate" or "distress." (See page 295 for an analysis of this word.)

55. **balk** bôk′ [*balka* (Old Norse), "a beam," "a ridge"] To hinder or stop as at an obstacle; to defeat; to disappoint; (of horses, to stop short and refuse to go).

93

I was willing to acknowledge my guilt in participating in the disorder in class, but when I was asked to inform on my colleagues, I *balked*, refusing adamantly to give their names.

Just as his plans for a Saturday night date looked most promising, Henry was *balked* by an unforeseen obstacle — lack of money.

Synonyms: frustrate, thwart, block, foil (noun and verb), impede, obstruct

Antonym: facilitate, ease

Phrases: balk at shoveling snow, a *balky* horse, thwarted *in* a plan, balked *in* his desires

56. ba-nal bā′năl bȧ-năl′ [*ban* (French), "an ordinance"] — Commonplace; made stale by constant use or repetition.

We had expected the dialogue to sparkle with wit; but we found, to our disappointment, that it was, on the contrary, *banal* and flat.

Related Form: banality

Synonyms: hackneyed, stereotyped, insipid, trite, stale, vapid, jejune

Antonyms: original, fresh, new, interesting, racy, piquant (*noun:* piquancy)

Note 1: In feudal times the lord of a manor had the power to issue a proclamation (called <u>bannum</u> in legal language) or a call to arms on pain of heavy penalties for disobedience. By the law of "banality" the lord had the right to require his vassals to use only his ovens, winepress, mills, and so on. The lord's mill was called the "banal mill," meaning "the mill that is common, at the service of all." Today <u>banal</u> means "commonplace" or "in common use." From the same root we get banish (to outlaw), <u>ban</u> (to prohibit by law), <u>contraband</u> (outlawed goods), and bandit (an outlaw).

Note 2: jejune has a number of meanings:
childish — jejune conduct; dull — a jejune piece of work; lacking substance — a jejune analysis

57. bane-ful bān′-fŏŏl [*bana* (Old English), "slayer"] — Destructive.

Corruption and vice will always exert a *baneful* influence upon, and will eventually destroy, anything it touches.

Synonyms: pernicious, poisonous, (noxious) ruinous

Antonyms: beneficial, salutary

Note: Do not confuse baneful, meaning destructive, with baleful, meaning "evil" or "sinister" or banal, meaning "commonplace" or "trite."

58. **bel-li-cose** bĕl'-ĭ-kōs [*bellicosus* (Latin), "warlike"; from *bellum*, "war"] — Inclined to quarrel or fight; warlike.

The *bellicose* manner of the witness caused the judge to hold him in contempt of court.

Related Forms: bellicosely, bellicoseness, bellicosity

Synonyms: quarrelsome, belligerent, pugnacious (*noun:* pugnaciousness, pugnacity), contentious, disputatious

Antonyms: pacific (pacifist — one who is opposed to war), peaceful, conciliatory

Note: Though bellicose and belligerent are often used interchangeably most authorities agree in pointing out distinct differences in meaning of the words. Bellicose means "inclined to pick a quarrel or fight readily; of a pugnacious or combative nature."
A bellicose temper; a bellicose mood.
Belligerent means "carrying on war."
The belligerent nations.

59. **be-nign** bĕ-nīn' [*benigne* (Middle English); from *bene* (Latin), "well" + *genus*, "birth," "origin," "kind," "race"] — Of gracious, gentle disposition; kindly; salutary.

Although the grizzly bear looks friendly and *benign*, he is really quite ferocious.

Related Forms: benignly, benignant, benignity

Synonyms: humane, amiable; mild; favorable

Antonyms: malignant (*noun:* malignancy), malevolent (*noun:* malevolence), rancorous (*noun:* rancor), venomous, malicious (*noun:* malice), spiteful

Phrases: α *benign* tumor; α *benign* disposition

60. bib-li-o-phile bĭb′-lĭ-ô-fīl [*biblion* (Greek), "book" +
philos, "loving"] — A lover of books.

Charles Lamb, the English essayist, was so great a *bibliophile*
that on closing a book he would kiss it reverently.

Note: Bibliophilism differs from bibliomania in this respect: a bibliophile is one
who loves books of any description, has a passion for reading, a profound respect for the written word; a bibliomaniac is one who has a craze
for owning and collecting books, especially choice or unusual books. For
every thousand bibliophiles one may find one bibliomaniac. Although the
word "mania" carries with it an unpleasant, unwholesome connotation,
when it is used in combination with books, man's great intellectual trea-
sure, it bears an aura of respectibility.

---

*"To desire to have many books, and never use them, is like the
child that will have a candle burning on him all the while he is
sleeping."*

HENRY PEACHAM, *The Compleat Gentleman*

EXERCISES

I. Words Out of Context

*In each group below, select the word or phrase that most
clearly expresses the meaning of the word at the left.*

1. averse (*a*) excessively desirous (*b*) reluctant
(*c*) the opposite side (*d*) prosaic

2. banal (*a*) fresh (*b*) ostracized (*c*) harsh-
sounding (*d*) commonplace

3. avarice (*a*) excessive love of money (*b*) ex-
travagance (*c*) hatred of many things
(*d*) jealousy

4. avid (*a*) hostile (*b*) unpossessive
(*c*) craving (*d*) disorderly

5. **baneful** (*a*) trite (*b*) destructive (*c*) antiseptic (*d*) deceptive

6. **bellicose** (*a*) quarrelsome (*b*) very beautiful (*c*) sticky (*d*) jubilant

7. **benign** (*a*) greedy (*b*) cowardly (*c*) aware (*d*) kindly

8. **bibliophile** (*a*) amateur (*b*) bookseller (*c*) critic (*d*) lover of books

9. **balk** (*a*) obstruct (*b*) deny (*c*) torment (*d*) pitch

10. **badger** (*a*) step aside (*b*) harass (*c*) encourage evil (*d*) soothe

II. Syllabication and Pronunciation

In each of the following pairs of words select the word which bears the correct accent.

1. a-verse' — a'-verse
2. be-nign' — be'-nign
3. aus-tere' — aus'-tere
4. a-nath-e-ma' — a-nath'-e-ma

III. Words in Context

A. One-Word Omissions

In each of the following sentences substitute for the blank an appropriate word selected from the Basic Vocabulary List for this lesson (Words 51-60):

1. Do not be so _avid_ of praise that you mistake flattery for sincere admiration of your virtues.

2. Until Eppie came into his life, Silas Marner had been a slave to _avarice,_ hoarding every penny he earned.

3. Disapproving of the work planned for the new agency, many Congressmen were _averse_ to appropriating any more funds for its use.

4. Berenson was a famous American *bibliophile* who bequeathed his thousands of books to Harvard University.

5. Dictators often appear as *demagogues* orators, whipping up the masses, and constantly threatening the world with impending war.

B. Words in Phrases

Select one of the four suggested words or phrases that most nearly expresses the meaning of the italicized word in each of the following expressions:

1. a *trite* remark (a) profound (b) concise (c) commonplace (d) insulting

2. *vapid* talk (a) without animation (b) vivacious (c) depressing (d) ceaseless

3. an *avid* reader (a) careless (b) retarded (c) enthusiastic (d) disinterested

4. a *proclivity* for mathematics (a) detestation (b) avidity (c) reputation (d) bent

5. motivated by *avarice* (a) stinginess (b) vengeance (c) distaste (d) greed

6. a *baneful* influence (a) sinister (b) pernicious (c) beneficial (d) belligerent

7. a *benign* countenance (a) beautiful (b) coarse (c) kindly (d) surly

8. *badgered* into action (a) convinced (b) harassed (c) compelled (d) inspired

9. a prominent *bibliophile* (a) philanthropist (b) lover of books (c) publisher (d) bookseller

10. an *aversion* to travel (a) predilection (b) inclination (c) eagerness (d) distaste

C. Words in Quotations

In each of the quotations below, certain words are underlined and numbered. Each numbered word is then followed by four words or expressions lettered (a) to (d). Select the letter of the item that is closest in meaning to each underlined word, as used in the quotation.

> Avarice[1] and luxury have been the ruin
> of every great state.
> — LIVY, *History of Rome*

1. *Avarice* (a) deprivation (b) desire of gain (c) jealousy (d) excessive wealth

> There is no greater bane[2] to friendship
> than adulation,[3] fawning[4] and flattery.
> — CICERO

2. *bane* (a) inspiration (b) aid (c) solace (d) ruination

3. *adulation* (a) indiscriminate praise (b) devotion (c) adoration (d) falsehood

4. *fawning* (a) envy (b) seeking favor by servility (c) gloating (d) approbation

IV. Analogies

Complete the following analogies:

1. whale : minnow = Gargantuan : _____
2. benign : benignity = malign : _____
3. itching palm : open hand = avarice : _____
4. witticism : amuse = tragedy : _____

V. Synonyms and Antonyms

A. *In each group of four words below, select the two that are synonyms:*

1. (a) loving (b) covetousness (c) cupidity (d) disguise

2. (*a*) loath (*b*) reluctant (*c*) prone (*d*) abhor

3. (*a*) zealous (*b*) rapacious (*c*) prejudiced (*d*) ravenous

4. (*a*) munificent (*b*) magnanimous (*c*) wealthy (*d*) assiduous

5. (*a*) bait (*b*) appease (*c*) harass (*d*) frustrate

B. *For each word in Column A find an antonym in Column B.*

A	B
1. facilitate	(*a*) malevolent
2. stereotyped	(*b*) original
3. ruinous	(*c*) peaceful
	(*d*) prodigal
4. belligerent	(*e*) balk
5. benignant	(*f*) salutary

WORD BUILDING

I. PREFIXES

The Latin prefix **a-, ab-** meaning "from" "away from" "off" is found in numerous English words, including *averse*, studied in this lesson.

abduct (literally, "to lead away") — to take away by force

abrupt (literally, "broken off") — sudden, hasty

abnormal (literally, "away from the normal") — exceptional

Other English words containing this prefix are *abhor*, *abrasion* (a "rubbing away"), *abdicate*, *abrogate*.

II. ROOTS

A. The Latin root **vertere, versus,** meaning "to turn," appears in *averse,* studied in this week's lesson.

> *avert* (literally, "to turn *from*") — to turn away, to prevent
>
> *adverse* (literally, "turned against") — opposed

B. The Latin root **bel-, bell-,** meaning "war" is found in several English words, including *bellicose,* studied in this lesson.

> *belligerent* — waging war; contentious
>
> *antebellum* — before the war
>
> *rebellion* — war against (re) authority; opposition to, or resisting, one in authority

C. The Latin root **bene,** meaning "well" "good," appears in *benign,* studied in this lesson. The antonymous root for **bene** is **male,** "bad," "evil."

> *benediction* (literally "speaking well") — a blessing
>
> *benevolence* (literally "wishing well") — generosity Antonym: *malevolence* — ill-will
>
> *benefactor* (literally "good-doer") — one who confers good on another. Antonym: *malefactor* — one who commits an offense against the law

D. The Latin root **gen-,** from **genus,** meaning "kind" "race" "birth," appears in the word *benign,* studied in this lesson.

> *genesis* — origin
>
> *generate* — produce
>
> *gentry* — those of high birth

EXERCISES

I. Etymology Mastery Test

1. Using a form of *mal*, give one word that conveys the meaning of each of the phrases below.

   (*a*) lacking adroitness
   (*b*) a discontented person
   (*c*) practicing medicine incompetently
   (*d*) pretending illness

2. What is the difference between a *"homogeneous group"* and a *"heterogeneous group"* of students?

3. What is *genocide?*

4. What would a *genealogist* most likely be interested in?

   (*a*) tracing pedigrees of persons
   (*b*) popular morality
   (*c*) study of electrical apparatus

5. *Define each of the following words. At first divide each word into its components in order to ascertain the meaning of the parts. Then give the definition of the whole word. Check the dictionary entries for your accuracy.*

divers	perverse	inadvertently
diverse	aversion	divert
avert	adversary	revert
animadversion	diversity	versatile

II. Word Analysis and Word Building

1. Give three English words derived from each of the following roots and prefixes: *gen-, vert-, bene-, ab.*

2. What kind of weapon is a *foil?* In which sport is it customarily used?

3. Why is a person who aims to undermine the authority of a government called *subversive*?

4. What is a *balkline*? In which sport is the term *balkline* commonly used? What is a "balky" horse? Specifically what is meant by the phrase "a pitchers balk" as used in baseball parlance?

5. What is a *foil* in a play on stage? Citing a contemporary play, or *Hamlet* or *Macbeth*, give an illustration and explanation of the use of a *foil* from the play cited?

6. The noted Reverend Austin Phelps said in one of his sermons: "Wear the old coat and buy the new book."

   What sort of person would this advice most likely appeal to? (*a*) a glutton (*b*) an ascetic (*c*) a bibliophile (*d*) a haberdasher (*e*) a bibliographer

7. Theodore Roosevelt condemned the idle rich in a phrase he coined: "the malefactors of great wealth." Explain the allusion in his phrase. What kind of "factors" did Roosevelt advocate?

8. What is a *malapropism*? From which character and in which play in this word derived? By consulting the play or an unabridged dictionary entry give two examples illustrating a *malapropism*.

9. Which one of the following dates would you associate with the expression "antebellum days of the Old South"; 1492, 1660, 1776, 1850, 1900? Explain your answer.

10. Explain the misuse of a word in each of the following:

    (*a*) The preacher announced the malediction as he wished the newly married couple godspeed.

    (*b*) Although the early types of prehistoric man did not belong to the same species as modern man, they belonged to the same genius.

    (*c*) The doctor declared that the patient has a benignant tumor on the brain and is not expected to live.

III. Fun With Words

A. What is the Difference?

The two words in each group below look alike and yet have different meanings. You will have to exercise special care in deciding which one will express the meaning you have in mind.

banal — baneful	belligerent — bellicose
adverse — averse	genus — genius

1. Define the two words in each group.

2. State specifically how they differ in meaning.

3. Select the word in parenthesis which correctly completes the meaning of each of the following sentences.

   (a) The critics declared that the author's (banal, baneful) treatment of the subject fails to move the reader; an unimaginative craftsmanship (banal, baneful) to its novel theme, wrecking a potentially popular work.

   (b) (Averse, Adverse) criticism often serves as a stimulant to a beginning writer.

   (c) I am (averse, adverse) to engaging in small talk and frivolous chatter; I prefer a hot argument over social issues any time.

   (d) The United Nations succeeded in making the two (belligerent, bellicose) nations cease fighting.

   (e) Harry hasn't kept a friend longer than a month because he is by nature (belligerent, bellicose) and self-opinionated.

   (f) One may question the truth of all of Kant's philosophical conclusions but one can have no doubt whatsoever that he was a (genus, genius).

   (g) Into what (genus, genius) are species like horses and zebras usually classified?

B. Books! Books! Books!

The words in Column **A** are all derived from the Greek word *biblion,* meaning "book." English has drawn on this stem for a great many words, all linked to the idea of the written or printed word.

*Match the English word in Column **A** with its meaning in Column **B**.*

A	B
bibliomancy	excessive reverence for the Bible
bibliography	a list of books
bibliomania	foretelling future events by opening the Bible at random to a significant verse
bibliolatry	enthusiasm for collecting books

IV. Review

*Match each word in Column **A** with its meaning in Column **B**.*

A	B
1. abstruse	(*a*) keen insight
2. admonition	(*b*) pertaining to agriculture
3. aesthetic	(*c*) angry dispute
	(*d*) friendly relationship
4. agrarian	(*e*) difficult to understand
5. alacrity	(*f*) anathema
6. altercation	(*g*) unjustly accused
	(*h*) to free from charge of guilt
7. acquit	(*i*) cheerful readiness
8. amity	(*j*) pertaining to a sense of beauty
9. anachronistic	(*k*) out of chronological order
	(*l*) gentle warning
10. acumen	

V. Building Your Own Thesaurus

Draw up in outline form in your notebook thesaurus entries and related notes for each word (except model word below) studied in this lesson. The form to be used is that patterned on the one followed in Roget's Thesaurus. You may refer to your own copy of Roget. Use as a model entry the following outline as an example on averse. You may add your notes to the entries as your studies in vocabulary building proceed from week to week.

Willingness

1. **NOUNS:** readiness, compliance, eagerness, alacrity, avidity, propensity, proneness, proclivity, disposition, inclination, bent, penchant

2. **VERBS:** be willing, disposed to, incline to, be prone to, have a mind to

3. **ADJECTIVES:** inclined, disposed, predisposed, eager, amenable

4. **ADVERBS:** willingly

5. **PHRASES:** of favorable disposition, would as lief as not, have a mind to, go in for, swallow bait hook, line and sinker, be in the mood for, enthusiastic about, with a will, with all one's heart and soul, con amore (Italian), with open arms, without reluctance.

Literary reference: "Barkis is willin' "
— Dickens

"Nothing is troublesome that we do willingly."
— Jefferson

Unwillingness

1. **NOUNS:** unwillingness, indisposition, disinclination, aversion, reluctance, misgiving, qualm, demur, hesitance, antipathy

2. **VERBS:** would rather not, cannot stomach; demur, scruple, recoil

3. **ADJECTIVES:** unwilling, disinclined, indisposed, reluctant, adverse, averse, loath, scrupulous

4. **ADVERBS:** unwillingly, grudgingly, distastefully

5. **PHRASES:** far be it from me! not at any price; under protest, goes against the grain, not for the world, fight shy of

Literary reference: "Nothing is so easy but it becomes difficult when done with reluctance."
— Terrence

Note: Suggested good sources for quotations involving the use in context of words you study you may refer to:
Bartlett's Familiar Quotations; Burton Stevenson's The Home Book of Quotations; Clifton Fadiman's The American Treasury; H. L. Mencken's A New Dictionary of Quotations and The Oxford Dictionary of Quotations

GENERAL REVIEW EXERCISES

(Lessons 1-6)

I. Words in Continuous Context

Select the letter preceding the word or phrase which most nearly expresses the meaning of the underlined and numbered word in each of the following passages.

"If this life is unhappy, it is a burden to us, which is difficult to bear; if it is in every respect happy, it is dreadful to be deprived of it: so that in either case the result is the same, for we must exist in anxiety and apprehension[1]."

— LA BRUYERE

1. apprehension (*a*) suspicion (*b*) understanding (*c*) freedom from fear (*d*) fear

A great man is affable[2] in his conversation, generous in his temper, and adamant[3] in what he has naturally resolved upon. As prosperity does not make him haughty[4] and imperious, so neither does adversity[5] sink him into meanness and dejection[6]: for if ever he shows more spirit than ordinary, it is when he is ill-used and the world frowns upon him. In short, he is equally removed from the extremes of servility[7] and arrogance[8], and scorns either to trample upon a worm or speak to an emperor.

— JEREMY COLLIER

2. affable (*a*) witty (*b*) cheerful (*c*) civil (*d*) imaginative

3. adamant (*a*) pertinacious (*b*) blunt (*c*) vacillating (*d*) perspicacious

4. haughty (*a*) conciliatory (*b*) parsimonious (*c*) scornfully proud (*d*) worthy of praise

5. adversity (*a*) reverses in fortune (*b*) hostility (*c*) catastrophe (*d*) affluence

6. *dejection* (*a*) regression (*b*) lowness of spirits (*c*) repulse (*d*) disappointment

7. *servility* (*a*) humility (*b*) menial employment (*c*) service (*d*) subservience

8. *arrogance* (*a*) meekness (*b*) cringing (*c*) overbearing manner (*d*) self-assurance

Yet such is Mr. Holroyd's skill as a biographer, and so assiduous[9] and perceptive[10] have been his researches into the prodigious[11] quantity of materials relating to Lytton Strachey's life put at his disposal, that there is scarcely a banal[12] page in either of his volumes constituting Lytton Strachey: A Critical Biography.

— MALCOLM MUGGERIDGE (adapted)

9. *assiduous* (*a*) shrewd (*b*) diligent (*c*) ingenious (*d*) dilatory

10. *perceptive* (*a*) showing acumen (*b*) comprehensive (*c*) intense (*d*) thorough

11. *prodigious* (*a*) burdensome (*b*) complicated (*c*) remarkable (*d*) enormous

12. *banal* (*a*) superabundant (*b*) original (*c*) dull (*d*) piquant

There never was any heart truly great and magnanimous[13] that was not also tender and compassionate[14]: it is this noble quality that makes all men to be of one kind[15]; for every man would be a distinct species to himself were there no sympathy among individuals.

— SOUTH

13. *magnanimous* (*a*) noble (*b*) popular (*c*) outstanding (*d*) pusillanimous

14. *compassionate* (*a*) intense (*b*) generous (*c*) enthusiastic (*d*) merciful

15. *of one kind* (*a*) heterogeneous (*b*) homogeneous (*c*) universal (*d*) specious

II. One-Word Omissions

In each of the following sentences substitute for the blank an appropriate word selected from Words 1-60 on the Basic Vocabulary List:

1. Talking to the sick man about his illness will *aggravate* not better his condition.

2. To win a case at court demands that the attorney have not only the ability to convince the jurors but also the *acumen* to reach to the heart of the issues involved.

3. The judge was impeached because his decisions, instead of being fair and equitable, were *arbitrary*

4. The contrast between the two witnesses was most striking: one was phlegmatic and *ambivalent* while the other was fiery and *adamant*

5. The preacher drew an *analogy* between the love of the parent for his child and that of the Lord for the repentant sinner.

6. Overwhelmed by the complexities of civilization, he gave up his worldly goods and retired to a hut in the woods, there to live the life of a(n) *ascetic*

7. When the bugler blows the mess call, the hungry recruits respond to the summons with *alacrity*

8. It was shocking to hear the *acrimonious* tone in which the angry woman addressed her browbeaten husband.

9. No matter how *abstruse* the idea may be, our instructor has the knack of explaining it in simple terms.

10. The storm is almost over; the force of the wind will now rapidly *abate*

III. Words Out of Context

In each group below, select the word or phrase that clearly expresses the meaning of the word at the left.

1. **altruistic**   (*a*) genuine   (*b*) unselfish   (*c*) exalted (*d*) sympathetic

2. **avid**   (*a*) munificent   (*b*) hostile   (*c*) detestable   (*d*) extremely eager

3. **bellicose**   (*a*) gorgeous   (*b*) pugnacious   (*c*) complaining   (*d*) untruthful

4. **banal**   (*a*) stale   (*b*) destructive   (*c*) exclusive   (*d*) arbitrary

5. **ascetic**   (*a*) bitter   (*b*) redolent   (*c*) rigidly self-denying   (*d*) pertaining to beauty

6. **apostate**   (*a*) one who deserts his party   (*b*) disciple   (*c*) adherent   (*d*) cynic

7. **amity**   (*a*) courtesy   (*b*) understanding   (*c*) repugnance   (*d*) friendly relationship

8. **alleviate**   (*a*) lighten   (*b*) cure   (*c*) arouse   (*d*) protest

9. **abet**   (*a*) lessen   (*b*) encourage   (*c*) tease (*d*) undermine

10. **abstemious**   (*a*) aesthetic   (*b*) prohibitionist   (*c*) self-indulgent   (*d*) temperate

11. **acumen**   (*a*) common-sense   (*b*) sarcasm   (*c*) keenness of insight   (*d*) bitterness

12. **abstruse**   (*a*) too profound for popular understanding   (*b*) moderate in habit   (*c*) acute (*d*) resentful

13. **alacrity**   (*a*) eagerness   (*b*) sharpness   (*c*) great need   (*d*) insolence

14. anathema   (*a*) disbelief   (*b*) benediction   (*c*) sermon   (*d*) object of intense dislike

15. apathy   (*a*) callousness   (*b*) indifference   (*c*) pertinence   (*d*) lack of skill

IV. Synonyms and Antonyms

A. *Select the two words in each of the following groups that are synonyms.*

1. (*a*) mordant, (*b*) inexorable, (*c*) acerb, (*d*) vulnerable, (*e*) inept

2. (*a*) obtuseness, (*b*) discernment, (*c*) perspicacity, (*d*) acidulousness, (*e*) blandness

3. (*a*) mitigate, (*b*) intensify (*c*) arbitrate, (*d*) moderate, (*e*) abet

4. (*a*) banal, (*b*) obdurate, (*c*) inflexible, (*d*) abstemious, (*e*) esoteric

5. (*a*) testy, (*b*) affable, (*c*) irritable, (*d*) agnostic, (*e*) stoical

6. (*a*) candor, (*b*) briskness, (*c*) sprightliness, (*d*) keenness, (*e*) resemblance

7. (*a*) execration, (*b*) aptness, (*c*) splendor, (*d*) malediction (*e*) apathy

8. (*a*) charlatan, (*b*) cantankerous, (*c*) highhanded, (*d*) imperious, (*e*) capricious

9. (*a*) ascetic, (*b*) austere, (*c*) gluttonous, (*d*) assiduous, (*e*) aesthetic

10. (*a*) auspicious, (*b*) sedulous, (*c*) ameliorative, (*d*) indefatigable, (*e*) abstinent

B. *Give two antonyms for each of the following words:*
bumptious, aggravate, convivial, capricious, anathema

LESSON SEVEN

61. bicker	66. cadaverous
62. bigoted	67. cajole
63. brochure	68. callous
64. bucolic	69. calumny
65. bumptious	70. candid

61. bick-er bĭk'-ēr [*bicken* (Middle English), "to thrust"] — To engage in petty, irritating argument or quarreling.

The conference began with an amicable discussion of relevant issues but soon deteriorated as the participants began to *bicker* over minor details of procedure.

Related Form: bickering

Synonyms: altercate (*noun:* altercation), wrangle, squabble, quarrel

Antonyms: accord, harmonize

62. big-ot-ed bĭg'-ŭt-ĕd [Probably derived from the French *bigot*, "a hypocrite and superstitious fellow," a word that the French applied to the Normans as a term of reproach.] — Intolerant of an opinion, creed or belief that is different from one's own.

In order to continue to learn, one must be neither arbitrary in judgment or *bigoted* in opinion.

Related Forms: bigot, bigotry

Synonyms: (*adjectives*) intolerant, prejudiced, narrow-minded, hidebound, fanatical, opinionated; (*nouns*) zealot, fanatic, fanaticism

Antonyms: tolerant, liberal, open-minded

The mind of the bigot is like the pupil of the eye; the more light you pour upon it, the more it will contract.

— OLIVER WENDELL HOLMES

How it infuriates a bigot when he is forced to drag into the light his dark convictions!

— LOGAN PEARSALL SMITH

That Word!
DIEHARD

This characterization was originally used more than a century ago by a badly wounded English commander who exhorted his troops: "Die hard, men, die hard!" The term "diehard" was later applied to a recalcitrant faction in the House of Lords. Today, the term "diehard" means "one who vigorously and stubbornly clings to a hopeless position or outdated point of view or lost cause."

63. **bro-chure** brŏ-shoor' [*brocher* (French), "to stitch" (a book)] — A booklet dealing with a subject of current interest, a pamphlet.

In an interesting five-page brochure, the Department of Health sets forth the dangers inherent in smoking cigarettes.

Synonyms: booklet, leaflet, tract, treatise

64. **bu-col-ic** bū-kŏl'-ĭk [*boukolos* (Greek), "a cowherd"] — Of, or pertaining to, shepherds or herdsmen; of, or pertaining to, country life.

Theocritus has been called the father of *bucolic* poetry because his pastoral verses have been the model for many great poems about simple country life.

Synonyms: pastoral, rustic, rural

113

Antonyms: urban, metropolitan

Do not confuse *urban*, meaning "pertaining to the city" with *urbane*, "polished in manners, elegantly polite, suave."

Note: Used as a noun, bucolic means "a poem about country life." Webster's Collegiate Dictionary clarifies the distinctions in the use of rural, rustic, pastoral and bucolic. "Rural refers to the country itself, esp. in its pleasant aspects; rustic implies a contrast with the refinements of the city, and often connotes a lack of polish. That is pastoral which has to do with the life of shepherds or (esp.) with conventional rural life. Bucolic is a literary synonym of rustic."

65. **bump-tious** bŭmp'-shŭs [*bump* (English), "a swelling"] — Offensively and often noisily conceited; inclined to demand too much attention for one's opinion; self-assertive.

Helen fancied herself a great personality, though in reality her tendency to dominate all conversations could cause her only to be described as *bumptious.*

Related Forms: bumptiously, bumptiousness

Synonyms: overbearing, forward, obtrusive, pert, arrogant (*noun:* arrogance), presumptuous, haughty

Antonyms: diffident, modest, humble (*nouns:* humility, humbleness), meek, obsequious, fawning, cringing, servile

Phrase: a swell-head (*inf.*); highfalutin (*colloq.*), pretentious, pompous

66. **ca-dav-er-ous** ka-dăv'-ẽr-ŭs [*cadaver* (Latin), "corpse"; from *cadere*, "to fall"] — Having the qualities of a corpse; hence, pale, haggard and thin.

The effect on Linda of a crash diet too long maintained was to make her look not more attractive but *cadaverous.*

Related Form: cadaver (a dead body)

Synonyms: wan, sallow, pallid (*noun:* pallor), ghastly, gaunt, emaciated

Antonyms: florid, ruddy

114

67. **ca-jole** kȧ-jōl′ [from *cajoler* (French), probably a blend of *caresser*, "to caress," and *enjoler*, "to wheedle"] — To persuade or seek to influence by flattery or deceit.

Since Miss Nelson demands dedication and hard work from her creative writing students, any attempt to *cajole* your way into her favor will be fruitless.

Related Forms: cajolery, cajolement

Synonyms: wheedle, inveigle, coax, induce

Antonyms: dissuade, deter

Phrase: soft-soap (persuasive flattery)

We love flattery even though we are not deceived by it.

— EMERSON

What really flatters a man is that you think him worth flattering.

— G. B. SHAW

---

68. **cal-lous** kăl′-ŭs [*callosus* (Latin), "thick-skinned"] — Hardened in feeling and mind; unfeeling; insensitive.

Seeing the wretched conditions under which the poor of our so-called affluent society live must make the most *callous* observer sensitive to the problem of poverty.

Related Forms: callously, callousness, callosity

Synonyms: hardened, toughened, thick-skinned, insensible, indurate, inured, apathetic

Antonyms: soft, soft-hearted, thin-skinned, sensitive, tender, compassionate, empathic

Note: Observe the difference in meaning and spelling between <u>callous,</u> the basic word of this lesson, and the noun <u>callus,</u> meaning "a hardened or thickened part of a skin."

Phrase: callously indifferent *to*

69. cal·um·ny kăl'-ŭm-nĭ [*calumnia* (Latin), "deception," "slander"] — A false accusation maliciously made to injure another's reputation.

Senator Bachelor was defeated in the election as a result of *calumny* spread by people who cared more for the success of the political machine than for the truth.

Related Forms: calumniate, calumniation, calumniator, calumnious

Synonyms: slander, defamation (*adjective:* defamatory), aspersion (*verb:* asperse), detraction, libel (*adjective:* libelous), vilification (*verb:* vilify)

Antonyms: flattery, blandishment, cajolery (see page 115), adulation

Note: The Winston Senior Dictionary makes these distinctions among the more common synonyms of calumniate:

"To <u>calumniate</u> is to invent and circulate lies about another.

"To <u>slander</u> is to repeat and help spread whatever lies or evil reports are already in circulation, especially behind the back of the person concerned.

"To <u>defame</u> is publicly to speak or write serious accusations against the character and reputation of another.

"To <u>asperse</u> is to cast reflections upon another's goodness or good name by insinuating things to his discredit."

70. can·did kăn'-dĭd [*candidus* (Latin), "white"; from *candere*, "to glisten"]

1. Impartial, as in the expression "a candid opinion."

We believed that Tom gave a *candid* view of the incident because he was a disinterested observer of the dispute.

Let facts be submitted to a *candid* world.
— DECLARATION OF INDEPENDENCE

---

2. Frank, outspoken.

When tempted to give your honest opinion of someone else, make sure that what you assume to be *candid* is not merely cruel.

116

3. Informal, unposed.

> Patricia is so pretty that even *candid* snapshots of her are works of art.

Related Forms: candidly, candidness, candor

Synonyms: unprejudiced, straightforward, truthful, artless, guileless, sincere, ingenuous, outspoken

Antonyms: biased, prejudiced, insincere, disingenuous, artful, guileful, evasive, crafty, equivocal (*noun:* equivocation, meaning "deliberately ambiguous")

Note: In ancient Rome a man who wished to be elected to public office wore a white robe or toga so that he might be recognized more easily wherever he went. Since the Latin word for "white" is candidus, an office-seeker became known as a candidatus, meaning "clothed in white." This is the derivation of the English word candidate.

EXERCISES

I. Words Out of Context

In each group below select the word or expression that most clearly expresses the meaning of the word at the left.

1. candid   (*a*) picturesque (*b*) frank (*c*) ingenious (*d*) competitive

2. calumny   (*a*) grudge (*b*) unjust criticism (*c*) a salve (*d*) false accusation

3. bicker   (*a*) engage in peevish argument (*b*) cudgel (*c*) complain (*d*) evade

4. bigoted   (*a*) reproduced (*b*) exaggerated (*c*) intolerant (*d*) prodigious

5. brochure (*a*) pamphlet (*b*) decoration (*c*) lengthy speech (*d*) advertisement

6. bucolic   (*a*) sophisticated (*b*) ill-tempered (*c*) provincial (*d*) rustic

7. **cajole** (*a*) praise (*b*) persuade deceptively
(*c*) insinuate (*d*) calumniate

8. **bumptious** (*a*) awkward (*b*) swollen (*c*) presumptuously self-assertive (*d*) obsequious

9. **callous** (*a*) thick-skinned (*b*) cautious
(*c*) harsh (*d*) senseless

10. **cadaverous** (*a*) slender (*b*) sinister (*c*) insensitive (*d*) ghastly

II. Words in Context

A. Two-Word Omissions

In each of the following selections, you will find two blanks indicating a pair of words has been omitted. Following the selections are four choices lettered (a) to (d). Select the letter preceding the pair of words that will most satisfactorily complete the meaning of the selection.

1. A report that is circulated deliberately to _____ another's reputation may be characterized as _____.

(*a*) downgrade — candid   (*c*) upgrade — slanderous
(*b*) degrade — calumnious   (*d*) humiliate — contemptuous

2. A(n) _____ person is one who is customarily _____.

(*a*) equivocal — unbiased   (*c*) insincere — tactless
(*b*) guileful — tactful   (*d*) candid — straightforward

3. The umpire's decision hit most of the spectators in the bleachers like a bombshell. They reacted furiously, catcalling, stamping their feet and hissing in outraged _____; _____ vociferously with neighbors who ventured to disagree with them over the injustice of the verdict.

(a) objection — dickering
(b) eulogy — arguing
(c) dissent — bickering
(d) invective — struggling

4. To be _____ is to be _____.

(a) diligent — recondite
(b) inured — hardened
(c) diffident — bumptious
(d) biased — unconcerned for the truth

5. One who is _____ is _____ obstinate in his opinions.

(a) illiberal — moderately
(b) bigoted — unreasonably
(c) conservative — reasonably
(d) recalcitrant — always

6. A(n) _____ is a severe _____.

(a) upbraiding — reprimand
(b) reproach — affirmation
(c) admonition — judgment
(d) rebuke — refusal

B. One-Word Omissions

In each of the following sentences substitute for the blank an appropriate word selected from the Basic Vocabulary List for this lesson (Words 61-70).

1. "Unless we cease this _____ among ourselves about trivial issues, how can we ever hope to present a unified front against our opponents on the critical issues?" exclaimed Mr. Balfour pleading for harmony at his party caucus.

119

2. I keep telling my uncle what a superb driver he is in the hope that I might thereby _____ him into giving me driving lessons in his new car.

3. An attractive _____ will often do more to bring a message to the people than a hundred dull speeches.

4. The children, innocent victims in a senseless war, became listless and _____ from lack of food.

5. If one can look at these starving children, and remain unmoved, one is _____ indeed!

C. Words in an Extended Passage

In the passage below, certain words are underlined and numbered. Each word is followed by four words or phrases lettered (a) to (d). Select the letter of the item that best completes the sentence.

The professional historian who is an active participant in the events he is depicting faces a dilemma[1]: to what degree shall he let his bias[2] encroach[3] upon and mar[4] the authenticity[5] of the account? One erudite[6] historian avers[7] that it is impossible for any historian to make any claim to absolute objectivity. All that one can demand from a contemporary historian writing of events in which he has played a role is an assiduous[8] study of all the facts available, and candor[9] and sincerity. One hopes that out of the comparison of many sincerities the truth will ultimately emerge. Arthur Schlesinger in his book on President John F. Kennedy in whose decisions he participated satisfies this criterion.[10]

1. A phrase that is synonymous with *dilemma* is (a) curious question (b) perplexing argument (c) puzzling situation (d) logical choice

2. *Bias* means (a) strongly held opinion (b) tolerance of another's viewpoint (c) conservatism (d) prejudgment blocking a fair consideration of another viewpoint

3. To *encroach* is to (*a*) enforce (*b*) make improper inroads upon (*c*) engender (*d*) determine

4. To *mar* is to (*a*) damage (*b*) enhance (*c*) inure (*d*) restrain

5. *Authenticity* is (*a*) originality (*b*) ingenuity (*c*) spuriousness (*d*) genuineness

6. An *erudite* man is (*a*) thoughtful (*b*) bigoted (*c*) scholarly (*d*) acknowledged

7. When a person *avers*, he (*a*) argues (*b*) declares positively (*c*) denies (*d*) charges

8. An *assiduous* pupil is (*a*) careful (*b*) creditable (*c*) painstaking (*d*) perfunctory

9. *Candor* means (*a*) frank honesty (*b*) knowledge (*c*) accuracy (*d*) tolerance

10. A *criterion* is a(n) (*a*) objection (*b*) quality (*c*) criticism (*d*) standard

III. Synonyms and Antonyms

A. *In each group of four words below select the two that are are synonyms.*

1. (*a*) rabble (*b*) squabble (*c*) dicker (*d*) quarrel

2. (*a*) showing excessive zeal (*b*) gauche (*c*) fanatical (*d*) hypercritical

3. (*a*) ancient (*b*) delightful (*c*) pastoral (*d*) rural

4. (*a*) haughty (*b*) obsequious (*c*) fawning (*d*) caustic

5. (*a*) overbearing (*b*) superfluous (*c*) exciting (*d*) arrogant

6. (*a*) consumed (*b*) pallid (*c*) wan (*d*) lacking

7. (*a*) inveigle (*b*) spur (*c*) spurn (*d*) coax

8. (*a*) unreasonable (*b*) cruel (*c*) insensitive (*d*) callous

9. (*a*) destruction (*b*) aspersion (*c*) vilification (*d*) hope

10. (*a*) ingenuous (*b*) guileless (*c*) clever (*d*) deceptive

B. *For each word in Column A select an antonym in Column B.*

A	B
1. cadaverous	(*a*) urbane
2. crafty	(*b*) unsympathetic
3. crude	(*c*) defamation
	(*d*) ruddy
4. compassionate	(*e*) erudite
5. adulation	(*f*) artless

IV. Related Forms

Give the noun form of each of the following adjectives.

1.	bigoted	6.	defamatory
2.	callous	7.	equivocal
3.	calumnious	8.	fanatical
4.	candid	9.	arrogant
5.	pallid	10.	humble

V. Analogies

Complete the following analogies.

1. cadaverous : florid (*a*) ornate : flamboyant (*b*) ponderous : flowery (*c*) sinister : pompous (*d*) pallid : ruddy

2. prodigious : diminutive (*a*) elephant : mouse (*b*) minnow : whale (*c*) gigantic : mammoth (*d*) greyhound : collie

3. calumny : reputation (*a*) defamation : notoriety (*b*) gossip : rumor (*c*) brochure : facts (*d*) slander : good name

4. bigoted : tolerance (*a*) callous : sensitivity (*b*) candid : truth (*c*) open-minded : secrets (*d*) bumptious : apprehension

5. famine : food (*a*) plague : health (*b*) saturation : liquid (*c*) drought : rainfall (*d*) deficiency : ability

WORD BUILDING

The Latin root **cad-, cas-,** and **cid-** meaning "fall" is the source of many English words, including *cadaverous,* studied in this lesson.

    cadaver — a corpse
    decadent — (*de,* "down" + *cad* "fall") — falling into ruin
    cascade — a waterfall
    deciduous — (*de,* "off" + *cid,* "fall") — falling off at certain seasons, as some leaves, horns, etc.

Other English words derived from this Latin root include *cadence* ("a fall of the voice"), *casual,* and *occasion.*

EXERCISES

I. Word Building Activities

1. "The words *case, casualty, mischance* are verbal blood relatives, though you could never tell it from their faces." Explain this statement.

2. *Which word is out of place in the following group from the point of view of root origin?*

    incidentally   causal   coincide   casually   **elevate**

3. What have *occidental* and *accidental* in common? Explain this relationship. What is the antonym of *occidental?*

4. Name two *Occidental* nations. Name two *Levantine* nations.

5. Give the meaning of the italicized words in the following phrases.

a *casual* acquaintance

a *happening*

merely a *coincidence*

II. Word Analysis and Development

1. Candide, the main character of Voltaire's novel by that name, sets forth his philosophical views of man and life in a fearless outspoken manner. Why is the name of the main character appropriately descriptive?

2. George Canning said "Save, save me from the *candid* friend!" Which of the following reasons would Canning select to justify his view?

(*a*) No one likes to be reminded of his deficiencies.

(*b*) The truth may hurt, but it is preferable to flattery.

(*c*) Criticism is valuable only if it is objective.

3. If you should come across a *cadaver* on a lonely road, would you notify (*a*) the postman (*b*) the prison warden (*c*) the police (*d*) sanitation department. Why?

4. Give four words which are derived from the Latin root *cas-*, *cid-*.

5. Here are several synonyms, each descriptive of a disagreeable manner, speech, or disposition: *curt, acrimonious, caustic, acerb.*

(*a*) Use each in a sentence.

(*b*) With or without the use of a dictionary, list other synonyms for the italicized words. (One suggestion: *crabbed*)

III. Fun with Words

A. Credo

Read the two selections below. Then fill each blank with a word that completes the sentence appropriately.

> A thing of beauty is a joy forever;
> Its loveliness increases; it will never
> Pass into nothingness . . .
>
> JOHN KEATS, "Endymion"

> The sacrifice most acceptable to God is complete renunciation of the body and its passions. This is the only real piety.
>
> — CLEMENT OF ALEXANDRIA (193 A.D.)

1. Keats believed in _____, while Clement advocated _____ as a guiding principle of life.

   (a) calumny-accord   (b) sensuousness-abstinence
   (c) affability-abstemiousness

2. When John Keats wrote in "Endymion":

   "A thing of beauty is a joy forever,"
   he was praising _____

   (a) asceticism   (b) aesthetics   (c) austerity

3. The branch of philosophy which deals with the nature and function of the beautiful standard is _____

   (a) ethics   (b) theology   (c) aesthetics

B. Which Size?

1. *Each of the following words carries a connotation of size. Assign the letter "A" to those which mean large, and the letter "B" to those which mean small.*

   Gargantuan   Lilliputian   midge   prodigious
   bantam   macrocosm   microcosm   snippet   obesity
   mote

2. *Each word in Column* **A** *contains in its meaning a reference as to size. Match the word in Column* **A** *with its meaning in Column* **B**.

A	**B**
1. **brochure**	(*a*) a small volume, usually with a soft binding
2. **tome**	(*b*) a pamphlet
3. **leaflet**	(*c*) a ponderous volume
4. **pocket book**	(*d*) a small folded sheet of printed matter

IV. A Dictionary Project

To Coin a Phrase: BLENDS

Certain English words are called *blends* because they are a combination of elements taken from two or more words. For example, "Eurasia" is a component of Europe and Asia. Usually this new combination word is invented by a clever writer. Gelett Burgess, the humorist, coined the word "blurb," which he intended to mean persuasive advertisement or announcement of an extravagantly laudatory nature. Many of the comments found on the colorful book jackets of novels today puff the merits of the book they cover and are characterized by the word "blurb." Lewis Carroll popularized his own inventions: burble, jabberwocky.

1. The word *travelog* is a coined word. On what other word (or words) was it probably modeled? What does *travelog* mean? What two words or word elements make up *travelog*?

2. Who first coined the word *chortle*? In what famous book does the word first appear? What two words make up the word. Define *chortle*.

3. The word *smog* is younger than the advent of the automobile and is as modern as the jet plane. What are the two component words which comprise *smog*. Define *smog*.

4. Define by tracing to their original elements the following blend words: *linsey - woolsey, dandle, scurry, rustle, brunch, anecdotage, technocracy.*

5. Consult the dictionary for the meaning of the phrase *portmanteau word*, a term invented by Lewis Carroll, author of *Alice in Wonderland.*

V. For the Ambitious Student

Define each of the following words, give its etymology, and use it in a sentence. You may use your dictionary.

1. bigamy	3. biopsy	5. blasé	7. bludgeon	9. browbeat
2. bilk	4. bizarre	6. bloc	8. boggle	10. buffoon

VI. Review

In the following paragraph, certain words are underlined and numbered. Read the paragraph carefully; then answer the questions that follow concerning the underlined words.

The search for peace is not for the timid[1] or the weak, it must come from a nation of high purpose — firm without being belligerent,[2] resolute[3] without being bellicose,[4] strong without being arrogant.[5] And that's the kind of America that will help build the peace of this world.

— H. H. HUMPHREY

1. An antonym of *timid* is (*a*) candid (*b*) craven (*c*) persuasive (*d*) bumptious

2. *Belligerent* means (*a*) unfriendly (*b*) waging war (*c*) conceited (*d*) beautiful

3. An antonym of *resolute* is (*a*) vacillating (*b*) persevering (*c*) valiant (*d*) tough-minded

4. A synonym of *bellicose* is (*a*) waging war .(*b*) venturesome (*c*) pugnacious (*d*) argumentative

5. *Arrogant* means (*a*) insolently proud (*b*) boastful (*c*) condescending (*d*) contemptible

LESSON EIGHT

71. canine
72. cantankerous
73. capricious
74. captious
75. castigate

76. catholic
77. caustic
78. charlatan
79. chastise
80. chauvinism

71. **ca-nine** kā'-nin [*canis* (Latin), "dog"] — Pertaining to dogs; doglike.

Sometimes I think that dogs show many human characteristics, while people behave in a manner which could be characterized as *canine*.

Related Form: caninity

Synonyms: doggish, snarling, churlish, sullen, morose, doggy, churlish (rude)

Note 1: The canine family includes dogs, wolves, foxes and jackals, but specifically the characteristics of the wolf and the fox are denoted by the adjectives lupine and vulpine respectively.

Note 2: Feline, "belonging to the cat family," includes tigers, lions, and leopards in addition to cats.

A feline person is sly, stealthy, treacherous.

Bovine, "oxen." Hence to be bovine is to be stolid or dull.

Ursine, "bears." Hence to be ursine is to be bearish, that is gruff, hard.

Vulpine, "pertaining to, or characteristic of, a fox"; that is, cunning, crafty

Lupine, "pertaining to, or characteristic of, a wolf"; that is, ravenous, greedy, savage

Phrases: a "dog-eat-dog" attitude (fiercely competitive); a "dog in the manger" (to be like the dog in the fable who appropriated something useless to himself so that others who might need it could not have it)

a "dog" (a despicable fellow)

"put on the dog" (colloquialism, to put on airs, or conduct oneself pretentiously)

128

Note 3: Our English word canaille (pronounced ka'-nāl'), is derived from the Latin canis "dog" and means "the rabble" — a mob, a disorderly crowd, the lowest class of people. Synonyms for canaille, besides rabble are riff-raff, scum of society, ragtag and bobtail.

72. can-tan-ker-ous kăn-tăng'-kĕr-ŭs [probably from contak (Middle English), "contention," "argument"] — Ill-natured; quarrelsome.

No one dares speak to me in the morning since all people know that my disposition at that time of day can only be described as *cantankerous*.

Related Forms: cantankerously; cantankerousness

Synonyms: crabbed; intractable (unamenable), contentious, petulant, peevish, perverse (noun: perversity), pugnacious, cross-grained, spiteful, contrary, grouchy

Antonyms: good-natured, amiable, equable, even-tempered, amenable, affable (see page 21), reasonable

73. ca-pri-cious kȧ-prĭsh'-ŭs [capricieux (French); from capriccio, "a sudden start"; from caper (Latin), "goat." The goat is noted for its prancing and jumping about.] — Inclined, through some whim or fancy, to change the mind, purpose or actions suddenly.

Mary is too *capricious* by nature to study medicine; to be successful she would have to have a steady purpose and the perseverance to work hard and steadily.

Related Forms: capriciously, capriciousness, caprice (a sudden change of mind without apparent motive)

Synonyms: fickle, changeable, erratic, fitful, inconstant, irregular, variable, freakish, crotchety, whimsical, wayward; (nouns) whim, vagary, quirk, whimsey, fancy

Antonyms: steady, steadfast, constant, invariable, undeviating, firm, even-tempered

74. cap-tious kăp'-shŭs [captieux (French); from capere (Latin), "to seize or take"] — Quick to take offense or find fault, especially about trifles.

Only a *captious* critic would endeavor to find fault with such a remarkable and original book.

Related Forms: captiously, captiousness

Synonyms: hypercritical, caviling, carping, faultfinding, censorious

Antonyms: laudatory, complimentary, approving

75. **cas-ti-gate** kăs'-tĭ-gāt [*castus* (Latin) "pure" + *agere* "to make"] — To criticize severely; to punish for the purpose of correction.

Johnny was roundly *castigated* by his parents for his sloppy appearance.

Related Forms: castigation, castigator

Synonyms: chastise, chasten, reprove, discipline, reprimand, upbraid

Antonyms: eulogize, commend, laud, extol

Phrases: "take to task" "dress down" "haul over the coals"

AN ANECDOTE

A friend once told Voltaire: "Many of your literary competitors say such nasty things about you. But it is pleasant to know that you say such pleasant things about them."

Voltaire smiled. "Perhaps" he said, "we are both mistaken."

---

76. **cath-o-lic** (adjective) kăth'-ô-lĭk kăth'-lĭk [*katholikos* (Greek), "universal" "general"]

1. Broad-minded, liberal, broadly sympathetic.

My taste in music is *catholic*; I like all types — from Bach to Beatles.

Related Forms: (nouns) catholicity, catholicism

Synonyms: humanitarian; broad-minded

Antonyms: narrow-minded, bigoted, provincial, parochial

130

2. Widely inclusive.

> The great Leonardo da Vinci was *catholic* in his interests: he was a painter, draftsman, scientist, sculptor, architect, engineer, musician and mathematician.

Synonyms: comprehensive, universal, ecumenical (When applied to church matters, *ecumenical* means "pertaining to the whole Christian church." The recent *ecumenical* conference in Rome consisted of church representatives from the four corners of the globe.)

Note: When capitalized, Catholic is a theological designation: it refers to the whole Christian church (but usually and specifically to the Church of Rome), to its practices, or membership in the Catholic church. Catholicism is "the faith, system, and practice of the Catholic church."

Uncapitalized, the word catholic denotes the two ideas set forth above in the analysis of the basic word 76.

77. caus-tic kôs′-tĭk [*caustique* (French); from *kaustikos* (Greek), "burnt"] — Inclined to eat away by chemical action; biting, burning, severe, sharp.

> For fear of his *caustic* wit, few dared to challenge Peterson to debate.

Related Forms: caustically, causticity

Synonyms: corrosive, mordant, stinging, tart, pungent (see page 395), acidulous, sarcastic, trenchant (see page 422), acrimonious (see page 6), virulent (see page 426)

Antonyms: mild, soft, sweet, dulcet, saccharine

Note: In ancient days, heat was used in the preparation of the pigments used in writing fluids. The Roman emperors signed their edicts with a purple-red fluid, which was called encaustum (literally, "a burning-in fluid"). From that word has come our word ink.

78. char-la-tan shär′-là-tăn [*ciarlatano* (Italian), "a chatterer"] — A fraudulent pretender to skill or knowledge.

> Surely only a *charlatan* could claim that a machine which flashed colored lights could cure cancer if the victim had faith.

Related Forms: charlatanism, charlatanry, charlatanic

Synonyms: quack, mountebank, impostor (*noun:* imposture), humbug (deception, fraud)

Note: A <u>quack</u> (shortened form of "quacksalver") is one who makes fraudulent claims for the salves and other medications that he sells; therefore anyone who makes fraudulent claims to skills or knowledge. A <u>mountebank</u> (literally, "one who mounts a bench") is a charlatan who uses clownish tricks to sell his goods; also applied to any unscrupulous pretender who is loud and boastful.

79. chas-tise chăs-tīz′ [*chastisen* (Middle English) from *castigare* (Latin), "to punish"; from *castus,* "pure" + *agere,* "to lead"] — To punish, usually by whipping, or other corporal punishment, often in order to reform.

Believing that experience is the best teacher, the father was disinclined to *chastise* his unruly son.

Related Forms: chastisement, chastiser, chasten

Synonyms: correct, discipline, castigate, tone down

He that spareth the rod hateth his son.

— THE BIBLE

---

80. chau-vin-ism shō′-vĕ-nĭzm [Nicholas Chauvin, a soldier, who worshipped Napoleon] — Excessive or blind patriotism; extravagant and belligerent devotion to any cause.

The slogan "My country above all, right or wrong" expresses *chauvinism* in its most common form; a more balanced and mature view of patriotism was expressed by Carl Schurz who said: "Our country, right or wrong! When right, to be kept right; when wrong, to be put right!"

Related Forms: (*noun*) chauvinist, (*adjective*) chauvinistic

Synonyms: super-patriotism, jingoism (extreme nationalism marked by a belligerent foreign policy). The term *jingoist* is applied to a super-patriot who is itching to go to war on the slightest provocation.

> *We don't want to fight,*
> *But, by Jingo, if we do,*
>
> *We've got the ships, we've got the men,*
> *We've got the money too.*
>
> — G. W. HUNT, "We Don't Want to Fight," an English music hall song of 1878 when England was on the verge of intervening in the Russo-Turkish war on behalf of the Turks.

EXERCISES

I. Words Out of Context

In each group below select the word or expression that most clearly expresses the meaning of the word at the left.

1. **captious** (*a*) inclined to be a leader (*b*) finding fault reasonably (*c*) excessively critical (*d*) aggressive

2. **chastise** (*a*) punish (*b*) defame (*c*) pursue (*d*) purify

3. **capricious** (*a*) starlike (*b*) frugal (*c*) spicy (*d*) tending to change one's mind often

4. **cantankerous** (*a*) of great capacity (*b*) ill-natured (*c*) unreasonable (*d*) overpowering

5. **caustic** (*a*) productive (*b*) chemical (*c*) sarcastic (*d*) happening by chance

6. **canine** (*a*) cunning (*b*) voracious (*c*) dogged (*d*) doglike

7. **charlatan** (*a*) fakir (*b*) pretender to a throne (*c*) chatterer (*d*) pretender to a skill

8. **chauvinism** (*a*) super-patriotism (*b*) sarcasm (*c*) zeal (*d*) militarism

9. **castigate**   (a) push aside (b) eulogize (c) discard (d) criticize severely

10. **catholic**   (a) religious (b) broad-minded (c) parochial (d) provincial

II. Words in Context

A. Words in Continuous Passage

In the passage below, certain words are underlined and numbered. Each numbered word is then followed by four words or expressions lettered (a) to (d). Select the letter of the item that best answers the question asked or is closest in meaning to each underlined word, as used in the selection.

It is hard for us today who find no outrage or novelty in strong-minded gifted women competing with men and running multi-million dollar corporations or sitting in council chambers fashioning legislation for the whole country, to imagine that there ever was a time when such opportunities for women did not or could not exist. Only a short hundred years span back a woman, however prodigious[1] her gifts, would have been cast beyond the pale of respectability had she dared to flout[2] the contemporary mores[3] and assert her right to an equal share in society management. Such a woman was Mary Ann Evans who eventually created an international literary reputation for herself. But she had to do it by disguising her sex in the process and risking anathema.[4] She accomplished the impossible. Adopting a pseudonym[5] with a male ring to it, George Eliot, she threw the Victorian prudes[6] off track. She became an accepted, tolerated, versatile[7] critic and journalist. She was also an editor of the Westminster Review — in covert[8] truth, the authentic[9] if not the nominal[10] editor. Her integrity,[11] her plausible[12] arguments, her unorthodox[13] opinions — all helped break down the ostracism[14] that literary women received who dared venture into print. When decorous[15] ladies were pouring tea and painting pastels, George Eliot, née Mary Ann Evans, was a professional writer, turning out novels of social significance.

1. **prodigious**   (a) versatile   (b) extraordinary   (c) exceptionable   (d) comprehension

2. **flout**   (a) scorn   (b) avoid   (c) criticize   (d) object to

3. **mores**   (a) majority opinion   (b) large quantity   (c) morals   (d) traditional customs

4. **anathema**   (a) anachronism   (b) disapprobation   (c) damnation   (d) unpopularity

5. **pseudonym**   (a) assumed name   (b) pretext   (c) postscript   (d) false claim

6. **prudes**   (a) stalwarts   (b) pompous judges   (c) hierarchy   (d) those who affect extreme modesty

7. **versatile**   (a) hostile   (b) adept in various fields   (c) knowledgeable   (d) ingenious

8. **covert**   (a) essential   (b) insidious   (c) clandestine   (d) forthright

9. **authentic**   (a) veritable   (b) inimitable   (c) patent   (d) acknowledged

10. **nominal**   (a) known   (b) in name only   (c) authorized   (d) chosen

11. **integrity**   (a) homage   (b) wholesomeness   (c) fame   (d) incorruptibility

12. **plausible**   (a) reasonably valid   (b) cogent   (c) effective   (d) convincing

13. **unorthodox**   (a) irreverent   (b) unconventional   (c) sacrilegious   (d) heterodox

14. **ostracism**   (a) curse   (b) unpopularity   (c) social condemnation   (d) lack of prestige

15. **decorous**   (a) social-minded   (b) conventionally proper   (c) prudish   (d) modest

B. One-Word Omissions

In each of the following sentences substitute for the blank an appropriate word selected from the Basic Vocabulary List for this lesson (Words 71-80).

1. My uncle who is a very _____ old gentleman becomes highly enraged when a neighbor's child puts a foot on his lawn.

2. The maxim "Spare the rod and spoil the child" means that a parent who never _____ a naughty child cannot expect him to become a decent person.

3. Although Jack is a specialist in ornithology, he is _____ in his tastes, his interests ranging over many subjects, including poetry, politics and sociology.

4. The dramatist insisted that the _____ criticism indicated that the reviewers lost sight of the most important aspects of his play.

5. For all his noisy protestations of love for his country, the _____ is not necessarily the only true patriot — genuine patriotism often goes deeper and is marked by quiet constant devotion.

C. Words in Phrases

Each of the phrases below contains an italicized word and is followed by four words or expressions lettered (a) to (d). Select the letter preceding the item that is closest in meaning to each italicized word as used in the phrase.

1. a *caustic* remark (*a*) introductory (*b*) of the nature of a warning (*c*) bitingly critical (*d*) civil

2. the *canine* world — (*a*) deceiving (*b*) industrious (*c*) characteristic of dogs (*d*) characteristic of pets

3. *capricious* behaviour — (*a*) peculiar (*b*) silly (*c*) sedate (*d*) erratic

136

4. the speech of a *charlatan* — (*a*) true patriot (*b*) impostor (*c*) churchman (*d*) zealot

5. *castigated* by his teacher — (*a*) lauded (*b*) appointed (*c*) criticized severely (*d*) corrected

D. Two-Word Omissions

In each selection below, you will find two blanks which indicate that a pair of words or phrases which will make the sense complete has been omitted. Following the selection are four choices lettered (a) to (d). Select the item that you think will best complete the meaning of the selection.

1. Propaganda is the most _____ weapon so far developed. It is worse than poison gas. If the wind is in the right direction, gas may kill a few and injure others; but the possibilities of manipulating the public mind by withholding or discoloring the facts are appalling. No one can think intelligently without knowing the facts, and if the facts are controlled by interested men, the very idea of democracy is destroyed. Let us, therefore, _____ propaganda in order to preserve democracy.

(*a*) noxious — deprecate   (*c*) perfidious — condone
(*b*) archaic — mitigate   (*d*) capricious — deprecate

2. Matters dealing with _____ may be termed _____.

(*a*) law — legacies   (*c*) beauty — aesthetic
(*b*) war — chauvinistic   (*d*) religion — catholic

3. "Nobody has a right to put another person in such a _____ that he must choose one of two alternatives: either hurt that person by being _____, or hurt himself by telling what is not true."

SAMUEL JOHNSON, *adapted*

(*a*) bewilderment — biased   (*c*) quandary — erratic
(*b*) dilemma — candid   (*d*) predicament — curt

4. A(n) _____ leader cannot effectively hold a nation together, for by constantly changing his mind he confuses his people, by vacillating when he should be firm he makes them stumble.

Principles, firmly held, mark the true leader; demagogic appeals to the highly wrought feelings in the masses rather than their reason, mark the _____, rather than the true patriot.

(a) chauvinistic —demagogue
(b) fickle — toady
(c) obdurate — zealot rabblerouser
(d) capricious — charlatan

5. "_____ critics have ruined my play," lamented the Broadway producer. Instead of assessing the major, significant aspects of this production, they have pounced on trifling flaws; they have been _____ when they should have been mild. They should have tried to weigh this drama on its inherent merits instead of trying to flaunt their own malicious wit in public print."

(a) Captious — caustic
(b) Acrimonious — candid
(c) Forthright — acrimonious
(d) Cantankerous — ponderous

III. Syllabication and Pronunciation

Syllabicate each of the following words correctly, then place the major stress mark (') after the syllable which is accented when the word is pronounced.

EXAMPLE: ma'jor

1. canine
2. cantankerous
3. capricious
4. castigate
5. captious
6. catholic
7. caustic
8. charlatan
9. chastise
10. chauvinism

IV. Antonyms

For each word in Column A select an antonym from Column B.

A	B
1. sullen	(a) extol
2. aristocracy	(b) lambaste
	(c) acrimonious
3. intractable	(d) amenable
4. upbraid	(e) dulcet
	(f) trifling
5. commend	(g) liberal
6. whimsical	(h) jovial
	(i) vulpine
7. momentous	(j) steady
8. mild	(k) downtrodden
	(l) permanent
9. tart	(m) canaille
10. bigoted	

WORD BUILDING

A. The Latin root **cap-, cep-,** (**cip-**), **cept** — from *capere, cepi, captus,* meaning "take" is the source of many English words, including *captious,* studied in this lesson.

> *captive* — one who is taken and held by force, as by an enemy

Other words from this root are *captivate, receptacle, incipient, intercept, recipe,* and *recipient.*

B. The Greek root **kaustikos,** from *kaiein,* meaning "to burn" is the source of the word *caustic,* studied in this week's lesson.

Other English words from this root are:

> *cauterize* — to burn or sear with a hot iron or a caustic drug

holocaust — destruction, especially by fire, of a large number of people.

ink — from (*encaustum*, literally a burning-in) — writing fluid

C. The Latin root **agere**, meaning "to do" "to drive" "to make" is the source of *castigate* studied in this lesson.

Other English words containing this root include *transact*, *agent* and *agile*.

EXERCISES

I. Etymology Mastery Test

1. A word widely used in recent years is *activist*. What is an *activist*? Many people of a conservative bent tend to use the word *activist* in a *pejorative* sense, somewhat like *agitator* or *extremist*. What quality or tone is indicated by the term *pejorative*?

2. The word *prodigal* derived from *agere* is a long standing word in the English language. What does *prodigal* mean? What is the story behind the phrase "the Prodigal Son"?

3. Consult the dictionary for the origin of *synagogue* and *pedagogue*, both of which have their origin in the Latin root *agere*.

4. What is *caustic* wit?

5. *Which word is* etymologically *out of place in the following* group.

participate   precept   capital   perceptive

II. Word Analysis and Word Building

1. The word *capriccio* (pronounced ká-prē-chĭ-ō) is a musical term. From its derivation tell whether this term refers to a musical piece that is (*a*) somber and solemn (*b*) slow-moving (*c*) military in tempo (*d*) light and fanciful.

2. What is the difference between a *carping* critic and a *caviling* critic?

3. A *catholicon* is a "panacea, or cure-all." Explain in the light of its origin the relationship between the word *catholicon* and its meaning.

4. *Supply an adjective that fits each blank below.*

As _____ as a bear
As _____ as a cat
As _____ as an ox
As _____ as a fox
As _____ as a wolf

5. *In each sentence below substitute for the blank an appropriate word from the following list.*

ingenious   ingenuous   disingenuous

(*a*) The _____ boy built an elaborately constructed airplane from matchsticks.

(*b*) The _____ child is incapable of telling a lie or giving an evasive answer to a question.

III. Dictionary Projects

A. Information Please

The following exercises are designed to acquaint you with the many sources of information a good unabridged dictionary provides about words and other general knowledge.

Answer the following questions briefly.

1. Define the phrase "man on horseback."

2. When did Pericles live?

3. What is the fine difference in meaning among *predicament, dilemma, quandary, plight*?

4. What is the meaning of *quid pro quo*? Of *tempus fugit*?

5. Who coined the term "beat generation." What does the phrase mean?

B. African and Other Continental Loan Words

A *loan word* is a word in English that has been borrowed from another language. In this lesson we noted that our current word *chauvinism* was taken from the name of one of Napoleon's loud-mouthed super-patriotic soldiers Nicholas *Chauvin*. Out of Africa, too, have come a number of word loans to enrich our English language. Borrowings from Egypt, for example, have included *paper, oasis, lion, gypsy*. From Africa we have adopted *gorilla, zebra, banana, voodoo*.

Locate the place of origin of each of the following current English words:

1. tsetse	6. canoe	11. boomerang
2. kumquat	7. mahogany	12. kowtow
3. yam	8. potato	13. thug
4. ammonia	9. skunk	14. gong
5. caucus	10. gingham	15. bulk

C. Church Terms

How accurately can you identify common reference to religious structures? Match each word listed in Column A associated with a cathedral or other religious structure with the appropriate descriptive phrase in Column B.

A	B
1. chancel	(*a*) reading desk from which scripture lessons are read in a church service
2. spire	(*b*) space about the altar reserved for choir and clergy
3. pew	
4. nave	(*c*) vault under main church floor
5. lectern	(*d*) room for choir and clergy for storing clerical vestments and meeting of officials
6. crypt	(*e*) tower; steeple
7. vestry	(*f*) middle lengthwise part of the church
	(*g*) enclosed seat or compartment reserved for the congregation

D. Real People behind English Words

Many of our words are derived from proper names with whom certain useful words are linked. We have seen an example of this in this week's basic word *chauvinism*. Other examples are:

boycott — from Captain Boycott, a land agent in Ireland who was the first victim of ostracism by the Irish Land League.

comstockery — from Anthony Comstock, an American crusader against vice who tended to interpret honesty in works of art as pornography. *Comstockery* means a fanatical censorship of literature and others of the fine arts; an excess of zeal in hunting down obscenity in works of art.

Explain the source of each of the following words:

1. dunce
2. nicotine
3. macadam
4. sandwich
5. pasteurize

6. John Doe
7. lynch
8. mesmerize
9. derby
10. guillotine

IV. For the Ambitious Student

Define each of the following words, give its etymology, and use each in a short sentence. You may use your dictionary.

1. bulwark 3. byword 5. canny 7. caption 9. cartel
2. burgeon 4. callow 6. cant 8. careen 10. categorical

V. Review

Use each of the following words in a sentence that explains clearly its meaning:

1. abate
2. askance
3. askew
4. arbitrary
5. acumen

6. atavism
7. apathy
8. apostate
9. aberration
10. aggravate

11. alacrity
12. assuage
13. abeyance
14. avarice
15. anachronism

16. amity
17. austere
18. authentic
19. augment
20. altercation

LESSON NINE

81.	chicanery	86.	clandestine
82.	circuitous	87.	clement
83.	circumspect	88.	cliché
84.	circumvent	89.	coerce
85.	clamorous	90.	cogent

81. **chi-ca-nery** shĭ-kā′-nĕ-rĭ [*chicaneri* (French), "deception," from *chicane*, "to pervert justice"] — Deception by fraud, sophistry (subtle reasoning to avoid the main issue), trickery or evasion.

The dictator used the half-truth, a device that is pure *chicanery*, to convince the people of the rightness of his cause.

Related Forms: chicane (variant form of *chicanery*), to chicane (to use chicanery — that is, to trick, cheat)

Synonyms: tricks, subterfuge, stratagem, sophistry, quibbling, duplicity, wiles

Antonyms: candor, sincerity, frankness, forthrightness

Phrases: sharp practice, quibble over, skulduggery (mean dishonesty or trickery)
In bridge, *chicane* is a hand without trumps.

82. **cir-cu-i-tous** sẽr-kū′-ĭ-tŭs [*circuitus* (Latin), "going around"; *circum* "around" + *ire* "to go"] — Indirect; roundabout.

Instead of taking the direct road home, Bill took a *circuitous* route.

Synonyms: circumlocutory (indirect or redundant in expression), devious, sinuous (winding, "the sinuous course of the stream"), rambling, oblique

Antonym: direct

144

Related Forms: circuitousness — circuit (a going around from place to place, as in "a circuit of the globe" "an electric circuit")

83. **cir-cum-spect** sûr'-kŭm-spĕkt [*circumspicere, circumspectus* (Latin), "to look about"; from *circum,* "about" + *specere* (spicere), "to look"] — Guarded in conduct; cautious, prudent.

Before setting out on his trip, John was warned by his father to be *circumspect* in his dealings with strangers, for there were always some persons waiting to take advantage of the inexperienced.

Related Forms: circumspective, circumspectness, circumspection

Synonyms: vigilant, discreet, wary, careful, watchful, well-considered, gingerly (warily)

Antonyms: rash, indiscreet, imprudent, careless, wanton, heedless, headlong, precipitate, temerarious, reckless, foolhardy

Synonyms in the sense of *judicious: considerate, calculating, sober* (as in *sober* reflection), deliberative

---

Discretion is the better part of valor.

---

84. **cir-cum-vent** sûr-kŭm-vĕnt' [*circumvenire, circumventus* (Latin), "to come around"; from *circum,* "around," + *venire,* "to come"] — To gain an advantage by the use of trickery; to evade by the use of stratagem or deception, to go around.

During Prohibition many citizens adopted all kinds of devices to *circumvent* the law restricting the sale of alcoholic beverages.

Related Forms: circumventive, circumvention, circumventor

Synonyms: entrap, frustrate (see page 282), thwart, balk, foil, baffle, disconcert, outwit, outmaneuver, obstruct, elude, checkmate, discomfit (to frustrate the plans of), *noun:* discomfiture

Antonyms: assist, abet (see page 1), help, facilitate

Note: In ancient Rome the circus was a racetrack. It was a large oval enclosure without a roof in which chariot races and public shows were held. It was called a circus because the literal meaning of circus is "ring." The Circus Maximus in Rome could accommodate 250,000 spectators. In England a circular area at the intersection of streets is called a circus. It is usually surrounded by rows of houses and shops. A famous example is Piccadilly Circus, located in the heart of London.

85. **clam-or-ous** klăm'ẽr-ŭs [*clamor* (Latin), "an outcry"] — Noisy; demanding loudly, urgently and persistently.

A *clamorous* mob crowded the central square demanding the resignation of the Premier.

Related Forms: noun and verb: clamor (a loud and persistent demand or complaint) clangorous (*noun:* clangor)

Synonyms: uproarious, obstreperous, riotous, vociferous, hubbub, racket, din, turbulence, vociferate (exclaim noisily)

Antonyms: peaceful, quiet, silent, dim

Phrases: a general *hue and cry* (public clamor, protest or alarm); *declamatory speech* (one that is delivered loudly)

I sound my barbaric yawp on the roofs of the world.

— WALT WHITMAN

---

86. **clan-des-tine** klăn-dĕs'-tĭn [*clandestinus* (Latin), "secret"] — Concealed for an evil purpose; secret.

The conspirators laid their plans in the dead of night at a *clandestine* meeting in the mountains.

Related Forms: clandestinely, clandestineness

Synonyms: surreptitious, furtive, stealthy, underhand, covert, hidden, private (for deceptive or illicit purposes)

Antonyms: open, frank, undisguised, avowed, manifest, apparent, obvious, patent, overt

87. clem-ent klĕm'-ĕnt [*clemens, clementis* (Latin), "merciful"]

1. Inclined to be forgiving or merciful; lenient.

   Is it at all possible to be *clement* in one's attitude toward anyone who tries to lure young people into the trap of narcotics addiction?

2. Mild (referring to the weather).

   The *clement* weather, the balloon venders, the people lying on the grass, all heralded the arrival of spring.

Related Forms: clemency, clemently

Synonyms: compassionate, gentle, humane, forbearing, forgiving, merciful, temperate (of weather)

Antonyms: cruel, pitiless, severe, vengeful, relentless, ruthless, inclement, inexorable, vindictive

88. cli-ché klē-shā' [*cliché* (French), "stereotype reproduction of picture or writing"] — A hackneyed phrase, idea, practice; a verbal formula; a stereotyped expression.

Did you ever stop to think that trite and unoriginal as a *cliché* may be, it frequently expresses a thought in a very few words?

Synonyms: stereotype, banality, shibboleth, trite phrase, bromide, platitude, commonplace, cant, catch word

89. co-erce kō-ûrs' [*coercere* (Latin); from *co,* "together" + *arcere,* "to confine or enclose"] — To compel a person to do something against his will by applying physical force or other means, such as intimidation.

"There are more ways of coercing a man than pointing a gun at his head."

— DEAN INGE

Related Forms: coercion, coercive (*synonym:* forcible)

Synonyms: constrain (*noun:* constraint), force, impel, throttle

Phrases: high-pressure methods; strong-arm tactics; bring pressure upon; to be *coerced into* doing something

90. co-gent kō'-jĕnt [*cogens* (Latin), "driving"; from *cogere*, "to drive"] — Having the force to compel, usually by appealing to reason; to the point.

> There are many *cogent* arguments against smoking cigarettes, and none in favor of it.

Related Forms: cogency, cogently

Synonyms: convincing, potent, forceful, compelling, persuasive
Synonyms for "to the point": relevant, pertinent, valid

Antonyms: weak, ineffective, inefficacious, impotent, unconvincing, invalid, untenable

EXERCISES

I. Words in Context

A. One-Word Omission

In each of the following sentences substitute for the blank an appropriate word selected from the Basic Vocabulary List for this lesson (Words 81-90):

1. Machiavelli in *The Prince* advised _____, duplicity and stratagem as the most effective, though not necessarily the most virtuous, way for a sovereign to attain success over rival governors.

2. A _____ investor never puts all his eggs in one basket.

3. The moving picture began like a typical cloak-and-dagger melodrama — a shot in the night, a cryptic message, a _____ meeting of foreign agents.

4. By taking a _____ route through the countryside rather than the high-speed highways one can get a more enjoyable view of a country and its places of interest.

5. The judge may appear curt and harsh but in cases of this kind he's apt to be _____ rather than vindictive.

6. Upon being told that their plane would be delayed for two hours, the passengers became angry and set up a _____ outcry of protest.

7. Your arguments against capital punishment are not very _____; you should buttress your statements with a few telling facts.

8. Since the statute had loopholes, many citizens succeeded in _____ the law by taking advantage of them.

9. Great and powerful nations sometimes _____ weaker neighbors into accepting alliances the latter do not desire.

10. _____ are trite rhetorical expressions which often lead the reader to doubt the writer's capacity for original thought or expression.

B. Two-Word Completions

Below you will find a number of short passages from each of which a pair of words has been omitted. At the end of each selection are four suggested pairs of words or phrases. Select the letter preceding the pair of words which will best complete the meaning of the passage.

1. A(n) _____ person is usually _____.

   (a) arbitrary — fair-minded

   (b) cantankerous — zealous

   (c) circumspect — cautious

   (d) ingenious — devious

2. Throughout his career, that smasher of idols H. L. Mencken poked satiric fun at stale formulas and mediocrity. He was a merciless critic of _____ humbug, pious fraud, and outworn slogans. In his long campaign against _____ he succeeded in refreshing American literature with a wholesome realism and unhypocritical sincerity.

(a) clichés — banality
(b) trite phrases — tirades
(c) cogency — hackneyed expressions
(d) novelty — commonplaces

3. "The battles in the streets of urban America" declared the Senator "will be won not by _____ or suppression but by frank dialogue, not by _____ evasion of the issues but by a direct confrontation of the facts."

(a) compromise — clandestine
(b) coercion — circuitous
(c) constraint — forthright
(d) intimidation — open

4. Lombroso, the great physiognomist, believed that the face is an index to character. He said that one can reliably detect motives as well by the way a man looks at people he meets. If the man looks you squarely in the face, he is _____, honest, unweighted down by feelings of guilt or wrong-doing. Lombroso's conclusion is no longer credited, for he overlooked many cracks in his hypothesis. How about the hypocrite whose cherubic countenance and frank direct eyes may be masking a most villainous piece of _____ and double-dealing?

(a) vigilant — subterfuge
(b) unconscionable — subterfuge
(c) incontrovertible — connivery
(d) candid — chicanery

C. Words in a Continuous Passage

In each of the following passages, certain words are underlined and numbered. Each numbered word is followed by four words or phrases lettered from (a) to (d). Select the letter of the item that is closest in meaning to each underlined word as it is used in the selection.

Mr. Edgar seldom mustered courage to visit Wuthering Heights openly. He had a terror of Earnshaw's reputation, and shrunk from encountering him; and yet he was always received with our best attempts at civility[1]: the master himself avoided offending him, knowing why he came; and if he could not be gracious, kept out of the way. I rather think his appearance there was distasteful to Catherine: she was not artful[2], never played the coquette, and had evidently an objection to her two friends meeting at all; for when Heathcliff expressed contempt[3] of Linton in his presence, she could not half concur[4], as she did in his absence; and when Linton evinced[5] disgust and antipathy[6] to Heathcliff, she dared not treat his sentiments with indifference, as if depreciation[7] of her playmate were of scarcely any consequence to her. I've had many a laugh at her perplexities and untold troubles, which she vainly strove to hide from my mockery. That sounds ill-natured: but she was so proud, it became really impossible to pity her distresses, till she should be chastened[8] into more humility. She did bring herself, finally, to confess, and to confide in me; there was not a soul else that she might fashion into an adviser.

— EMILY BRONTE, *"Wuthering Heights"*

1. civility (a) attention (b) courtesy (c) duty (d) civilized behavior

2. artful (a) ostentatious (b) ingenuous (c) unnaturally affected (d) strategic

3. contempt (a) scorn (b) insult (c) dissatisfaction (d) disapprobation

4. concur (a) disagree (b) contest (c) gainsay (d) assent

5. *evinced* (*a*) displayed (*b*) expressed (*c*) evoked (*d*) bore

6. *antipathy* (*a*) disinclination (*b*) lack of evidence (*c*) antithesis (*d*) aversion

7. *depreciation* (*a*) earnest disapproval (*b*) disparagement (*c*) derision (*d*) adverse criticism

8. *chastened* (*a*) pursued (*b*) prevailed from (*c*) subdued (*d*) coerced

There must have been a good idea in this long, lumpy, <u>circumlocutory</u>[9] novel, but it has probably disappeared under the pounding of a style that has more <u>clichés</u>[10] than a chamber of commerce <u>brochure</u>[11]. Its technique is <u>inept</u>[12], fumbling, of a kind that gives naturalism a bad name, of a psychology that would be an insult to an afternoon soap opera. The push behind this novel has as much <u>cogency</u>[13] as a yawn.

9. *circumlocutory* (*a*) redundant (*b*) concise (*c*) tedious (*d*) talkative

10. *clichés* (*a*) epithets (*b*) commonplace expressions (*c*) archaisms (*d*) witticisms

11. *brochure* (*a*) poster (*b*) tome (*c*) caricature (*d*) descriptive pamphlet

12. *inept* (*a*) inappropriate (*b*) inaccurate (*c*) ineffective (*d*) inexpedient

13. *cogency* (*a*) thoughtfulness (*b*) perception (*c*) effectiveness (*d*) convincing force

II. Words Out of Context

A. Synonyms

In each group of five words below, select the two that are most nearly alike in meaning.

1. (*a*) clement (*b*) partisan (*c*) compassionate (*d*) callous (*e*) soft-hearted

2. (*a*) silent (*b*) clamorous (*c*) insistent (*d*) noisome (*e*) noisy

3. (*a*) vociferous (*b*) convincing (*c*) expressive (*d*) pertinacious (*e*) cogent

4. (*a*) electrified (*b*) roundabout (*c*) circuitous (*d*) rambling (*e*) deceptive

5. (*a*) force (*b*) authorize (*c*) importune (*d*) compose (*e*) coerce

B. Antonyms

Give two antonyms for each of the following words.

1. furtive	6. foil
2. candor	7. rash
3. cogent	8. direct
4. pitiless	9. subterfuge
5. vociferous	10. humane

III. Pronunciation and Syllabication

Syllabicate the following words correctly. Place the major stress mark (') after the syllable which is accented when the word is pronounced.

EXAMPLE: *ma'jor*

1. chicanery	6. clandestine
2. circuitous	7. clement
3. circumspect	8. cliché
4. circumvent	9. coerce
5. clamorous	10. cogent

WORD BUILDING

I. PREFIXES

A. The Latin prefix **circum-**, "around; about," is the basis of many English words, including *circuitous, circumspect,* and *circumvent,* studied in this week's lesson.

circumnavigate — sail around, as the globe

circumscribe — enclose, encircle

circumference — perimeter of a circle

circumlocution — use of many words to express an idea; hence, a roundabout, rather than a concise, expression

B. The Latin prefix **co-, col-, com-,** derived from **cum,** meaning "together," appears in several forms in many English words and is one of the derivative elements in *coerce,* studied in this lesson.

co-operate — to work together, or act together

coexist — to exist together at the same time

coeducation — education of both sexes together

cohere — to stick together

collapse — to fall together

Note: In Latin words (or English words derived from Latin), the prefix com is used before b, m, p, and sometimes i; col before l; cor before r; con before all consonants except b, h, l, m, r and w; co before vowels and h and w; co is also used to make new English words, and in those words may be placed before either a vowel or a consonant, as coexist, codefendant, etc.

II. ROOTS

A. The Latin verb **specere, spicere, spect,** "to look" is the source of many English words including *circumspect,* studied in this lesson.

inspect — to look into

despicable — deserving to look down upon

perspicacious — of keen insight; able to penetrate or see into a problem

retrospect — a looking back on, or review of, the past

prospect — act of looking forward

B. The Latin root **ven-, vent-,** from *venire, veni, ventus,* meaning "come," contributes many words to English, among them *circumvent,* studied in this lesson.

advent (literally, "a coming to") — arrival, coming, approach (usually of importance)

convene (literally, "to come together") — to meet

prevent (literally, "to come beforehand") — to hinder or obstruct

intervene (literally, "to come between") — to interfere

EXERCISES

I. Etymology Mastery Test

1. Give the meaning of the following words in the light of the meaning of their original roots: *circumflex, circumvent.*

2. What is *circumstantial* evidence? How does it differ from *prima facie* evidence?

3. Define the following expressions. (You may consult the dictionary.)

> graduated cum laude
> a national policy of coexistence
> a cum dividend
> corresponding angles
> the confluence of two rivers

4. The basic root of each of the following words, *spec, spectus,* is modified by a prefix. Define each word below using the English proposition which qualifies the root.
prospectus   retrospection   introspection   perspicuous

5. What are "covenants openly arrived at"?

II. Word Analysis and Development

1. *Explain the meaning of the following expressions.*

   (*a*) pleading for clemency
   (*b*) resist coercion
   (*c*) a circumspect attitude
   (*d*) cogent reasons

   (*e*) circumvent the law
   (*f*) clandestine plotters
   (*g*) the advent of spring

2. **What does each of the following Biblical expressions mean?**

   (*a*) an eye for an eye
   (*b*) the salt of the earth
   (*c*) Ye cannot serve God and Mammon.
   (*d*) casting pearls before swine

3. In this lesson your attention was called to the use in English of a Latin adverb *circa*, meaning "about" and is placed before a date that is approximate. Thus: *circa 1861* (sometimes abbreviated to *ca.* or *c.*) means occuring "about 1861."

   Define each of the abbreviations of foreign words and phrases below. You may consult a dictionary to trace the original phrase for which they stand.

e.g.	Q.E.D.
et al.	R.S.V.P.
N.B.	ibid.
i.e.	

4. Many phrases have been absorbed into English from Latin without change and serve to express an idea concisely. You will find these Latin relatives used as legal terms, in formal and informal writing, and in conversation.

   Each of the following sentences contains a Latin-English expression. Explain or define its meaning.

   (*a*) During school hours, your teachers are called on to act *in loco parentis.*
   (*b*) The traitor was adjudged guilty *in absentia.*
   (*c*) The list of petitioners could be extended *ad infinitum.*
   (*d*) His remarks were quoted *in toto.*
   (*e*) Frank is a *per diem* employee in a garment factory.

5. Like Latin, other languages have donated to English many phrases or characterizations which serve handily the purpose of incisive expression.

*Each of the following sentences contains a foreign phrase.
Explain its meaning and indicate the country of origin.*

(a) This is not quite my cup of tea; after all, *chacun à son
goût.*

(b) Nothing ever turns out right for this *schlemiel.*

(c) His *wanderlust* has taken him to all sorts of outlandish places.

(d) *Entre nous,* do you really think Peggy's miniskirt is in
good taste?

(e) Black tie is *de rigueur* for a special occasion like this.

III. One-Word Titles

A. Adages

*Select the word from the four suggested which best sum-
marizes each of the adages below:*

1. Look before you leap.

(*a*) aggression   (*c*) prudery
(*b*) apprehension   (*d*) circumspection

2. Haste makes waste.

(*a*) timidity   (*c*) prevarication
(*b*) alacrity   (*d*) profligacy

3. Strike while the iron is hot.

(*a*) **expediency**   (*c*) audacity
(*b*) aggression   (*d*) fervor

4. Give an inch, he'll take an ell.

(*a*) parsimony   (*c*) cupidity
(*b*) deception   (*d*) proclivity

B. By Their Actions

Below in Column A you will find a list of actions of famous persons. In Column B are one-word characterizations which can reasonably be made about them in light of the action. Match the characteristic in Column B with the appropriate action in Column A.

A

1. Lord Cardigan of "Charge of the Light Brigade" fame paid his men a shilling each to line the London streets on Sundays and salute him as he passed.

2. The philosopher Immanuel Kant led a highly routinized existence. His neighbors at Koenigsberg set their clocks by Kant's afternoon walks, which he started punctually at 4 p.m.

3. Charles Kingsley, famous author, poet and social reformer, gave up his chair of Modern History at Oxford because he thought history is "largely a lie."

4. John Stuart Mill began to study Greek at age 3. By the time he was 8, he had read the whole of the *Iliad*.

5. Thomas Jefferson invented the waffle iron, the swivel chair and many other practical devices for household convenience.

B

(a) punctiliousness

(b) integrity

(c) ingenuity

(d) vanity

(e) precocity

IV. For the Ambitious Student

Define each of the following words, give its etymology, and use each in a short sentence. You may use a dictionary.

1. caucus	4. charisma	6. chunky	8. clarion
2. caveat	5. chequered	7. clamber	9. climactic
3. crestfallen			10. clod

V. Review

A Glance Back

Read the selection below. Then select the letters preceding the word which best completes the meaning of each sentence.

"It would be an abject[1] surrender of our integrity[2] as broadcasters, if we were to sugarcoat or close our eyes to the stark, ugly and often violent realities of our times and attempt to substitute a bland[3] and Pollyanna[5] point of view in our news and public affairs programming, and even in our dramatic entertainment schedule."

— RUSSELL CORY

1. An *abject* surrender is one that is (*a*) involuntary (*b*) despicable (*c*) laudable (*d*) callous

2. A man of *integrity* is one who (*a*) is honest (*b*) favors racial integration (*c*) abhors violence (*d*) possesses exceptional courage

3. A synonym for *bland,* as used in the selection, is (*a*) unrealistic (*b*) flattering (*c*) non-stimulating (*d*) cantankerous

4. According to the writer, broadcasters should continue to present their programs with (*a*) magnanimity (*b*) candor (*c*) acumen (*d*) pertinacity

5. A *Pollyanna* is a person who (*a*) is unmoved by moral principles (*b*) is sincerely honest (*c*) shows a firm, resolute character (*d*) is excessively or blindly optimistic

159

LESSON TEN

91. collaborate	98. condone
92. comely	99. conjecture
93. compatible	100. connive
94. complacent	101. connoisseur
95. con	102. construe
96. concur	103. consummate
97. condolence	104. contrite
105. contumely	

91. **col-lab-o-rate**   kŏ-lăb'-ô-rāt   [*collaborare, collaboratus* (Latin), "labor together"; from *col-(cum)*, "with" + *laborare*, "to work"] — To act in union with another. (Sometimes used in an evil sense, to conspire)

The French general was found guilty of *collaborating* with the Nazis during the days of the occupation.

Related Forms: collaboration, collaborator

Synonyms: co-operate, share, band

Antonyms: disunite, dissociate

92. **come-ly**   kŭm'-lĭ   [*cymlic* (Anglo-Saxon), "beautiful"] — Pleasing to the sight.

Kathie is a *comely* child, and her disposition is as pleasant as her appearance.

Related Form: comeliness

Synonyms: good-looking, attractive, personable, lovely, beautiful, handsome

Antonyms: plain, unattractive, homely, ugly, hideous, repulsive

Note: According to Webster's <u>International Dictionary</u> (Second Edition), "Comely, in present usage, as applied to persons, is a term of lower praise than beautiful. . . . Comely usually suggests a well-proportioned figure and wholesomeness of aspect."

160

93. **com-pat-i-ble**   kŏm-păt′-ĭ-b'l   [*cum* (Latin), "together" + *pati*, "to feel or endure"] — Harmonious; able to get along together.

Mr. Earle and Mr. Waterson decided to dissolve their partnership because, despite almost identical backgrounds and interests, their personalities were not *compatible*.

Related Forms: compatibly, compatibleness, compatibility

Synonyms: agreeable, accordant, suitable, congruous, consistent

Antonyms: inharmonious, discordant, antagonistic, conflicting, clashing, incongruous, inconsistent

94. **com-pla-cent**   kŏm-plā′sĕnt   [*complacens* (Latin), "pleasing very much"; from *complacere*, from *cum*, "very" + *placere*, "to please"] — Self-satisfied.

Pleased because she felt that she had delivered herself of a crushing retort, Amy sat back in her chair with a *complacent* expression on her face.

Related Forms: complacently, complacence, complacency

Synonyms: content, smug, gratified

Antonyms: dissatisfied, discontented

Note: Do not confuse **complacent,** meaning "self-satisfied," with **complaisant,** meaning "inclined to make others satisfied"; hence, "compliant," "courteous."

95. **con**   kŏn   [*can, con* (Old English) "to learn to know"] — To examine or study closely.

I did not merely glance at the letter; I *conned* it for such a long time that I was sure I would never forget it.

Related Forms: conning, conned

Synonyms: peruse, scrutinize, ponder over

Phrases: pore over; *desultory reading* (unmethodical, fitful)

Note the use of con in the following phrases:

the conning tower — a raised structure on a submarine deck used as an observation post

con amore — with love and tenderness

con brio (musical directive) — vivaciously

From contemplation one may become wise, but knowledge comes only from study.

— A. NEWTON

---

96. con-cur kŏn-kûr′ [concurrence (Latin), "to run together"; from *cum*, "together + *currere* "to run"]

1. To agree (in opinion).

   Chief Justice Burger *concurred* in the decision of the majority; Justice Douglas dissented.

2. To happen or exist at the same time.

   Since my birthday and April Fool's Day *concur*, you can imagine the sort of gifts I receive from my friends.

Related Forms: concurrent, concurrently, concurrence

Synonyms: assent, approve, coincide

Antonyms: disagree, demur, dissent (noun: dissension), disapprove, discordant (*adjective*), differ

Phrases: view with disfavor
        give it the nod
        turn thumbs down

97. con-do-lence kŏn-dō′-lĕns [condolere (Latin), "to suffer with," from *cum*, "with" + *dolere*, "to grieve"] — Expression of sympathy with another in his sorrow, pain, or misfortune.

While the *condolences* of my friends upon my failure to graduate did not remedy the situation, it did make me feel better.

162

Related Forms: condole, condolence, condolent

Synonyms: commiseration, compassion (*adjective:* compassionate), consolation, solace

Antonyms: indifference, apathy; exultation (with over)

Note the difference in meaning of the following words each of which contains the element <u>dol</u>:

<u>dolorous</u> — distressed; expressing pain or sorrow

<u>doleful</u> — sorrowful; gloomy

<u>indolent</u> — lazy

<u>dole</u> (out) — to give out sparingly or in small quantities

<u>redolent</u> — fragrant

<u>dolt</u> — blockhead

<u>dolor</u> — grief (poetical)

98. con-done   kŏn-dōn'   [*condonare* (Latin), "to give away," "to give up to"; from *cum*, "with" + *donare*, "to give"] — To forgive (an offense) or overlook it by treating the offender as though he had done nothing wrong or reprehensible.

The mayor was accused of *condoning* his commissioner's offense by maintaining silence in the face of a flood of hostile criticism.

Related Forms: condoner, condonation

Synonyms: pardon, excuse, extenuate

Antonyms: arraign, indict, condemn, charge, avenge, impugn, to be vindictive

Note: To <u>forgive</u> or <u>pardon</u> connotes the idea that an offense has been recognized and excused but not forgotten. To <u>condone</u> means to overlook the offense completely, as though it had not been committed.

Tout comprendre c'est tout pardonner.

— MADAME DE STAEL

(To understand everything is to pardon everything.)

---

99. con-jec-ture kŏn-jĕk'-tūr [*conjectura* (Latin), from *conjicere, conjectus,* "throw together," "conjecture"; from *cum,* "together" + *jacere,* "to throw"] — Opinion or inference drawn from inadequate evidence; guess, theory, surmise.

Our opponent's argument is nothing but *conjecture,* for even the evidence on which it is based is questionable.

Related Form: conjectural

Synonyms: supposition, presumption, speculation

Antonyms: factual; certainty

Phrase: hazard a guess

Note: Observe the difference in meaning between conjecture and two of its synonyms — surmise and guess.

A conjecture is a conclusion arrived at on insufficient evidence. A surmise is an opinion formed on a still flimsier basis. A guess is a hasty opinion formed at random or without any real evidence, as in "Three guesses — who is coming down the street?"

The use of guess to connote probability — as in "I guess I'll see a play tonight" — is colloquial and should be avoided in formal communication.

Conjecture may also be used as a verb.

100. con-nive kŏn-nīv' [*connivere* (Latin), "to close the eyes," "to wink at or let pass unnoticed"]

1. To give passive consent to; to shut one's eyes to a fault or wrong of another. *The Winston Senior Dictionary* explains the special use of the word thus: "To *connive* is to permit wrong-doing to go on while feigning ignorance of it; one who *connives* does not actively take part in the wrong act or deed, but he gives guilty assent to it."

Since he was secretly in agreement with the rioters, the official *connived* at their acts of violence.

2. To co-operate with or encourage secretly (followed by *with*).

164

In order for such a daring robbery to be carried out someone must have *connived* with those who committed it.

Related Forms: connivance, conniver

Synonyms: (*nouns*) collusion, conspiracy, machination, plot,
cabal (a small group of plotters engaged in intrigue or secret
scheming); (*verbs*) collude (to cooperate for the purpose of
committing a fraud), conspire

Phrase: to wink at, act in collusion

Note: One connives <u>with</u> a person; one connives <u>at</u> an action: "Constable Skeat
connived <u>with</u> his brother <u>at</u> the violation of the state law."

101. con-nois-seur   kŏn-ĭ-sûr'   [French: from *cognoscere*
(Latin) "to become acquainted with," "to learn"] — A
person qualified to act as a judge, of art or literature, or
in matters of taste.

Her knowledge of Chinese porcelain, which has been acquired
through many years of study, qualifies Jane to be called a
connoisseur.

Synonyms: pundit (expert — makes judgments in a solemnly
authoritative manner), virtuoso

Antonym: novice (a beginner)

Phrases: know-how (faculty or skill for a particular thing)
knowledgeable (possessing knowledge or understanding of a subject)

noun: expertise (pronounced ĕk-spĕr-tēz') — expert skill or
knowledge

Note: <u>Amateur</u> and <u>dilettante</u> both refer to someone who studies or practices a
branch of the arts for his own amusement, but dilettante now carries with
it a meaning of "dabbler — one who is not very serious. A <u>connoisseur</u>
has sufficient knowledge to serve competently as a critic.

102. con-strue   kŏn-stroo'   [*construere* (Latin), "to heap up
together"; from *cum*, "together" + *struere*, "to build"] —
To interpret or explain the meaning or intention of words
or actions.

The jury *construed* the silence of the accused as an admission of guilt.

Related Forms: construable, construction

Synonyms: infer, deduce, translate

Antonyms: misconstrue, misinterpret

Note: In grammar, to <u>construe</u> means "to explain or analyze the relations of words in a sentence and thus make clear their meaning." In connection with a foreign language, to <u>construe</u> means "to translate."

103. **con-sum-mate** (*adj.*) kŏn-sŭm'-ĭt (*verb*) kŏn'-sŭ-māt [*consummare, consummatus* (Latin), "add together," "complete"; from *cum* "with" + *summare*, "to sum up"]

1. (*adjective*): Carried to the highest degree or quality; perfect.

   Henry is a perfectionist in everything; he drives his car with *consummate* skill.

2. (*verb*): To raise to the highest degree; to complete, to achieve, to perfect, to accomplish.

   We expect to *consummate* the deal without any further delay.

Related Forms: consummation, consummately

Synonyms: supreme, pre-eminent, accomplished, virtuoso

Antonyms: inept, bungled, botched, deficient, mediocre

Synonyms: achieve; finalize (colloquial)

104. **con-trite** kŏn'-trīt kŏn-trīt' [*contritus* (Latin), "bruised"; from *cum*, "together" + *terere, tritus*, "rub"] — Penitent; humble with sorrow for sin.

A broken, *contrite* heart, O God, thou wilt not despise.
                                              — *Fifty-first Psalm*

Related Forms: contritely, contriteness, contrition

Synonyms: repentant (*noun:* repentance), remorseful, conscience-stricken, compunctious (*noun:* compunction); penitent (*noun:* penance)

Antonyms: impenitent, unremorseful, remorseless, obdurate

To do it no more is the truest repentance.

— MARTIN LUTHER

---

105. con-tu-me-ly kŏn'tū-mē-lĭ [*contumelia* (Latin), "insult"]
— Arrogant or humiliating treatment; scornful rudeness
in speech or action.

To act toward one's elders with *contumely* not only is very
rude but accomplishes nothing.

Related Forms: contumelious, contumeliously

Synonyms: insult, scorn, disdain, insolence, contempt, opprobrium, scurrility

Antonyms: graciousness, civility, affability, complaisance

EXERCISES

I. Words Out of Context

*In each group below select the word or phrase that most
nearly expresses the meaning of the word at the left.*

1. **contrition** (*a*) hostile criticism (*b*) solicitude (*c*)
   sorrow for wrongdoing (*d*) sincere af-
   firmation

2. **compatible** (*a*) self-satisfied (*b*) satisfactory (*c*)
   competitive (*d*) consistent

3. **construe** (*a*) erect (*b*) interpret (*c*) hold back
   by force (*d*) protest

4. **contumely** (*a*) scornful rudeness (*b*) rebellious-
   ness (*c*) humiliation (*d*) quarrel

5. **complacent** (*a*) courteous (*b*) well adjusted (*c*)
   self-satisfied (*d*) intricate

6. **collaborate** (*a*) toil (*b*) work in association with others (*c*) decorate (*d*) unify

7. **consummation** (*a*) indictment (*b*) expenditure (*c*) ease of mind (*d*) completion

8. **connoisseur** (*a*) art lover (*b*) artist (*c*) expert (*d*) (*d*) scholar

9. **connive** (*a*) defraud (*b*) cooperate secretly with (*c*) abate (*d*) transpire

10. **conjecture** (*a*) a discarded opinion (*b*) rejection (*c*) guess (*d*) estimation

II. Synonyms and Antonyms

Give two synonyms and one antonym for each of the following words.

1. personable	4. arraign	7. contrite
2. smug	5. pundit	8. compatible
3. commiseration	6. concur	9. consummate (*adj.*)
		10. contumely

III. Words in Context

A. One-Word Omissions

In each of the following sentences, substitute for the blank an appropriate word selected from the Basic Vocabulary List for this lesson (Words 91-105).

1. Two of our teachers _____ in the writing of the grammar textbook we use.

2. I do not know why the President vetoed that bill, but my _____ is that he considered it extreme as well as unconstitutional.

3. No _____ of art would accept this painting as a genuine Rembrandt.

4. This measure, declared Congressman Morelli, is not _____ _ with the best interests of our country; in fact, he added, it violates the spirit of fundamental civil rights.

5. How can you remain so _____ in the face of dangers to civilization inherent in the mere existence of the atom bomb?

6. If I were to show you how to get out of the building without an authorized pass, I would be _____ with you in the commission of the offense.

7. Please do not _____ my leaving for home now as an indication of boredom. I don't want to be caught in the approaching storm.

8. Maurice's _____ skill as an interpreter enabled us to follow the foreigner's conversation easily.

9. Sam is not at all _____; he appears to be convinced that he was justified in what he did.

10. Among life's burdens, Hamlet lists "the pangs of despised love," "the insolence of office," and "the proud man's _____."

B. Two-Word Omissions

In each selection below, you will find two blanks indicating the omission of a pair of words or phrases which will make the sense complete. Select the letter preceding the pair that you think will best complete the meaning of the selection.

1. While one candidate has proved by his indifference and public record to be _____ in the face of turmoil and fear in the streets, the other has shown himself to be deeply _____ in all the implications of this pressing problem.

    (*a*) complaisant — contumelious

    (*b*) empathic — apathetic

    (*c*) complacent — involved

    (*d*) solicitous — concurrent

2. To _____ a misdeed when you are in a position to do something positive to check it is to _____ it.

    (*a*) renounce — condone

    (*b*) concur in — deter

    (*c*) mitigate — exacerbate

    (*d*) overlook — condone

3. The concert master often faces an enigma when it comes to filling the vacant post of first violinist: whether to choose the talented _____ who is new to the orchestra but certain to give a superb account of himself, or the _____ performer who has been with the group for years without perfecting his art.

    (*a*) virtuoso — mediocre

    (*b*) dilettante — perfunctory

    (*c*) consummate artist — neophyte

    (*d*) connoisseur — accomplished

4. Tears stirred by _____ within him welled up in the young man's eyes when he realized the nature of his misdeed. He apologized profusely, and the _____ judge, moved by his penitence, declared that though the law must exact a penalty it can also show that it respects the heart and intention of the transgressor.

    (*a*) compunction — dispassionate

    (*b*) contrition — clement

    (*c*) remorse — obdurate

    (*d*) apathy — compassionate

5. It is the nature of _____ to fumble for truth. Inventions have sometimes come about through wild surmises. The light at the end of the tunnel appears only after laborious groping but the chances are that persistence, hope, imagination or intuition may turn out to be better guides to the ultimate truth than seeming _____.

(*a*) intuition — hypotheses

(*b*) speculation — probabilities

(*c*) conjecture — certainties

(*d*) certainty — surmises

C. Words In Phrases

Each of the numbered phrases below contains an italicized word and is followed by four words or expressions lettered (a) to (d). Select the letter of the item that is closest in meaning to each italicized word, as used in the phrase.

1. An *incompatible* couple (*a*) misunderstood (*b*) obnoxious (*c*) ostentatious (*d*) inharmonious

2. A notorious *collaborator* (*a*) protagonist (*b*) fellow conspirator (*c*) prevaricator (*d*) antagonist

3. *Condoned* the mischief (*a*) condemned (*b*) extenuated (*c*) accomplished (*d*) initiated

4. A *comely* girl (*a*) personable (*b*) repulsive (*c*) strikingly beautiful (*d*) silly

5. Sheer *conjecture* (*a*) outrage (*b*) hostility (*c*) surmise (*d*) insight

6. Act in *collusion* (*a*) competition (*b*) connivance (*c*) misapprehension (*d*) at cross purposes

7. Executed with *expertise* (*a*) expert skill (*b*) efficiency (*c*) good taste (*d*) creativity

8. *Misconstrued* my motives (*a*) objected to (*b*) distorted (*c*) questioned (*d*) misinterpreted

9. *Consummate* a deal (*a*) enter into (*b*) complete (*c*) break off (*d*) sum up

10. An act of *contrition* (*a*) vindictiveness (*b*) hostility (*c*) deceit (*d*) penitence

D. Words in a Continuous Passage

In each of the passages below, certain words are underlined and numbered. Each of these words is followed by four words or phrases lettered from (a) to (d). Select the letter of the item that best defines the word as it is used in the selection.

Not in the clamor[1] of the crowded street,

Not in the shouts and plaudits[2] of the throng,

But in ourselves, are triumph and defeat.

— H. W. Longfellow

1. *clamor* —   (a) protest   (b) popular outcry   (c) argument   (d) jostle

2. *plaudits* —   (a) platitudes   (b) condemnation   (c) enthusiastic expression of approval   (d) commotion

The British Empire and the United States will have to be somewhat mixed up together in some of their affairs for the mutual and general welfare. For my own part, looking out upon the future, I do not view the process with any misgivings.[3] I could not stop it if I wished; no one can stop it. Like the Mississippi it just keeps rolling along. Let it roll. Let it roll on full flood, inexorable,[4] irresistible, benignant,[5] to broader lands and better days.

— Winston Churchill

3. *misgivings* —   (a) regret   (b) criticism   (c) apprehension   (d) mistake in judgment

4. *inexorable* —   (a) unalterable   (b) incapable of being exhausted   (c) unconquerable   (d) dynamic

5. *benignant* —   (a) fulsome   (b) mighty   (c) happy   (d) beneficial

IV. Fun with Words

A. *In each of the following select the expression that best completes the sentence:*

1. Canon law is a body of laws governing (*a*) the church (*b*) the use of ammunition (*c*) valleys and mountains (*d*) a lodge.

2. If a person gets a subpoena, should he (*a*) consult an astronomer (*b*) report to the proper court officer (*c*) hire a lawyer (*d*) apply to a bank for a bill of higher denomination?

3. If you should come across a *corpus delicti*, should you (*a*) codify it (*b*) notify the police authorities (*c*) carry him to the barracks (*d*) ask him to identify himself or to submit to arrest?

4. If a jury is said to be *hung*, is it so called because (*a*) it cannot reach a decision (*b*) it has been bribed to bring in a favorable decision (*c*) one of its members could not attend because of illness (*d*) it is unable to decide whether or not the defendant should be hanged?

5. To *whitewash* a person charged with a crime is to (*a*) cover up or gloss over his guilt (*b*) ascribe to him virtues which he does not possess (*c*) prescribe an unduly mild punishment (*d*) allow him to plead guilty to a lesser charge.

B. *What is wrong with the logic in each of these sentences? Substitute the word that will make the meaning more plausible.*

1. Mr. Johnson was arraigned in court because he refused to obey a statue of long standing.

2. The prisoner was let off easily because the jury found that he had committed only a felony rather than a misdemeanor.

3. The President, refusing to grant the draft evader his freedom, reprieved the man in no uncertain terms.

4. As the police commissioner had done nothing to reduce crime in the city, he was charged with malfeasance of duty. (Hint: What is the difference between *malfeasance* and *nonfeasance*? You may consult the dictionary.)

5. The ordnance that the man acknowledged he had broken had been passed just the year before.

C. Words in Titles

Complete each statement below by selecting the appropriate completing item from among the three lettered choices given.

1. *The Clandestine Lover* is most probably about a lover who

   (*a*) hides his love   (*b*) suffers from his love   (*c*) is a trickster

2. In the title "A Matter of *Conjecture*" the italicized word means

   (*a*) recognition   (*b*) surmise   (*c*) perplexity

3. In "A Misdeed *Condoned*" a wrongful act is

   (*a*) plotted with consummate skill   (*b*) frustrated   (*c*) extenuated

4. "The *Unrepentant* Sinner" is most probably about a sinner who is

   (*a*) not contrite   (*b*) unapprehended   (*c*) remorseful

D. Medically Speaking

1. What is a *psychopath*?

2. What is a *placebo*? Why do some physicians prescribe *placebos*? What is a *nostrum*, a *panacea*?

3. *What is the special concern of each of the following:*

pediatrician   dermatologist pathologist   ophthalmologist

podiatrist   orthodontist   osteopath   gynecologist

4. What is the difference between *hydropathy* and *homeopathy?*

WORD BUILDING

I. PREFIXES

The Latin prefix **co-, col-, con-,** is derived from *cum,* "with" "together" and is the source of one element in a number of words studied in this lesson.

> *connive, collaborate, concur, consummate, condolence complacent, compatible*

> (See p. 154 for a detailed study of this Latin prefix.)

II. ROOTS

A. The Latin root **dol-** from *dolere,* "to suffer pain" "to grieve," is a source of several English words including *condolence* studied in this lesson.

> *dolorous* — dismal, dreary

> *doleful* — sorrowful

> *indolent* (literally, "not suffering") — avoiding labor, lazy

B. The Greek root **pathy,** from *pathos* "suffering," is a derivative of several English words including *compatible,* studied in this week's lesson. It is an element that denotes "feeling," "disease," or "treatment."

> *pathetic* — arousing feelings of sorrow or pity

175

apathy — indifference

antipathy — aversion, repugnance

Other English words containing this Greek root include

sympathy — feeling for another's suffering

compassion — a feeling of sorrow or pity for another's suffering

empathy — a psychological term that is often used today meaning "mental entering into the spirit or feeling of another person"

osteopathy — a system of treatment involving manipulation of the bones

C. The Greek root **gnosis** "knowledge" from *gignoskein*, "to know" is the source of many English words including *connoisseur*, studied in this week's lesson.

diagnose (*noun:* diagnosis, *adjective:* diagnostic) — to learn by analytical study

prognosis — a knowing beforehand, a forecasting of the course of an event or disease

Other English words derived from this root include *prognosticate* (foretell), *reconnaissance* (a fact-finding preliminary examination study or search), as in the phrase "a reconnaissance flight."

D. The Latin root **cur-, curs,** — from *currere* "to run," is found in many English words including *concur* studied in this lesson.

recur — to happen again

current — a running stream

precursor — a forerunner, one that precedes

E. The Latin root **plac-,** from *placere* "to please," is the source of several English words, among them *complacent*, studied in this lesson.

176

placate — to appease, soften, or pacify

complaisant — inclined to please, gracious, affable

placid — peaceful

F. The Latin root **jacere** "to throw" is the source of a number of English words, including *conjecture*, studied in this lesson.

eject (noun: ejection) — to drive out

ejaculate — to exclaim

dejected — cast down; despondent

EXERCISES

I. Etymology Mastery Test

1. Thomas Hood in his poem "Song of the Shirt" describes a woman singing "with a voice of dolorous pitch." This woman was obviously (*a*) exhilarated (*b*) sorrowful (*c*) lazy

2. Explain the following phrases: (*a*) living on the dole (*b*) play a piece on the piano *doloroso* (*c*) *la dolce vita*.

3. If your friend harbors aversion to television commercials, would you say that he is *apathetic* to them or *antipathetic* to them? Explain the difference in meaning between these two words.

4. "The picture by Duchamp was appreciated at its first exhibit only by the *cognoscenti*."

   Who are the *cognoscenti* (pronounced kô-nyô-shĕn′-tē)?

   What is the singular of *cognoscenti*?

   Give a synonym for this word.

5. Show how the prefix alters the meaning of the root *cur-*, *curs*, in each of the following words:

   recur precursor concur excursion incursion concourse

6. Give an adjectival form for *placate*, a noun form for *placid*, *complaisant* and *complacent*.

7. Define each of the following words which are derived from the Latin root *jacere*. You may consult the dictionary.

   jetsam   jetty   trajectory   gist   jut

II. Word Analysis and Development

1. What is the meaning of the phrase *flotsam and jetsam*?

   A synonymous word or phrase for this phrase is:

   (*a*) ship   (*b*) cargo   (*c*) odds and ends

2. *Connoisseur, reconnaissance, reconnoiter* are French words that have been taken into English and that stem from the Latin *noscere* and the Greek *gnoskein*. How many more English words do you know that have the same root?

3. Use a derivative of *cognoscere* in each of the following sentences.

   The airplane was dispatched on a _____ flight to ascertain the weak spots in the enemy lines.

   Bernard Berenson was the acknowledged dean of art _____ in the world in the early twentieth century.

4. *In each sentence below substitute for the blank an appropriate word selected from the following list. (All words on the list are derived from the Latin root* **currere**.*)*

   currency   excursion   cursory   courier   discourse
   succor   incur   recur   recourse   recurrent   precursor

   (*a*) He will probably _____ their enmity by winning all the prizes at graduation.

   (*b*) We did all we could to _____ the stricken passenger.

(c) Frances, who was my _____ in the G. O. office, explained to me in an interesting _____ all the duties of my new post.

(d) If the pain should _____, take this medicine.

(e) The news came by _____.

(f) The speaker referred to his past in a _____ manner.

(g) The only _____ the tenant had for redress of his grievance was to apply to court.

5. What is the difference between:

notorious and *famous*
complacent and *complaisant*
gentle and *genteel*
uninterested and *disinterested*

IT DOES MAKE A DIFFERENCE

"What is the difference between a misfortune and a calamity?" somebody asked Disraeli. Disraeli replied, "Well, if my opponent Gladstone fell into the Thames, that would be a misfortune, and if anybody pulled him out, that I suppose would be a calamity."

The Story Behind a Word
CONCLAVE

When Cardinals gather in concourse in Rome to select a Pope, they are closeted in one or more private rooms. The chamber is locked <u>con</u> *(Latin meaning "with") a* <u>clavis</u> *(Latin meaning "key") and the Cardinals are kept continuously secluded, under lock and key, until they have arrived at a decision. Hence, the word conclave has come to mean any meeting held in secret. The expression in conclave means "engaged in a secret conference."*

III. Building Your Own Thesaurus

In this lesson the word con was traced to its source, and defined and analyzed for study purposes. This word is one of many that are used in connection with reading and books. The nature of the subject matter as well as the difficulties imposed by vocabulary, style, etc. will dictate the method of reading. As Bacon put it with finality: "Some books are to be tasted, others to be swallowed, and some few to be chewed and digested."

Answer the following questions in the thesaurus section of your notebook. Use your dictionary and/or a standard thesaurus.

1. Read Bacon's essay "On Studies." Jot down three maxims which appear in the essay.

2. Study the section entitled "Learning" in the thesaurus and answer the following questions:

   (a) What is the difference between *skimming* and *perusing*?

   (b) Give three synonyms for *diligent*.

   (c) Explain the following phrases: *learning by rote, burn the midnight oil, read between the lines.*

IV. For the Ambitious Student

Define each of the following words, give its etymology, and use each in a short sentence. You may use a dictionary.

1. cloture	3. cogitate	5. comatose	7. compact	9. complex (*n.*)
2. cloy	4. cohort	6. comity	8. concordat	10. comstockery

V. Review

Use each of the following words in a sentence that explains its meaning clearly:

1. bigoted	6. averse	11. chauvinistic	16. florid
2. assiduous	7. caprice	12. capricious	17. pallid
3. agnostic	8. acumen	13. cajole	18. charlatan
4. asperity	9. altruistic	14. deter	19. abstemious
5. benign	10. cantankerous	15. bicker	20. avaricious

LESSON ELEVEN

106. convivial	111. credence	116. cult	121. dapper
107. copious	112. criterion	117. cupidity	122. deadlock
108. corroborate	113. culinary	118. cursory	123. debonair
109. coterie	114. culmination	119. curtail	124. decorum
110. crass	115. culpable	120. cynical	125. deference

106. **con-viv-i-al** kŏn-vĭv′-ĭ-ăl [*convivium* (Latin), "a feast"; from *cum*, "together" + *vivere*, "to live"] — Of or pertaining to a feast; jovial.

We were in such a *convivial* mood, even the dull speeches could not dampen our high spirits.

Related Forms: convivially, conviviality

Synonyms: festive, joyous, jocund, mirthful, sportive, social, sociable; merriment, jollity, revelry

Antonyms: dismal, cheerless, unsociable, saturnine, mirthless, mournful, gloomy

Note: Convivial, social, sociable have the same general meaning of enjoyment of company:

convivial — pertaining to jovial fellowship or good fellowship in eating and drinking

social — pertaining to society in general, or human intercourse in general; sometimes referring to contacts or activities in pursuit of pleasure, or to society in its narrow sense of the leisure class

sociable — inclined toward friendliness or enjoyment of human contacts; of a friendly character (as a sociable evening)

107. **co-pi-ous** kō′-pĭ-ŭs [*copia* (Latin), "abundance"] — Large in number or quantity.

The child shed *copious* tears at the loss of her dog.

Related Forms: copiously, copiousness

181

Synonyms: plenteous, profuse (*noun:* profusion), bountiful, superabundant, overflowing, ample, exuberant (*noun:* exuberance), numerous, multitudinous

Antonyms: meager, scanty, scarce, sparse, inadequate, insufficient

Note: Webster's Students' Dictionary states: "That is plentiful of which there is great or sufficient supply; that is abundant which is very plentiful, or of which there is more than enough. That is copious which is supplied in great abundance; exuberant implies superabundant richness."

108. cor-rob-o-rate kŏ-rŏb'-ŏ-rāt [*corroborare, corroboratus* (Latin), "strengthen"; from *cum*, "together" + *robur*, "strength"] — To make more certain or establish the truth of a report.

Witnesses were produced in court to *corroborate* the defendant's statement that he was confined to the hospital on the day on which the robbery took place.

Related Forms: corroborative, corroboration, corroborator

Synonyms: substantiate, verify, authenticate, confirm, establish, ascertain, strengthen, ratify, sanction

Antonyms: refute, contradict, rebut, confute, gainsay, impugn

Note: Webster's Students' Dictionary states: "To confirm is to give certainty, often to that before regarded as doubtful. Corroborate suggests the strengthening of one statement by another; as, the bystanders corroborated his story. To authenticate is to confirm as genuine."

109. co-te-rie kō'-tĕ-rĭ [*coterie* (French), "society"] — A group of people or a circle that meets for social, political, or some other common interest.

Three centuries ago, a *coterie* of intellectuals ruled the social life of France and dictated the laws of fashion and literary taste.

Synonyms: set, clique (pronounced klēk), junto, cabal (a small group of secret plotters), cadre (a political or religious faction highly trained to lead or train an expanding organization)

Cadres of experienced soldiers went about the countryside organizing and training groups of men for guerrilla warfare.

Note: A clique prides itself on being exclusive. A faction is a coterie or party whose aims are usually selfish and who employ irregular or underhand means to accomplish their ends.

110. crass krăs [*crassus* (Latin), "thick," dense," "fat"] — Gross in mind, insensitively coarse; utterly stupid. (*Crass* often conveys the suggestion of "utterly" in a degrading sense.)

Don't you think it is a bit *crass* of you to eat a chocolate fudge sundae in front of me when I am trying so hard to diet?

Related Form: crassness

Synonyms: crude, boorish, dense, obtuse, graceless, notorious

Antonyms: polished, suave, refined

Phrases: crass stupidity, crass ignorance, crass commercialism

111. cre-dence krē'-dĕns [*credens* (Latin), "believing"; from *credere*, "to believe"] — Belief or trust.

The general refused to give *credence* to the prisoner's story that the enemy had fled from their positions.

Related Forms: credential, credulous (inclined to believe on slight or uncertain evidence), credible

Synonyms: credit, faith

Antonyms: distrust, skepticism, doubt, unbelief, disbelief

Note: Observe the difference between credible and creditable: credible means trustworthy or capable of being believed; creditable means deserving of praise.

A creed (or credo) is any system of belief or formula of belief, usually religious.

112. cri-te-ri-on krī-tĭr-ē-ŭn [*kriterion* (Greek) "test," "standard"] — A standard on which a judgment or decision may be based; an established principle for testing anything.

John Ruskin laid down morality of purpose as a basic *criterion* for judging a work of art.

Related Form: criteria (plural of *criterion*)

Synonyms: touchstone, gauge, yardstick, canon

Calamity is man's true touchstone
— BEAUMONT AND FLETCHER

Gold is tried with the touchstone, and men with gold.
— CHILO

THAT WORD
DEADLINE

Originally, deadline was a line around a military prison beyond which a prisoner may be shot. Today it signifies a limit, particularly of time, past which one may not go.

---

113. **cu-li-nar-y** kū'-lĭ-nĕr-ĭ [*culinarius* (Latin); from *culina*, "kitchen"] — Pertaining to the kitchen or to cookery; used in cooking.

The first dinner at home confirmed the young man's doubts about his bride's *culinary* skill.

114. **cul-mi-na-tion** kŭl-mĭ-nā'-shŭn [*culmen* (Latin), "top"] — Attainment by anything of its highest point.

It is thought that Pasteur's discovery of the cure for rabies was the *culmination* of his career as a scientist.

Related Forms: culminate, culminant

Synonyms: climax, acme, zenith, consummation, apogee, height, apex, crown, summit, peak, pinnacle, crest

Antonyms: nadir, bottom

184

Note 1: Observe the difference in meaning among the following synonyms of culmination (from Webster's New Collegiate Dictionary):

climax — suggests more definitely (than culmination) the movement or ascent which leads to the culminating point; as, the climax of a play

acme — the culminating point itself; as, the acme of his fame

zenith (in its literal sense, the point of the heavens highest overhead) — in its figurative sense differs from acme in connoting more of splendor; as, the zenith of his career

(The literal and figurative antonym of zenith is nadir.)

Note 2: Climax comes from the Greek word meaning "ladder" or "staircase." In a play the climax is the point in the ascending (ladder-like) succession of events at which interest in the outcome of the plot is greatest. In a sentence or paragraph climax is achieved by arranging the details so that each one is more forceful than its predecessor. Anticlimax is the arrangement of details so that each one is less forceful than its predecessor. For the purpose of anticlimactic humor the climactic progress may be followed until the last detail, when there is a sudden turn to the ridiculous or absurd.

Climax: I accuse these scoundrels of misdemeanors, felonies, petty and grand larceny, sedition, and treason.

Anticlimax: The first four courses of the dinner were hors d'oeuvres, pamplemousse frappé, crème des asperges, and sole au vin blanc. Then came the pièce de résistance — a hamburger on a roll with ketchup and onion.

115. cul-pa-ble   kŭl'-pà-b'l   [culpare (Latin), "to blame"; from culpa, "fault"] — Deserving blame.

Because the children were unkempt and undernourished, their parents were held by the court to be *culpable* of neglecting their children's welfare.

Related Forms: culpably, culpability

Synonyms: censurable (*noun:* censure), blameworthy, blameful, blamable, faulty, guilty, delinquent

Antonyms: commendable, laudable, praiseworthy, blameless, meritorious

Phrases: The Latin phrase *mea culpa* (meaning "my sin or guilt," "I am guilty.") is often used in religious services.

116. cult kŭlt [*cultus* (Latin), "worship"]

1. A system of religious belief and observance; a body of disciples drawn to such a system.

   Among today's hippies there is a *cult* of worshippers of the Hindu god Krishna.

2. The more common sense of *cult* is that of a faddish homage or devotion paid to a person, theory, or idea; an intellectual fad.

   Although James Joyce, the author of *Ulysses*, merits acclaim as a literary figure, many devotees have gone to extreme lengths in idolizing him and have turned their homage into a *cult*.

Related Forms: cultist, cultish

Synonyms: venerate, idolize, adulation, fetish, craze

Phrases: a cult of youth; a drug cult; an ancient cult

Note: Cult often carries the pejorative or depreciating meaning of "idolization of something or belief that is weird or odd, almost in the sense of fetish, that is, an object regarded unreasonably or superstitiously sacred or magical." the long hair and beard cult

117. cu-pid-i-ty kū-pĭd'-ĭ-tĭ [*cupidus* (Latin), "longing"; from *cupere*, "to long for"] — Eager or excessive desire for possessions.

His whole life was an example of the stupidity of *cupidity*; no sooner had he acquired one possession than he set about gaining another.

Synonyms: greed, avidity, craving, covetousness (*adj.* covetous), rapacity (*adj.* rapacious), avarice (*adj.* avaricious), miserliness, voracity (*adj.* voracious)

Antonyms: munificence, generosity, lavishness

Note: According to Roman mythology, Cupid was the son of Venus, the Goddess of Love. He is usually represented as a winged, mischievous-looking child, carrying a bow and arrows of two sorts. Some of the arrows were tipped with lead, to produce hatred in those they struck; the others were tipped with gold, to incite love. Cupid was identified with the Greek god Eros. The English word <u>erotic</u> means "pertaining to love." Thus <u>cupidity</u> has changed in meaning; it now signifies only "love of wealth."

What is a man profiteth, if he shall gain the whole world, and lose his own soul.

— THE BIBLE

---

118. **cur-so-ry** kûr'-sȯ-rĭ [*cursor* (Latin), "a runner"; from *currere, cursus,* "run"] — Superficial; hasty.

The examination, *cursory* though it was, convinced the doctor that his patient required immediate hospitalization.

Related Forms: cursorily, cursoriness

Synonyms: hurried, hasty, careless, unmethodical, desultory, fitful, superficial, perfunctory

Antonyms: thorough, exhaustive, comprehensive, painstaking, methodical, systematic, critical, protracted, prolonged

119. **cur-tail** kŭr-tāl' [*curtal* (English), "pertaining to a horse with a docked or shortened tail"; from *cortald* (Old French); from *curtus* (Latin), "short"] — To shorten; to lessen.

Business difficulties forced him to *curtail* his vacation at the seashore, and rush back to the city.

Related Form: curtailment

Synonyms: reduce, abbreviate, abridge, retrench (usually in connection with expenses), diminish, cut short, shorten, dock (deduct from wages usually as a punishment)

Antonyms: lengthen, increase, dilate, amplify

Note: Webster's New International Dictionary makes the following distinctions between curtail and three of its synonyms:

"Curtail, abridge, abbreviate, and retrench agree in denoting reduction in both compass and content.

"Curtail denotes a cutting off in such fashion as to impair completeness; as 'photo' curtailed from 'photograph.'

"Abridge expresses the reduction in compass of an object which still remains relatively complete, as, an abridged dictionary.

"Abbreviate implies reduction by contraction; as the abbreviation of Eng. for England.

"Retrench suggests the reduction of something felt to be in excess; as, to retrench one's expenses."

---

120. cyn-i-cal sĭn'-ĭ-k'l [*kynikos* (Greek) "like a dog"] — Inclined to distrust or deny the goodness or sincerity of human motive; sneering faultfinding.

Bert is so *cynical* that if anyone says a nice word to him he questions the motive behind it.

Related Forms: cynic, cynicism

Synonyms: (*adjectives*) sarcastic, distrustful, scornful, derisive, (*noun*) scoffer

Antonyms: idealistic, optimistic

The cynic is one who never sees a good quality in a man, and never fails to see a bad one. He is the human owl, vigilant in darkness, and blind to light, mousing for vermin, and never seeing a noble game.
— H. W. BEECHER

---

121. dap-per dăp'ẽr [*dapyr* (Middle English) "pretty, elegant"] — Trim, neat; spruce and stylish.

His trim moustache, his fashionably cut suit, and his gleaming shoes made him the model of a *dapper* gentleman.

Related Form: dapperness

Synonyms: natty (coll.), chic (pronounced shēk), dashing, stylish

Antonyms: dowdy, blousy, frowzy, untidy, sloppy (coll.), slovenly, frumpy, shabby

---

Apparel oft proclaims the man.

— WILLIAM SHAKESPEARE

---

122. dead-lock dĕd'-lŏk [dead + lock] — A complete standstill, as in a dispute.

Since neither of the opposing forces would yield an inch to the other side, the parley ended in a *deadlock*.

Related Form: deadlock (*verb*)

Synonyms: impasse, stalemate, checkmate (to block)

123. deb-o-nair dĕb-ŏ-nâr' [*de bonne aire* (Old French) "of a gentle, pleasing disposition"] — Pleasant in manner; gayly charming.

His pride was such that he hid his many problems behind a gay and *debonair* exterior.

Related Forms: debonaire (*variant spelling*), debonairly, debonairness

Synonyms: (Of persons and manners) genial, affable, sprightly, easy, urbane, gracious
(Of mood) cheerful, carefree, jocund, blithe, light-hearted, dashing (lively, spirited)

Antonyms: brusque, curt, surly, crude, boorish, morose, splenetic (bad-tempered), dejected (cast down, doleful, despondent)

Phrase: free and easy

124. de-co-rum dĕ-kō'-rŭm [*decorus* (Latin), "suitable," "beautiful"] — Propriety of speech, appearance, behavior, or character adherent to requirement of polite society.

The children who are customarily obstreperous behaved with exceptional *decorum* because there were guests present.

Related Forms: decorous, decorously, decorousness

Synonyms: propriety, seemliness, conventionality, tradition, appropriateness, suitability, fitness, dignity, etiquette, punctilio

Antonyms: indecorum, impropriety, unseemliness, unsuitability, inappropriateness, unfitness

Note: Décor is a style of decoration or ornamentation. The living room was furnished in an ultra-modern décor.

Phrases: social usage

Grundyism, or dictates of Mrs. Grundy

The tyranny of Mrs. Grundy is worse than any other tyranny we suffer under.

—HERBERT SPENCER

---

125. def-er-ence dĕf'-ẽr-ĕns [*deference* (French); from *deferre* (Latin), "to carry down"; from *de*, "down" + *ferre*, "to carry"] — Submission to another's opinion or wishes, usually out of respect for the latter's age or unquestioned wisdom and experience.

I had little confidence in his judgment, but out of *deference* for his age I acceded to what he suggested.

Related Forms: defer (also signifies "to act in a delaying or dilatory manner"; the noun form of *defer* in this sense is *deferment*), deferent, deferential, deferentially

Synonyms: regard, respect, respectful, esteem, complaisance, reverence, veneration

Antonyms: disrespect, disregard, irreverence, defiance, recalcitrance (*adj.* recalcitrant), flout (to treat with contempt)

Phrase: in deference *to*

190

EXERCISES

I. Words in Context

A. One-Word Omissions

In each of the following substitute for the blank an appropriate word selected from the Basic Vocabulary List for this lesson (Words 106-125):

1. Even a _____ reading of the article will convince the reader that it was written with malicious intent.

2. Since I am aware that Sally is a bit of a prevaricator, I give no _____ to anything she tells me.

3. Dale Carnegie's book tells you how _____ to the wishes and interests of others will help you to win friends, but it doesn't tell you what to do with them after you've won them.

4. The _____ of the conference was the speech made by the American delegate in defense of the plea.

5. My father said that business being what it was, we would have to _____ our expenses.

6. The lawyer declared that if ambition, initiative, and courage even in the face of unpopularity, were crimes, then his client was indeed _____.

7. The motion picture portrayed the destructive effect of _____ on the lives of two grasping shopkeepers.

8. It was not the décor, which was abominable, but rather the _____ skill of the chef which was responsible for the success of the restaurant.

9. The social reformer attacked the _____ commercialism of his day as being crude, insensitive, shortsighted, and detrimental to the good of the people.

10. In "L'Allegro" Milton characterizes the goddess of sprightliness and pleasant manners picturesquely in the line "So buxom, fair and _____."

B. Words in a Continuous Passage

In each passage below, certain words are underlined and numbered. Following each passage is a group of questions in which each of the numbered words is followed by the letters (a) to (d). Select the identifying letter of the word or phrase that is closest in meaning to each underlined word as it is used in the selection.

ALL IN FUN

Haste thee, Nymph, and bring with thee
Jest[1] and youthful jollity,[2]
Quips,[3] and cranks, and wanton[4] wiles,[5]
Nods, and becks, and wreathéd smiles . . .
Sport that wrinkled Care derides,[6]
And Laughter holding both his sides.
Come and trip it as you go
On the light fantastic toe.

— JOHN MILTON

1. **Jest**   (a) prank (b) hilarity (c) pleasantry
(d) joy

2. **jollity**   (a) gay festivity (b) pleasure (c) vivacity (d) orgy

3. **Quips**   (a) tricks (b) puns (c) practical jokes
(d) witty sayings

4. **wanton**   (a) eager (b) cruel (c) unrestrained
(d) wearisome

5. **wiles**   (a) malicious sport (b) trickery (c) undisciplined enthusiasm (d) caprices

6. **derides**   (a) mocks at (b) joins in (c) dispossesses (d) approves

Sainte-Beuve, speaking of that exquisite master of language, the Italian poet Leopardi, remarks how often we see the alliance, singular though it may at first sight appear, of the poetical genius with the genius for scholarship and philology.[7] Dante and Milton are instances which will occur to everyone's mind. Byron is so negligent in his poetical style, he is often, to say the truth so slovenly,[8] slipshod, and infelicitous,[9] he is so little haunted by the authentic[10] artist's fine passion for the correct use and consummate[11] management of words, that he may be described as having for this artistic gift the insensibility of the barbarian. . . . Shakespeare and Milton, with their secret of consummate felicity in diction,[12] are of another and altogether higher order from Byron, nay, for that matter, from Wordsworth also. . . . With a poetical gift and a poetical performance of the very highest order, the sloveliness and tunelessness of much of Byron's production, the pompousness[13] and ponderousness[14] of much of Wordsworth's are incompatible.[15]

— MATTHEW ARNOLD

7. **philology** (*a*) linguistics (*b*) instructional poetry (*c*) love of music (*d*) moral philosophy

8. **slovenly** (*a*) tiresome (*b*) imprecise (*c*) apt (*d*) untidy

9. **infelicitous** (*a*) unattractive (*b*) inappropriate (*c*) mournful (*d*) harsh

10. **authentic** (*a*) apocryphal (*b*) creative (*c*) aberrant (*d*) genuine

11. **consummate** (*a*) perfect (*b*) thorough (*c*) complete (*d*) expressive

12. **diction** (*a*) saying (*b*) doctrine (*c*) choice of words (*d*) assertion

13. **pompousness**   (a) ostentatious loftiness   (b) dignity
       (c) dogmatism   (d) ornamentation

14. **ponderousness**   (a) insight   (b) discrimination
       (c) deep reflection   (d) heavy dullness

15. **incompatible**   (a) beyond compare   (b) inconsistent
       (c) unutterable   (d) intolerable

AN ANTHOLOGY OF CRITICISM

Criticism is a study by which men grow important and formidable[16] at very small expense. — SAMUEL JOHNSON

16. **formidable**   (a) impressive   (b) prodigious
       (c) superior   (d) inspiring fear

Criticism is a disinterested[17] endeavor to learn and propagate[18] the best that is known and thought in the world.

— MATTHEW ARNOLD

17. **disinterested**   (a) impartial   (b) dull   (c) profitless
       (d) righteous

18. **propagate**   (a) create   (b) spread   (c) endorse
       (d) advocate

A wise skepticism[19] is the first attribute[20] of a good critic.

— J. R. LOWELL

19. **skepticism**   (a) an attitude marked by petty fault-finding   (b) shrewd evaluation of the facts presented   (c) disbelief in a divinity   (d) systematic doubt and judgment

20. **attribute**   (a) attitude   (b) requirement   (c) inherent characteristic   (d) attractive quality

The sting of a reproach[21] is the Truth of it.

— BENJAMIN FRANKLIN

21. **reproach**   (*a*) rejection (*b*) vilification
                    (*c*) rebuke (*d*) retaliation

A poet that fails in writing becomes often a morose[22] critic; the weak and insipid[23] white wine makes at length excellent vinegar.

WILLIAM SHENSTONE

22. **morose**   (*a*) sullenly ill-humored (*b*) boring
                   (*c*) perspicacious (*d*) hypercritical

23. **insipid**   (*a*) unpalatable (*b*) succulent
                   (*c*) piquant (*d*) flat

II. Words Out of Context

In each group below, select the word or expression that best defines the word at the left.

1. **culpable**   (*a*) selective (*b*) offensive (*c*) competitive (*d*) deserving blame

2. **culmination** (*a*) catastrophe (*b*) result (*c*) peak attainment (*d*) climax

3. **cult**   (*a*) mystery (*b*) intellectual enlightenment (*c*) faddish devotion (*d*) refinement

4. **deference**   (*a*) submission out of respect (*b*) postponement (*c*) challenge (*d*) swerving from a course

5. **criterion**   (*a*) adverse criticism (*b*) standard of judgment (*c*) denunciation (*d*) verdict

6. **copious**   (*a*) abundant (*b*) pertaining to copyright (*c*) deceitful (*d*) imitative

7. cynical   (*a*) hypocritical   (*b*) distrustful of another's motives   (*c*) morose   (*d*) pessimistic

8. curtail   (*a*) assuage   (*b*) abet   (*c*) allot   (*d*) reduce

9. cursory   (*a*) hasty   (*b*) rude   (*c*) blasphemous   (*d*) banal

10. cupidity   (*a*) angelic   (*b*) rapacity   (*c*) assiduity   (*d*) asperity

III. Synonyms

In Other Words

1. Give three phrases that mean approximately the same as the *italicized* phrase.

   "On with the dance — let *joy be unconfined*."

2. Give three words or phrases which mean "to give confirmation or formal sanction."

3. What specifically is a *cadre*?

4. Give three words that one can appropriately substitute for the underlined word in the expression "crass ignorance."

5. *Match each word in column A with two synonyms in column B.*

A	B
1. **suave**	(*a*) gauge
2. **touchstone**	(*b*) zenith
	(*c*) munificent
3. **apex**	(*d*) polished
4. **lavish**	(*e*) desultory
	(*f*) prodigal
5. **cursory**	(*g*) perfunctory
	(*h*) urbane
	(*i*) yardstick
	(*j*) pinnacle

196

IV. Related Forms

1. *Give an adjectival form of each of the following words.*
   conviviality   profusion   corroborate   credence   censure

2. *Give the plural of each of the following words.*
   criterion   addendum   millennium

3. *Give a noun form of each of the following words.*
   corroborate   cursory   curtail   cynical   decorous
   recalcitrant

V. Syllabication and Pronunciation

Syllabicate the following words correctly, and place the major stress mark (') after the syllable which is accented when the word is pronounced. Indicate the correct pronunciation by inserting the diacritical marks on each vowel.

EXAMPLE: dĭ-vīde'

1. credence	6. cupidity
2. criterion	7. curtail
3. culinary	8. deadlock
4. culmination	9. debonair
5. cursory	10. decorum

WORD BUILDING

I. PREFIXES

A. The Latin prefix **con-, com-, col-,** "together," is an important element in the structure of numerous English words, including *convivial* and *corroborate,* studied in this lesson. (A detailed analysis of this prefix is provided on p. 154.)

B. The Latin prefix **de-,** "down," "away," "off," contributes an important element of qualification to the core meaning of many words including *deference* (**de,** "down" + **ferre** (Latin), "to carry"), studied in this week's lesson.

   dejected (literally "cast down") — despondent

descend — to go down

devolve (literally, "to roll down") — to transmit or transfer from one person to another; to pass by through transmission

Since the employer became ill, full responsibility for running the business *has devolved* upon the manager.

dethrone — to remove from the throne

II. ROOTS

A. The Latin root **vivere,** "to live" is the source of many English words including *convivial,* studied in this week's lesson. Another form of the word in Latin is *vita,* meaning "life."

vivid — full of vigor or life; bright

vital — essential to life

victual (substance to promote living) — food

vivisection — cutting of a living animal for scientific investigation

revive — to return to life or consciousness

B. The Latin root **cred-,** from credere, "to believe," has contributed the core meaning of many English words, including *credence,* studied in this week's lesson.

creed — a statement of belief

accredit — to invest with credit and authority

credo — a set of professed opinions

C. The Latin root **cur- curs-,** meaning "to run" is the source of many English words, including *cursory,* studied in this week's lesson.

current — a running stream

excursion (literally, "the act of running out") — an expedition or jaunt

precursor — a forerunner; a harbinger

D. The Latin root **fer-**, from *ferre*, meaning "to carry or bear" is the source of many English words, including *deference*, studied in this lesson.

> *transfer* — to carry across (*trans*); to cause to pass from one place or person to another

> *prefer* (literally, "to carry before") — to esteem more than something else

E. The Greek word *kriterion*, meaning "standard" "test" contributes our English words critic, critical, and criticism.

EXERCISES

I. Etymology Mastery Test

1. Many English words so closely resemble their Latin originals that one need not have studied Latin to be able to understand some phrases in that language. Try your skill in construing these well known maxims or phrases some in the original Latin, some in the derivative French or Spanish. You may consult the dictionary to check upon your accuracy.

viva voce	vive le roi	vivace (musical term)
vive la bagatelle	ars longa vita brevis	a bon vivant

2. Consult the dictionary for the origin and meaning of *miscreant*. Why were the Saracens characterized by the medieval crusaders as *miscreants*?

3. What is a *credit* union? *Credit standing?* An ambassador's *credentials?*

4. *Define, trace the origin of, and use in a short sentence the following words containing the prefix* **de.**

debris	debunk	decapitate	delete	delinquent
debut	decamp	dejection	delineate	depreciate

5. *Explain the following phrases.*

hard currency, a report that has gained general currency, current assets, par for the course

6. *Define, in the light of their origin, and use in a short illustrative sentence, the following words containing the Latin root* **ferre.**

afferent   indifference   referendum   toleration   odoriferous
prelate   fertile   circumference   vociferate   conifer

II. Word Analysis and Word Building

1. Each of the following is a term that denotes a certain kind of "combination" of persons: (*a*) coterie, (*b*) set, (*c*) faction, (*d*) cabal. Distinguish each term from the others.

2. (*a*) In law, what is meant by *cumulative evidence*?
   (*b*) In finance, what is meant by a *cumulative dividend*?

3. The word *cupidity* is associated with the name Cupid, the mythical god of love. Can you suggest any other words in current English usage that stem from classical mythology or names of planets? Give their meaning. Here are a few hints to start you off: *mercurial*, meaning "flighty," is derived from the god Mercury; *martial*, meaning "war-like" is derived from Mars, the god of war.

4. *The following words denote creeds. Give the principle of belief each suggests.*

stoicism   skepticism   idealism   epicureanism   deism

5. *Read the following passage from the Times Literary Supplement.*

   "Every reader must make up his mind about Disraeli, adventurer or statesman, *charlatan, cynic,* or *romantic,* and the answer is bound to be *subjective.*"

   (*a*) Briefly give the meaning of this sentence.
   (*b*) Define the italicized words.

III. Fun With Words

A. The Seven Deadly Sins

Lust, a synonym for *cupidity,* studied in this week's lesson, is regarded in certain religious teachings as one of seven deadly sins. Note that one sin may slightly obtrude into the area covered by another sin. Consult your dictionary.

Below you will find seven deadly sins listed in column A. In column B you will find the areas covered by these sins. Match each sin in column A with its appropriate definition.

A	B
1. **pride**	(*a*) indolence
2. **sloth**	(*b*) longing jealously to possess what someone else possesses
3. **gluttony**	(*c*) arrogant self-esteem
4. **lust**	(*d*) a feeling of ill-will or discontent over seeing someone else's superiority or advantage
5. **covetousness**	
6. **anger**	(*e*) wrath
	(*f*) given to excessive eating; voracious
7. **envy**	(*g*) intense desire, as for power, strong sexual desire

B. Short Expressive Words

The words in column A are short and expressive of acts of disparagement. How many of these do you know? Match the word in column A with its meaning in column B.

A	B
1. **sneer**	(*a*) reproach or provoke insultingly
2. **snarl**	(*b*) smile or curl the lips in contempt
3. **chaff**	(*c*) harass persistently with questions or objections
4. **taunt**	(*d*) tease good-naturedly
5. **heckle**	(*e*) growl angrily

C. "Apparel Oft Proclaims the Man"

Match each word or phrase in column A with its definition in column B.

A	B
1. **Beau Brummel**	(*a*) pretentiously elegant or stylish
2. **a fop**	(*b*) a maker of fashionable attire
3. **chi chi** (pronounced *she she*)	(*c*) a man wearing the newest fashion in clothes
4. **modiste**	(*d*) a man who is excessively concerned about his clothes
5. **chic** (pronounced *sheek*)	(*e*) in fashion

D. Coteries

Each word in column A expresses the idea of a collection. Match each of these words with the kind of being or thing listed in column B with which it is usually associated.

A	B
1. cluster	(*a*) grapes
2. clump	(*b*) airs
3. medley	(*c*) girls
4. bevy	(*d*) bees
5. herd	(*e*) partridges
6. swarm	(*f*) cattle
7. covey	(*g*) trees
8. school	(*h*) sticks
9. faggot	(*i*) well-wishers
10. claque	(*j*) fish

E. Cults

Explain each of the following types of cults in the light of its historical significance.

the cult of Apollo, the cult of violence, the Shelley cult

IV. Building Your Own Thesaurus

Are You Dead Sure?

Strangely, the word *dead* does not always mean "no longer existing." Often, when used in certain context, *dead* means just the reverse, "pulsing" "strongly moving" — as in the sense: "If there is anything I am in *dead* earnest about, it is the question of civil rights."

The unabridged dictionary defines dozens of words and expressions using *dead* as one word apart or in a combination. The index in Roget's International Thesaurus has more than a whole column of entries indicating the wide diversity in the use of the word *dead* as a separate entity or in a special context.

Deadlock is one of a group of English words in which the word *dead* is used in conjunction with another word to form a graphic combination. Here are a few other examples:

dead heat — a race in which the competitors end in a tie

dead shot — with perfect accuracy

dead-beat (colloquial) — exhausted

dead beat — one who tries to avoid paying for anything

dead end — a street that is closed at one end; a blind alley, a *cul de sac*

dead right — absolutely

dead pan — expressionless immobile face

dead weight — a heavy unrelieved burden; inert

dead set — firmly opposed

dead center — precise

deadline — the latest time for finishing something

a dead letter — meaningless or impotent

Jot down in your notebook as many words, phrases or expressions involving the word *dead*. Use your thesaurus and dictionary.

Answer each of the following questions dealing with the word **dead.**

1. *Give the phrase containing* **dead** *which expresses the meaning of each of the following.*

   (*a*) a race in which the competitors end in a tie

   (*b*) with unerring accuracy

   (*c*) (a colloquial expression) tired to the point of exhaustion

   (*d*) an expressionless mobile face

   (*e*) meaninglessness or impotence

   (*f*) firmly opposed

   (*g*) an unrelieved burden; inert

   (*h*) the last time for finishing something

   (*i*) a street that is closed at one end

   (*j*) one who tries to avoid paying his debts

2. *What is the difference between* **deathly** *and* **deadly**? *Fill in each blank with the correct word.*

   a _____ pallor

   _____ sick

   a _____ fear of attack

3. Consult the entry in your dictionary for the word *deadly.* In one dictionary you will find several synonyms for deadly: *mortal, fatal, lethal.* In another dictionary the fine distinction is drawn between *dead, deceased, extinct,* and *lifeless.* In a short sentence or phrase for each word show the differentiation in implication suggested by these words.

V. Analogies

Complete each of the following analogies.

1. culinary : fare = (*a*) cupidity : money (*b*) sartorial :

   clothes (*c*) boutique : shoes (*d*) convivial : celebration

2. thermometer : temperature = (a) stricture : morality
   (b) transgression : culpability (c) criterion : value
   (d) myriad : stars

3. dapper : untidy = (a) debonair : jaunty (b) uptight :
   serene (c) unkempt : urbane (d) chic : dowdy

4. impulsive : cautious = (a) deliberate : intuitive
   (b) peruse : ponder (c) impetuousness : circumspection (d) premeditative : instinctive

5. cheerful : hilarious = (a) jubilant : jocund
   (b) despondent : dejected (c) lively : vivacious
   (d) unhappy : inconsolable

VI. Review

A. *In the following paragraph substitute for each blank an appropriate word selected from Words 1-125 on the Basic Vocabulary List (including derivations). The first letter of the appropriate word is given in each case. Eight of these words are
especially difficult. Synonyms are provided at the end of the
paragraph to guide you in your choice.*

An argument based upon a..(1).. is not at all c..(2)..un-
less the comparison made between the two cases is really
a..(3)..; that is, unless the cases c..(4).. are exactly paral-
lel. As an extended form of this type of reasoning, we might
mention the type of literature known as the a..(5)..in which
imagined events and characters are symbolic of u..(6)..
problems and characters in human life. To devise exact paral-
lels requires c..(7).. thinking and is not c..(8).. with the
preciseness of reasoning essential in argumentation. Loose
thinking no conscientious teacher of logic can c..(9)...

Yet, to advise mere d..(10).. in the art of debating to be
very c..(11).. in their resort to this type of reasoning is not to
imply a wish to d..(12).. its use by experienced debaters
who display great a..(13).. in their selection of comparisons.
We should, however, be d..(14).. in our duty if we did not

warn beginners against the excessive use of arguments so vulnerable to the refutations of d..(15).. opponents.

Synonyms of Difficult Words in Passage Above

1. comparison
3. suitable, well-fitted
6. genuine
7. perfect, finished
8. harmonious

10. dabblers
11. cautious, careful
14. negligent
15. clever, skillful

B. *In each of the following sentences substitute for the blank an appropriate word selected from Words 1-125 (including derivations) on the Basic Vocabulary List. The first letter of the appropriate word is given in each case.*

1. If the Great Powers do not learn to live together in a_____ there will surely be a third world war.

2. I'd like you to tell me quite c_____, Professor Smith, what you think of my son's progress thus far.

3. The question is this: "Does a _____ make a man wealthy, or does wealth make a man a _____ious?"

4. This isn't my idea of a lively party; you fellows have been about as c_____ as a group of professional mourners at a funeral.

5. He's the kind of politician who would gladly c_____ with the enemies of his country.

6. Astronomers are scientists; astrologers are c_____.

7. The teacher spoke with considerable a_____: "So this is how the class behaves when I leave the room!"

8. "I do not consider it c_____ with my dignity to engage in an altercation with a teacher," remarked the student.

9. The number of enlistments was greatly a_____ when the pay-increase provisions were announced.

10. The benign pastor sought in his funeral address to a____ the grief of the widow.

LESSON TWELVE

126. deleterious	136. deviate
127. demagogue	137. dexterous
128. demur	138. didactic
129. demure	139. diffident
130. denigrate	140. dilatory
131. deprecate	141. dilemma
132. derelict	142. dilettante
133. derogatory	143. discomfiture
134. destitute	144. disparage
135. desultory	145. disparity

126. del-e-te-ri-ous dĕl-ĕ-tē′-rĭ-ŭs [*deleterios* (Greek), "injurious"] — Morally or physically harmful.

According to many critics, gangster films have had a *deleterious* effect upon the youth of our country.

Related Forms: deleteriousness, deleteriously

Synonyms: injurious, detrimental, hurtful, baneful, unwholesome, noxious, pernicious, destructive

Antonyms: beneficial, helpful, salutary, wholesome, advantageous, constructive

Note: Do not confuse forms of <u>deleterious</u> with those of the verb <u>delete</u> (n. <u>deletion</u>), "to take out something written or printed." Synonyms of <u>delete</u> are: expunge, excise (n. <u>excision</u>).

127. dem-a-gogue (variant spelling *demagog*) dĕm′-à-gŏg [*demos* (Greek) "the people" + *agogos*, "leading"] — An insincere, unprincipled leader who stirs up the passions and prejudices of the masses for his own advantage; a mob leader.

If you think about the issues involved, your judgment will never be swayed by the rantings of a *demagogue.*

Related Forms: demagoguery (methods, practices, or the insincere appeal by a mob leader), demagogic (děm-ȧ-gǒj'-ik or děm-ȧ-gǒg'-ĭk), demagoguism

Synonyms: agitator, ringleader, rabble-rouser

Originally, in Athenian democracy, a demagogue was a leader of the people, recognized as an orator who could sway large groups of people by his eloquence and cogent logic. He was a skilled rhetorician who was closely identified with the people. Current usage lends an unsavory connotation to this word, as one who is trying to make capital of social discontent, who resorts to catch words and a clever tongue to advance his own interests.

---

128. de-mur dě-mûr' [*demorari* (Latin), "to delay" "to linger"]

1. To take exception or offer objections to something, often because of scruples.

   When asked to support the anti-strike legislation, the Senator *demurred* on the ground that such a law would be unjust.

2. In law, to interpose a pleading that although the facts as presented by the other side are true they are not sufficient on which to build a case.

   When the defendant's attorney *demurred*, the judge suspended the trial until the following week.

Related Forms: demurrer (a term used in law to mean the objection raised or the exception taken when one demurs; also the person who demurs), demurral, demurrage

Synonyms: pause, scruple, object, vacillate, waiver, boggle

Antonyms: accede, agree, concur

129. de-mure dě-mūr' [*de* (Latin), "very" + *mure* (Middle English), "mature"]

1. Affectedly or unnaturally modest.

> Her career as an actress has embraced roles ranging from that of a *demure* ingenue to that of an openly sharp-tongued vixen.

2. Of sober and becoming behavior.

> The *demure* young lady sat by herself in the front pew, her gloved hands folded in her lap.

Related Forms: demurely, demureness

Synonyms: sedate (dignified, composed), reserved, decorous, diffident, shy, staid, coy, prim (stiffly neat), priggish (affectedly precise or superior), prudish (exaggeratedly or self-consciously modest)

Antonyms: frivolous, bold, forward, immodest, openly self-confident, conceited, imprudent, blunt

Note: Shyness is genuine modesty; demureness often is affected or pretended shyness.

130. **den-i-grate**   dĕn'-ĭ-grāt   [*de* (Latin intensive), "very much" + *nigrare, nigratus* "to blacken"] — To besmirch another's good fame, reputation, or ability; to criticize with the intention of belittling.

> The blistering attack on the Councilman was obviously made to *denigrate* his reputation among the electorate.

Related Form: denigration

Synonyms: defame, vilify, blacken, sully; disparage, asperse (noun: aspersion)

Antonyms: exalt, elevate, ennoble, glorify, extol, praise

Phrases: cast aspersions on the character of, a derogatory reference to

131. **dep-re-cate**   dĕp'-rĕ-kāt   [*deprecari, deprecatus* (Latin), "pray hard," "curse"; from *de*, "away from" + *precari*, "to pray"] — To disapprove of, or argue strongly against, a course of action.

Bob's judgment is usually sound; therefore if he *deprecates* a plan it should be reconsidered.

Related Forms: deprecation, deprecatory (apologetic), deprecatingly, deprecative

Synonyms: protest, reject, remonstrate, decry (denounce disparagingly), expostulate (reason earnestly with a person)

Antonyms: approve, commend, laud, sanction

Phrase: to expostulate *with* a person *on* or *about* something; protest *against* a scheme, express disapproval *of*

Note: <u>Deprecate</u> means to plead against a course of action, not necessarily belittling its importance or value.

<u>Depreciate</u> means to belittle, undervalue or underrate.

---

132. **der-e-lict**   dĕr'-ĕ-lĭkt   [*derelinquere, derelictus* (Latin), "forsake," "abandon"; from *de*, "completely" + *re*, "back" + *linquere*, "to leave"]

1. An abandoned vessel.

> The deep-sea divers went far below the surface of the ocean in search of a *derelict* supposedly laden with Spanish gold.

2. A social outcast, a "human castaway."

> A plan of rehabilitation was proposed by which society could salvage many *derelicts* whom the community once regarded as beyond hope.

3. Neglectful, unfaithful to one's duties, morally blamable.

> A week after the prisoners had escaped, a departmental hearing was held to determine whether the police captain had been *derelict* in his duty.

Related Form: dereliction

Synonyms: shipwreck, wreckage, flotsam, pariah (social outcast); deserted, delinquent

Antonyms: punctilious, attentive

Phrase: dereliction of duty

133. de-rog-a-to-ry dĕ-rŏg'-ȧ-tō-rĭ [*derogare, derogatus* (Latin), "repeal part of a law," "to take away from or diminish"; from *de*, "away" + *rogare*, "to ask"] — Belittling, or expressing a low opinion of, a person.

Several persons in the audience objected to the *derogatory* remarks which the speaker had made about his opponent.

Related Forms: derog'a-tive, de'rogate (followed by from), deroga'tion, derog'atorily, derog'atoriness

Synonyms: degrading, disparaging, detracting, depreciating (*adj.* depreciatory), vilifying, discrediting, defaming (*adj.* defamatory), calumniating (*nouns:* calumniation, calumny) decrying, disdainful (*noun:* disdain), insulting

Antonyms: flattering, eulogistic, laudatory, commendatory, encomiastic (*noun:* encomium), panegyrical (*noun:* panegyric)

134. des-ti-tute dĕs'-tĭ-tūt [*destitutus* (Latin), "abandoned"] — Lacking in something needed; hence, extremely poor.

The countryside of Appalachia is beautiful, but most of its people lack the barest necessities of life and are indeed *destitute.*

Related Form: destitution

Synonyms: deprivation, impecunious, indigent (*noun:* indigence), penniless, necessitous, impoverished

Antonyms: opulent, affluent

Phrases: a man of substance (wealthy), a destitute patient

Note: The word <u>destitute</u> may sometimes denote "deficiency," as in the phrase <u>destitute of</u> (meaning "lacking in") help.

135. des-ul-to-ry dĕs'-ŭl-tō-rĭ [*de*, "down" + *salire*, (Latin) "to leap"] — Shifting from one thing to another without method or rational connection; digressive.

The test on study habits showed that fifteen minutes of concentration had produced better results than two hours of *desultory* study.

Related Forms: desultoriness, desultorily

Synonyms: disconnected, aimless, rambling, straying, unmethodical, erratic, roving, fitful, discursive, cursory, random, spasmodic (intermittent, given to brief spells of activity)

Antonyms: systematic, constant, concentrated, methodical, steadfast, painstaking

Phrase: by fits and starts

Note: Cursory is applied to an action that is superficial because of rapidity; it does not necessarily denote carelessness. The idea inherent in desultory is that of fitfulness, veering from course to course, a sense of incoherence. A cursory examination is quick and hence superficial; a desultory application to a task is one that is unmethodical, careless, unthorough.

136. de-vi-ate dē′-vĭ-āt [de (Latin), "away from" + *viare*, "to travel"; from *via*, "a way," "a road"] — To turn aside from a customary direction or the right course.

To *deviate* from accepted codes of behavior simply because they are the rules of the Establishment is just as wrong as to conform rigidly to them.

Related Forms: deviation, deviative

Synonyms: digress, divagate, veer, stray, wander, diverge (noun: divergence), deflect

Antonyms: undeviating, unswerving

Phrases: take a circuitous route, in a roundabout way

Note: As a noun, deviate is used to mean an individual who differs markedly from the average.

137. dex-ter-ous dĕks′-tĕr-ŭs [*dexter* (Latin), "right"] —Skillful in the use of the hands.

Barry's experiment in carpentry proved to him that he was not as *dexterous* as he had thought; he could not keep the shelves steady long enough to hammer them in place.

Related Forms: dexterously, dexterousness, dexterity, dexter (meaning, on the right side; as the *dexter* wings of the house), dextral (pertaining to the right side)

Synonyms: clever, proficient, adept, deft, nimble, quick, expert, adroit (derived from French *droit*, meaning "right")

Antonyms: gauche, clumsy, awkward, inept, maladroit

Note 1: <u>Dextrous</u> is a variant spelling of <u>dexterous,</u> the preferred form.

Note 2: Originally, <u>dexterous</u> meant "right-handed." <u>Sinister,</u> originally meaning "toward the left," now means "ill-omened," "unlucky."

138. di-dac-tic dī-dăk'-tĭk [*didasktikos* (Greek), from *didaskein*, "to teach"] — Designed to instruct; imparting a lesson.

A good example of *didactic* poetry is Alexander Pope's *Essay on Criticism*, a versified treatise on rhetoric.

Related Forms: didactical, didactically, didactics (plural used as a singular noun), didacticism

Synonyms: instructive, pedagogical, explanatory

Note: <u>Didactic</u> has an unfavorable sense when used to refer to a person. It means "too much inclined to instruct others against their will or at unsuitable occasions." A synonym is <u>pedantic</u> (showing off one's book learning).

139. dif-fi-dent dĭf'-ĭ-děnt [*diffidens* (Latin), "having no confidence"; from *diffidere*, from *dis*, "not" + *fidere*, "to trust"] — Lacking confidence in oneself.

The great English essayist Addison was *diffident* in the company of people he did not know, but self-confident the moment he sat down to write.

Related Forms: diffidence, diffidently

Synonyms: modest, reserved, retiring, shy, humble, hesitant, timid

Antonyms: self-confident, self-reliant, aggressive, forward, arrogant

Note: <u>Coy</u> is used in respect to women who pretend to be modest.

<u>Diffident</u> is used usually to describe individuals who are really modest or reserved.

140. dil-a-to-ry dĭl'-à-tō-rĭ [*dilator* (Latin), "a loiterer"; from *differre, dilatus,* "delay"] — Inclined to, or causing delay.

The "ten-o-clock scholar" and the "schoolboy creeping like a snail unwillingly to school" aptly describe the *dilatory* pupil.

Related Forms: dilatorily, dilatoriness

Synonyms: dawdling, delaying, sluggish, deferring, procrastinating, tardy, lethargic

Antonyms: prompt, expeditious, speedy, punctual

Note: Do not confuse <u>dilatory</u> with <u>dilating</u> "expanding, spreading" which comes from the Latin verb <u>dilatore</u>, "to spread out."

141. di-lem-ma dĭ-lĕm'-à [*di* (Greek), "two" + *lemma* (Greek), "assumption." The word *dilemma* is a Greek word meaning "a double proposition."] — A choice of a situation in which one must choose between equally unsatisfactory courses; hence, a difficult, perplexing situation.

There I was in the midst of a *dilemma;* should I cut my hair to please my parents, or should I leave it long and maintain my individuality but lose my allowance.

Synonyms: quandary, plight, perplexity, predicament, option (power or right of choosing)

HOBSON'S CHOICE

When customers wished to rent a horse from Thomas Hobson's stable at Cambridge, England, Mr. Hobson insisted on each customer's taking in his turn the horse nearest the door or no horse at all. Thus, in current usage, a Hobson's choice is a choice that is no choice at all: either take what is offered or nothing.

Thomas Ward offers an apt quotation:

"Where to elect there is but one,
'Tis Hobson's choice — take that or none."

Phrases: to be *on the horns of a dilemma* (a form of argument in which two or more alternatives are presented, each of which holds out an unfavorable choice for the chooser)

to *opt for* something (to make a choice) be *nonplused* (be in a state of utter perplexity)

caught between Scylla and Charybdis

142. dil-et-tan-te dĭl-ĕ-tăn′-tĭ dĭl-ĕ-tänt′ [*dilettare* (Italian), "to delight"; from *delectare* (Latin), "to delight"] — One who dabbles in the fine arts or in a branch of knowledge for amusement only and without serious or concentrated study.

His income was now so large that he felt he could afford to become an expert in his hobbies and be a *dilettante* in his business.

Related Form: dilettantism

Synonyms: amateur, trifler, dabbler

Antonyms: expert, professional, connoisseur (See page 165)

Note 1: The plural of dilettante is dilettanti or dilettantes.

Note 2: The Winston Dictionary makes the following general distinction between amateur and dilettante: "An amateur chooses his art or sport for love of it, and, though not ranked as a professional, he may be expert and accomplished. The dilettante shares the amateur's love for his chosen field, but not his application; hence, he is a dabbler, one who toys with a subject, a mere trifler."

143. dis-com-fi-ture dĭs-kŭm′-fĭ-tūr [*dis* (Latin), "with intensive force" + *conficere*, "to finish, or bring about," "to accomplish"] — Utter defeat in battle, rout; frustration of the plans of another; confusion of mind resulting from perplexity or frustration of hopes or plans.

Confident of the *discomfiture* of the enemy, our troops rushed into the battle to take full advantage of their new opportunity to effect utter rout of the opposing forces.

The sternness of his expression so *discomfited* me that I found it difficult to answer his questions.

Related Form: discomfit

Synonyms: frustration, thwarting, abashment, disconcertment, confusion; ruffled, foiled

Antonyms: poised, unruffled, composed, self-possessed

Note: Do not confuse discomfit, which means "to put to rout, to overwhelm, to defeat utterly," "to baffle," "to be so disturbed by perplexity as to be unable to collect one's thoughts," with discomfort, which means to "rob of comfort," "to make uneasy," "to embarrass."

144. dis-par-age dĭs-păr'-aj [*desparagier* (Old French), "to marry a person of inferior rank"; from *dis* "apart" + *par* (Latin), "equal"] — To speak slightingly of; to discredit or undervalue.

Michael rebuked his friend for *disparaging* all immigrants, pointing out that all Americans except American Indians were themselves immigrants or descendants of immigrants.

Related Forms: disparagingly, disparagement

Synonyms: belittle, underrate, minimize, depreciate, vilify, decry, derogate

Antonyms: enhance, magnify, extol, laud, eulogize

Note: The Winston Senior Dictionary makes the following distinctions between disparage and some of its synonyms:

"To depreciate is to lessen in value, standing, esteem, or rank; as, a centralized government tends to depreciate the power of the states; Russian currency was greatly depreciated. To discredit a person is to bring reproach upon him or his integrity; to discredit evidence, testimony, etc. is either to impugn it or prove that it is unworthy of belief.

"To disparage a person, quality, or achievement, is to belittle him or it by implying a lack of merit."

145. dis-par-i-ty dĭs-păr'-ĭ-tĭ [*disparite* (French), from *dis* (Latin), "not" + *par* (Latin), "equal"] — Difference (in age, quantity, character, or rank); inequality.

Among the members of this class there is similarity in respect to age and number of years in school, but great *disparity* in respect to reading ability and cultural interests.

Related Forms: disparate, disparately, disparateness

Synonyms: disproportion, inconsistency

Antonyms: parity, likeness, equality, similarity

EXERCISES

I. Words in Context

A. One-Word Omissions

In each of the following sentences substitute for the blank an appropriate word selected from the Basic Vocabulary List for this lesson (Words 126-145), including derivatives.

1. The candidate's _____ remarks about his rival led members of the audience to rise to the defense of the maligned person.

2. His essay, "Clerks and Mechanics," deplored the _____ in the wages of the two groups although they do comparable work.

3. John could have been class valedictorian had he not been too _____ to speak before a large public audience.

4. Having profited by methods that were, to say the least, _____, he would be last to admit that straightforwardness is an admirable trait.

5. When he realized what a blunder he had made, his _____ was so acute that he left the room unceremoniously.

6. The old lady, her heart touched by the plight of homeless unfortunates, gave the _____ lodging for the night.

7. I really must organize my reading better; up to now it has been very _____.

8. The humid air of these low-lying regions has a _____ effect on the lungs of tubercular patients.

B. Words in Quotations

Select the word which is closest in meaning to the underlined word in each quotation below:

> But knowledge to their eyes her ample page,
> Rich with the spoils of time, did ne'er unroll;
> Chill <u>penury</u>[1] repress'd their noble rage,
> And froze the genial current of the soul.

> — THOMAS GRAY, "Elegy Written in a Country Churchyard"

1. *penury* (*a*) isolation (*b*) solitude (*c*) destruction (*d*) deprivation

> Excess of wealth is cause of <u>covetousness</u>.[2]

> — MARLOWE

2. *covetousness* (*a*) cupidity (*b*) impecuniosity (*c*) condolence (*d*) parsimony

> There is nothing in this world constant but <u>inconstancy</u>[3]

> — SWIFT

3. *inconstancy* (*a*) cantankerousness (*b*) persistency (*c*) inevitability (*d*) fickleness

> The heart of the wise is in the house of mourning;
> But the heart of the fool is in the house of <u>mirth</u>.[4]
> It is better to hear the <u>rebuke</u>[5] of the wise,
> Than for a man to hear the song of fools.
> For as the crackling of thorns under a pot,
> So is the laughter of the fool;
> This also is <u>vanity</u>.[6]

> — ECCLESIASTES

4. *mirth* (*a*) exaltation (*b*) despair (*c*) illusion (*d*) joyous gaiety

5. *rebuke*   (*a*) repulsion (*b*) reproof (*c*) contradiction (*d*) counsel

6. *vanity*   (*a*) emptiness (*b*) merriment
(*c*) sagacity (*d*) smugness

The man who cannot laugh is not only fit for treasons, stratagems[7] and spoils; but his whole life is already treason and a stratagem.

— CARLYLE

7. *stratagems*   (*a*) sinister designs (*b*) tactics
(*c*) sedition (*d*) plans

Poetry teaches the enormous force of a few words, and, in proportion to the inspiration, checks loquacity.[8]

— EMERSON

8. *loquacity*   (*a*) terseness (*b*) art of speaking
(*c*) freedom of thought (*d*) prolixity

II. Words Out of Context

In each group below select the word or expression that is closest in meaning to the word at the left.

1. **demur**   (*a*) liberate (*b*) speak softly
(*c*) show modesty (*d*) take exception to

2. **denigrate**   (*a*) upbraid (*b*) defame (*c*) deny
(*d*) accuse

3. **derelict**   (*a*) remiss (*b*) drunkard (*c*) balance
(*d*) abandoned as worthless

4. **dexterous**   (*a*) insidious (*b*) sugary
(*c*) maladroit (*d*) deft

5. **demagogue**   (*a*) turncoat (*b*) plebeian
(*c*) civic leader (*d*) rabble-rouser

III. Synonyms and Antonyms

A. Synonyms

Match each word in Column A with its synonym in Column B.

	A		B
1.	eulogistic	(a)	thwart
2.	gauche	(b)	waver
3.	deferring	(c)	maladroit
4.	foil	(d)	procrastinating
5.	vacillate	(e)	encomiastic

B. Antonyms

Match each word in Column A with its antonym in Column B.

	A		B
1.	inept	(a)	ruffled
2.	punctual	(b)	derogate
3.	composed	(c)	pernicious
4.	extol	(d)	deft
5.	salutary	(e)	tardy

IV. Related Forms

1. The noun form of *deleterious* is _____.
   The verb form of *deletion* is _____.

2. To excise is to make a(n) _____.

3. The methods and practices of a *demagogue* is termed
   d_____y or d_____ism.

4. A young lady who is *demure* possesses d_____.

5. Two adjective forms for *deprecate* are _____ and _____.

6. Give the noun form of each of the following:

   disparage calumniate detract defame derogate
   eulogize

WORD BUILDING

I. PREFIXES

The Latin prefix **dis** "away from" in the sense of negation, absence of, is a source of numerous English words including *diffident* (dis + fides), studied in this week's lesson.

disagree — to not agree

disorderly — not orderly

discomfort — to not comfort; hence, to cause embarrassment, pain, or lack of comfort.

II. ROOTS

A. The Latin root **fid-** from *fides-* meaning "faith" "trust" is the source of many English words including *diffident*, studied in this week's lesson.

fidelity — loyalty

infidel — an unbeliever

B. The Latin root **via,** "way" "road" is the source of many English words including *devious* and *deviate*, studied in this week's lesson.

viaduct — a bridge

via (pronounced vī'-ȧ) — by way of

C. The Latin root **sal-** (**sil-**), from *salire, saltus,* "leap" "jump" is a source root of several words in English including *desultory* studied in this lesson.

salient (literally, jumping about, capering) — noticeable

resilient (literally, springing back) — elastic

sally (literally "a leaping forth") — an attack; a jaunt; a witty outburst

D. The Latin root **rog,** from *rogere,* "to ask" is the source of *de-rogatory,* studied in this week's lesson.

arrogate — to assume unto oneself

abrogate — to revoke or abolish

prerogative (literally, calling first) — exclusive right or privilege

Other words derived from the same root include *arrogant* (insolently proud), *surrogate* (literally, put into another's place — a substitute), and *interrogate.*

E. The Greek root **demos,** "the people" is a source of many words including *demagogue,* studied in this lesson.

endemic — peculiar to a people, nation, or locality

Malaria was for a long time *endemic* to Central America.

A synonym for *endemic* is "indigenous"; an antonym, "exotic."

epidemic (*epi,* "away" + *demos*) — widespread

democracy (*demos* + *kratos* "power") — government by the people

F. Many English words are derived from the Latin root **par,** meaning "equal," including *disparage* and *disparity,* studied in this week's lesson.

parity — equality

peer — a person of the same civil rank; (also a nobleman)

G. The Latin root **ficere, fac- fic- factus** meaning "do" "make" is the source of many English words, including *discomfiture,* studied in this lesson.

factotum — a servant who performs all kinds of duties

factory — a place where articles are made

EXERCISES

I. Etymology Mastery Test

1. *Define and indicate the origin of the following words.*
    fiduciary   fealty   bona fide   high-fidelity

2. What does the Latin phrase *via media* mean?

3. In what respect does a *cursory* reading of a book differ from a *desultory* reading of the book?

4. *What is meant by the following expressions?*
    the king's prerogative   a surrogate father   abrogate a treaty

5. *What do the following phrases mean?*
    be judged by one's peers
    peer of the realm
    par for the course
    up to par

6. *Give the meaning and etymology of the following words.*
    benefactor   magnify   facsimile   facilitate   faction
    feasible

II. Word Analysis and Word Building

1. In the sentence, "Jack was caught on the *horns* of a dilemma," the italicized word means (*a*) bull's-eye (*b*) unpleasant alternatives (*c*) horrors (*d*) ticklish points

2. What are the language stories behind *dilettante* and *disparage*?

3. If a man were an expert who made his living by judging the value of literary or art masterpieces, which of the following epithets would he resent having applied to him: (*a*) connoisseur (*b*) aficionado (*c*) dilettante (*d*) agent provocateur?

4. (a) The custom of extending the hand in a friendly greeting was instituted to show that the right hand contained no weapon. How, then, did *sinister* come to mean "dangerous"? (b) Would an *ambidextrous* person be less dangerous than a person who was, in the original sense of the word, *sinister*?

5. Explain why the young man in the following anecdote may be said to have been guilty of a *gaucherie*.

> A young man arose in a crowded bus and offered his seat to a rather unattractive woman of uncertain age.
>
> "Thank you very much," the lady gushed. "Such courtesy is most unusual these days."
>
> "You said it, Lady," remarked the young man, "but my mother brought me up to be polite to all ladies, not just those that are young and pretty."

III. A Dictionary Project

A. Vogue Words

Consulting an unabridged dictionary of *recent date, Give the meaning of each of the following words that have achieved considerable vogue in current English usage. Use each word in a short sentence that clearly illustrates its meaning. Consult an unabridged dictionary of recent date.*

(a) syndrome	(d) snob appeal	(g) cadres
(b) extrovert	(e) proliferation	(h) dialogue
(c) a building complex	(f) a "put-on"	(i) charisma

B. Differences in Synonyms

1. Most dictionaries differentiate, and give illustrative details between the words *deviate, digress, diverge,* and *swerve,* all of which have the general connotation of going aside from a path. Study the entries under these words carefully and supply the correct form of the italicized words above in each of the following sentences.

(a) Want forced him to _____ from the path of honesty.

(b) Bill _____ from his set speech to tell a personal anecdote.

(c) The new political party was formed from two groups who had _____ from the main party.

(d) The man _____ to the left to avoid being thrown down by the oncoming runner.

2. *Indicate the difference between the words in each pair below. Use each word in the pair in a short sentence that clearly illustrates its meaning.*

discomfiture — discomposure	affect — effect
dilettante — virtuoso	malfeasance — nonfeasance
felicitate — facilitate	fiat — feat
factious — factitious	deprecate — depreciate

3. Consult an unabridged dictionary for the fine distinctions in the meaning of predicament, dilemma, plight and quandary.

IV. A Glance Back

Graphic Phrases

Give the meaning of each of the following phrases.

1. to soft-soap a person
2. the bone of contention
3. a diehard
4. high-falutin language
5. circulate a round robin
6. to be at loggerheads
7. a red-letter day
8. keep a weather-eye open
9. put on the dog
10. dog-eat-dog attitude

LESSON THIRTEEN

146. **dis-traught** dĭs-trôt′ [*distractus* (Latin), "distracted"]
— Anguished; greatly disturbed in mind; deeply agitated.

At the realization that she had lost her mother's much-treasured bracelet, Mary became utterly *distraught* and began to search frantically about.

Synonyms: distressed, distracted, bewildered (*noun:* bewilderment), unnerved, frantic, perturbed (almost to the point of insanity)

Antonyms: equable, composed; self-composure

147. **di-vulge** dĭ-vŭlj′ [*divulgare* (Latin), "to spread among the people"; from *vulgus*, "the common people"] — To make public; to disclose, as a secret.

The District Attorney refused to *divulge* the names of his witnesses before he brought the case to trial.

Related Forms: divulgence, divulgement

Synonyms: reveal, impart, publicize

Antonyms: conceal, hide

148. doc-ile dŏs'-ĭl [*docere* (Latin), "to teach"] — Easy to manage, teach, or discipline.

Although usually good-natured and *docile*, Ted could be driven into a frenzy by any remark which implied that he was somewhat overweight.

Related Form: docility

Synonyms: submissive, gentle, teachable, amenable, tractable, compliant, obedient, acquiescent, subservient

Antonyms: intractable, obdurate (*noun:* obduracy), fractious, unmanageable, headstrong, ungovernable, willful, ineducable

149. dog-mat-ic dŏg-măt'ĭk [*dogma* (Greek), "opinion"] — Insistent and positive in manner or utterance, arrogant in expressing an opinion, asserting opinion as if it were an undisputed fact.

Bill tends to deliver his opinions in a *dogmatic* manner as if they are proven facts.

Related Forms: dogma, dogmatist, dogmatical, dogmatically, dogmatism, dogmatize

Synonyms: dictatorial, imperious, opinionated, self-opinionated, assertive, illiberal, intransigent (refusing to conciliate)

Antonyms: gentle, unassertive, diffident, liberal, moderate

Phrase: impervious to reason

150. dras-tic drăs'-tĭk [*drastikos* (Greek), "active"] — Acting with force or quickness; extreme in effect.

In order to rid our country of air and water pollution, it will be necessary to apply not half-hearted, but *drastic*, measures.

Related Form: drastically

Synonyms: thoroughgoing, vigorous, stern

Antonyms: moderate, mild

Phrase: drastic changes

151. du-plic-i-ty dū-plĭs'-ĭ-tĭ [*duo* (Latin), "two" + *plicatus*, "folded"] — Intentional double-dealing or deception; deceit in speech or conduct.

He concluded his sermon on the evils of hypocrisy and *duplicity* by quoting Polonius' lines in Hamlet:

> "To thine own self be true;
> And it must follow, as the night the day,
> Thou canst not then be false to any man."

Synonyms: guile (*adj.* guileful), deceit, trickery, dissimulation, chicanery, imposture, artifice

Synonyms for deceive: hoodwink, cozen, beguile, dupe, gull, bilk, bamboozle (*colloquial*)

Antonym: straightforwardness

Phrases: sharp practice (deception), under false colors, an artful dodge

---

> "O, what a tangled web we weave
> When first we practice to deceive."
>
> — Scott

---

152. dy-nam-ic dī-năm'-ĭk [*dynamis* (Greek), "power"] — Having power or physical energy; energetic.

A man of *dynamic* personality, he tackled his problems with force and determination, and executed his plans with enthusiasm and vigor.

Related Forms: dynamical, dynamically

Synonyms: forceful, powerful, effective, strenuous, energetic; (*nouns*) drive, dash, ebulliency

Antonyms: static, inert, passive, torpid (*noun:* torpidity), sluggish, lethargic, phlegmatic, quiescent (*noun:* quiescence)

153. ef-fete   ĕ-fēt′ [*effetus* (Latin), "worn out by breeding"; from *ex*, "out" + *fetus*, "offspring"] — No longer productive, because of age; exhausted, worn out.

"Soft living has rendered the democracies *effete*," said the demagogue; "therefore our energy and purpose will easily beat them to their knees."

Related Form: effeteness

Synonyms: barren, withered, sterile

Antonyms: fertile, productive, fecund (*noun:* fecundity), prolific, ripe

154. ef-fi-ca-cious   ĕf-ĭ-kā′-shŭs [*efficere* (Latin), "to accomplish," from *ex*, "completely" + *facere*, "do"] — Having the power to produce a desired effect.

Since we are talking about misdirected energy, do you happen to know the story about the doctor who invented an amazingly *efficacious* medicine to cure a disease that didn't exist?

Related Forms: efficacy, efficaciously, efficaciousness

Synonyms: effective, effectual, powerful, potent (*noun:* potency)

Antonyms: ineffective, powerless

155. ef-fi-gy   ĕf′-fĭ-jĭ [*effigies* (Latin), "image," "likeness"] — A crude likeness of a person who is disliked, usually in the form of a stuffed figure.

During the opening days of the American Revolution, King George III was hanged in *effigy* many times in many American towns.

Synonyms: image, representation, figure, icon (usually a sacred personage)

An iconoclast (*adj.* iconoclastic) is literally, "an image smasher" and in current usage means "one who attacks cherished tradition."

156. ef-fron-ter-y ĕ-frŭn'-tĕr-ĭ [*effrons, effrontis* (Latin), "barefaced," "shameless;" from *ex*, "without" + *frons*, "forehead"] — Boldness without shame.

After twice breaking a date with Janey, Bob had the *effrontery* to ask her to help him write his English report.

Synonyms: impudence, audacity (*adj.* audacious), presumption (*adj.* presumptuous), temerity, brass (*colloquial*), impertinence, gall (*slang*), brazenness

Antonyms: timidity, modesty, diffidence, shyness, meekness

Phrases: barefaced audacity, put on a bold front

157. e-gre-gious ĕ-grē'-jŭs [*egregius* (Latin), "out of the herd," that is, "distinguished, extraordinary"; from *e*, "out" + *grex, gregis*, "herd"] — Conspicuous by undesirable qualities.

In criticizing this composition I must say that I am concerned not with your typical mistakes in sentence structure, but rather with the *egregious* intolerance it betrays.

Related Forms: egregiously, egregiousness

Synonyms: flagrant, shocking, outrageous, glaring, extraordinary, gross, enormous

Note: Egregious once meant "distinguished" or "extraordinary," like its Latin equivalent. That meaning of the English word is now obsolete. The word egregious is used in current usage in a pejorative (derogatory) sense.

Pete is such an egregious liar: he can look you squarely in the face and tell you the most obvious falsehood.

158. e-lic-it ē-lĭs'-ĭt [from e, "out of" + *lacere*, (Latin) "to draw"] — To draw out, of, or forth; that is, to bring to light; to draw out against inclination.

Since both sides were so obviously biased, it was impossible to *elicit* a true version of what had taken place.

Related Form: elicitation

Synonyms: extract, educe, exact, extort, evoke

Phrase: wring or wrest from

Note: Do not confuse elicit with illicit, meaning "unlawful."

159. e-ma-ci-at-ed ē-mā'-shĭ-āt-ĕd [e, "thoroughly" + *ma-ciare* (Latin) "to make lean"; from *macies,* "leanness"] — Wasted or reduced in weight by starvation or disease.

It is hard to believe that in a country as rich as ours there are still children who are listless and *emaciated* because of lack of food.

Related Form: emaciation

Synonyms: shriveled, withered, raw-boned, pinched

Antonyms: battened, fattened, plump

160. em-a-nate ĕm'-ă-nāt [e, "out" + *manare,* (Latin) "to flow"] — To issue forth, as from a source (as of something intangible or immaterial, like light, ideas, inspiration, etc.)

The aura of kindness and serenity that *emanates* from Joanne makes her a very pleasant person to be with.

Related Forms: emanation, emanative

Synonyms: flow, arise, originate, radiate, send forth, emit, emerge

Note 1: <u>Emanate</u> often appears in "spelling demon" lists. Note the order of the vowels: e a, a, e.

Note 2: <u>Emanation,</u> in the scientific sense, refers to that which issues from a radioactive substance.

161. em-bez-zle ĕm-bĕz'-'l [*embeseler* (Anglo-French), "to destroy by fraud"] — To appropriate or misuse fraudulently money entrusted to one's care.

The teller, who was urgently in need of money, *embezzled* a huge sum from the bank.

Related Forms: embezzler, embezzlement

Synonyms: misappropriate, defalcate (misappropriation held by a trustee), peculate (*noun:* peculation — embezzle public money), purloin

Other synonyms for *stealing:* filch (of small value) pilfer (petty thieving — *noun:* pilferage)

Good name in man and woman, dear my lord,
Is the immediate jewel of their souls:
Who steals my purse steals trash; 'tis something, nothing;
'Twas mine, 'tis his, and has been slave to thousands:
But he that filches from me my good name
Robs me of that which not enriches him,
And makes me poor indeed.

— SHAKESPEARE, *Othello*

---

162. **e-mol-u-ment** ē-mŏl'-ū-mĕnt [*emolumentum* (Latin), "profit"] — Salary or profits derived from an occupation or office.

He's altogether too pretentious; now that he has been granted a four-dollar-a-week increase, he refers to his salary as his *emolument.*

Synonyms: remuneration, fee, compensation, stipend (usually a fixed fee or a periodic payment, like a pension), honorarium (a payment for professional services on which no fee is set)

163. **em-u-late** ĕm'-ū-lāt [*aemulari* (Latin), "to strive to equal"] — To try to equal or excel (usually with some degree of success).

Young people of the late nineteenth century were advised to *emulate* the hard-working young heroes of Horatio Alger's novels.

Related Forms: emulation, emulator, emulative, emulous

Synonyms: imitate, rival, vie with (*participle:* vying), compete, strive, contend

164. en-dem-ic ĕn-dĕm'ik [*endemos* (Greek), "belonging to a people"] — Peculiar to a locality or a definite people.

Many diseases which are *endemic* to certain areas can be eradicated by the addition of vitamins and minerals to the diet of the people.

Related Form: endemical

Synonyms: indigenous, native

Antonyms: epidemic, pandemic (epidemic over a large area)

Phrases: an endemic disease

Note: Epidemic differs from endemic in that epidemic has the meaning of a disease which spreads rapidly among many people at the same time without regard to group or locality.

165. en-hance ĕn-hăns' [*enhaucier, enhalcier* (Old French); probably from *in* (Latin), "intensive meaning" + *altiare*, "to raise"] — To heighten or add to the qualities of something; as, to *enhance* the beauty of a room.

Can't someone convince Margie that the long earrings and false eyelashes she insists on wearing do not *enhance*, but on the contrary detract from her natural good looks?

Related Form: enhancement

Synonyms: raise, intensify, magnify, augment, increase, adorn

Antonyms: detract (from), depreciate, minimize, decrease, reduce, diminish.

EXERCISES

I. Words in Context

In each group below, select the word or expression that best defines the word at the left:

1. **embezzle** (*a*) appropriate dishonestly (*b*) drink quickly (*c*) underestimate (*d*) fortify

2. **effigy** (*a*) delineation (*b*) figurative language (*c*) representative image (*d*) treachery

3. **dynamic** (*a*) exhaustive (*b*) energetic (*c*) like a motor (*d*) static

4. **drastic** (*a*) warlike (*b*) hostile (*c*) rigorous (*d*) devious

5. **efficacious** (*a*) efficient (*b*) fanciful (*c*) protracted (*d*) effective

6. **duplicity** (*a*) two-step (*b*) veracity (*c*) deception (*d*) disparagement

7. **effete** (*a*) worn out (*b*) effectual (*c*) pertaining to a festival (*d*) a solemn ceremony

8. **docile** (*a*) learned (*b*) tractable (*c*) reproachable (*d*) pertaining to a doctor

9. **effrontery** (*a*) encounter (*b*) extinction (*c*) boldness (*d*) opposition

II. Words in Context

A. Two-Word Omissions

In each of the following selections, you will find two blanks indicating that a pair of words has been omitted. Following the selections are four choices lettered (a) to (d). Select the letter preceding the pair of words that will most satisfactorily complete the meaning of the selection.

1. When Philip of Macedon wrote the Spartan leaders, "If I enter Laconia, I will level Lacedemon to the ground," he received for answer the single but significant word "If." This is, perhaps, the finest example of _____ utterance on record, and was indeed worthy of the people who gave not only a local habitation but a name to _____ speech.

(*a*) conjectural — cogent

(*b*) laconic — pithy

(*c*) prolix — bombastic

(*d*) dubious — caustic

2. That civilization is _____ which has lost its basic vigor. It takes a prolonged period of renascence to _____ it.

    (*a*) effete — rejuvenate

    (*b*) anachronistic — wreck

    (*c*) in abeyance — alleviate

    (*d*) benign — circumvent

3. The great, in _____, bear a countenance more princely than they are wont; for it is the temper of the highest hearts, like the palm tree, to strive most upwards, when it is most _____.

    (*a*) altercation — assuaged

    (*b*) discomfiture — assiduous

    (*c*) affliction — burdened

    (*d*) austerity — contumelious

B. One-Word Omissions

In each of the following sentences substitute for the blank an appropriate word selected from the Basic Vocabulary List for this lesson (Words 146-165), including derivatives.

1. As my knock failed to _____ any response, I tried the door. It was locked.

2. Leonard Bernstein has often declared his admiration for Sergei Koussevitzky, his mentor, and Bernstein has in turn been _____ by many up-and-coming symphony orchestra conductors.

3. How can you have the _____ to apply for a really important post after showing yourself to be incompetent in a minor position?

4. The correct answer to the problem is 12; your answer of 1200 was caused by an _____ error at the beginning of the computation.

5. Was it illness, worry, or a crash diet which caused Sue to become so haggard and _____ in appearance?

6. I do not expect any _____ for my work with these slum children. I am led to do this work by purely altruistic motives.

C. Words in Headlines

In each headline below, certain key words are underlined and numbered. Each numbered word is then followed by four words or expressions lettered (a) to (d). Select the letter of the item that is closest in meaning to each underlined word as used in the headline.

BANKER INDICTED[1]
EMBEZZLEMENT[2] CHARGED

1. *indicted*   (a) angry (b) charged with an offense
(c) horrified (d) poverty stricken

2. *embezzlement*   (a) robbery (b) deceit (c) lack of funds (d) fraudulent appropriation

RIOTERS CONVERGE ON SQUARE
HANG TRAITORS IN EFFIGY[3]

3. *effigy*   (a) indignation (b) ridicule
(c) image (d) protest

DRASTIC[4] REGULATIONS CURTAILED[5]
NEW LAW IN EFFECT TOMORROW

4. *drastic*   (a) rigorous (b) inhumane
(c) efficacious (d) punitive

5. *curtailed*   (a) abolished (b) abridged
(c) attacked (d) intensified

D. Words in Quotations

In each passage below, certain words are underlined and numbered. Each numbered word is then followed by four words or expressions lettered (a) to (d). Select the letter of the item that is closest in meaning to each underlined word, as used in the selection.

In a case of dissension,[1] never dare to censure[2] till you've heard the other side.

— EURIPIDES

1. *dissension* (*a*) argument (*b*) doubt (*c*) concurrence (*d*) disagreement

2. *censure* (*a*) reprimand (*b*) examine critically (*c*) laud (*d*) reach a conclusion

In the adversity[3] of our best friends we often find something that is not exactly displeasing.

— LA ROCHEFOUCAULD

3. *adversity* (*a*) criticism (*b*) misfortune (*c*) repugnance (*d*) effrontery

III. Analogies

Complete the following analogies.

1. galleon : cruiser = _____ : modern (*a*) grotesque (*b*) archaic (*c*) bucolic (*d*) recent

2. war : treaty = (*a*) aggression : conquest (*b*) bargain : bickering (*c*) deadlock : strike (*d*) altercation : agreement

3. embellishment : enhance = (*a*) cosmetic : brighten (*b*) adornment : fascinate (*c*) ire : mollify (*d*) trimming : adorn

4. honors : diploma = (*a*) bonus : salary (*b*) emolument : compensation (*c*) graduation : degree (*d*) award : merit

WORD BUILDING

I. PREFIXES

The Latin prefix **e-, ex,** meaning "from" "out of" "without" has served as an important derivative element in innumerable English words.

> *emigrate* — to migrate out of a country
> *expel* — to drive out

II. ROOTS

A. The Latin root **greg-,** from *grex, gregis,* "flock" "herd" is the source of a number of English words, including *egregious,* studied in this lesson.

> *congregate* — to collect into a group
> *segregate* — to separate from the group

B. The Latin root **duo,** meaning two, has contributed to a number of scientific terms and is the source of many other words in our language, including *duplicity,* studied in this lesson. It is related to the Latin prefix *bi* "twice" and *di* meaning "double" "twice," from the Greek prefix *dis.*

> *dichromatic* — having two colors
> *dihedral* — made by two planes, as a *dihedral* angle
> *duplex* — double, doublefold

C. The Latin root **plic-,** from *plicare, plicatus,* meaning "fold," is the source of several English words, including *duplicity* studied in this lesson.

> *complicate* (literally, "to fold together") — to make intricate or involved
> *implicate* — to involve
> *duplicate* — an exact copy; to make a copy of

D. The Latin root **doc-, doct-,** from *docere, doctus,* meaning "teach," contributes the core meaning of many English words, including *docile,* studied in this lesson.

> *doctrine* (literally, "teaching, instruction") — something taught; a principle of belief
>
> *indoctrinate* — to teach or inculcate a doctrine

EXERCISES

I. Etymology Mastery Test

1. Trace the origin of the word *egregious* from the Latin root *grex-, gregis* to its present meaning.

2. *Bi,* a shorter form of *bis,* is a Latin prefix meaning "twice."

   What do the following words mean? Try to arrive at the meaning of each word by tracing the derivative meanings of the elements composing it.

   > biped   biennial   bilateral

3. *What is the meaning of the following Latin number derivatives? Give an English word example derived from each number.*

mono	quarto	sextus	octavus
tri	quint	septus	decem

4. *Trace the meaning of each of the following words through its etymology. You may consult the dictionary.*

   replica   pliant   exploit   accomplice   ply

5. "Patrick used a *ploy* to gain admission to the secret conference." Which of the following words does *ploy* mean?

   (*a*) jest (*b*) stratagem (*c*) coercion

II. Word Analysis and Word Development

1. What did the word *biscuit* mean originally?

2. Note that the English word *endemic* is taken with little change from the Greek. Give three other words in this

lesson that are so derived. After consulting the Basic Word List, select as many words as possible that come without change from the Latin.

3. If you were asked to consult a *frontispiece*, would you turn to (*a*) the front part of a piece of armor, (*b*) an illustration facing the first page or the title page of a book, (*c*) the cover of a book?

4. Would you be most likely to find an *equilibrist* (*a*) in a church, (*b*) in a graveyard, (*c*) in Tin Pan Alley, (*d*) at the circus, (*e*) on a college faculty?

III. Review

In each of the following sentences substitute for the blank an appropriate word selected from Words 1-145 (including derivatives) on the Basic Vocabulary List. The first letter of the appropriate word is given in each case.

1. The sleight-of-hand artist manipulated a pack of cards with such c_____ skill that the audience sat amazed.

2. God will pardon all who are truly repentant. The Scriptures say: "A humble and a c_____ heart the Lord will not despise."

3. Although casualties caused by motor accidents are decreasing, we still have no reason to feel c_____ about the situation.

4. Living on the fruits of his tiny garden and blueberries gathered in neighboring swamps and pastures, Thoreau certainly led a very a_____ existence.

5. We chatted for an hour on all manner of subjects; it was indeed a rather d_____ conversation.

6. When I asked the bus driver to let me out at an unscheduled stop, he at first d_____, but finally acceded to my request.

7. "Tiger : feline = wolf : c_____" is a common analogy.

General Review

(Words 1-165)

I. Words Out of Context

In each group below, select the word or phrase that is closest in meaning to the word at the left. Some of these words are not on the Basic Vocabulary List but have been referred to and defined in the foregoing lessons.

1. *mirthful*   (*a*) sardonic   (*b*) slovenly   (*c*) jocund   (*d*) fantastic

2. *copious*   (*a*) plenteous   (*b*) emulating   (*c*) mimicking   (*d*) envious

3. *bicker*   (*a*) bargain   (*b*) quarrel over trifles   (*c*) complain   (*d*) disagree

4. *distraught*   (*a*) ruined   (*b*) untaught   (*c*) deeply disturbed   (*d*) disillusioned

5. *elicit*   (*a*) beg   (*b*) do wrong   (*c*) permit   (*d*) draw forth

6. *crass*   (*a*) unintellectual   (*b*) disorderly   (*c*) flamboyant   (*d*) grossly stupid

7. *petulant*   (*a*) peevish   (*b*) trifling   (*c*) affectionate   (*d*) pleading

8. *charlatan*   (*a*) jingoist   (*b*) connoisseur   (*c*) vassal   (*d*) quack

9. *catholic*   (*a*) reverent   (*b*) pious   (*c*) broad-minded   (*d*) religious

10. *circumspect*   (*a*) cautious   (*b*) circuitous   (*c*) surrounded   (*d*) possessing insight

II. Words In Context

A. Words in Phrases

Explain the meaning of each of the following phrases. Use each phrase in a sentence that will clearly show that you understand the meaning of the phrase.

11. putting on the dog
12. an equivocal reply
13. a bone of contention
14. an ecumenical conference
15. Hobson's choice
16. sibling rivalry
17. a red-letter day
18. quid pro quo
19. in a pejorative sense
20. pinnacle of success

B. Words in a Continuous Passage

In each of the following passages, certain words are underlined and numbered. Each numbered word is followed by four words or phrases lettered (a) to (d). Select the letter of the item that best defines the numbered word as it is used in the passage.

To an Author

Your leaves bound up compact[21] and fair
In neat array[22] at length prepare
To pass their hour on learning's stage,
To meet the surly[23] critic's rage;
The statesman's slight,[24] the smatterer's sneer[25] —
Were these, indeed, your only fear,
You might be tranquil[26] and resigned;[27]
What most should touch your fluttering mind
Is that, few critics will be found
To sift your works, and deal the wound.

            — Philip Frenau

21. *compact*   (*a*) harmonious (*b*) attractive
                     (*c*) packed together (*d*) scented

22. *array*   (*a*) orderly arrangement (*b*) brilliance
                     (*c*) adjustment (*d*) circle

23. *surly*   (*a*) overconfident (*b*) rude
                     (*c*) critical (*d*) carping

24. *slight*   (*a*) stricture (*b*) caution (*c*) dissent
                     (*d*) discourteous inattention

25. *sneer*   (*a*) disapprobation (*b*) revulsion
                     (*c*) smirk (*d*) contemptuous expression

26. *tranquil*   (*a*) offended (*b*) calm (*c*) ill at ease
                     (*d*) conciliatory

27. *resigned*   (*a*) acquiescent (*b*) hopeless
                     (*c*) reprieved (*d*) respondent

On Genius

The first virtue of all really great men is that they are candid.[28] They eschew[29] hypocrisy. They bravely unveil their frailties,[30] their doubts, their defects. They do not cower.[31] Boldly they ride a-tilt against biases.[32] No civil, moral nor immoral power overawes them. They love their fellow-men profoundly. They are magnanimous.[33] They allow their hearts to expand. They have compassion[34] for the pathetic.[35] Pity is the very foundation of Genius.

             — Anatole France (adapted)

28. *candid*   (*a*) unafraid (*b*) free from duplicity
                     (*c*) honorable (*d*) efficacious

29. *eschew*   (*a*) shun (*b*) denounce
                     (*c*) reprehend (*d*) oppose

30. *frailties*   (*a*) inabilities (*b*) quirks
                     (*c*) eccentricities (*d*) weaknesses

31. cower   (a) crouch in fear   (b) envy
                     (c) desire wrongfully   (d) renege

32. biases   (a) creeds   (b) dogmas   (c) proclivi-
                     ties   (d) preformed judgments

33. magnanimous   (a) generous   (b) vindictive
                     (c) self-important   (d) ignoble

34. compassion   (a) fervor   (b) forgiveness   (c) intui-
                     tive understanding   (d) feeling for
                     another's woes

35. pathetic   (a) arousing an emotion of pity
                     (b) downtrodden   (c) trite
                     (d) miserable

C. Two-Word Omissions

In each statement below, you will find two blanks which indicate that a pair of words or phrases lettered (a) to (d) which will make the sense has been omitted. Select the letter preceding the item that you think will best complete the meaning of the sentence.

36. Matters that pertain to ———— are termed ————.

    (a) motives — mercenary

    (b) cooking — culinary

    (c) money — impecunious

    (d) religion — iconoclastic

37. To ———— opinion is to ————.

    (a) question another's — be querulous

    (b) listen to another's — be opinionated

    (c) suppress — throttle it

    (d) permit expression of — endorse it

38. To _____ is to be _____.

    (*a*) diligent in one's studies — recondite

    (*b*) biased — captious

    (*c*) abrupt in manner — brusque

    (*d*) reticent — meek

39. To _____ an action is to _____ it severely.

    (*a*) balk at — condemn

    (*b*) castigate — criticize

    (*c*) exult at — indulge in

    (*d*) sanction — disapprove

D. Quotations

Below, you will find five quotations each containing a clue word which will give meaning to the quotation. Read each quotation and then complete the statement that follows it.

40. The hearts of good men admit *atonement.* — HOMER

    This means that good men

    (*a*) will always listen to *reason.*

    (*b*) are always prepared to *make amends* for a misdeed.

    (*c*) are *subject to temptation.*

41. Where true *fortitude* dwells, loyalty, bounty, friendship, and fidelity may be found — SIR THOMAS BROWNE.

    This means that

    (*a*) One can possess loyalty only if one has good *fortune.*

    (*b*) Faithfulness in friendship is impossible without *honesty.*

    (*c*) *Spiritual strength to endure suffering is an essential* associate of true friendship.

42. A *cynic* can chill and dishearten with a single word. — R. W. EMERSON

The kind of person referred to in the foregoing quotation who can chill and discourage with one word is one who

(a) questions the existence of God.

(b) is inclined to sneer at and doubt the good motives of others.

(c) is inclined to tell a joke at the expense of others.

43. O thou, whose days are yet all spring,

Faith, *blighted* once, is past retrieving.

— J. R. LOWELL

According to Lowell, in early life

(a) faith once blasted or ruined can never be repaired.

(b) faith, once born, can never be destroyed.

(c) faith, once strengthened, needs to be nourished or it will die.

44. Open covenants openly arrived at.

— WOODROW WILSON, Fourteen Points.

In this provision Wilson favors

(a) treaties for peace to be negotiated in the open.

(b) secret treaties to be agreed on unanimously.

(c) plans for war openly declared.

III. Synonyms and Antonyms

In each group below select the two words that are either synonyms or antonyms.

45. (a) discursive (b) effete (c) drastic (d) rambling (e) deferential

46. (a) derogatory (b) desultory (c) deleterious (d) salutary (e) dilatory

47. (a) momentous (b) pallid (c) presently (d) paltry (e) cadaverous

48. (a) cadaverous (b) patrioteer (c) jingoist (d) callous (e) complacent

49. (a) excessive (b) curt (c) aggressive (d) notorious (e) flagrant

50. (a) sully (b) deceive (c) beseech (d) sneer (e) besmirch

51. (a) egregious (b) abject (c) clandestine (d) overt (e) excessive

52. (a) introvert (b) ascetic (c) fitful (d) condescending (e) capricious

53. (a) esoteric (b) devoid (c) circumspect (d) exotic (e) bereft

54. (a) raucous (b) dulcet (c) catastrophic (d) obtuse (e) symmetrical

IV. Etymology

55. *Give the meaning and etymology of each of the following words.*

    agnostic diehard capricious connive candidate

56. *Define each of the following prefixes and give two words — with their definitions — which have their origin in these source elements.*

    ab- ex- con- de- di-

V. Related Forms

57. *Give a noun form of each of the following adjectives.*

    apathetic atavistic bigoted clement didactic

58. *Give an adjective form of each of the following nouns.*

    assiduity coercion deference dogmatism calumny

59. *Give a verb form of each of the following nouns or adjectives.*

    aspersion authentic cajolery deviation discomfiture

LESSON FOURTEEN

166. enigma	176. exacerbate
167. epicure	177. execration
168. epithet	178. exigency
169. epitome	179. exonerate
170. equitable	180. exotic
171. erudite	181. expatiate
172. esoteric	182. expatriate
173. ethnic	183. expedient
174. eulogy	184. expiate
175. euphony	185. explicit

166. **e-nig-ma** ĭ-nĭg'-mȧ [*ainigma* (Greek), "a mysterious saying"] — A riddle or puzzle; figuratively, a situation difficult to understand; also, a mysterious, baffling person.

Most modern poetry is characterized by unconventional syntax, occult and obscure allusions. It is a complete *enigma* to the average reader.

Related Forms: enigmatic, enigmatical, enigmatically

Synonyms: conundrum, obscurity, riddle, perplexity

In classical mythology, the sphinx was a monster having the head of a woman, the body of a lion, and the wings of an eagle. She was represented as crouching on a block of stone outside Thebes. This female oddity was said to confront travelers with a riddle intended to stump them. The traveler who could not answer the riddle was killed. When Oedipus solved the riddle, the sphinx killed herself.

Ancient Egyptians constructed a colossal recumbent figure of the sphinx near the pyramids of Gizeh.

Derived from the mythology of this imaginary creature is our current word sphinx, *a person who habitually asks unsolvable riddles, or is engaged in mysterious actions, or has an enigmatic facial expression, or is equivocal (deliberately evasive) in his answers.*

---

167. ep·i·cure ĕp′-ĭ-kūr [from *Epicurus*, a Greek philosopher of the fourth century B. C., who taught that the desire for pleasure should be the chief motive in life. He believed that pleasure is produced by "peace of mind" and the "absence of bodily pain," and he advocated the simple life. But his ideas were misunderstood and distorted, so that now an epicure or epicurean (not capitalized) is understood to mean one who is a refined sensualist, a connoisseur of fine food and drink.] — One who is extremely fastidious in his tastes or pleasures, especially in matters of food and drink.

Is it necessary to enjoy only exotic foods in order to be considered an *epicure* or may one enjoy a hamburger as well?

Related Forms: epicurean, epicureanism, epicurism

Synonyms: gourmet, hedonist

Note 1: A <u>gourmet</u> is a discriminating connoisseur of food and drink.
A <u>gourmand</u> is less fastidious about the quality of food than a gourmet.
A synonym for gourmand is <u>glutton.</u>

Note 2: By extension, an <u>epicure</u> can also mean a person who has developed refined taste in music or the arts as well as in food. A synonym for <u>epicure</u> in this sense is <u>connoisseur.</u>

A gourmet is just a glutton
with brains.

— P. W. HABERMAN

---

168. ep·i·thet ĕp′-ĭ-thĕt [*epitheton* (Latin); from *epithitenai* (Greek), "to add"; from *epi*, "upon" + *tithenai*, "to place"] — An expression (usually an adjective and a a noun) that denotes so characteristic or significant a quality of the person or thing described that one part of the expression always suggests the other; as, "*rosy-fingered* dawn," or "Alexander the *Great*."

Among some well-known Homeric *epithets* are "winged words," "the trackless sea," "the swift Achilles," "the blue-eyed Pallas," and "Zeus, the cloud-gatherer."

Synonyms: characterization, appelation, designation

Note: In current usage, epithet also has the meaning "a brief, explosive, un-complimentary description; a characterization expressing utter detestation."

Synonyms: invective, vituperation

> He referred to his detractors in a string of vile epithets (that is, demeaning characterizations).

169. e-pit-o-me ĕ-pĭt′-ō-mē [*epitome* (Greek), "cut," "abridgment"; from *epi*, "upon" + *tennein*, "to cut"]

1. A summary or a brief condensation of the leading points of a book or an article.

   > Bob stated the *epitome* of Herman Hesse's *Steppenwolf* in his excellent report.

2. A part that is typical of the whole.

   > A man so various that he seemed to be
   > Not one, but all mankind's *epitome*. — DRYDEN

Related Forms: epitomize, epitomist

Synonyms: compendium, syllabus, abridgment, digest, abstract, synopsis (*adj.* synoptic), condensation, microcosm (a little world, one that reflects on a smaller scale the structure of the larger world)

Antonyms: amplification, enlargement, periphrasis, macrocosm

Phrases: in a word, in short, in brief, in substance; *multum in parvo* (Latin), "a great deal in a little space"; to make a long story short; the gist of his address

---

Brevity is the soul of wit — SHAKESPEARE

---

170. eq-ui-ta-ble ĕk′-wĭ-tà-b'l [*aequitas* (Latin), "justice"] — Impartial, just.

> Anthony and the other seniors were satisfied that the distribution of awards at graduation had been as *equitable* as possible.

Related Forms: equitably, equitableness, equity

Synonyms: fair, reasonable, honest, righteous, unbiased

Antonyms: inequitable, biased, unfair, partial

Note: Do not confuse equitable with equable, which means "uniform," "unvarying," "tranquil."

171. **er-u-dite** ĕr'-ŏŏ-dīt ĕr'-yŏŏ-dīt [*erudire* (Latin), "to bring out of the rough; hence, to instruct"; from e, "out of" + *rudis*, "rude"] — Of profound learning.

Lord Chesterfield advised his son never to appear more *erudite* than the company he was in: he might have great learning but he should refrain from displaying it unless those around him were also learned.

Related Forms: eruditely, eruditeness, erudition

Synonyms: scholarly, learned

Antonyms: ignorant, unlettered, superficial (in scholarship)

172. **es-o-ter-ic** ĕs-ō-tĕr'-ĭk [*esoterikos* (Greek), "inner"] — Understood, or intended for understanding, by only a select, initiated few; hence, secret.

Only a few of the members of the executive committee knew all the *esoteric* rites of our fraternity.

Related Forms: esoterical, esoterically

Synonyms: recondite, occult, abstruse, profound

Antonyms: exoteric, manifest, clear

Note: A subject is recondite when it is profound. It is abstruse when it is hard to understand because it is advanced or abstract. It is esoteric when only the initiated have the key to an understanding of it.

173. **eth-nic** ĕth'-nĭk [*ethnos* (Greek), "nation"] — Pertaining to, or belonging to, racially or historically relative groups having culture, speech, customs, and characteristics in common.

America's population is made up of a large number of different ethnic groups from all parts of the world.

Related Form: ethnical

Synonyms: cultural, endemic (peculiar to a particular people or locality)

Note 1: The sociological term ethnic group designates a group of people who, being historically or racially related, have a common distinctive culture.

Note 2: Do not confuse the core meaning of the following words which look alike but have a different denotation: ethical (derived from the Greek ethos, meaning "character" "moral" [upright]) and ethnical (derived from the Greek root ethnos meaning "nation" "race" "culture.")

Note 3: Ethnology is the science that treats of the division of mankind according to race, origin and other characteristics.

174. eu-lo-gy ū'-lŏ-jĭ [*eulogia* (Greek); from *eu*, "well" + *logos, logein*, "speak," "speech"] — A speech or statement, written or oral, in praise of a person or his character, frequently a funeral oration; high commendation or praise.

The minister delivered an eloquent *eulogy* in praise of the great humanitarian who had devoted his life to the service of others.

Related Forms: eulogistic, eulogistically, eulogize, eulogist

Synonyms: praise, encomium, laudation (*verb:* laud; *adj.* laudatory), panegyric (an elaborate public speech of praise)

Antonyms: opprobrium (*adj.* opprobrious), disapproval, depreciation, disparagement (*verb:* disparage; *adj.* disparaging), defamation (*verb:* defame; *adj.* defamatory), calumniation (*verb:* calumniate; *adj.* calumniatory), abuse

Note the difference between eulogy (as explained above) and elegy, "a mournful poem, usually a funeral song or lament for the dead." Here are four well-known lines from Thomas Gray's Elegy Written in a Country Churchyard:

"The boast of heraldry, the pomp of power,
And all that beauty, all that wealth e'er gave
Awaits alike th' inevitable hour: —
The paths of glory lead but to the grave."

An adjectival form of elegy is elegiac; an adjectival form of eulogy is eulogistic, meaning "expressive sorrow or grief."

175. eu-pho-ny ū'-fŏ-nĭ [*euphonie* (French); from *euphonia* (Greek); from *eu*, "well" + *phone*, "sound"] — A pleasing sound; a pleasant effect on the ear produced by words or music.

In an effort to depart from established forms, many modern composers write music which lacks *euphony*, and which may sound discordant.

Related Forms: euphonious, euphoniously, euphonic, euphonize

Synonyms: harmony, concord (*adj.* concordant), melodious, mellifluous

Antonyms: cacophony (*adj.* cacophonous), discordance (*adj.* discordant), dissonance (*adj.* dissonant), discord

176. ex-ac-er-bate ĕg-zăs'-ēr-bāt [*ex* (Latin), "completely" + *acerbare*, "to embitter"] — To increase anger, bitterness, or violence of.

John's already existing feelings of hostility were *exacerbated* by his mother's insistence that he return his new puppy to the pet shop.

Related Form: exacerbation

Synonyms: irritate, aggravate, intensify, embitter, exasperate, inflame, infuriate, acerbate

Antonyms: lessen, moderate, mollify, palliate, allay, pacify

Phrase: add fuel to the flame

177. ex-e-cra-tion ĕk-sĕ-krā'-shŭn [*execratio* (Latin), from *execrare*, *execratus*, "call accursed"; from *ex*, "completely" + *sacer*, "accursed"] — A curse, expressing intense hatred; utter detestation.

When sentence was pronounced, the leader of the crime syndicate lost his control and hurled *execrations* at the judge.

Related Forms: execrate, execrable, execrably, execrative, execratory

Synonyms: curse, oath, malediction, imprecation, anathema, abomination

Antonyms: benediction, benison, blessing

178. ex-i-gen-cy ĕk′-sĭ-jĕn-sĭ [*exigere* (Latin), "to drive out,' "to demand"] — State of urgency or a case demanding immediate attention or action.

The President took drastic steps to meet the *exigencies* imposed on the economy by inflation and rising unemployment.

Related Forms: exigence, exigent

Synonyms: emergency; pressing need

179. ex-on-er-ate ĕg-zŏn′-ēr-āt [*exonerare*, *exoneratus* (Latin), "unload"; from *ex*, "from" + *onus, oneris,* "a load"] — To free from blame.

The officer was *exonerated* by a board of inquiry from any suspicion of having been derelict in his duty.

Related Forms: exoneration, exonerative

Synonyms: absolve, exculpate, acquit (*noun:* acquittal), vindicate (not to be confused with *vindictive*, "revengeful"), excuse

Antonyms: blame, inculpate, accuse, condemn, indict, arraign (*noun:* arraignment), impugn, convict

180. ex-ot-ic ĕks-ŏt′-ĭk [*exotikos* (Greek), "outside"] — Not native; strange because of its distant or foreign association.

"Exotic" does not mean "non-American." A South Sea festival is *exotic* to us, as an Automat would be *exotic* to a South Sea Islander.

Related Forms: exotical, exotically, exoticness, exoticism

254

Synonyms: foreign, alien, bizarre, outlandish, grotesque

Antonyms: native, endemic, indigenous (not to be confused with *indigent,* "needy"), peculiar (to a region)

Phrases: exotic dress, an *exotic* plant

181. **ex-pa-ti-ate** ĕks-pā'-shĭ-āt [*ex,* "out of" + *spatiari* (Latin), "to walk about"; from *spatium,* "space"] — To write or speak at great length.

Goldsmith *expatiated* on the scenes of his childhood in his long poem "The Deserted Village."

Related Form: expatiation

Synonyms: (*verbs*) dilate, enlarge, swell, paraphrase, amplify; (*adjectives*) copious, discursive, circumlocutory

Antonyms: (verbs) compress, condense, abbreviate, abridge; (*adjectives*) succinct, laconic, concise, terse

182. **ex-pa-tri-ate** ĕks-pā'-trĭ-āt (verb) [*expatriare, expatriatus* (Latin); from *ex,* "away from" + *patria,* "native land"; from *pater,* "father"] — To exile, or banish from one's native land; to go into voluntary exile.

Before World War II, many German scholars preferred to be *expatriated* rather than endure the repressive measures of the Nazis.

Related Form: expatriation

Synonym: expel

Note 1: A person who is <u>ostracized</u> is banned socially; a person who is <u>expatriated</u> is either forced out of his country or leaves it of his own accord, renouncing his citizenship to take on that of another country.

Note 2: <u>Expatriate</u> can also be used as a noun or as an adjective.

183. **ex-pe-di-ent** ĕks-pē'-dĭ-ĕnt [*expediens* (Latin), "freeing (one) caught by the foot," "extricating"; from *expedire,* from *ex,* "from" + *pes, pedis,* "foot"] — Advantageous; based on the desire for special advantage or selfish profit rather than on principle or right; proper under the circumstances.

"The difference between a politician and a statesman," said the cynic, "is this: a politician does whatever is *expedient* and defends his action by pleading the pressure of circumstances; a statesman does whatever is *expedient* but convinces us that he was motivated solely by principle."

Related Forms: expediently, expediential, expediency

Synonyms: convenient, suitable, fit, favorable, opportune, seasonable, timely, propitious, meet, befitting, politic, practical, wise

Antonyms: inexpedient, disadvantageous, impolitic, inadvisable, unfit, unseemly, inept, improper

Note: <u>Expedient</u> can also be used as a noun. <u>Expedient</u> may be used to mean a resource adopted in an emergency. The only <u>expedient</u> left in his pressing need was to close his shop altogether or face bankruptcy.

184. ex·pi·ate ĕks'-pĭ-āt [ex*piare* (Latin), from *ex*, "out" + *piare*, "to cleanse with sacred ritual"; from *pius*, "devout"] — To atone for, or pay the penalty of, as a sin; or to make satisfaction for or make amends for, as for an offense or wrong committed.

The culprit attempted to *expiate* his crime by giving all his property to the family of his victim.

Related Forms: expiation, expiator, expiatory

185. ex·plic·it ĕks-plĭs'-ĭt [ex*plicite* (French); from *explicare*, *explicitus* (Latin), "unfold"; from *ex*, "out" + *plicare*, "to fold"] — Distinctly and clearly stated; outspoken, as, he was ex*plicit* in his answer.

The Declaration of Independence includes an *explicit* listing of the colonists' grievances against England.

Related Forms: explicitly, explicitness

Synonyms: frank, open, expressed, unambiguous, unequivocal, plain, positive, definite

Antonyms: implicit, implied, tacit, unexpressed, ambiguous, equivocal

EXERCISES

I. Words in Context

A. One-Word Omissions

In each of the following sentences, substitute for the blank an appropriate word or its related form from Words 166-185 of the Basic Vocabulary List.

1. Many of the customs brought to America by the various _____ groups who came here as immigrants have taken root and have served to enrich our culture.

2. Why Mary insists on taking singing lessons with an atonal voice like hers is a(n) _____ to me.

3. The executor of the estate did his best to make a(n)____ distribution of the property among the heirs.

4. Of all Shakespearean scholars, Professor George L. Kittredge of Harvard was certainly among the most _____.

5. The drivers of the two trucks which had collided leaned from their cabs to hurl insulting _____ at each other.

6. "I can't understand how you came to take that wrong turning," said my friend; "I certainly tried to make my directions very _____."

7. The murderer _____ his crime on the scaffold.

8. In a section of the Botanical Gardens reserved for _____ plants bloom strange and lovely flowers from many foreign climes.

9. Faced with the _____ of the bank's inevitable failure, the Federal Deposit Insurance Corporation took steps to indemnify the depositors.

10. In the 1920's, Paris was swarming with American _____ poets who thought it a more hospitable environment in which to live than their native grounds.

B. Words in a Continuous Passage

In each passage below, certain words are underlined and numbered. Each numbered word is then followed by four words or expressions lettered (a) to (d). Select the letter of the item that is closest in meaning to each underlined word as used in the selection.

The Governor, after being ceremonially sworn in to the thudding cadence of a 19-gun salute, defined his Just Society as one "where government is courageous, power is benign,[1] learning abounds,[2] prosperity is general, law is honored, compassion[3] is practiced and brotherhood is lived."

1. *benign* (a) illusory (b) kindly (c) deceptive (d) treacherous

2. *abounds* (a) increases (b) hems in (c) is limited (d) prevails

3. *compassion* (a) intense emotion (b) profound love (c) pity for the misfortune of others (d) mild affection

If I had influence with the good fairy who is supposed to preside over the christening of all children, I should ask that her gift to each child in the world be a sense of wonder so indestructible that it would last through life, as an unfailing antidote[4] against the boredom[5] and disenchantments[6] of later years, the sterile[7] preoccupation[8] with things that are artificial, the alienation[9] from the sources of our strength.

— RACHEL CARSON

4. *antidote* (a) inducement (b) protection (c) counteractive agent (d) provocation

5. *boredom* (a) ennui (b) nostalgia (c) nonchalance (d) solace

6. *disenchantments* (a) disintegration (b) disengagement (c) disinterestedness (d) disillusionments

7. *sterile* (a) meaningless (b) barren (c) prolific (d) feeble

8. **preoccupation** (*a*) complete absorption (*b*) prejudice
   (*c*) prelude (*d*) apprenticeship

9. **alienation** (*a*) adjustment (*b*) ostracism (*c*) transfer
   (*d*) estrangement

> Lounging, <u>languid</u>¹⁰ Lord Melbourne, the elderly
> mentor of the young Queen Victoria, impaled Macau-
> lay on a sharp-pointed <u>epigram:</u>¹¹ "I wish I were as
> sure of any one thing as Macaulay is of everything."
>
> — W. H. Chamberlin

10. **languid** (*a*) lugubrious (*b*) taciturn (*c*) torpid
    (*d*) indolent

11. **epigram** (*a*) short speech (*b*) pointed saying
    (*c*) tombstone (*d*) boast

II. Words Out of Context

*In each group below, select the word or expression that most
clearly expresses the meaning of the word at the left.*

1. **erudite** (*a*) boorish (*b*) learned
   (*c*) wipe out (*d*) dispatch

2. **epitome** (*a*) origin (*b*) a thick volume
   (*c*) summary (*d*) plateau

3. **expiate** (*a*) be no longer religious (*b*) drug
   (*c*) die (*d*) atone for a wrong

4. **enigma** (*a*) symbol (*b*) riddle (*c*) stipend
   (*d*) inquiry

5. **expedient** (*a*) inconvenient (*b*) advantageous
   (*c*) speedy (*d*) harsh response

6. **eulogy** (*a*) funeral song (*b*) high commendation (*c*) pun (*d*) criticism

7. **equitable** (*a*) just (*b*) biased
   (*c*) even-tempered (*d*) discouraged

WORD BUILDING

I. PREFIXES

A. The Greek prefix **epi-** "upon " "over" is a source element in several English words including *epithet* and *epitome* studied in this lesson.

epidermis — outer layer of the skin

epiglottis — (literally, *epi*, "upon" + *glotta*, "tongue") — a thin plate of cartilege in front of the glottis

Other words containing this prefix are *epigram*, *epilogue*, *episode*, *epistle*

B. The Greek prefix **eu-** meaning "good" occurs chiefly in English words of Greek origin like *eulogy* and *euphony* studied in this lesson.

II. ROOTS

A. The Greek root **equi-** meaning "just" "equal" is the source of many English words, including *equitable* studied in this lesson.

equilateral — equal-sided
equidistant — equally distant

B. The Latin root **pater,** meaning "father" is the source of many English words including *expatriate* studied in this lesson.

patriot — one who loves his fatherland
paternal — pertaining to a father

C. The Latin word **sacer,** meaning "accursed" "sacred" is the source of *execration* studied in this lesson.

sacrament — a holy right
desecrate — to profane
sacrilegious — treating sacred objects irreverently

> sacrifice — literally "to make sacred"; hence, to give up something cherished for something thought more desirable
>
> sacristan — one who is in charge of a church

D. The Latin root **ped-**, meaning "foot," is the source of several English words including *expedient*, studied in this lesson.

EXERCISES

I. Etymology Mastery Test

1. Define *epigram* in the light of its origin. What is the adjectival form of this word? Cite an epigram referred to in a previous lesson.

2. What is an *equivocal* answer? Give two synonyms for this word. The porter in *Macbeth* who imagines he guards the gates of Hell, says: "Faith, here's an equivocator, that could swear in both the scales against either scale; who committed treason enough for God's sake, yet could not equivocate to heaven; Oh, come in, equivocator."
Why is the equivocator being doomed to go to Hell?
Define *equivocator* in the light of its origin.

3. Define *eugenics, euphemism, euthenics, euphoria* in the light of their origin. Give two examples of a euphemism.

4. What is the feminine of *paternal, patriarch,* and *patricide*? Define, in the light of its origin, *patronage*.

5. Many English words are to be found related to the *sacer* family. What is a *sanctuary*? What is *sanctimonious*? Would you feel flattered if you were called *sanctimonious*? Explain your answer.

6. What is meant by the phrase "sanctioned by law"? What are "economic sanctions?"

7. *Define in the light of their origin the following words, some of which are partly derived from the Latin root* **pes- pedis-.**
pew   expedition   podium   impediment   pedigree

II. Word Analysis and Development

1. The Greek word element *ethnos* is somewhat distantly related to the Greek root *ethos*, meaning "character."
   Consult the dictionary for the meaning of the following English words that are derived from one or the other of the above Greek roots.
   ethos   ethics   ethnology

2. *Define the following phrases:*
   ethnic group   an ethical physician   the German ethos
   ethnic taboos

3. What do we mean when we say that someone is "caught on the horns of a dilemma"?

4. Consult the dictionary for the fine distinction in meaning between *puzzle*, *riddle*, and *enigma*.

5. How does the sphinx differ from the Delphic Oracle, the sibyls, Cassandra?

III. Syllabication and Pronunciation

Syllabicate the following words correctly and place the major stress (') after the syllable which is accented when the word is pronounced.

EXAMPLE: en-dure'

epicure	enigma	exacerbate
epithet	esoteric	execration
epitome	ethnic	exigency
equitable	eulogy	exonerate
erudite	euphony	exotic

IV. Analogies

Complete the following analogies:

1. epithet : exacerbate = (a) condolence : condone
   (b) epigram : amuse   (c) epitaph : instruct
   (d) compliment : placate

2. epicure : food = (a) aesthete : beauty (b) philatelist
   : currency (c) philosopher : learning
   (d) lexicographer : law

3. exonerate : responsibilty = (a) extricate : difficulty
   (b) arraign : offense (c) absolve : guilt
   (d) incarcerate : crime

4. opprobrium : vandal = (a) conundrum : sphinx
   (b) eulogy : hero (c) accolade : transgressor
   (d) greeting : traveler

5. duplicity : deceptive = (a) audacious : forthright
   (b) chicanery : dapper (c) complacency : affable
   (d) veracity : true

V. Fun With Words

A. Stories Behind Words

*Each of the following words derives from a story connected
with a well-known person, myth, a literary work, or notable
event. Tell the story of each in a short paragraph. Define each
word.*

1. babbitt	6. maverick
2. herculean	7. utopian
3. mesmerize	8. tantalize
4. malapropism	9. boycott
5. bowdlerize	10. dunce

B. What Square Are You?

"Many years ago," observed Maine's Senator Margaret
Chase Smith, 66, at a dinner in Manhattan, "the word square
was one of the most honored words in our vocabulary. The
square deal was an honest deal. A square meal was a full and
good meal. It was the square shooter rather than the sharp-
shooter who was admired. What is a square today? He's the
fellow who never learned to get away with it, who gets choked

up when the flag unfurls. There has been too much glorification of the angle players, the corner cutters, and the goof-offs. One of America's greatest needs is for more people who are square."

1. What is a *square* deal?

2. What is a *square* meal?

3. What do we mean when we call a person a *square*? An *egg head*?

4. What is a *square* shooter?

C. Vogue Words

Match each vogue word or expression listed in Column A with the phrase in Column B which gives its meaning.

A	B
1. **activist**	(*a*) make a choice
2. **phase out**	(*b*) unyielding element in a group
3. **hard core**	(*c*) those ahead of the majority in artistic tastes, political opinions, etc.
4. **avant-garde**	(*d*) eliminate something by degrees
5. **opt**	(*e*) a vigorous advocate of a cause

VI. Using the Dictionary

Exotica

Where do the words below originate? These words have been absorbed into English from practically every continent, including Africa.

Consulting the dictionary, trace the following items to their country or continent of origin. Describe the exotic item.

1. **sari**	4. **fakir**	7. **thug**	10. **algebra**
2. **boomerang**	5. **pow-wow**	8. **intelligentsia**	
3. **mandarin**	6. **voodoo**	9. **jubilee**	

VII. Using the Library

Which library aid would you consult to answer the following questions? Answer each question briefly.

1. What is the exact meaning of the expression *status symbol?*

2. Who coined the word *debunk?* the word *genocide?*

3. What is the title of a good dictionary of American slang?

4. In a dictionary one finds several definitions of a word arranged according to frequency of usage — most often, occasional, seldom. Where does one learn the order of presentation in a particular dictionary? How is the entry presented in the reference dictionaries below?

   > *The American College Dictionary*
   > *Webster's New Collegiate Dictionary*
   > *The Winston Senior Dictionary*

VIII. Building Your Own Thesaurus

Answer each of the following questions in your notebook.

1. Study the section in *Roget's Thesaurus* under the heading *Success* and *Failure*. Answer the following questions.
   (*a*) What is a trump card?
   (*b*) What does *veni, vidi, vici,* mean?
   (*c*) Define the following expressions:

hors de combat	win one's spurs
to checkmate	a stalemate
a wild goose chase	

   (*d*) Explain the biblical saying: "Thou art weighed in the balance, and art found wanting."

2. Consulting your thesaurus, draw up a comprehensive list of words which denote actions that stem from feelings of anger.
   Examples: *rave fume fulminate*

LESSON FIFTEEN

186. expunge	196. fallacy
187. extemporize	197. fathom
188. extenuate	198. fatuous
189. extirpate	199. feasible
190. extol	200. feign
191. extradite	201. felicitous
192. extraneous	202. fetish
193. extrovert	203. fiasco
194. facetious	204. fickle
195. facsimile	205. filch

186. ex-punge ĕks-pŭnj′ [*expungere* (Latin), "to strike out"; from *ex*, "out" + *pungere*, "to puncture"] — To blot out, to erase.

It is impossible for me to *expunge* from my mind the memory of the mangled bodies of the accident victims.

Synonyms: strike out, delete, cancel, delete (*noun:* deletion), obliterate, efface, censor (*adj.:* censorial, not to be confused with censorious, "severely critical")

187. ex-tem-po-rize ĕks-tĕm′pŏ-rīz [*ex* (Latin), "out" + *tempus, temporis*, "time"] — To utter or to do (something) without preparation or previous study.

Bill is so well-informed that he is able to *extemporize* eloquently on many subjects.

Related Forms: extempore, extemporary, extemporal, extemporization, extemporizer, extemporaneous

Synonym: improvise (*noun:* improvisation), impromptu (*noun and adjective*)

Phrases: speak off the cuff
an *impromptu* speech

188. ex·ten·u·ate ĕks-tĕn'-û-āt [*extenuare*, *extenuatus* (Latin), "make thin or small," "reduce"; from *ex*, "out" + *tenuare*, "to make thin"] — To make smaller or weaker in degree; to lessen, or treat as less severe than it is (said of a crime, an illness, and the like).

If one understands the circumstances surrounding a particular situation, one may be able to *extenuate* a seemingly unpleasant act.

Related Forms: extenuating, extenuation, extenuatory

Synonyms: mitigate (*adj.*: mitigatory, mitigative), lessen, diminish, excuse, palliate (*adj.*: palliative), underestimate

Antonyms: aggravate (see p. 22) intensify, increase, heighten

---

> Speak of me as I am; nothing *extenuate*,
> Nor set down aught in malice.
>
> — SHAKESPEARE, *Othello*

---

189. ex·tir·pate ĕks-tĕr'-pāt [*extirpare*, *extirpatus* (Latin), "tear up by the root"; from *ex*, "out" + *stirps*, "stem," "root"] — To pluck out by the root; to eradicate.

It is important to make every effort to *extirpate* the evils of poverty and intolerance from our society.

Related Form: extirpation

Synonyms: root out, uproot, exterminate, destroy

Antonyms: plant, root, establish; nourish, foster

190. ex·tol ĕks-tōl' [*ex*, (Latin), "from" + *tollere*, "to raise"] — To praise highly.

Such is the fickleness of fame: in one year the Russian general was *extolled* as a superpatriot, even given the Star of Stalin; in the next, the climate of opinion having changed, he was condemned as a traitor and executed.

Synonyms: commend, eulogize, glorify, laud, idolize, acclaim; homage (*noun*)

Antonyms: vilify, berate, condemn, censure, castigate, upbraid

Phrases: win golden opinions
find favor with

---

*You can tell the character of every
man when you see how he receives praise.*

— SENECA

---

191. **ex-tra-dite** ĕks-trȧ-dīt′ [*ex,* (Latin), "out" + *traditio,*
"giving over"] — The surrender by a state or national
government of a fugitive from justice or one person accused of a crime in another state to the province where
the crime is alleged to have been committed.

The American Government formally requested that the alleged
culprit who had fled our shores be *extradited* and tried here
where the crime was committed.

Related Forms: extradition, extraditable

Phrase: an *extraditable* offense

192. **ex-tra-ne-ous** ĕk-strā′-nĭ-ŭs [*extraneus* (Latin), "foreign"] — Nonessential.

Develop the ability to separate the main facts of an issue from
its *extraneous* details, and you will find it easier to study.

Synonyms: external (not basic), extrinsic (not proper or belonging to a thing), alien, adventitious, irrelevant, foreign

Antonyms: basic, intrinsic, inherent, innate, pertinent, germane,
relevant (*noun:* relevance), relative

193. **ex-tro-vert** (variant spelling: extravert) ĕks′-trō-vûrt
[*extro* (Latin), "outside" + *vertere* "to turn"] — One
who is concerned chiefly with the outside world or objects
outside his inner self.

One tends to find the outgoing *extrovert* personality attractive; however, the quiet, shy introvert, upon closer acquaintance, will often reveal great charm and depth.

Related Form: extroversion

Antonyms: introvert, introspective, introverted (turned inward)

194. fa-ce-tious fă-sē'-shŭs [*facetiae* (Latin), "jests"] — Humorous; in a manner or spirit of levity.

Christopher Morley's method in the essay is to surprise and delight the reader by an abrupt change in tone; for example, he will end a solemn discussion by a series of *facetious* remarks.

Related Forms: facetiously, facetiousness

Synonyms: witty, waggish, jocular, jocose, pleasant, droll, comic, funny

Antonyms: serious, grave, solemn, earnest, humorless, saturnine, sermonizing

195. fac-sim-i-le făk-sĭm'ĭ-lē [*fac* (Latin), "make" + *simile* "like"] — An exact copy.

The painting, supposedly a long-lost Rembrandt, was so good a *facsimile* that only an x-ray study proved it to be a forgery.

Synonyms: stereotype, counterpart, replica, transcript

Phrase: a carbon copy

196. fal-la-cy făl'-ă-sĭ [*fallax* (Latin), "deceitful"]

1. Faulty reasoning, not based on logic; an invalid argument.

   Explain the *fallacy* in the following argument: "All cows are quadrupeds; all mules are quadrupeds; therefore, all cows are mules."

2. A false or erroneous idea.

   The effort to relate physical characteristics to personality usually results in an absurd *fallacy;* for example, "red hair indicates a quick temper," "close-set eyes indicate dishonesty," and "a receding chin indicates weakness."

Related Forms: fallacious, fallaciously, fallaciousness

Synonyms: error, sophism, deception, misconception, falsification; specious

Phrases: a non sequitur, "an illogical conclusion"
  quibble — "deliberately shifting the point or issue in order to evade it"

  specious reasoning — "seemingly sound but on closer investigation without merit"

Note the meaning and use of fallible, which is related to fallacious in origin and denotation.

fal-li-ble făl'-ĭ-b'l [fallere (Latin), "to deceive"] — Liable to make mistakes or to be deceived; liable to be inaccurate.

"I agree," said the teacher to the boy, "that all human beings are fallible, but it seems to me that when you write 'Too err is humane,' you are taking unfair advantage of the privilege."

Related Forms: fallibility, fallibly

Synonyms: errable, erring, questionable, unreliable, debatable, untrustworthy

Antonyms: infallible, unerrable, unerring, reliable, trustworthy, unfailing

197. **fath-om** făth'-ŭm [*faethm* (Anglo-Saxon), "the outstretched arms"] — To get to the bottom of.

So abstruse was his reasoning that I found it impossible to *fathom* his meaning.

Related Forms: fathomless (*synonym:* inexplicable), unfathomable

Synonyms: gauge, comprehend, sound (to measure the depth of), grasp (get the meaning of)

Phrases: get the drift, beyond comprehension

Note: In nautical measurement, a fathom is a measure of length, approximately six feet or the spread of a man's outstretched arms.

198. **fat-u-ous** făt'-ū-ŭs [*fatuus* (Latin), "foolish"] — Unconsciously foolish; vain or stupid in a silly way.

Richard's effort to present a façade of charm and urbanity resulted only in making him appear to be a *fatuous* fool.

Related Forms: fatuity, fatuously, fatuousness

Synonyms: inane, dull, silly, senseless, witless, puerile, vapid (without flavor or sharpness, insipid, vacuous)

Antonyms: sensible, sagacious (*noun:* sagacity), acute

199. fea-si-ble fē′-zĭ-b′l [*faisible* (Old French), "capable of being done"; from *facere* (Latin), "to do"]

    1. Capable of being carried out.

        Although his plan sounded *feasible*, it proved impossible of execution when put to the test.

    2. Capable of being controlled or dealt with.

        Much as I would like to invite everyone I know to my party, this is not *feasible* because my house is too small.

Related Forms: feasibly, feasibility, feasibleness

Synonyms: possible, practicable, accomplishable, manageable, suitable

Antonyms: unfeasible, impracticable, unworkable

Note: <u>feasible</u> — capable of being carried out — a feasible plan

    <u>possible</u> — not contrary to the nature of things

    <u>practicable</u> — capable of being used (as a tool, or a method)

    <u>practical</u> — pertaining to that which exists in practice and action (as practical politics, opposed to political theory), or capable of being put to good use (as a suggestion)

    <u>nonfeasance</u> — omission of an act that should have been performed

    <u>malfeasance</u> — wrongful commission of an act which one has no legal right to perform

    <u>misfeasance</u> — wrongful performance of lawful authority

200. feign fān [*fingere* (Latin), "to shape" "pretend"] — To make up deceptively or fictitiously, as an excuse or story; to imitate or disguise in order to deceive; to assume (as a name).

    Tommy *feigned* illness so that he could stay home from school.

Related Forms: (*adj.*) feigned, (*noun*) feint

The boxer made a *feint* with his left hand but threw a blow with his right.

Synonyms: simulate, pretend, sham, affect, assume, counterfeit

---

*Methinks the lady doth protest
too much.* — SHAKESPEARE

---

201. fe-lic-i-tous fĕ-lĭs′-ĭ-tŭs [*felicitas* (Latin), "happiness"; from *felix*, "happy"] — Happy in expression; appropriately or gracefully expressed.

The letter of regret for our misconduct which the class wrote to Miss Martin was not especially *felicitous*, but in spite of its awkwardness it was sincere.

Related Forms: felicitously, felicitousness, felicity, felicitate (congratulate)

Synonyms: apt, well-chosen, appropriate, pertinent

Antonyms: inept, awkward, inappropriate

202. fe-tish (or **fe-tich**) fĕ′-tĭsh, fē′-tĭsh [*fetiche* (French); from *feitico* (Portuguese), "a charm"; from *facticius* (Latin), "artificial"]

1. A material object, either natural (as a root) or carved (as an idol), thought to have magical powers and therefore worshipped. The name was first used for idols and talismans, or charms, of the West Africans.

   Today many shops display small human images carved from ebony typical of the *fetishes* found in Africa.

2. An object of unreasoning devotion or worship.

   Photography, which had started as a hobby, became for Fred a *fetish*: it was his one means of recreation and his one topic of conversation.

Related Forms: fetishism (also spelled *fetichism*), fetishist (also spelled *fetichist*)

Synonyms: idol, talisman, charm, amulet

Phrase: blind reverence

203. fi·as·co fē-ăs′-kō [*fiasco* (Italian), "a flask"; relation to English word doubtful] — A ludicrous and complete failure.

Poor planning and inadequate equipment caused the venture to end in an utter *fiasco*.

Synonyms: crash, disaster, debacle

Phrase: an ignominious (disgraceful) failure

204. fick·le fĭk′-′l [*ficol* (Anglo-Saxon), "deceitful"] — Changeable; without apparent reason; inconstant; irresolute.

So *fickle* is the public that today's fashion will be markedly out-of-date tomorrow.

Related Form: fickleness

Synonyms: variable, unsteady, vacillating (*noun:* vacillation), capricious, whimsical (moved by sudden whim or fancy), moody, unstable (lacking in emotional balance), mercurial (changeable in mood, ranging from exaltation to depression), volatile

Antonyms: steadfast, constant, unwavering, obstinate

Phrase: La donna è mobile (Italian for "Woman is fickle.")

205. filch fĭlch [Source uncertain] — To steal slyly, especially petty things.

The grocer complained that the butcher's boy had *filched* an apple from the basket on the counter.

Synonyms: purloin, pilfer, thieve, crib, peculate (steal public funds), embezzle (*noun:* embezzlement — appropriate trust funds), larceny (*adj.:* larcenous)

EXERCISES

I. Words Out of Context

In each group below, select the word or expression that most clearly expresses the meaning of the word at the left.

1. **fickle**
   (*a*) impressionable (*b*) silly
   (*c*) imaginative (*d*) capricious

2. **felicitous**
   (*a*) appropriately expressed (*b*) congratulatory (*c*) awkward (*d*) envious

3. **fiasco**
   (*a*) wisecrack (*b*) celebration
   (*c*) ludicrous failure (*d*) decree

4. **feasible**
   (*a*) impracticable (*b*) capable of achievement (*c*) fearful (*d*) probable

5. **extirpate**
   (*a*) root out (*b*) call out
   (*c*) exacerbate (*d*) denounce

II. Words in Context

A. One-Word Omissions

In each of the following sentences, substitute for the blank an appropriate word selected from Words 186-205 including derivatives, on the Basic Vocabulary List.

1. The insulting remarks of the speaker were _____ from the Congressional Record.

2. Charles Lamb says that the idea that a bully is always a coward is a popular _____.

3. Every person likes to hear himself _____ though few would be willing to admit his eagerness for praise.

4. Of course you are being _____ when you say that schools should give instruction in the fine art of prevarication.

5. I can't for the life of me _____ what most of our modern poets are trying to say; to my conservative mind it is all a gigantic hoax.

B. Words in Phrases

Select the one of the four suggested words or phrases which most clearly expresses the meaning of the italicized word in each of the following expressions.

1. A *fatuous* smile is (a) fateful (b) silly (c) queer (d) meaningful

2. To speak *extemporaneously* is to speak (a) off the cuff (b) deliberately (c) at great length (d) haltingly

3. *Extenuating* circumstances are those which (a) cause severe hardship (b) are effective only externally (c) serve to make an offense less serious (d) injure a person's character

4. A *facetious* remark is (a) acute (b) humorless (c) sarcastic (d) jocular

5. An *infallible* judgment is (a) invaluable (b) unerring (c) unprejudicial (d) specious

III. Synonyms and Antonyms

In each group below select either two words that are synonyms or two words that are antonyms.

1. (a) improvise (b) change (c) delete (d) expunge (e) altercate

2. (a) perceive (b) mitigate (c) extend (d) falsify (e) aggravate

3. (a) idolize (b) nullify (c) revive (d) vilify (e) gratify

4. (a) deleterious (b) rude (c) pertinent (d) fortuitous (e) germane

5. (a) evasiveness (b) scrutiny (c) introspection (d) perversion (e) introversion

WORD BUILDING

I. PREFIX

The Latin prefix **extra, extro,** meaning "outside," is the source of *extrovert* studied in this lesson.

II. ROOTS

The Latin root **tempus, temporis,** meaning "time," is the basis of a number of English words, including *extemporize*, studied in this lesson.

contemporary — existing at the same time

temporary — for a limited time

EXERCISES

I. Etymology Mastery Test

1. Give the meaning of the following phrases that have been adapted *in toto* from the Latin into English. Use each expression in a brief illustrative sentence.

ex post facto	*ex libris*
ex cathedra	*ex officio*
extempore	

2. What is a "chairman pro tem"?
    What do we mean when we say "John is *temporizing*"?

3. In a recent lesson you studied words that are derived from *chronus*, the Greek equivalent of *tempus*. Who was Chronus in Greek mythology? What is meant by "synchronizing" watches? What is an *anachronism*?

II. Word Analysis and Development

1. When the dying Hamlet says to his dearest friend, Horatio, who wishes, by committing suicide, to join Hamlet in death: "Absent thee from *felicity* a while," is Hamlet encouraging Horatio to commit suicide or seeking to dissuade him from doing so? What does he ask him to do?

2. (a) Select the appropriate word from those in the parentheses.

An (extrovert, introvert) is gregarious; an (extrovert, introvert) likes to be by himself.

(b) Why is an introvert likely to be given to introspection? Explain.

3. Select the correct word from those in parentheses.
The speaker suggested some (practical, practicable) steps to help remedy the situation. Frederick is not a (practical, practicable) person, being inclined to be visionary.

III. Using the Dictionary

1. With the help of a dictionary define and give an example of each of the following words:
archaic   slang   obsolete   colloquial   dialectal

2. What do the following abbreviations, usually found in dictionary entries mean?

Var. O.E. Gk. Obs. Ant. n.

3. Psychological terms have become popular in recent days and are referred to frequently in every medium of communication. Explain the meaning of the following psychological terms.

neurosis paranoid inhibition psychosomatic
schizophrenia

IV. Fun With Words

Vogue Words

Use each of the following words or phrases in a sentence that clearly shows its meaning.

the Establishment	confrontation	dialogue
escalate	to opt for	instant history
a put-down	charisma	hangup

V. Review

In the following paragraph substitute for each blank an appropriate word selected from Words 1-205 (including derivatives) on the Basic Vocabulary List. Synonyms are provided at the end of the paragraph to guide you in your choice.

THE CHARACTER OF FRANKLIN

Benjamin Franklin was active in many fields. Although without formal scientific training, he became a really e..(1).. scientist, competent to deal with the most a..(2).. scientific problems of his day. Trained only in the school of practical political experience, he proved himself to be not a mere politician, activated only by what was e..(3).., but a true statesman, a..(4).. in his efforts toward the welfare not only of America but of mankind as well. Although not a profound philosopher, he produced in his *Poor Richard's Almanac* c..(5).. common sense maxims, d..(6).. in content, but so f..(7).. in wording that even today few of them sound t..(8)... Moreover, in his more popular effort as a writer, his *Autobiography*, he proved himself to be so c..(9).. an artist that it is no mere hyperbole to characterize him as one of the great masters of this type of writing.

But Franklin's c..(10).. quality was a quality of the soul: he was a humanitarian and an a..(11).. From one invention alone, that of the Franklin stove, for example, he might with his native business a..(12).. have realized a fortune had he been moved by a..(13).., but although well-meaning friends urged him to patent this device, he d..(14).., declaring that the only e..(15).. he desired for conferring a benefit upon mankind was the joy of adding to human comfort and happiness.

Synonyms or Definitions of Difficult Words Above

1. learned
2. difficult to comprehend
4. diligent
6. instructive

9. finished, perfect
10. outstanding
13. cupidity

LESSON SIXTEEN

206.	filial	216.	fulsome
207.	fiscal	217.	furtive
208.	flagrant	218.	futile
209.	fluctuate	219.	garish
210.	foible	220.	garnish
211.	forensic	221.	garrulous
212.	formidable	222.	gregarious
213.	fortuitous	223.	grimace
214.	frugal	224.	hackneyed
215.	frustrate	225.	haggard

206. fil-i-al fĭl'-ĭ-'l [*filius* (Latin), "son"; *filia*, "daughter"] — In the nature of, befitting, or pertaining to, a son or daughter.

A lively and lasting sense of *filial* duty is more effectually impressed on the mind of a son or daughter by reading King Lear, than by all the dry volumes of ethics, and divinity, that ever were written.

— THOMAS JEFFERSON

Like father, like son. — THE BIBLE

---

207. fis-cal fĭs'-kăl [*fiscalis* (Latin), "belonging to the state treasury"] — Pertaining to the revenue, expenditures or financial affairs, public or general.

The Secretary of the Treasury recommended a new *fiscal* policy to the Congress in order to meet the threat of inflation.

Synonyms: monetary, financial, pecuniary

Phrases: the *fiscal* year, a *monetary* reward, *pecuniary* obligations

208. fla-grant flā′-grănt [*flagrans -antis* (Latin), "burning"] — Conspicuously wicked, outrageous, scandalous (as a crime).

A drug addict is guilty not only of a *flagrant* offense against society, but also of an offense against himself as well.

Related Form: flagrancy

Synonyms: rank (extremely objectionable), notorious, monstrous, atrocious, glaring, flagitious, heinous (extremely wicked)

Antonym: inoffensive

Phrases: a *flagrant* breach, a *heinous* crime, a *glaring* fault, a *rank* offense

209. fluc-tu-ate flŭc′-tŭ-āt [*fluctuare, fluctuatus* (Latin), "move up and down," "wave"; from *fluere*, "to flow"] — To move alternately up and down; hence, to vary irregularly in degree or quantity; to be unstable.

Because of the lack of an atmospheric envelope, temperatures on the moon *fluctuate* widely — from 215° F. during the day to —250° F. at night.

Related Form: fluctuation

Synonyms: waver, vacillate, undulate, oscillate, vibrate, sway, teeter, see-saw

Phrases: in a state of flux (continuous change), ups and downs, ebb and flow

210. foi-ble foi′-b'l [*faible* (Old French), "weakness"] — A slight frailty or defect in a person's character or personality; hence, a peculiarity.

Superstition was one of Samuel Johnson's *foibles;* he would pause to touch with his cane every lamp post he passed.

Synonyms: failing, weakness, whim, idiosyncrasy, quirk, crotchet, oddity, eccentricity

Note: When a **foible** takes an extreme nature, it is termed an **obsession** or a **phobia**. A noun form indicating the possessor of such a **phobia** ends in **phobe**. A person who has **claustrophobia** is a **claustrophobe**.

211. fo-ren-sic   fô-rĕn'-sĭk   [*forensis* (Latin), "pertaining to the forum or public place"] — Pertaining to public speaking or courts of law; argumentative; rhetorical.

The headmaster urged his students who wish to study law to prepare themselves in the art of *forensic* debate.

Note: In ancient Rome, the public square, flanked by shops, public buildings, and especially the law courts, was the center of public discussion and judicial business. Here could be found the more important temples, imposing imperial buildings, and markets. The square was called Forum Romanarum, or Forum (literally the marketplace). Hence, in modern times, a public meeting place or an auditorium for discussion of burning issues of the day, or the organization that provides the medium for public discussion, is called a forum. Today a forum is not necessarily an open square; it may be a pulpit, a platform, a meeting, or a discussion group. Forensic medicine deals with medical law.

Forensic chemistry deals with the legal aspects of chemistry.

Phrase: to engage in a public *dialogue*

212. for-mi-da-ble   fôr'-mĭ-dȧ-b'l   [*formidare* (Latin), "to fear"]

1. Difficult to accomplish because of obstacles, difficulties, size, etc.

   The seemingly *formidable* task of clearing away the debris after the storm was accomplished with the co-operation of everyone in the community.

2. Inspiring fear or awe; hence, capable of preventing another from undertaking opposing steps.

   The President declared that a *formidable* sentinel system was a sure means of saving the nation from attack by other countries.

Related Forms: formidably, formidableness

Synonyms: menacing, redoubtable, dangerous, terrible, fearful, dreadful, tremendous, awful, appalling

Antonyms: powerless, weak, helpless

213. for-tu-i-tous fôr-tū'-ĭ-tŭs [*fortuitus* (Latin), from *forte*, "by chance"; from *fors*, "chance"] — Occurring by chance.

A *fortuitous* meeting in the park changed his whole life: the stranger he happened to speak to was later instrumental in getting him his first commissions to paint portraits.

Related Forms: fortuitously, fortuitousness, fortuity

Synonyms: accidental, chance, adventitious, random, casual

Antonyms: deliberate, considered

214. fru-gal frōō'-găl [*frugalis* (Latin), "thrifty"] — Using rigid economy.

Having married a man of moderate means, my sister, who had always been a spendthrift, became a *frugal* housekeeper.

Related Forms: frugally, frugality, frugalness

Synonyms: sparing, economical (using resources carefully), parsimonious (stingy, miserly, penurious), provident, inexpensive, stinting, scrimping

Antonyms: prodigal, extravagant, lavish, squander, improvident

Phrases: penny-wise, fritter money away, tight-fisted, penny-pinching, dissipate funds

---

As ye sow, so shall ye reap — THE BIBLE

---

215. frus-trate frŭs'-trāt [*frustrare, frustratus* (Latin), from *frustra*, "in vain"]

1. To bring to naught or make ineffectual, as efforts.

My plans for the trip were *frustrated* by an unforeseen attack of the flu.

282

2. To prevent from reaching a goal, as a person.

> He had been so *frustrated* in his efforts to improve his position in the firm that he had little ambition left to seek any advancement.

Related Form: frustration

Synonyms: balk, defeat, thwart, circumvent (see page 145), foil, nullify, check, obstruct, discomfit, impede (see page 312)

Antonyms: aid, encourage, abet, promote, effect, accomplish, achieve, perform

Note: To <u>baffle</u> means to confuse in order to prevent action.

> To <u>thwart</u> is to prevent action by placing obstacles in the way of an opponent.

> To <u>frustrate</u> means to nullify the effects of an action, or prevent (a person) from attaining a goal.

216. ful-some fo͞ol'-sŭm fŭl'-sŭm [full (in the sense of "foul") + some] — Offensive (from excess) to good taste or sensibility; hence, grossly insincere. (Usually used in connection with flattery)

> We were revolted when the speakers lauded the dictator with such *fulsome* phrases as "immortal genius" and "benefactor of the people."

Related Forms: fulsomely, fulsomeness

Synonyms: gross, repulsive, disgusting, nauseating, offensive

Antonyms: scant, moderate, modest

Phrase: ad nauseam (Latin) "to a sickening or disgusting extent"

Damn with faint praise. — ALEXANDER POPE

---

217. fur-tive fûr'-tĭv [*furtivus* (Latin), "stolen"] — Done in a secret or underhand manner.

The plotters, who were engaged in a nefarious scheme to steal the jeweled idol, behaved in a *furtive* manner as they left their clandestine meeting.

Related Forms: furtively, furtiveness

Synonyms: stealthy, surreptitious, clandestine (see page 146), sly, secretive, covert, masked; cloak, veil muffle; subterfuge (an artifice employed to escape detection)

Antonyms: unconcealed, aboveboard, overt, open, frank, straightforward, revealed, divulged, exposed

Phrases: underhanded, a cover up, keep one's own counsel, keep under wraps, close-mouthed,
in camera (in private)
sotto voce (an aside)
sub-rosa (in secret)
behind the veil of secrecy
off the record
entre nous (literally, "between ourselves")

218. fu-tile fū'-tĭl [*futilis* (Latin), "leaky"; hence, "worthless] — Not accomplishing the intended end; ineffectual.

The lifeguard made a heroic though *futile* attempt to save the woman from drowning.

Related Forms: futilely, futility, futileness

Synonyms: vain, fruitless, bootless, profitless, nugatory, idle

Antonyms: effective, effectual, efficacious, advantageous

219. gar-ish gâr'-ish [source uncertain] — Excessively or crudely or obstrusively showy.

The overblown plot, the gawdy costumes, the glaring lights, the *garish* makeup of the actors made the entire performance a show well worth missing.

Related Form: garishness

Synonyms: gaudy, ornate, flashy, dazzling, glaring, striking, tawdry, pretentious, meretricious

Antonyms: chaste, unadorned, stark, somber

Phrases: tawdry furnishings, *gaudy* colors, a *pretentious* style of writing

220. gar-nish gär′-nĭsh [*garnishen* (Middle English), "to equip"] — To add savory or decorative touches to a table or a dish; to equip with decorative accessories.

> The roast pig, *garnished* with a necklace of holly, lay proudly on his bed of parsley.

Related Forms: garnish (noun), "a relish" or "decoration"; garnisher, garnishment

Synonyms: adorn, embellish (n. embellishment), deck (also bedeck), bedizen (to adorn gaudily), beautify

Note: In law, to **garnish** (var. **garnishee**) means "to attach money belonging to a debtor."

221. gar-ru-lous gär′-ŏŏ-lŭs [*garrulus* (Latin), "chatter"] — Talking much, especially on trivial matters.

> My *garrulous* traveling companion insisted on telling me her entire life history from babyhood on.

Related Forms: garrulity, garrulousness

Synonyms: talkative, chatty, loquacious, diffuse (use of words to excess), verbose, voluble, glib, prolix (in speech as well as in writing)

Antonyms: taciturn, reticent, laconic

Phrases: the gift of gab (glib speech), long-winded

Much talk, much foolishness. — THE TALMUD

---

222. gre-ga-ri-ous grē-gâ′-rĭ-ŭs [*grex, gregis* (Latin), "a flock" (See page 238 for a discussion of this root)]

1. Habitually associating in a company or herd.

> Extroverts are by nature *gregarious;* they are unhappy without company.

2. Pertaining to a company, herd or group, as *gregarious* instinct.

> Prehistoric man banded into tribes, not only for mutual protection, but also to satisfy his *gregarious* instinct for sociability.

Related Forms: gregariously, gregariousness

Synonyms: social, social-minded, extrovert, fraternizing, outgoing, companionable

Antonyms: hermitic, antisocial, unsocial

Phrase: esprit de corps (persons associating with a sense of common purpose)

living in *an ivory tower* (withdrawn from the world)

223. gri-mace (noun and verb) grĭ-mās′ grĭ′mǎs [*grima* (Old English), "fright"] — A facial expression which twists the features to indicate disapproval, disgust, or pain.

> Mother's *grimace* told me more clearly than words that she did not approve my decision.

Synonyms: smirk (a sardonic grin in a self-satisfied way) snicker (laugh with a suggestion of disrespect)

Phrases: to make a *wry* (distorted) face; make faces

224. hack-neyed hăk′-nēd [Source uncertain] — Worn out through frequent use; hence, commonplace or meaningless.

> The critics charged the writer with using *hackneyed* expressions, such as "red as a rose" and "white as snow".

Related Form: hackney (a coach for hire; let out for common use)

Synonyms: banal (see page 94), trite, bromidic, jejune, over-worked, platitudinous

Phrases: a shop-worn expression
a stock phrase (a cliché)
corny (slang)

225. hag-gard hăg′-ērd [Source uncertain] — Having a worn expression or appearance, as though harried by hunger or anxiety.

A prolonged heat spell and lack of sleep caused most of the employees to become worn and *haggard* and unable to work.

Related Forms: haggardness, haggardly

Synonyms: wan, gaunt, pale, wasted, drawn, pinched, cadaverous

Antonyms: healthy, florid, well-fed

EXERCISES

I. Words Out of Context

In each group below, select the word or expression that most clearly expresses the meaning of the word at the left.

1. **fiscal**
   (*a*) calculating (*b*) strenuous
   (*c*) monetary (*d*) fishy

2. **grimace**
   (*a*) queer smile (*b*) severity
   (*c*) filth (*d*) facial contortion

3. **garrulous**
   (*a*) talkative (*b*) ornate
   (*c*) ludicrous (*d*) fortified

4. **flagrant**
   (*a*) criminal (*b*) glaring
   (*c*) callous (*d*) declamatory

5. **garnish**
   (*a*) corrupt (*b*) cultivate
   (*c*) wreathe (*d*) adorn

II. Words in Context

A. One-Word Omissions

In each of the following sentences substitute for the blank an appropriate word selected from Words 206-225 or their derivatives on the Basic Vocabulary List.

1. In a period of industrial unrest, prices have a tendency to _____; today they rise, tomorrow they fall.

2. The champion soon found that he had in the young, energetic and skillful challenger a most _____ adversary.

3. An essay filled with such _____ expressions as "to cap the climax" will not impress the reader as highly original.

4. After their long forced march the troops looked tired and _____.

5. The British National Anthem, referring to the Sovereign's political opponents, says:

   "Confound their politics!
   _____ their knavish tricks!"

B. Words in Continuous Passages

Below, you will find several passages in which certain words are numbered and underlined. Select the letter preceding the item which is closest in meaning to the underlined word.

The news writer is a consummate[1] artist. In its simplest terms, art is the business of selecting for effect — plus deftness.[2] The writer is the creative manipulator of the most plastic, the most resistant, the most mercurial,[3] and yet the stickiest substance known to man — the written word.

— CARL LINDSTROM (adapted)

1. *consummate* (*a*) circumspect (*b*) clever
   (*c*) accomplished (*d*) destructive

288

2. *deftness*   (*a*) carefulness (*b*) dexterity
                     (*c*) sincerity (*d*) design

3. *mercurial*   (*a*) excitable (*b*) morbid
                     (*c*) voluble (*d*) flighty

It was <u>ingeniously</u>[4] secured at vacant hours by a withe
twisted in the handle of the door and stakes set against
the window shutters, so that, though a thief might get in
with perfect ease, he would find some embarrassment in
getting out — an idea most probably borrowed by the
architect, Vost Van Houten, from the mystery of an eel-
pot. The school-house stood in a rather lonely but
pleasant situation, just at the foot of a woody hill, with
a brook running close by and a <u>formidable</u>[5] birch tree
growing at one end of it. From hence the low murmur of
pupils' voices, <u>conning</u>[6] over their lessons, might be
heard in a drowsy summer's day like the hum of a bee-
hive, interrupted now and then by the <u>authoritative</u>[7] voice
of the master in the tone of <u>menace</u>[8] or command, or,
peradventure, by the <u>appalling</u>[9] sound of the birch as he
urged some tardy loiterer along the flowery path of
knowledge. Truth to say, he was a conscientious man,
and ever bore in mind the golden <u>saw</u>.[10] "Spare the rod
and spoil the child." Ichabod Crane's scholars were not
spoiled.

— Washington Irving, "The Legend of Sleepy Hollow"

4. *ingeniously*   (*a*) artlessly (*b*) deceptively
                    (*c*) cleverly (*d*) insipidly

5. *formidable*   (*a*) awesome   (*b*) well-shaped
                    (*c*) gigantic (*d*) antediluvian

6. *conning*   (*a*) hurrying over (*b*) eluding
                    (*c*) committing to memory
                    (*d*) reverberating

7. *authoritative* (*a*) pedagogical (*b*) forceful
                    (*c*) creative (*d*) domineering

8. menace   (*a*) insolence   (*b*) malice
                (*c*) threat   (*d*) evil

9. appalling   (*a*) low-pitched   (*b*) frightful
                (*c*) reassuring   (*d*) raucous

10. saw   (*a*) maxim   (*b*) creed
                (*c*) cliché   (*d*) platitude

C. Words in Maxims

In each passage below, certain words are underlined and numbered. Each numbered word is then followed by four words or expressions lettered (a) to (d). Select the letter of the item that is closest in meaning to each underlined word as used in the selection.

> There is no possible success without some opposition as a fulcrum: force is always aggressive[1] and crowds something.
>
> — O. W. HOLMES

1. aggressive   (*a*) advanced   (*b*) obnoxious
                (*c*) making the first attack   (*d*) illegal

> Adversity[2] has the effect of eliciting[3] talents which in prosperous circumstance would have lain dormant.[4]
>
> —HORACE

2. Adversity   (*a*) hostility   (*b*) opposition   (*c*) competition   (*d*) unfavorable fortune

3. eliciting   (*a*) breeding   (*b*) drawing forth
                (*c*) reducing   (*d*) discouraging

4. dormant   (*a*) quiescent   (*b*) dreaming
                (*c*) futile   (*d*) unused

> All good abides[5] with him who waiteth wisely.
>
> — THOREAU

5. abides   (*a*) cooperates   (*b*) waits for
                (*c*) stays   (*d*) puts up with

WORD BUILDING

The Latin root **fluere, fluctus,** "to flow" is the source of many English words, including *fluctuate* studied in this lesson.

fluent — flowing (i.e. speaking) smoothly and readily
mellifluous — flowing sweetly (as *mellifluous* language)

EXERCISES

I. Etymology Mastery Test

1. *Define and trace the origin of the following words.*
   influx   confluence   affluent   superfluous

2. Give two antonyms of *mellifluous*.

3. What is meant by the following expressions?
   a state of *flux*   a *fluctuating* market   an *influx* of visitors

II. Word Analysis and Development

1. What are *fluid* assets? A *flume* is a ravine or gorge with water streaming through it. What common Latin root in the two italicized words betrays their meaning in English.

2. What does *forensic* medicine mean? Would *forensic psychiatry* most probably refer to (*a*) the law about insanity (*b*) capital crimes (*c*) insane asylums (*d*) canon law?

3. *Explain the following expressions.*

sotto voce	in camera
ad nauseam	entre nous
sub rosa	esprit de corps

4. What is the difference between *baffle*, *thwart* and *frustrate*? Use each in a short sentence that clearly illustrates its special usage.

5. Explain what is meant by the term "garnishing a person's salary"?

III. Fun with Words

A. Bon!

Match the "bon" word in Column A with its appropriate meaning in Column B.

A	B
1. **embonpoint**	(a) a spectacular windfall
2. **bon mot**	(b) an obvious blunder
3. **bona fide**	(c) a confectionery store
	(d) pleasant trip
4. **bon vivant**	(e) a good-natured manner
5. **bonanza**	(f) in good faith
6. **bonbonniere**	(g) innkeeper
7. **boner**	(h) a person who enjoys good food and drink
8. **bonhomie**	(i) excessive plumpness
9. **boniface**	(j) clever saying
10. **bon voyage**	

B. A Diverting Quiz

1. Explain the meaning of the French word "divertissement," which is also proper *English* usage, by showing how it is derived from its Latin root.

2. Why is a person who is *apt* at many things called *versatile*?

3. If a person were afflicted with *vertigo*, would he be most likely to have (a) green sickness (b) dizzy spells (c) kleptomania?

4. If you were asked to express your *animadversion* about a subject, would you be expected (a) to criticize it unfavorably (b) satirize it (c) explain it clearly?

292

IV. Building Your Own Thesaurus

Look!

In this week's lesson we learned a new word *grimace*. The English language is rich in words descriptive of facial expressions.

The index in *Roget's Thesaurus* lists references to many words and expressions that convey the idea inherent in the word *look*.

1. Consulting a thesaurus, draw up a list of expressions which either contain the word *look* or describe a person's facial expressions that indicate his feeling or attitude. (Do not use any expression indicated in question 2 below) Some suggestions: look daggers, look down one's nose.

2. Define the following; then list them in your book for further reference.

a *cursory* look	a *leering* look
a *scowl*	to *ogle*
a *seductive* look	look *askance*

3. Draw up a list of ten words that are synonymous with *see*. (You may consult Section 441. *Vision* in *Roget's Thesaurus*.)

V. Review

Define and use in a short illustrative sentence each of the following words:

1. abstemious	6. dapper	11. demure
2. anathema	7. didactic	12. cult
3. adjudicate	8. endemic	13. bibliophile
4. crass	9. emolument	14. chicanery
5. criterion	10. distraught	15. contumely

LESSON SEVENTEEN

226.	harangue	236.	hilarious
227.	harbinger	237.	histrionic
228.	harrow	238.	hoax
229.	haughty	239.	hoodwink
230.	headstrong	240.	hue
231.	heinous	241.	hybrid
232.	herculean	242.	hyperbole
233.	heresy	243.	idiosyncrasy
234.	hiatus	244.	ignominy
235.	hibernate	245.	illicit

226. ha-rangue (noun and verb) hȧ-răng' [*harenga* (Late Latin), "a public address"] — A long, noisy, vehement public speech (the object being to arouse the feelings of people in the audience).

The quiet reason of the community leader quieted the mob which had been aroused by the demagogue's *harangue*.

Related Form: haranguer

Synonyms: declamation (a rhetorical formal speech), address, tirade (a prolonged denunciatory speech). While *oration*, *address* and *harangue* are united in the idea of communication, each has singular characteristics.

An *oration* is a polished, eloquent speech delivered at a special ceremony. An *address* is a formal, well-planned speech directed to a discussion of a particular subject. A *harangue* is an unrestrained informal passionate speech intended to arouse strong feeling or action in a mob.

---

*She speaks poignards
and every word stabs.*

— SHAKESPEARE

294

227. har-bin-ger (noun and verb) här′-bĭn-jĕr [*herbergeor* (Old French), "one who provides lodgings"]

1. Originally, a messenger who was sent on ahead to prepare lodging and entertainment for the royal family or nobles; hence, in modern English, a forerunner or a messenger.

   The wild geese flying south are *harbingers* of winter.

2. To foretell or indicate beforehand the approach of an event.

   Tradition has it that the groundhog emerging from his winter quarters *harbingers* spring.

Synonyms: precursor, herald, vanguard, omen (*noun:* ominous, "foreboding"), courier

Phrase: an *avant-courier*

If Winter comes, can spring
be far behind?

—SHELLEY

---

228. har-row hăr′-ō [*harwe* (Anglo-Saxon), "a harrow"] — To afflict the mind or feelings; to torment; to vex severely.

Although she tried hard, Janey's fear of water was so great that the mere thought of learning to swim left her feeling *harrowed* and almost hysterical.

Related Form: harrowing (*adjective*)

Synonyms: lacerating, agonizing (*verb:* agonize), distressing, vexing (*adj.* vexation; *verb,* vex)

The English word *harrow* is intended to describe with metaphorical vividness the action of a harrow.

The harrow is a farming instrument having sharp spikes of iron which serve to break up clods or lumps of earth and smooth them into pulverized soil.

A *harrowing* experience then, tears at one's nerves as a harrow might tear one's flesh. The action lacerates and torments.

Phrases: heart-rending, an excruciating, heart-breaking experience, a *racking* (distressing) headache, make the flesh creep, make the hair stand on end, set the teeth on edge

229. haugh-ty hô'-tǐ [*haut* (French), "high"; from *altus* Latin), "high"] — Scornfully proud.

Amy's habitually *haughty* expression and her air of condescension do little to make people feel that she is a warm and pleasant person.

Related Forms: haughtiness, hauteur (haughty spirit or manner)

Synonyms: arrogant, supercilious, presumptuous, lordly, condescending, overbearing, disdainful, vainglorious (boastful, arrogant display of skill, achievement, etc.)

Antonyms: meek, unpretentious, unassuming, lowly, servile

Phrases: proud-hearted, acting the role of *grande dame*, give oneself airs, put on the dog, stiff-necked, proud as a peacock, purse-proud (arrogantly proud of his wealth)

Pride goeth before destruction, and a haughty spirit before a fall.
— BIBLE

---

230. head-strong hĕd'-strông [head + strong] — Stubborn, possessing an ungovernable will.

In order to be a good executive one must learn not to be *headstrong* but to listen to and evaluate the advice of one's co-workers.

Synonyms: obstinate, obdurate, wilful, intractable, inflexible, positivistic

Antonyms: malleable, docile (*noun: docility*), tractable (*noun:* tractableness)

Phrases: impervious to reason, stand pat, a die-hard

It is only an error of judgment to make a mistake, but it argues an infirmity of character to adhere to it when discovered.

— C. N. BOVEE

---

231. hei-nous hā'-nŭs [*hainos* (Old French), "hateful"] — Atrocious or deeply offensive.

It was hard to believe that the mild-mannered man they had known as a neighbor could have committed a crime so *heinous* that they shuddered at the thought of it.

Related Forms: heinousness, heinously

Synonyms: odious (*noun:* odium), hateful, disreputable, wicked, infamous, loathesome, gross, flagrant, villainous, nefarious (see page 360), abhorrent (*verb:* abhor), monstrous, damnable, diabolical, flagitious, execrable (*noun:* execration)

Antonyms: laudatory (*verb:* laud; *adj.:* laudable), praiseworthy, commendable, panegyric

Phrase: committed an unpardonable offense

Note: **Venial** means "not seriously wrong" as opposed, in theological matters, to "mortal" or "deadly"; hence pardonable, or excusable, being regarded as an unintentional transgression.

A <u>venial</u> sin is minor, in contrast to a <u>mortal</u> sin, which is major.

Do not confuse <u>venial</u> with <u>venal,</u> "corrupt" "mercenary."

232. her-cu-le-an hêr-kū'-lē-ăn hûr-kū-lē'-ăn [*Hercules*, the Greek mythical hero] — Requiring great strength or courage to perform; of extraordinary size.

It took years of planning and work to accomplish the *herculean* task of putting a man on the moon.

Synonyms: gigantic, titanic, prodigious, colossal, mammoth, laborious, leviathan, gargantuan

Legendary characters other than Hercules have been known for their size and strength. Some of these are:

Titan   Goliath   Atlas   Samson

Antonyms: Lilliputian, diminutive, insignificant, minute, puny

---

The Greek hero Hercules was celebrated for having performed twelve hitherto impossible extraordinary "labors" or tasks. Consult an unabridged dictionary under the entry Hercules or a book of Greek mythology for the nature of these tasks.

---

233. her-e-sy hĕr'-ĕ-sĭ [*heresie* (Old French); from *hairesis* (Greek), "a choosing," "choice," "sect," "heresy"] — A doctrine or opinion held in opposition to accepted views in religion or other fields. Usually said of the views of a member of a religious group who differs from the group only in those views.

During the Middle Ages, anyone suspected of religious practices differing from those of the established church was charged with *heresy* and burned at the stake.

Related Forms: heretic, heretical, heretically

Synonyms: heterodoxy, recusant (one who refuses to comply or conform), nonconformity (*adj.* nonconformist)

Antonyms: orthodoxy, conformity

Phrases: to commit heresy
a heresiarch (a leader in heresy)
true blue (consistently faithful)

234. hi-a-tus hī-ā'-tŭs [*hiare* (Latin), "to gape"] — A gap, break or missing part.

The death of their leader left a *hiatus* in the ranks of the party which was difficult to fill.

Synonyms: breach, vacancy, respite (a brief period of rest or relief), lacuna (*plural:* lacunae), interruption, lapse (in continuity)

Phrases: the generation gap; a breach (lapse) of faith

235. hi-ber-nate hī'-bẽr-nāt [*hibernare* (Latin), "to pass the winter"] — To pass the winter (or, figuratively speaking, any extended length of time) in a state of sleep or suspended animation; hence, to be inactive for a long time.

I so hate the cold weather that I wish I could crawl into my bed and *hibernate* as soon as the first snow falls.

Related Forms: hibernation, hibernator, hibernal (pertaining to winter)

Synonyms: winter, quiescence, comatose

Phrases: remain in seclusion; estivate — "to spend the summer"

236. hi-la-ri-ous hĭ-lā'-rĭ-ŭs   hĭ-lā'-rĭ-ŭs   [*hilaris* (Latin), "cheerful"] — Boisterously merry.

Albert was such a good story teller that even when he told a joke that was only mildly funny, his audience would become *hilarious.*

Related Forms: hilariously, hilariousness, hilarity

Synonyms: jolly, (n. jollity), joyous, jocund, convivial, frisky, mirthful

Antonyms: solemn, serious, pensive, lugubrious, grave, saturnine (see page 409), gloomy, morose, taciturn (see page 420)

Phrases: engaged in highjinks (slang), rollicking humor

237. his-tri-on-ic hĭs-trĭ-ŏn'-ĭk [*histrio* (Latin), "an actor"]

1. Pertaining to the stage or actors.

A polished Shakespearean actor is the result of considerable *histrionic* ability and years of hard work and experience.

2. Intended for effect; stagy, affected.

> Mary's tears are only *histrionic;* she isn't so deeply touched as she wants us to believe.

Related Forms: histrionics (theatricals; acting), histrionical

Synonyms: theatrical, dramatic; artificial

238. hoax hōks [Probably contracted from *hocus* in the expression *hocus-pocus,* a meaningless magic formula in mock Latin used by jugglers a few centuries ago.] — A false story circulated through mischief; a fraud played as a joke; a practical joke.

> The report of a two-day holiday from school turned out to be a *hoax;* the freshman who had spread the rumor said he had done it "just for fun."

Synonyms: prank, canard; *blague* (French word for *hoax*)

Note: <u>Hoax</u> is also a verb (<u>Synonym:</u> flimflam).

239. hood-wink hood'-wĭngk [hood + wink] — Literally, to blind by covering the eyes; hence, to deceive by giving (something) a false appearance.

> The medicine man of years ago was frequently a charlatan who *hoodwinked* his audience into believing in the magical properties of his often worthless potions.

Synonyms: dupe, trick, mislead, dissemble, gull, humbug, cozen, delude, swindle, beguile

Phrases: sharp practice; palm off

240. hue hū [*hiw* (Anglo-Saxon), "color"] — Gradation or variety of color; shape or aspect; an outcry.

> Although we know that the *hue* of Homer's "wine-dark sea" was not red, we find the phrase beautifully descriptive.

Related Form: hued (*adjective*)

Synonyms: shade, dye, tint, tincture, complexion, tinge

Phrase: hue and cry — "a general public outcry of alarm or pursuit, usually of a criminal; a public clamor or protest."

Note: According to The American College Dictionary, the term spectrum, in physics, is "an array of entities, as light waves or particles, ordered in accordance with the magnitude of a common physical property, as wavelength or mass: often the band of colors produced when sunlight is passed through a prism, comprising red, orange, yellow, green, blue, indigo and violet."

The series is usually arranged in order of wave lengths.

By extension, a spectrum is a wide range of varied but related objects, opinions, or concepts in which the salient traits overlap or merge to form a continuous range or sequence.

The spectrum of public reaction to the news of the disaster ranged from horror at one end to indifference at the other.

241. hy-brid hī'-brĭd [*hybrida* (Latin), "the offspring of a wild boar and a tame female swine"] — Of mixed origin.

The mule, the *hybrid* offspring of a donkey and a horse, was much used as a beast of burden during the settlement of the West.

Related Forms: hybridism, hybridity, hybridize

Synonyms: crossbreed, mongrel, interbreed, half-breed

Antonyms: pure, purebreed, thoroughbred, pedigreed

242. hy-per-bo-le hĭ-pûr'-bō-lē [*hyperbole* (Greek), "an overshooting"; from *hyper*, "over" + *ballein*, "to throw"; that is, "to throw beyond the mark"]

1. A figure of speech in which an obvious overstatement is used to give emphasis or effect and is not intended to be taken literally.

    In order to convince people of her sincerity, Ursula will frequently use *hyberboles* such as, "If you gave me ten million dollars . . ."

2. Extravagant exaggeration.

    John resorted to *hyperbole* so often to express his feelings about even humdrum matters that his friends had learned to make allowances for his exaggerations.

Related Forms: hyperbolic, hyperbolical

> *Somebody has said of the boldest figure in rhetoric, the* hyperbole,
> *that it lies without deceiving.*
>
> — THOMAS B. MACAULAY

---

243. id-i-o-syn-cra-sy ĭd-ĭ-ȏ-sĭng′-kră-sĭ [*idios* (Greek), "one's own" + *syn,* "together" + *krasis,* "a mixture"] — A constitutional eccentricity peculiar to an individual; a personal mannerism.

One of Lamb's *idiosyncrasies* was that of wearing black clothes at festive occasions and of appearing solemn at joyous affairs.

Related Form: idiosyncratic

Synonyms: oddity, foible, vagary, idiocrasy, queerness, kink, aberration, peculiarity, quirk, whimsey, singularity, crochet, peccadillo (a petty fault or offense)

Phrase: a maggot in the brain (a little bit of madness)

Note: An idiosyncrasy is not necessarily either good or bad. A foible is usually indicative of a minor defect or weakness.

An extreme of idiosyncrasy is an obsession or craze.

> *Though this be madness,*
> *yet there is a method in't.*
>
> — SHAKESPEARE

---

244. ig-no-min-y ĭg′-nȏ-mĭn-ĭ [*ignominia* (Latin), "the taking away of one's good name"; from *in,* "not" + *nomen,* "name"] — Public disgrace, contempt or dishonor sometimes as a result of ignoble or contemptible conduct.

Laura wondered if she would ever live through the *ignominy* of being the only girl in her class who was not invited to the prom.

Related Forms: ignominious, ignominiously

Synonyms: infamy, humiliation, opprobrium (*adj.* opprobrious), obloquy (see page 364), disrepute, degradation

Antonyms: honor, fame, glory, repute

245. il-lic-it ĭ-lĭs'-ĭt [*in* (Latin), "not" + *licere* "to be allowed"] — Not authorized; unlawful.

> Part of the American tax dollar must be used each year to control the *illicit* traffic in narcotics and to rehabilitate drug addicts.

Related Form: illicitness

Synonyms: unlicensed, forbidden, illegitimate

Antonyms: authorized, legal

Note: Our English word <u>veto</u> comes from the Latin, meaning, "I forbid."

EXERCISES

I. Words in Context

A. Words in Phrases

Select the one of the four suggested words or phrases which most nearly expresses the meaning of the italicized word in each of the following expressions.

1. a *harrowing* experience (*a*) thrilling (*b*) sensational (*c*) agonizing (*d*) eye-opening

2. a *purse-proud* man (*a*) arrogantly proud of his wealth (*b*) greedy (*c*) philanthropic (*d*) one whose wealth is self-earned

3. a *stand-patter* one who (*a*) is stubborn in asserting his rights (*b*) is reactionary (*c*) is a rabble-rouser (*d*) refuses to consider changing

4. a *venial* offense (*a*) flagitious (*b*) excusable (*c*) odious (*d*) flagrant

5. a *true-blue* ally (*a*) undependable (*b*) helpful (*c*) consistently faithful (*d*) pessimistic

B. One-Word Omissions

In each of the following sentences substitute for the blank an appropriate word selected from Words 226-245 of the Basic Vocabulary List.

1. The _____ of the sky at dawn this morning was a beautiful rosy pink.

2. To a strong believer in religion, _____ seems as grave a crime as treason does to a patriot.

3. The _____ stare of the headwaiter as he said, "I beg your pardon, sir, but you may not enter without a tie," froze me to the marrow of my bones.

4. It was a(n) _____ of the immortal Babe Ruth that he always stepped on second base when he came in from the outfield between innings.

5. I am sure that with my _____ ability I will be able to show such distress that my father will allow me to take the car.

II. Words Out of Context

In each group below, select the word or expression that most clearly expresses the meaning of the word at the left.

1. **ignominious**   (*a*) deficient in learning (*b*) ill repute
                        (*c*) crude (*d*) incognito

2. **hybrid**   (*a*) arrogantly proud (*b*) pedigreed
                        (*c*) of mixed origin (*d*) thoroughbred

3. **hoodwink**   (*a*) delude (*b*) conspire
                        (*c*) disguise (*d*) perceive

4. **harrow**   (*a*) hasten (*b*) harness
                        (*c*) devastate (*d*) distress painfully

5. **hibernate**   (*a*) remain in seclusion (*b*) sleep
                        (*c*) censure (*d*) exclude

III. Antonyms and Synonyms

A. Antonyms

Match the word in Column **A** with its antonym in Column **B**.

A	**B**
1. vainglorious	(a) inflexible
2. malleable	(b) gargantuan
3. execrable	(c) unpretentious
4. diminutive	(d) heterodox
5. morose	(e) inoffensive
6. obloquy	(f) fame
7. orthodox	(g) mirthful

B. Synonyms

Match the word in Column **A** with its synonym in Column **B**.

A	**B**
1. wilful	(a) insignificant
2. nefarious	(b) inactive
3. puny	(c) cozen
4. lacuna	(d) hoax
5. quiescent	(e) obdurate
6. canard	(f) gap
7. gull	(g) quirk
8. kink	(h) flagitious

IV. Related Forms

A. Give a noun form of the following words.

hilarious	jolly	heinous
heretical	docile	

B. Give an adjectival form of the following words.

hyperbole	idiosyncrasy	ignominy
hauteur	abhor	

WORD BUILDING

I. PREPOSITION

The Greek preposition **hyper-**, meaning "above" or as an adverb "over" in the sense of excess or exaggeration, is the source of many English words including *hyperbole*, studied in this lesson. It is used in many medical terms to denote excess or beyond the normal amount. The Latin preposition for *hyper-* is *super-*.

> *hyperacidity* — state of being too strongly acid
>
> *hypercritical* — excessively critical

II. PREFIX

The Latin prefix **in-**, "not," is one of the elements in our English word *illicit*, studied in this week's lesson. Note that the prefix *in-* before *l* becomes *il-* (example, *illusion*); before *r* it becomes *ir-* (example, *irreparable*); before *p, b, m,* it becomes *im-* (example, *impossible*).

> *inelastic* — not elastic; rigid
>
> *inarticulate* — not articulate: not able to speak distinctly

III. ROOT

The Latin root **nomen, nominis,** meaning "name" and its Greek kinsman **onoma, onyma,** also meaning "name," are the source of many English words including *ignominy*, studied in this lesson.

> *cognomen* (literally, "with the name") — a surname or last name
>
> *nominal* — in name only

EXERCISES

I. Etymology Mastery Test

1. What is a hypochondriac? Define in the light of their derivation *hypocrite, hypothetical.*

2. *Change the following "positives" to "negatives" by the use of* in- *or its variations.*

imitable	credulous
mobile	curious
moderate	delicate
palpable	licit
apt	tractable

3. *Define and give the origin of each of the following words.*
anonymous denomination pseudonym onomatopoeia
nominate

II. Word Development and Analysis

1. *Explain the meaning and origin of the following words.*

histrionic	ignominy	patronymic	synagogue
hoax	hyperbole	synchronize	symposium
hybrid	hypercritical	hypodermic	

2. In Ancient Rome the family name came third. For example, the name of Gaius Julius Caesar indicated that he belonged to the famous Caesars. Give two synonyms for the term "family name."

3. *What does each of the following patronymics mean?*

Atkinson	MacTavish	Van Loon	Ben Adhem
O'Reilly	Ivanovich	Fitz William	

4. Animals that *estivate* are seldom seen (*a*) on cold days, (*b*) on wet days (*c*) on hot days (*d*) on windy days

5. What is a "hibernal" expedition?

6. Define *nomenclature.* Which two of the following words belong in the *nomenclature* of subjects studied in high school? (*a*) binomial (*b*) therapy (*c*) predicate (*d*) philatelist

7. What is a *hyperbola*? Draw one. If a person were termed *hyperbolic,* what would he most likely be?

III. Fun with Words

A. Graphic Phrases

What do the following phrases mean?

1. a beggar on horseback
2. hiding one's light under a bushel
3. the whole spectrum of political dissent
4. the generation gap
5. cleansing the Augean stable

B. Out of Place

Which word or expression is for one reason or another out of place?

1. swagger   blusterer   swank   windjammer
2. in the groove   hang-up   tension   uptight
3. daub   gull   smear   gloss
4. recant   rant   hector   lambaste

IV. Building Your Own Thesaurus

TALK   TALK   TALK

The Basic Vocabulary List of this week includes the analysis of *harangue*, a specific graphic word in the long catalogue of synonyms of the simpler or more general words *say* or *talk*.

Draw up in your notebook three lists under headings as follows.

Talk	Say	Shout

In consultation with *Roget's Thesaurus* and an unabridged dictionary list correctly under each heading synonyms that cover the whole spectrum of speech, from a whisper through moderate articulation to extreme loudness.

Whither Mankind?

In the following paragraphs substitute for each blank an appropriate word selected from Words 1-165 (including derivatives) on the Basic Vocabulary List. Synonyms are provided at the end of the passage to guide you.

Today only the most e..(1).. optimist can look with c..(2).. upon the c..(3).. condition of the world. A..(4).. impulses stemming from the era of the Cave Man seem to be urging us on to the dreadful task of e..(5).. the entire human race.

In the face of this impending catastrophe, some of us are simply a..(6).., regarding every attempt to build a Brave New World as c..(7).. and f..(8).. Others are c..(9).., remaining unmoved by the possibility of incalculable misery soon to be visited upon millions of their fellow human beings. Still others are c..(10).., speaking d..(11).. of all humanity and seeming to believe that its utter extinction would be a blessing rather than a calamity.

No one of these attitudes is, of course, c..(12).. to the solution of the great e..(13)..: Whither is Mankind heading? Will man eventually become sufficiently civilized to live in a..(14) with his neighbors, or will he e..(15).. his primitive forbears, the Cave Men, in the dreadful task of self-destruction?

Synonyms and Definitions of Words to be Supplied

1. extreme, out of the common run	8. useless
2. self-satisfaction	9. unfeeling
3. disorganized	10. scornful
4. relating to a reversal to the primitive	11. in a derogatory manner
5. destroying, rooting out	12. contributing to
6. indifferent	13. puzzle
7. fantastic	14. friendship
	15. try to equal

LESSON EIGHTEEN

246. immaculate	**256.** inarticulate
247. immutable	**257.** incarcerate
248. impasse	**258.** incense
249. impeccable	**259.** incipient
250. impediment	**260.** incognito
251. impervious	**261.** incongruous
252. implacable	**262.** incumbent
253. impugn	**263.** indigent
254. impunity	**264.** indiscreet
255. inane	**265.** indomitable

246. im-mac-u-late ĭ-măk′-ū-lăt [*in*, "not" + *maculatus*, "spotted"; from *macula*, "a spot"] — Spotlessly clean; unblemished; error-free.

Despite the heat and dirt of a summer day in the city, Doris managed somehow to look cool and *immaculate*.

Related Forms: immaculateness, immaculacy

Synonyms: flawless, spotless, impeccable, stainless, untarnished, undefiled, perfect, unsullied

Antonyms: stained, blotched, speckled, blemished, impure, foul, sullied, defiled, tarnished

Phrases: unsullied reputation

247. im-mu-ta-ble ĭ-mū′-tà-b'l [*im* (Latin), "not" + *mutabilis*, "changeable"] — Not capable of being changed.

The scientist explained that although man could understand the workings of some of the *immutable* laws of nature, he was powerless to change them.

Related Forms: immutably, immutability

310

Synonyms: changeless, unchangeable, constant, unalterable, steadfast, resolute

Antonyms: mutable, alterable, variable, fickle, wavering, inconstant, unstable, unsteady

---

*Plus ça change, plus
c'est la même chose —*
— ALPHONSE KARR

(*The more it changes, the
more it's the same thing.*)

---

248. im-passe ĭm-pȧs′ ĭm′pȧs [*impasse* (French), "an impassable road"] — A predicament that leaves one no escape.

Having tried all means to resolve the *impasse* reached in their negotiations, the diplomats decided to adjourn their conference.

Synonyms: deadlock, cul-de-sac, blind alley

Phrase: lead up a blind alley

249. im-pec-ca-ble ĭm-pĕk′-ȧ-b'l [*im* (Latin), "not" + *peccare*, "to sin" (See page 306 for discussion of the prefix)]

1. About persons: not inclined to error or sin.

   Only a person of no humor and little wisdom could believe himself to be *impeccable* at all times.

2. About things: free from blemish or fault; beyond reproach.

   Having been trained for the stage, John has *impeccable* speech.

Related Forms: impeccability, impeccably, impeccant

Synonyms: flawless, consummate, perfect, irreproachable, unerring, infallible

Antonyms: peccable, peccant, blemished, defective, errant, mistaken, culpable, fallible, reproachable

Phrase: impeccable taste

The only impeccable *writers are those that never wrote.*

— WILLIAM HAZLITT

---

250. **im-ped-i-ment** ĭm-pĕd′-ĭ-mĕnt [*impedire* (Latin), "to entangle the feet"; from *im*, "in" + *pes, pedis*, "foot" (See page 261 for a discussion of this root)] — Anything that obstructs or hinders.

As soon as John became aware that his overlong hair was an *impediment* to him in his search for a job, he decided to have a haircut.

Related Forms: impede, *impedimenta* (Latin plural meaning "baggage")

Synonyms: obstacle, encumbrance, bar, resistance, block

Antonyms: aid, help, assistance

Phrase: a speech impediment

251. **im-per-vi-ous** im-pûr′-vĭ-ŭs [*im* (Latin), "not" + *per*, "through," + *via*, "a way" (See page 221 for a discussion of this root.)] — Incapable of being penetrated, hence, figuratively, incapable of being reached by ideas.

All my histrionic efforts failed; my mother remained *impervious* to my pleas for a higher allowance.

Related Forms: imperviousness, imperviable

Synonyms: impenetrable, impermeable, impassable; insensible, callous, adamant (to reason)

Antonyms: pervious, penetrable, permeable, flexible, susceptible

252. **im-pla-ca-ble** ĭm-plā′-kȧ-b'l [*im* (Latin), "not" + *placare*, "to appease"] — Incapable of being made peaceful or forgiving.

The two rivals at school had been *implacable* enemies since early childhood; nothing would make them friends now.

Related Forms: implacableness, implacably, implacability

Synonyms: unappeasable, immitigable, inexorable (see page 324), obdurate (see page 363), inflexible, unrelenting, inclement, unallaying, pitiless, relentless, remorseless, merciless, unbending

Antonyms: placable, appeasable (*verb:* appease), mitigative (*verb:* mitigate), conciliatory, propitiatory (*verb:* propitiate), yielding, forbearing, merciful

253. im-pugn ĭm-pūn' [*im* (Latin) "against" + *pugnare*, "to fight"] — To attack as false; call into question another's motives, statements, etc.

Marge is so proud of her vocabulary that she is likely to say, "Do you *impugn* my veracity?" when she means, "Are you telling me that I'm lying?"

Related Forms: impugnment, impugnable

Synonyms: question, assail, challenge, refute, rebut, gainsay

Antonyms: confirm, substantiate, affirm, authenticate, corroborate

Phrase: to impugn another's motives

254. im-pu-ni-ty ĭm-pū'-nĭ-tĭ [*im* (Latin), "not" + *poena*, "punishment"] — Freedom or exemption from penalty or punishment.

In the legislative chamber a member enjoying the privilege of legislative *immunity* may make libelous statements and reckless charges without incurring legal recrimination.

Synonym: immunity

Phrase: acted *with impunity*

255. in-ane ĭn-ān' [*inanis* (Latin), "empty"] — Without sense or intelligence; empty; void.

Florence was so embarrassed at being caught in a lie that she could do nothing but stand there sheepishly with an *inane* smile on her face.

Related Forms: inanely, inanity, inanition

Synonyms: fatuous, silly, foolish, pointless, dull, insipid, vapid, trivial, petty, banal, frothy, frivolous

Antonyms: significant, meaningful, witty, sapient, sage, sententious

256. in-ar-tic-u-late ĭn-är-tĭk'-ū-lăt [*in* (Latin), "not" + *articulatus*, "spoken distinctly"]

1. Incapable of speaking distinctly; mute; without words.

   My joy at hearing that I had gotten into the college of my choice made me completely *inarticulate*.

2. Unable to express one's ideas and feelings intelligently.

   If you make a systematic effort to improve your vocabulary, you will not find yourself *inarticulate* when you wish to express yourself.

Related Forms: inarticulately, inarticulateness, inarticulation

Synonyms: inexpressible, ineffable, dumb, mute, speechless, indistinct

Antonyms: vocal, fluent, voluble

257. in-car-cer-ate ĭn-kär'-sẽr-āt [*in* (Latin), "in" + *carcer*, "prison"] — To put in prison; to confine.

In our democratic system of government anyone may express his opinion without fear of being *incarcerated*.

Related Forms: incarceration, incarcerator

Synonyms: imprison, jail, coop, impound, intern, constrain, immure

Antonyms: liberate, free, emancipate, release

258. in-cense (verb) ĭn-sĕns' [*in* (Latin), "on" + *cendere*, "to burn"] — Stir up to violent anger.

Incensed at what they considered to be unjust taxation, the American colonists rose in revolt.

Related Forms: incendiary (pertaining to, or one who sets fire to (property); incendiarism

Synonyms: anger, infuriate, enrage, inflame, provoke, irritate, incite

Phrases: an incendiary speech
an incendiary bomb
rile (colloquial)
lash into fury
throw into a ferment
mad with rage
flush with anger

259. in-cip-i-ent ĭn-sĭp'-ĭ-ĕnt [*incipere* (Latin), "to begin"; from "to take" (See page 139 for discussion of this root)] — Beginning to appear.

The woods were so dry during the hot summer months that even the tiniest spark could mean an *incipient* forest fire.

Related Forms: incipiently, incipience, incipiency

Synonyms: commencing, initial, introductory, embryonic, budding, sprouting, burgeoning

Antonyms: terminal, concluding, closing, ending

260. in-cog-ni-to ĭn-kŏg'-nĭ-tō [*incognito* (Italian); from *incognitus* (Latin), "unknown"; from *in*, "not" + *cognoscere*, "to become acquainted with" (See page 176 for a discussion of the root.)] — Without being known; under an assumed name or character.

Today the faces of famous people are so well known, that it is well nigh impossible for them to travel *incognito*.

Synonyms: disguised, unidentified

261. in-con-gru-ous ĭn-kŏng'-grōō-ŭs [*in* (Latin), "not" + *congruere*, "to agree"] — Not agreeing with; hence, out of harmony or not suitable, sometimes almost absurd.

The lisping speech and childish manner which were thought attractive when she was a girl were *incongruous* in the grown woman.

Related Forms: incongruously, incongruity, incongruousness

Synonyms: inappropriate, inharmonious, unsuitable, discordant, inconsistent, incompatible

Antonyms: appropriate, suitable, fitting, consistent, compatible, consonant

262. in-cum-bent (*adj.*) ĭn-kŭm'-bĕnt [*in* (Latin) "upon" + *cumbens* "leaning"] — Obligatory.

It is *incumbent* upon every citizen over twenty-one to inform himself of the issues of the moment in order that he may vote wisely.

Related Forms: incumbent (*noun:* incumbency, the position or term of an incumbent)

Synonyms: mandatory, imperative, duty-bound

Antonym: optional

Phrases: call of duty
be *under* an obligation

Note: Incumbent as a noun means "an office-holder," one who holds a position that is the subject of a contest.

In the election for District Attorney, Frank is challenging Toynbee who is the incumbent.

263. in-di-gent ĭn'-dĭ-jĕnt [*indu* (Latin), "in" + *egere*, "to need"] — Poverty-stricken.

Private philanthropy in America provides the necessities of life for many *indigent* families who are not able to support themselves.

Related Forms: indigently, indigence

Synonyms: destitute, impecunious, needy, poor, necessitous, penniless, penurious

Antonyms: wealthy, affluent, moneyed, rich, opulent

264. in-dis-creet ĭn-dĭs-krēt' [*in* (Latin), "not" + *discreet*, from *discernere*, "to discern" "perceive" "discriminate"] — Imprudent; lacking good judgment.

I realize now that I should never have entrusted my secret to Jane, she is such an *indiscreet* blabbermouth.

Related Forms: indiscretion, indiscreetness

Synonyms: rash, precipitate, unwise, injudicious, incautious

Antonyms: circumspect, judicious, cautious, prudent, vigilant, deliberate, guarded

Phrases: indiscreet (lacking or uninhibited in judgment)

Note: Do not confuse **indiscreet** with **indiscrete**, meaning not separate; firmly joined.

Discretion is the better side
of valor.

---

265. in-dom-i-ta-ble ĭn-dŏm'-ĭ-tà-b'l [*in* (Latin), "not" + *domitere*, "to tame"] — Not capable of being overcome; unconquerable.

It took *indomitable* will for Franklin Delano Roosevelt to persist in his career despite the handicaps imposed upon him by an attack of polio.

Related Forms: indomitably, indomitability, indomitableness

Synonyms: invincible, untamable, irrepressible, unyielding, intractable, fearless

Antonyms: amenable, docile, submissive, tractable, yielding

EXERCISES

I. Words Out of Context

In each group below, select the word or expression that most clearly expresses the meaning of the word at the left.

1. **impugn**   (*a*) act impertinently (*b*) attribute
(*c*) assail as false (*d*) battle

2. **immutable**   (*a*) unchangeable (*b*) outspoken
(*c*) expressive (*d*) inconstant

3. **incarcerate**   (*a*) burn (*b*) imprison (*c*) foment
(*d*) incapacitate

4. **incensed**   (*a*) purged (*b*) stimulated
(*c*) unreasonable (*d*) infuriated

5. **impervious**   (*a*) having insight (*b*) impenetrable
(*c*) irreligious (*d*) mischievous

6. **incipient**   (*a*) spouting (*b*) absorptive (*c*) in the
initial stage (*d*) without interruption

7. **inarticulate**   (*a*) non-existent (*b*) incapable of
speaking distinctly (*c*) immeasurable
(*d*) incompetent

8. **immaculate**   (*a*) callous (*b*) inaccessible
(*c*) spotless (*d*) finicky

9. **indiscreet**   (*a*) imprudent (*b*) speechless
(*c*) indescribable (*d*) lacking in
confidence

10. **incumbent**   (*a*) obstructive (*b*) resilient
(*c*) obligatory (*d*) inflexible

II. Words in Context

A. One-Word Omissions

In each of the following sentences substitute for the blank an appropriate word selected from words 246-265 of the Basic Vocabulary List.

1. The negotiators seeking to settle the strike have now reached a(n) _____ since neither side will make any compromise.

2. The written prose of Joseph Conrad is _____, but his spoken English had a decided Polish accent.

3. Though it seemed an impossible task, the soldiers fought on with _____ courage against almost insuperable odds.

4. If the dethroned monarch of Belgravia is in the United States, he must be traveling _____, since the newspapers contain no reports on his visit.

5. The government dispatched food and clothing to aid the _____ and disabled victims of the flood.

6. Mark Twain's famous witticism: "The reports of my death are greatly exaggerated," is an example of the _____ in humor.

7. Of all the _____ remarks I have ever heard, "I like this food but it doesn't like me" strikes me as about the silliest.

8. "You cannot flout my authority with _____," said the irate professor. "You shall be duly punished for this infraction."

9. John does not actually stutter but he obviously has a slight _____ in his speech.

10. Although other French generals became collaborationists during World War II, DeGaule remained the _____ foe of the Germans.

B. Words in Quotations

In each selection below, certain words are underlined *and numbered. Each numbered word is followed by four words or phrases lettered (a) to (d). Select the letter preceding the item that is closest in meaning to each underlined word as used in the selection.*

Since the general civilization of mankind, I believe there are more instances of the abridgment[1] of the freedom of the people by gradual silent encroachments[2] of those in power than by violent and sudden usurpations.[3]

> — JAMES MADISON: "Speech in the Virginia Convention," 1781

1. *abridgment* (a) linking (b) increment
  (c) lessening (d) censure

2. *encroachments* (a) derision (b) hostilities
  (c) endeavors (d) inroads

3. *usurpations* (a) utilizations (b) dissents
  (c) wrongful seizures (d) interferences

There is nothing I more deprecate[4] than the use of the Fourteenth Amendment beyond the absolute compulsion of its words to prevent the making of social experiments that an important part of the community desires, in the insulated[5] chambers afforded by the several states, even though the experiments may seem futile[6] and even noxious[7] to me and to those whose judgments I most respect.

> —JUSTICE OLIVER WENDELL HOLMES

4. *deprecate* (a) deplore (b) advocate
  (c) sanction (d) detest

5. *insulated* (a) biased; privileged (b) unpopular; selfish (c) protected; selective
  (d) segregated; isolated

6. *futile* (*a*) insignificant (*b*) unreasonable
(*c*) efficacious (*d*) useless

7. *noxious* (*a*) baneful (*b*) baleful
(*c*) nauseating (*d*) repulsive

C. Words in Miscellaneous Contexts

Select the letter preceding the word or expression which is closest in meaning to the underlined and numbered word.

Headlines

U. S.-PERU PARLEY[1]
SEEN AT IMPASSE[2]

1. *Parley* (*a*) dispute (*b*) conference (*c*) truce
(*d*) contest

2. *Impasse* (*a*) crisis (*b*) denouement
(*c*) blocking point (*d*) crossroads

AVERS[3] F.C.C. RULE
FOSTERS[4] TV TIMIDITY[5]

3. *Avers* (*a*) affirms (*b*) hints (*c*) deplores
(*d*) decides

4. *Fosters* (*a*) promotes (*b*) promulgates
(*c*) influences (*d*) counteracts

5. *Timidity* (*a*) fearfulness (*b*) rashness
(*c*) tenacity (*d*) reaction

Book Titles

EXODUS[6] by Leon Uris

6. (*a*) rebirth (*b*) departure (*c*) urgency
(*d*) immigration

FORTITUDE[7] by Hugh Walpole

7. (*a*) strength (*b*) chance (*c*) good fortune
(*d*) courage under affliction

WORD BUILDING

I. PREFIX

1. The Latin prefix **per-**, "through," "throughout," is an element in many English words including *impervious*, studied in this week's lesson.

II. ROOT

2. The Latin root **placere**, "to please," "to appease," appears in many English words including *implacable*, studied in this lesson.

EXERCISES

I. Etymology Mastery Test

1. *Define in the light of their source elements each of the following words.*

    pervade   perspicuous   permeate   perspective

2. What is a *placebo*?

3. *Define and trace the origin of the following words. Use each in a short sentence.*

    placate   placid   complacent   complaisant   placable

II. Word Analysis and Development

1. *With the aid of a dictionary, give the meaning of each of the following words and classify them according to their derivation from* **pes, pedis** *(Latin), "foot" or* **pais, paidos** *(Greek), "child."*

peddler	pediatrics	pedantry
pedigree	pedestrian	pedant
pedicure	pedestal	pedagogy

2. Why is a prison called a *penal institution*? Give three words other than *penal* that are derived from the Latin root *poena*, meaning punishment.

322

3. Which of the following would be most likely to prevent a person from becoming an orator? (*a*) impedimenta (*b*) speech impediments (*c*) impecuniosity

4. Are *cognoscenti* (*a*) conspirators (*b*) connoisseurs (*c*) collaborators (*d*) revolutionaries?

5. Are *punitive* measures taken for the purpose of (*a*) healing (*b*) imparting scientific knowledge (*c*) chastising (*d*) making witticisms?

6. From what Latin root is the word *incensed* derived? "*Incentive, incandescent* are relatives of *incense.*" Explain.

7. What is a *recumbent* position? Explain etymologically why an "incumbent" candidate is so called? Why is *incubus* synonymous with "nightmare"?

8. What does the biological term "mutant" mean? Define *mutation*. What is meant by the expression "the mutability of fortune"?

9. What is:
   (*a*) an *immaculate* housekeeper?
   (*b*) an *inane* remark?
   (*c*) an *incendiary* bomb?
   (*d*) the *incipiency* of a disease?

10. Illustrate by an anecdote the maxim:
   "Discretion is the better side of valor."

III. Review

Define and use in a short sentence each of the following words.

1. grimace	6. fiscal	11. askew
2. connive	7. duplicity	12. alacrity
3. headstrong	8. heretical	13. fulsome
4. charlatan	9. garish	14. erudite
5. haughty	10. herculean	15. elicit

LESSON NINETEEN

266.	inert	**276.**	intrinsic
267.	inexorable	**277.**	inveigh
268.	inference	**278.**	inveigle
269.	ingenious	**279.**	inveterate
270.	ingratiate	**280.**	irascible
271.	inordinate	**281.**	irony
272.	inscrutable	**282.**	jaunty
273.	insidious	**283.**	jeer
274.	insipid	**284.**	jeopardize
275.	intrepid	**285.**	jostle

266. in-ert ĭn-ûrt′ [*in* (Latin), "not" + *ars, artis,* "skill," "art"] — Inactive, indisposed to activity; inherently lacking in power to move or act or resist.

Our long walk in the heat of the day had so tired us that all we could do was lie in the shade, *inert* as logs.

Related Forms: inertia, inertly, inertness

Synonyms: passive, torpid, lethargic, motionless, quiescent, sluggish, dormant, supine, cowardly

Antonyms: kinetic, mobile, dynamic, lively

Ars longa, tempus breve
— HORACE

*Art is long, and time
is fleeting.*
— LONGFELLOW

---

267. in-ex-o-ra-ble ĭn-ĕk′-sỏ-rá-b'l [ex (Latin), "out" + *orare,* "to pray"] — Not moved by prayer or entreaty; unyielding.

In view of the many past crimes committed by the convicted burglar, Judge Roberts was *inexorable* in his decision to impose the maximum penalty.

Related Forms: inexorably, inexorability, inexorableness

Synonyms: inflexible, adamant (see page 18), relentless, unrelenting, implacable (see page 312), resolute, obdurate (see page 363), immovable

Antonyms: placable, flexible, pliant, docile (see page 227), malleable, tractable; compassionate (merciful)

Phrases: an inexorable stance, the inexorable march of time

268. in-fer-ence ĭn'-fēr-ĕns [*inferre* (Latin), "to conclude"; from *in*, "in" + *ferre*, "to bring"] — A conclusion reached on the basis of reasoning from data or premises.

Although the speaker did not state his affiliation, the *inference* we drew from his remarks was that he was politically conservative.

Related Forms: infer, inferential, inferentially

Synonyms: deduction, implication

Phrases: a *non sequitur* (a Latin phrase meaning "It does not follow") — an inference that does not logically follow from a given premise
without rhyme or reason

Note: A syllogism is a set of three statements, a major premise, a minor premise, and a conclusion. Thus:

(Major:) All men are mortal.

(Minor:) Frank is a man.

(Conclusion:) Therefore, Frank is mortal.

Two common types of reasoning are: deductive and inductive. In deductive reasoning, one reasons from an accepted general statement to an individual case. The syllogism above is an example of deductive reasoning.

In inductive reasoning, one reasons from specific instances to a generalization. The basis for this kind of reasoning process is experimental (synonym: empirical), observations from which a general statement is developed.

A large number of today's rebellious young people come from upper middle class families. Their upbringing has been rather permissive and without much discipline. Therefore, it is possible that today's youth is in a state of rebellion because of the permissiveness of their upbringing.

269. in-gen-ious ĭn-jēn'-yŭs [*ingeniosus* (Latin), from *ingenium*, "natural capacity," "cleverness"] — Demonstrating originality, skill or inventiveness.

Paul's cousin invented an *ingenious* device that enables a fountain pen to hold five different colors of ink at one time.

Related Forms: ingeniously, ingeniousness, ingenuity

Synonyms: clever, adroit, skillful, dexterous, deft, cunning

Antonyms: gauche, clumsy, maladroit, inexpert, crude; banal, commonplace.

Note: Do not confuse **ingenious** with **ingenuous,** which means "artlessly frank" or "simple and unsophisticated."

Disingenuous means "not ingenuous; lacking in candor; insincere." (noun: **disingenuousness**)

Phrases: done with *finesse; a tour de force,* "a feat requiring exceptional originality, skill."

The play itself has little to recommend it, but Tony's performance is a *tour de force.*

270. in-gra-ti-ate ĭn-grā'-shĭ-āt [*in gratiam* (Latin), "into favor"] — To gain favor or bring oneself into another's good graces.

It is impossible for me to scold my dog Alfie, for when I do he sidles up to me, puts up his paw, and does his best to *ingratiate* himself.

Related Forms: ingratiatingly, ingratiation

Synonym: insinuate (oneself)

Antonyms: alienate, estrange, antagonize

Phrases: apple polishing (seeking favor by flattery); to curry favor; an ingratiating act

326

271. in-or-di-nate ĭn-ôr′-dĭ-năt [*in* (Latin), "not" + *ordinatus*, "arranged"] — Not within proper limits; unrestrained; excessive.

Seeing her young daughter's eyes hardly visible because of the use of an *inordinate* amount of eye makeup, Mrs. Eastman rebuked her for her excessive use of cosmetics.

Related Form: inordinately

Synonyms: uncurbed, unchecked, extravagant, immoderate, intemperate (as *inordinate* demands)

Antonyms: curbed, checked, moderate, temperate, restrained

272. in-scru-ta-ble ĭn-skroo′-tȧ-b'l [*in* (Latin), "not" + *scrutari*, "to search"] — Not capable of being interpreted or understood, mysterious.

The meaning behind the *inscrutable* smile of Da Vinci's *Mona Lisa* has long been a subject for speculation.

Related Forms: inscrutably, inscrutability, inscrutableness

Synonyms: unfathomable, incomprehensible, esoteric (see page 251), enigmatic, cryptic, occult (beyond the bounds of common knowledge, secret), inexplicable, baffling, arcane

Antonyms: patent, manifest, clear, explicable, comprehensible

Phrase: the Mona Lisa smile

273. in-sid-i-ous ĭn-sĭd′-ĭ-ŭs [*in* (Latin), "in" + *sedere*, "to sit"] — Full of deceit and cunning, working secretly or imperceptibly and intending to entrap.

Many young people are trapped into drug addiction by the false reasoning and other *insidious* tactics of the drug pusher.

Related Forms: insidiously, insidiousness

Synonyms: sly, crafty, deceptive, perfidious, underhanded, surreptitious, stealthy, furtive, treacherous, artful, guileful, beguiling, wily

Antonyms: frank, candid, guileless, ingenuous, naive

Phrases: an insidious virus; with insidious intent; underhand practice; parading under false colors

---

O, what a tangled web, we weave
When first we practise to deceive.

— SCOTT

---

274. in-sip-id ĭn-sĭp'-ĭd [*in* (Latin), "not" + *sapidus,,* "tasteful"] — Without taste; hence, uninteresting or dull; lifeless.

There is nothing *insipid* about G.B. Shaw's style; throughout his works the famous writer exhibits a keen, often a biting, wit.

Related Forms: insipidly, insipidity, insipidness

Synonyms: jejune, flat, vapid, vacuous, wishy-washy, unsavory, monotonous, unanimated, lackluster

Antonyms: savory, salty, pungent, lively, piquant, sparkling, coruscating, animated, sapid, racy

275. in-trep-id ĭn-trĕp'-ĭd [*in* (Latin), "not" + *trepidus,* "alarmed"] — Without fear; brave.

New ideas and discoveries can only be carried out by people *intrepid* enough to disregard personal safety and altruistic enough to ignore self-interest.

Related Forms: intrepidly, intrepidity

Synonyms: daring, doughty, valiant, stalwart, courageous, redoubtable, valorous, gallant, dauntless, undaunted, mettlesome

Antonyms: fearful, frightened, disheartened, apprehensive, timorous, cowardly, craven, pusillanimous (see page 395), poltroon

328

276. in-trin-sic ĭn-trĭn'-sĭk [*intra* (Latin), "within" + *secus*, "beside"] — Pertaining to the essential nature of a thing.

Stacy hoped that his friends would judge him by his *intrinsic* worth rather than by the fact that his father is a millionaire.

Related Form: intrinsical

Synonyms: inherent, basic, innate, inbred, ingrained, inborn, real, essential, constitutional

Antonyms: extrinsic, extraneous

277. in-veigh ĭn-vā' [*invehere* (Latin), "carry against," "attack with words"; from *in*, "against" + *vehere*, *vectus*, "carry"] — To speak reproachfully, angrily, or bitterly.

Surely only a cruel person would *inveigh* against government spending for aid to abandoned children.

Synonyms: reproach, vituperate, denounce, declaim, rail, fulminate

Antonyms: praise, eulogize, commend, laud, extol

Note: The preposition "against" is used with the verb "inveigh."

He inveighed against the manner in which the prize winner had been selected.

The noun "invective" means "violent accusation, wordy abuse."

278. in-vei-gle ĭn-vē'-g'l ĭn-vā'-g'l [*aveugler* (French), "to blind"; from *ab* (Latin), "from" + *oculis*, "eye"] — To lead astray or persuade by deception or flattery.

Beware of the door-to-door salesman who tries to *inveigle* you into buying things you do not want.

Related Form: inveiglement

329

Synonyms: decoy, allure, beguile, seduce (*adj.* seductive), entice, cajole, wheedle, trick, lure

Antonyms: dissuade, deter

Phrase: a slick (suave, smoothly adroit) talker

Note: To <u>allure</u> means to tempt by attractive promises.

To <u>entice</u> is to allure by clever means.

To <u>beguile</u> means to tempt by guile or trickery.

To <u>cajole</u> is to persuade by flattery.

To <u>inveigle</u> is to tempt by blinding the victim to the truth of the situation.

To <u>decoy</u> is to trick a person by false show.

To <u>seduce</u> is to lead away from the proper or the right course.

279. in-vet-er-ate ĭn-vĕt′-ēr-ăt [from *vetus* (Latin), "old"] — Deeply rooted; of long standing.

My uncle is an *inveterate* opera lover; every season he attends at least one performance of every opera presented in our Civic Auditorium.

Related Forms: inveterately, inveterateness

Synonyms: chronic, habitual, ingrained, persistent, hardened (as a hardened criminal), deep-seated, confirmed (in a belief or practice — an inveterate racing fan, a confirmed believer in God)

Antonyms: incipient (budding); *nouns:* novice, neophyte

280. i-ras-ci-ble ĭ-răs′-ĭ-b′l ĭ-răs′-ĭ-b′l [*ira* (Latin), "anger"] — Easily angered.

Scrooge is pictured in *A Christmas Carol* as an *irascible* old miser, lacking in compassion and quickly provoked to anger.

Related Forms: irascibly, irasicibility, irascibleness

Synonyms: choleric, petulant, testy, splenetic, cross, touchy, irritable, excitable

Phrases: an *irascible* temperament

330

an *irascible* retort

an *irate* (enraged) customer

281. i-ro-ny ĭ'-rŏ-nĭ [*eironia* (Greek), "pretended ignorance"]

1. A combination of circumstances or a line of conduct or a situation the result of which is the direct opposite of what would normally be expected or hoped for. The result is as though it were directed by malice or the perversity of fate or done to mock the proper result.

> Mussolini died strung up like a pig. It was one of life's *ironies* that such should be the ignominious end for a proud dictator who sought eternal glory in conquest.

2. *Verbal irony* is used when making a statement that intends to convey the opposite of what it says literally, as when Mark Anthony, in the famous lament over the dead body of Julius Caesar, calls Brutus and his fellow conspirators "honorable men, so are they all, all honorable men."

> The expression of disgust on the face of the art connoisseur made the *irony* in his voice unmistakable when he said, pointing to the piece of crushed metal on display, "Now, that is what I call *real* art."

3. *Tragic irony* is a dramatic quality in which a speech or an action on the stage is fully grasped by the previously informed audience but its full and real significance is lost on the actor who is not so informed. For example: Lady Macbeth hails with inordinate flattery her guest King Duncan whom she had made plans to murder in the castle presently. King Duncan replies to extravagant speech by saying he is pleased to come to the castle to be treated like a guest. The audience realizes that he is walking into a trap, but he, of course, is unaware of that fact.

Related Forms: ironic, ironical

Synonyms: sarcasm, satire, mockery, sardonic (bitterly ironical)

One of the late Mahatma Gandhi's followers once observed that "it costs a lot of money to keep Gandhi in poverty," referring to the costly arrangements that were necessary to provide for the Mahatma and his extensive entourage when the Indian leader carried his freedom crusade into the slums of Indian cities.

---

282. jaun-ty jôn'-tĭ jän'-tĭ [*gentil* (French), "gentle"] — Having an air of easy carelessness or liveliness.

Mr. Walther's lively curiosity, quick wit, and *jaunty* manner belied his age, which was well past seventy.

Related Forms: jauntily, jauntiness

Synonyms: swaggering, perky, pert, gay, airy, sprightly, jovial, light-hearted

Antonyms: somber, sedate, staid, lugubrious, solemn

Phrases: smartly dressed
a Beau Brummel (a fop or dandy, one who consciously tries to set the fashion)
walked at a jaunty pace

283. jeer jĭr (*verb* and *noun*) [Source uncertain] — To cry out mockingly or contemptuously.

The rebellious students *jeered* at the school administrator when he stated that he would expell anyone involved in the riot.

Synonyms: gibe, scoff, ridicule, deride, hoot, fleer, flout, sneer; twit, taunt (tease scornfully)

Antonyms: cheer; sulk (stand aloof in a sullen mood); fawn (seek favor by servile conduct), truckle

Phrases: a cutting remark
curled his lips in a sneer
jeered the speaker off the platform

284. jeop-ard-ize jĕp'-ēr-dīz [*jeu parti* (Old French), "literally, a divided game, in which the chances are equal; hence, a risk, a hazard"] — To bring into danger, loss, or injury.

A student who gets mediocre grades in high school *jeopardizes* his chances of being admitted to college.

Related Form: jeopardy

Synonyms: imperil, hazard, risk, expose

Antonyms: secure, protect, shield

285. jos-tle jŏs''l [*justil* (M. English), "to joust; to push vigorously in combat"] To push rudely or roughly against another.

The day was hot and tempers flared as the crowds of people *jostled* their way into the bus.

Related Form: jostler

Synonyms: collide (with), bump (against), elbow (roughly), joggle, hustle, jolt, jar, jog, jounce, buffet

EXERCISES

I. Words Out of Context

In each group below, select the word or expression that most clearly expresses the meaning of the word at the left.

1. **jostle**
   (a) banter (b) elbow roughly
   (c) compete (d) unsettle

2. **jeer**
   (a) jerk (b) exult over
   (c) scoff rudely (d) boast

3. **inert**
   (a) inactive (b) fatuous
   (c) irrepressible (d) swiftly flowing

4. **inordinate**
   (a) without calculation (b) insufficient
   (c) numerically inferior (d) excessive

5. **inveigh** (*a*) eulogize (*b*) abuse bitterly
(*c*) inspect closely (*d*) allure

6. **insidious** (*a*) besieged (*b*) scrupulously honest
(*c*) implacable (*d*) treacherous

7. **intrepid** (*a*) quivering (*b*) well-armed
(*c*) fearful (*d*) fearless

8. **inveterate** (*a*) deep-rooted (*b*) caustic
(*c*) mild-mannered (*d*) peevish

9. **inexorable** (*a*) compassionate (*b*) unyielding
(*c*) compliant (*d*) incorruptible

10. **jeopardize** (*a*) imperil (*b*) secure
(*c*) immunize (*d*) renege

II. Words in Context

A. One-Word Omissions

*In each of the following sentences substitute for the blank
an appropriate word (or its related form) from words 266-285
on the Basic Vocabulary List.*

1. Why are you so _____ this morning? Did you get out of
the wrong side of the bed?

2. When Professor Cutting referred to the most stupid fellow
in class as his "learned friend," the _____ of the Professor's remark was quite obvious.

3. The sailor, his hat perched on his head at a very precarious
angle, swung in a(n) _____ manner down the street.

4. The _____ value of my lost ring is not great, but to me its
sentimental value is considerable; it was a gift from my
grandfather.

5. Throughout the long, moving address of the defense attorney, Judge Black sat silent and _____; no one could
tell by looking at him whether he was at all touched by
the recital.

B. Words in a Continuous Passage

In each passage below, certain words are underlined and numbered. Following each passage is a group of questions in which each of the numbered words is followed by the letters (a) to (d). Select the identifying letter of the word or phrase that is closest in meaning to each underlined word as it is used in the selection.

No man ought to be molested[1] on account of his opinions, not even on account of his religious opinions, provided the avowal[2] of them does not disturb the public order established by the law.

— *Declaration of the Rights of Man*
(by the French National Assembly, X, 1789)

1. molested   (a) insulted (b) harassed
                   (c) questioned (d) jeered

2. avowal   (a) frank declaration (b) defamation
                   (c) refutation (d) investigation

One word is too often profaned[3]
For me to profane it.

One feeling too falsely disdained[4]
For thee to disdain it,

One hope is too like despair[5]
For prudence to smother,

And pity from thee more dear
Than that from another.

— PERCY BYSSHE SHELLEY

3. profaned   (a) abused (b) cursed
                   (c) desecrated (d) plagiarized

4. disdained   (a) proclaimed (b) disowned
                   (c) eulogized (d) scorned

5. despair   (a) lack of hope (b) forgiveness
                   (c) default (d) depression

III. Analogies

Complete the following analogies:

1. curb : foster = (a) expostulate : infiltrate
   (b) emigrate : immigrant (c) thwart : substitute
   (d) extirpate : engender

2. cactus : asparagus = (a) gray : green
   (b) unpalatable : edible (c) plant : legume
   (d) garnish : condiment

3. clamor : hum = (a) vociferation : drone
   (b) bang : strike (c) warble : sing
   (d) whisper : growl

4. excavate : slash = (a) mow : scythe
   (b) hollow out : sever (c) inter : lop (d) dig : slog

5. impede : retard = (a) hasten : delay (b) walk : run
   (c) stymie : crush (d) thwart : slacken

WORD BUILDING

I. PREPOSITION

The Latin preposition **intra-, intro-,** "within" "inside," is a source element in *intrinsic*, studied in this lesson.

> *intramural* — within the precincts (literally, walls) of a school
>
> *introspective* — looking within oneself

II. ROOTS

A. The Latin root **ira**, "anger" appears in a number of English words, including *irascible*, studied in this lesson.

B. The Latin element **in-**, "not" (*inscrutable*), and roots **ferre**, "to carry" (*inference*), **gen-** "kind" (*ingenious*) and **sed-** "sit" (*insidious*) were analyzed in a previous lesson.

EXERCISES

I. Etymology Mastery Test

1. *Define and trace the origin of each of the following words.*
   intravenous   interracial   obsession   sedative   irate
   progeny   genetics

2. *Give the negative form of each of the following words.*
   typical   existent   malleable   operative   revocable

3. What is the difference between *interstate* and *intrastate*?
   Define each of the following:
   extraterritorial rights   extrovert   introvert

4. Consult the dictionary for the story behind the phrase
   Dies Irae.

II. Word Building and Analysis

1. What is "inductive reasoning"? How does it differ from
   reasoning that is "deductive"? Illustrate each mode of reasoning by a group of sentences. Which of these processes
   does the modern scientist use most?

2. Give five English words that have the same root as that of
   inference. Explain the meaning of the name *Lucifer* by
   analyzing the component parts *lux* (meaning "light") and
   fer (meaning "to carry"). What is the name of the great
   English poet and of the epic he wrote in which Lucifer
   plays an important part?

3. Which of the following people would be most likely to use
   invective? (*a*) a Congressman recently elected to office
   (*b*) your closest friend   (*c*) a district attorney summing
   up a case against an accused murderer

4. What qualities have these words in common: *sarcasm,
   irony, satire?*

5. Referring to (*a*) a Shakespearean play or (*b*) an incident in the life of a person you know or have read about,
   illustrate the meaning of *irony.* You may cite an ironic
   anecdote about Gandhi.

III. Fun With Words

The Gen Family

Hundreds of English words are derived from the parent Latin root **gen-**, from *genus*, meaning "birth," "race," or "kind." The following exercises aim to help you see some interesting relationships in this prolific family.

1. *Generate* means "to produce." Explain the meaning of each of the following words, which have a close link to this word: *engender, degenerate, generation, unregenerate.*

2. (*a*) What is homogenized milk? Why is this milk so called? (*b*) What would heterogenized milk be, if such a product could be made? (*c*) What is the opposite of *homogeneous*?

3. *Ingenuous* means "free from guile or deceit." An *ingenuous* person is one who is simple by nature. *Ingenious* means "clever, resourceful, adroit." An *ingenious* person is one who is born with such ability. In the light of the distinction between *ingenuous* and *ingenious* explain the meaning of each of the following phrases or sentences:

   (*a*) an *ingenuous* comment;

   (*b*) an *ingenious* device;

   (*c*) Henry was too *ingenuous* to believe that the pedlar had intended to cheat him.

   (*d*) Only a person as *ingenious* as John would think up such a contraption.

4. What kind of character on the stage is called the *ingenue*?

5. (*a*) Define *gentleman*. (*b*) What is a *gentle* person? (*c*) Who were the *gentry* during the thirteenth century? (*d*) What quality in a person five hundred years ago would entitle him to be termed a gentleman? (*e*) Show how we can trace a number of fundamental changes in society during the past five or six centuries by noting the changes in the meaning of such words as *gentle* and *gentleman*.

LESSON TWENTY

286.	judicious	296.	magnanimous
287.	laconic	297.	marital
288.	latent	298.	matriculate
289.	laudable	299.	maudlin
290.	lethargy	300.	mendacious
291.	levity	301.	mendicant
292.	loquacious	302.	mercenary
293.	lucrative	303.	meticulous
294.	lugubrious	304.	mitigate
295.	lurid	305.	mollify

286 ju-di-cious jōō-dĭsh'-ŭs [*judicium* (Latin), "judgment"]
— Exhibiting or using sound judgment.

Thanks to Leo's *judicious* advice, we refrained from rushing into an unwise ill-considered course of action.

Related Form: judiciousness

Synonyms: discreet, sage, politic, prudent, sensible, discerning, sober, circumspect

Antonyms: unwise, indiscreet, impolitic, imprudent, ill-advised, rash

Note the difference between judicious and judicial, both of which basically have the core meaning of wise judgment. Judicious suggests the use or characteristic of carefully balanced judgment in action or in dealing with people, as a judicious measure for heading off inflation. Judicial connotes a fair and impartial judgment in a court of law, as a judicial manner in presiding at a trial.

Give every man thine ear, but few thy voice;
Take each man's censure, but
reserve thy judgment.
— SHAKESPEARE, *Hamlet*

---

287. la-con-ic lă-kŏn'-ĭk [*Laconicos* (Greek), "a dweller of Laconia, a state in southeastern Greece, of which Sparta was the capital"] — Given to the use of few words, to the point, succinct.

When reproached for his long silence, he made the *laconic* reply, "I had nothing worth saying."

Related Forms: laconical, laconically

Synonyms: terse, pithy, concise, sententious, brief, pointed

Antonyms: prolix, wordy, verbose, diffuse, circumlocutory, periphrastic

Note: In the southern peninsula of Greece lies Peloponnesus, which was divided into seven countries. From these lands the Greek language received a number of useful and interesting words, which in turn have been adopted by the English-speaking peoples. Arcadia, a mountainous country, gave us the word Arcadian, which means "simple, or rustic." Laconia contributed laconic. The inhabitants of Sparta, the capital of Laconia, being noted for their stern military discipline and stoicism, contributed the adjective spartan, meaning "rigid, severe, stern, austere." A spartan meal is one that is sparse or frugal. To be spartan is to be unflinching in courage and endurance.

288. la-tent lā'-tĕnt [*latens* (Latin), "hidden"] — Present in some form, but not visible or fully developed.

Given a more favorable environment John's *latent* talents which are now dormant could be brought out and developed to the fullest.

Related Form: latency

Synonyms: dormant, quiescent, potential

Antonyms: operative, manifest

Phrases: a latent disease; latent powers

Note the fine distinction between latent and potential, both of which refer to possibilities that exist but are not revealed. Latent suggests the idea of hidden character, as latent talent (not visible or apparent) while potential connotes a state of undevelopment but capable of fuller development at some future time, as a potential genius.

289. laud-able lôd'-á-b'l [*laudabilis* (Latin), from *laudare*, "to praise"] — Worthy of commendation or praise.

Mary is much deserving of praise for the *laudable* record she has made despite the handicap of a year of illness.

Related Forms: laudable, laudability, laud, laudatory, laudation

Synonyms: commendable, praiseworthy, meritorious

Antonyms: condemnatory, objectionable, exceptionable

290. leth-ar-gy lĕth'-ēr-jĭ [*lethargia* (Greek), "forgetfulness"] — Drowsiness or apathy.

Why is it that when I am doing something I enjoy, no matter how difficult, there is never any feeling of *lethargy* but only a sensation of exhilaration?

Related Forms: lethargic, lethargical, lethargize (to stupefy)

Synonyms: inaction, indifference, torpor (n. torpidity), languidness, inertness

Antonyms: alertness, nimbleness, readiness, alacrity, agility

---

According to Greek mythology, Lethe is a river in Hades. It has often been referred to by poets as the River of Oblivion, for anyone who drank its water lost remembrance of the past. The adjective lethean *denotes forgetfulness or oblivion.*

---

291. lev-i-ty lĕv'-ĭ-tĭ [*levis* (Latin), "light in weight"] — Frivolity or lack of seriousness.

My method is to take the utmost trouble to find the right thing to say, and then to say it with the utmost *levity*.

— GEORGE BERNARD SHAW

Synonyms: flippancy, jocularity, gaiety, triviality

Antonyms: gravity, seriousness, earnestness, solemnity, sobriety, grimness

292. lo-qua-cious lō-kwā'-shŭs [*loquax* (Latin), "talkative"; from *loqui*, "to speak"] — Disposed to an undue amount of talking.

I did not enjoy the movies Saturday afternoon, for the audience consisted mostly of *loquacious* children who chattered incessantly.

Related Forms: loquaciously, loquaciousness, loquacity

Synonyms: garrulous, talkative, chattering, babbling, prolix, wordy

Antonyms: reticent, taciturn, close-mouthed, tight-lipped, silent, laconic

Note: The word <u>loquacious</u> is gradually developing a <u>pejorative</u> (i.e. disparaging) sense, though it still retains the meaning "a disposition to talk freely," sometimes with too little restraint.

293. lu-cra-tive lū'-krǎ-tĭv [*lucrum* (Latin), "gain"] — Profitable.

During the eighteenth century New England enjoyed a *lucrative* "triangular trade" in molasses, rum, and slaves.

Related Forms: lucratively, lucrativeness, lucre (meaning "riches" — now used in a bad or scornful sense)

Synonyms: gainful, advantageous, remunerative, money-making

Antonyms: unprofitable, unremunerative

Phrase: filthy lucre (an echo of Timothy's phrase in the Bible: "not greedy of filthy lucre")

294. lu-gu-bri-ous lŭ-gū'-brĭ-ŭs [*lugere* (Latin) "to mourn"] — Mournful; dismal-looking.

We could tell by the *lugubrious* expression on Bo Peep's face that she had lost her sheep.

Related Forms: lugubriously, lugubriousness

Synonyms: funereal, doleful, melancholic, baleful, sorrowful, depressed, solemn, grievous, sad, dreary

Antonyms: lively, gay, sprightly, gladsome, jocund, joyous, blithe

295. lu·rid lū′-rĭd [*luridus* (Latin), "pale yellow"]

1. Sensational, shocking, as, for example, a *lurid* crime; glaringly vivid, as *lurid* details.

> Do you think that more copies of *Macbeth* would be sold if it bore a *lurid* cover depicting a distraught Lady Macbeth wringing her bloody hands?

Synonyms: gruesome, revolting

2. Ghastly; dimly glowing, as light seen through fog or smoke.

> Although we knew we were watching an eclipse of the sun, the *lurid* light it produced evoked in us a feeling of apprehension.

Synonyms: murky, lowering (lour′-ing), wan, pale, pallid

Related Form: luridness

296. mag·nan·i·mous măg-năn′-ĭ-mŭs [*magnanimus* (Latin), from *magnus,* "great" + *animus,* "mind"] — Possessing or showing greatness of soul; rising above pettiness or meanness.

> The losing contestant showed that he was *magnanimous* by rushing over to offer his hand to his opponent.

Related Forms: magnanimously, magnanimousness, magnanimity (pronounced măg-nă-nĭm′-ĭty)

Synonyms: high-minded, generous, noble, altruistic (see page 41), lofty, exalted, unselfish

Antonyms: ignoble, pusillanimous, despicable, petty, low-spirited, vindictive

Note: A <u>magnanimous</u> person is one who is generous in adversity, defeat, or victory.

A <u>generous</u> or <u>benevolent</u> person is one who is unselfish or noble in giving to others.

> *Magnanimity in politics is not seldom the truest wisdom; and a great empire and little minds go ill together.*
>   — BURKE, *Conciliation with America*

---

297. mar·i·tal măr′-ĭ-tăl [*maritus* (Latin), "married"] — Pertaining to marriage or the married state.

The marriage counsellor, after several conferences with both husband and wife, succeeded in adjusting the couple's *marital* difficulties.

Synonyms: conjugal, matrimonial, connubial, nuptial (the rites and ceremonies attending marriage)

Antonyms: celibate (*noun:* celibacy), spinsterish

Phrases: marriage of convenience (marriage for the sake of advancing one's social position); in holy wedlock

Note: Do not confuse marital with martial, "warlike."

298. ma·tric·u·late mȧ-trĭk′-ū-lāt [*matricula* (Late Latin), "a register"] — To enroll or be admitted to a college or a university.

The freshmen who *matriculated* at the college spent a week before classes began in an orientation course on the school courses and general procedures.

Related Form: matriculation

Synonym: register

299. maud·lin môd′-lĭn [*Madeleine* (Old French), "Magdalen," who is often pictured with eyes swollen with tears of penitence] — Foolishly sentimental to the point of being easily moved to tears; incapable of controlling emotion.

My mother claims that she misses the movies of her youth — particularly the *maudlin* ones that were called "tear jerkers."

Synonyms: mawkish, effusive, tearful, lachrymose

Antonyms: unsentimental, unemotional, stolid, restrained

300. men·da·cious měn-dā′-shŭs [*mendax, mendacis* (Latin), "lying"] — Given to falsehood.

It is ironical that a *mendacious* person so often comes to believe his lies that he lives two lives — a real one and an imaginary one.

344

Related Forms: mendaciously, mendaciousness, mendacity

Synonyms: false, lying, untruthful, deceitful, dissimulating, prevaricating, buncombe (*colloquial*), charlatanism

Antonyms: veracious, truthful

Phrases: a pathological liar; a put-on (slang vogue word); a trumped-up charge

---

The man who fears no truths has nothing to fear from lies.

— THOMAS JEFFERSON

---

301. men-di-cant (*noun and adjective*) [měn'-dǐ-kănt *mendicans, mendicantis* (Latin), from *mendicus,* "beggar"] — Begging; a beggar.

Touched by the sight of the man in tattered clothes I dropped a dime into the *mendicant's* cap.

Related Forms: mendicancy, mendicity (the practice of begging)

Antonym: spurning

Note: <u>Mendicant</u> is also a noun. It refers to one who makes a business of begging, and is used especially for the members of certain religious orders that live by alms.

The beggar fears no reverses in fortune.

— BHARTRIHARI

---

302. mer-ce-na-ry mûr'-sė-nȧ-rǐ [*merces* (Latin), "wages," "reward"] — Influenced by, or acting only for, profit or reward.

A person who is actuated by *mercenary* motives should not go into teaching or the ministry, for his material rewards will not be great in either of these professions.

Related Forms: mercenarily, mercenariness

345

Synonyms: greedy, selfish, hireling, venal, grasping, avaricious, covetous

Antonyms: altruistic, unselfish, generous

Note: As a noun, mercenary means a soldier who is hired by and paid by a foreign government; a hireling.

303. me-tic-u-lous mē-tĭk′-ū-lŭs [*meticuleux* (French); from *metus* (Latin), "fear"] — Originally, fearful; now, giving excessive attention to unimportant details or trifles.

The princess's playhouse was a replica of the palace, complete in every detail to a *meticulous* degree.

Related Forms: meticulously, meticulousness

Synonyms: careful, finical, fastidious, finicky, particular, punctilious, over-nice, fussy, precise, demanding

Antonyms: careless, slovenly, neglectful

304. mit-i-gate mĭt′-ĭ-gāt [*mitigatare* (Latin), "soften"] — To soften or make less severe or painful; to relieve.

The director of the youth center formulated a constructive program which he hoped would *mitigate* the problem of juvenile delinquency.

Related Forms: mitigation, mitigative, mitigatory

Synonyms: assuage, allay, alleviate, moderate, soothe, mollify

Antonyms: arouse, incite, aggravate, worsen

305. mol-li-fy mŏl′-ĭ-fī [*mollis* (Latin), "soft" + *facere*, "to make"] — To calm or pacify; to make less severe.

The mayor's promise to "investigate the situation" did little to *mollify* the anger of the people who had heard such promises before.

Related Forms: mollification, mollifier

Synonyms: soothe, quiet, placate, appease, mitigate, assuage, pacify

Antonyms: intensify, aggravate, sharpen, heighten

346

EXERCISES

I. Words Out of Context

In each group below, select the word or expression that most clearly expresses the meaning of the word at the left.

1. **latent**
   (*a*) quiescent (*b*) unpunctual
   (*c*) curt (*d*) pithy

2. **lucrative**
   (*a*) financial (*b*) profitable
   (*c*) unprofitable (*d*) very clear

3. **magnanimous**
   (*a*) courageous (*b*) generous in forgiving (*c*) vindictive
   (*d*) exhilarating

4. **matriculate**
   (*a*) master (*b*) enroll in college
   (*c*) supervise (*d*) graduate

5. **mendicant**
   (*a*) living by alms (*b*) audacious
   (*c*) lying (*d*) philanthropic

II. Words in Context

One-Word Omissions

In each of the following sentences substitute for the blank an appropriate word from Words 286-305 (including derivatives) on the Basic Vocabulary List.

1. Lincoln was so _____ that he harbored no ill will even against those who had done most to frustrate his plans.

2. When a friend is in trouble, help him without forcing him into telling you all the unhappy and possibly _____ details of his predicament.

3. The defense lawyer attacked the credibility of the witness for the prosecution, asserting that he could prove that this witness was notorious for his _____ stories.

4. Your new position will not at first be _____; until you learn the ropes, your salary will be merely nominal.

347

5. A _____ person is my bête noire, for I myself like a chance to get in a few words now and then.

6. An attitude of _____ is most indecorous at a funeral.

7. When my brother looks at me with that sad expression and begins to speak in a _____ tone of voice, I know he is about to ask me for something.

8. My 'mother sets the table with _____ care, seeing to it that every piece of silverware is exactly in the right position.

9. His friends were used to seeing him grow _____ as he talked about his boyhood; therefore they disregarded his tears.

III. Synonyms and Antonyms

A. Synonyms

Match the word in Column A with its synonym in Column B.

A	B
1. circumlocutory	(a) maudlin
2. quiescent	(b) jocund
3. gainful	(c) importunate
4. gruesome	(d) dormant
5. supplicating	(e) revolting
6. mawkish	(f) periphrastic
7. cheerful	(g) remunerative

B. Antonyms

Match the word in Column A with its antonym in Column B.

A	B
1. alacrity	(a) indiscreet
2. pusillanimous	(b) gravity
3. flippancy	(c) prevaricating
4. veracious	(d) torpidity
5. politic	(e) fearless

IV. Analogies

Complete the following analogies.

1. circumvent : law = (*a*) shirk : responsibility
   (*b*) quibble : issue   (*c*) sidestep : manhole
   (*d*) elude : pursuit

2. typhoon : zephyr = (*a*) hubbub : racket
   (*b*) bass : soprano   (*c*) clamorous : dulcet
   (*d*) jangle : jingle

3. secret : clandestine = (*a*) manifest : obvious
   (*b*) covert : overt   (*c*) latent : patent
   (*d*) circuitous : candid

4. coercive : permissive = (*a*) edict : will
   (*b*) policeman : parent   (*c*) refusal : allowance
   (*d*) must : may

5. chicanery : subterfuge = (*a*) deception : subversion
   (*b*) candor : frankness   (*c*) circumspection : evasion
   (*d*) hypocrisy : sincerity

WORD BUILDING

I. ROOTS

A. The Latin root **loqui, locutus,** "to talk," is the source of many English words, including *loquacious,* studied in this lesson.

elocution — the art of public speaking

eloquent — forcibly and movingly expressive

B. The Latin root **magnus,** "great," is a source element in the word *magnanimous* studied in this lesson.

magnify — to make great

C. The Latin root **merc-,** from **merces** "pay" "reward," is the source of a number of English words, including *mercenary* studied in this lesson.

merchant — one who trades (usually on a large scale)

mercy — a reward or favor (as from God)

D. The Latin root **anima** "mind," "soul," "living being," is the source of many English words including *magnanimous* studied in this lesson.

animate — to give life to

animosity — hostility in action or mind

II. SUFFIXES

The Latin suffix -**us** (other form **ose**) "full of" "characterized by" is used especially in adapting adjectives from Latin ending in -*us* and from Greek ending in -*os*.

beauteous — full of beauty

courageous — full of courage

EXERCISES

I. Word Building Activities

1. *Define in the light of their origin:*

   obloquy   interlocutor   soliloquy   mercantile

2. *Change the following words into adjectival form by adding the Latin suffix* -**us** *or* -**ose**.

verb	tedium	miscellany
error	right	bounty

3. *All of the following words contain the root* **anima**. *Define each word, give its etymology and use each in a short sentence.*

   animism   animus   equanimity   animadversion

II. Word Analysis and Development

1. A man referred to as a "baseball magnate" is probably (*a*) an outfielder (*b*) a sports writer (*c*) the owner of a professional team (*d*) an expert on the game.

2. If you were to purchase a *magnum opus*, would you be buying (*a*) a big animal (*b*) a literary masterpiece (*c*) a bottle of wine?

3. What is the difference in meaning and origin between *mendicant* and *mendacious*, *judicial* and *judicious*, *marital* and *martial*?

4. Each of the following words owes its meaning to a place noted in history, mythology, etc. Define the word and tell why the meaning is linked to its place of origin.

   Arcadian   laconic   spartan   sardonic   meandering

5. A *magnum* of wine contains (*a*) a pint (*b*) a quart (*c*) a gallon (*d*) two-fifths of a gallon

III. Using the Dictionary

A. Critical Attitudes

1. Each of the following words describes various critical attitudes such as dispraise, depreciation, or excessive flattery. Define each of them. You may consult a dictionary.

diatribe	philippic	tirade	obloquy	cavil
ingratiate	cajole	acclaim	eulogy	scorn

2. Arrange the words above in two columns, one headed by *dispraise*, and the other headed by *flattery*.

B. Emotional Attitudes

Define each of the following short words which express graphically a person's reaction to an event or his own sense of happiness or unhappiness. You may use the dictionary whenever necessary.

simper	whimper	chortle	snicker
guffaw	chuckle	whine	smirk

351

General Review III

(Lessons 1-20)

A. Words in a Continuous Passage

In the following paragraphs substitute for each blank an appropriate word selected from Words 1-305 (including derivatives) on the Basic Vocabulary List. The first letter of the appropriate word is given in each case. Synonyms of the more difficult words are provided at the end of the passage.

DIPLOMATS AND COMMON FOLKS

Diplomats deliver interminable speeches i..(1).. against war as an a..(2).., a throw-back to the Stone Age that is quite i..(3).. in the advanced civilization of today. Despite the i..(4).. verbal protestations of their pacific intentions, however, their actions j..(5).. world peace. For each diplomat seems intent on achieving not what is right in principle but what is e..(6).. as a means of a..(7).. the power and prestige of his own national group.

The great i..(8).. masses of the common folk in all lands, however, are a..(9).. toward this drive for power. These common folk long only for a protracted period of peace in which to bring order out of the c..(10).. of war. If it were f..(11).. to bring together in a peace conference these simple, common folk, they would soon put an end to every program of Power Politics. Only in these common folk lies our hope of averting a catastrophe that would e..(12).. all humanity and leave a vacant world drifting like a d..(13).. on the cosmic ocean of astral space.

Synonyms and Definitions of Difficult Words Above

1. denounc(ing)	8. unable to put into words
3. not appropriate	9. indifferent to
4. not ceasing	11. practicable
7. increasing	12. root out

B. Two-Word Omissions

In each selection below, you will find two blanks indicating the omission of a pair of words or phrases which will make the sense complete. Following the selection are four choices lettered (a) to (d). Select the item that you think will best complete the meaning of the selection.

14. One of the most hectic and _____ contested Presidential elections of the century took place in 1968, with public opinion polls suggesting that very possibly no candidate would obtain a majority of the electoral vote, so that the long, costly process would end in a(n) _____.

    (a) amiably — deadlock   (c) moderately — deadlock
    (b) intensely — impasse   (d) equitably — pandemonium

15. The Greek philosopher Diogenes was noted for his cold, _____ wisdom. He looked on the world sneeringly, regarding most men's actions as _____.

    (a) impartial — ignominious
    (b) compassionate — crass
    (c) dispassionate — altruistic
    (d) cynical — best

16. An assortment that is _____ is one that is _____.

    (a) miscellaneous — multitudinous
    (b) superabundant — heterogeneous
    (c) copious — profuse
    (d) diverse — homogeneous

17. To _____ a statement is to _____ it.

    (a) refute — corroborate
    (b) authenticate — ascertain
    (c) confirm — substantiate
    (d) verify — gainsay

18. In his famous book length eulogy of his parents, Edmund Gosse declares that he admired the detached way his mother endeavored to face the prospect of death with the _____ of a Roman matron, without the slightest _____,

calm in her conviction of the righteousness of divine judgment.

(a) fortitude — apprehension
(b) austerity — stoicism
(c) complacency — deference
(d) conviviality — dread

C. Words Out of Context

In each group below, select the word, or expression that most clearly expresses the meaning of the word at the left.

19. abject   (a) proud   (b) pessimistic   (c) degraded   (d) oppressed

20. laconic   (a) loquacious   (b) nebulous   (c) mocking   (d) sparing in words

21. accord   (a) disorder   (b) tieup   (c) separation   (d) agreement

22. exonerate   (a) free from blame   (b) relieve a person's burden   (c) swear falsely   (d) suspect

23. diffident   (a) unfaithful   (b) reserved   (c) contradictory   (d) divisive

24. dilemma   (a) challenge   (b) delay   (c) quandary   (d) a crucial error

25. epithet   (a) tombstone   (b) peak   (c) characterization   (d) witty saying

26. discomfiture   (a) frustration   (b) lack of comfort   (c) helplessness   (d) wrong size

27. epicure   (a) stoic   (b) hermit   (c) dandy   (d) connoisseur of food

28. esoteric   (a) exclusive   (b) queer   (c) superfluous   (d) insincere

29. exigency   (a) pressing need   (b) rebellion   (c) bribery   (d) opportunism

30. euphony　　　　　(a) hypocrisy　(b) harmony of sound
　　　　　　　　　　(c) religious holiday　(d) discord

31. accessory　　　　(a) supplement　(b) antagonist
　　　　　　　　　　(c) essential part　(d) gadget

32. disparity　　　　(a) indifference　(b) inequality
　　　　　　　　　　(c) contradiction　(d) in low spirits

33. exacerbate　　　(a) irritate　(b) curse
　　　　　　　　　　(c) mollify　(d) attack

34. abet　　　　　　(a) dissuade　(b) encourage
　　　　　　　　　　(c) challenge　(d) minimize

35. derogatory　　　(a) clamorous　(b) mocking
　　　　　　　　　　(c) depreciatory　(d) calling out

36. exotic　　　　　(a) not generally known　(b) imported
　　　　　　　　　　(c) peculiar　(d) strange

37. acrimonious　　(a) generous　(b) onerous
　　　　　　　　　　(c) thought-provoking　(d) biting

38. destitute　　　　(a) deprived　(b) lack of status
　　　　　　　　　　(c) hostility　(d) dilapidated

39. expatiate　　　　(a) spit　(b) be above board
　　　　　　　　　　(c) speak at great length　(d) expel

40. explicit　　　　(a) vague　(b) implicated
　　　　　　　　　　(c) obvious　(d) clearly stated

D. Words in Phrases

Each of the phrases below contains an italicized word or phrase and is followed by four words or phrases lettered (a) to (d). Select the letter preceding the item that is closest in meaning to the italicized word as used in the phrase.

41. A *cogent* reason　(a) plausible　(b) persuasive
　　(c) logical　(d) striking

42. Engaged in *skulduggery*　(a) long deliberation
　　(b) petty mischief　(c) assault and battery
　　(d) mean trickery

43. Took *circuitous* means to accomplish his end (*a*) round-about (*b*) direct (*c*) cautious (*d*) ineffectual

44. A general *hue and cry* (*a*) urgent demand (*b*) public cry of alarm (*c*) complaint (*d*) public demonstration

45. A *furtive* glance (*a*) fearful (*b*) distrustful (*c*) quick (*d*) stealthy

E. Analogies

Complete the following analogies.

46. ointment : burn = (*a*) palliative : peace (*b*) peace : rebellion (*c*) consolation : grief (*d*) levee : river

47. assuage : aggravate = (*a*) accord : discord (*b*) placate : worsen (*c*) allay : mitigate (*d*) alleviate : appease

48. attraction : fascination = (*a*) apathy : indifference (*b*) allergy : reaction (*c*) praise : adulation (*d*) love : affection

49. consolidate : unify = (*a*) merge : fusion (*b*) coalesce : diversify (*c*) synthesize : dichotomy (*d*) sunder : sever

50. toga : suit = (*a*) anachronism : fashionable (*b*) vogue : archaic (*c*) obsolete : contemporary (*d*) ensemble : apparel

F. Word Background

Define each of the following words, give its etymology, and use each in a short illustrative sentence.

51. bibliophile	54. ignominy
52. candid	55. impediment
53. harrowing	

356

LESSON TWENTY-ONE

306. moot	316. nocturnal
307. motley	317. noisome
308. mundane	318. nominal
309. munificent	319. nonchalance
310. murky	320. novice
311. mystique	321. noxious
312. naive	322. obdurate
313. nebulous	323. obese
314. nefarious	324. obliterate
315. neophyte	325. obloquy

306. moot mōot [*mot* (Anglo-Saxon), "a meeting for discussion"] — Subject to controversy, debate or discussion; doubtful.

The seemingly incontrovertible fact that one has a right to order one's own life becomes a *moot* point when this right interferes with the rights of others.

Synonyms: debatable, arguable, controvertible, disputable, controversial

Antonyms: incontrovertible, indubitable, indisputable, irrefutable

307. mot-ley mŏt'-lē [Source unknown] — Exhibiting various colors or elements.

A group of people composed of rich men, poor men, beggarmen, thieves, doctors, lawyers, and Indian chiefs would be a *motley* crew indeed.

Synonyms: dappled, multi-colored, variegated, diverse, checkered (usually used to refer to a varied career), piebald; a medley; heterogeneous

Antonym: monotone, homogeneous

357

Phrases: to wear the motley (the many-colored garment of the
medieval jester)
a motley (made up of diverse elements) crowd

Note 1: Motley is also a noun, meaning a woolen fabric of mixed colors; a
garment made from such material; a mixture of colors.

Note 2: Mottled is derived from motley and means "marked with spots or
blotches of varied colors."

> *They stripped Joseph out of his*
> *coat, his coat of many colors.*
>
> — THE BIBLE

---

308. mun-dane mŭn'-dān [*mundus* (Latin), "world"] —Pertaining to the world, universe, or earth (as contrasted
with heaven).

The group of savants interrupted their discussion about the effect of belief in God on the morality of man to turn their attention to the *mundane* matter of the restaurant menu.

Synonyms: worldly, earthly, terrestrial, secular, temporal;
banal, unimaginative

Antonyms: spiritual, heavenly, ecclesiastical, religious

Phrases: worldly success
mundane pursuits
the terrestrial globe

309. mu-nif-i-cent mū-nĭf'-ĭ-sĕnt [*munus* (Latin), "gift" +
facere, "to make"] — Liberal in giving; pertaining to a
gift that is vast in amount.

The philanthropist Harry Elkins Widener bestowed a great
library on Harvard College, one of the most *munificent* gifts that
the institution had ever received.

Related Forms: munificence, munificently

Synonyms: generous, bountiful, free-handed, lavish, benev-
olent, philanthropic, ungrudging, unsparing

---

*If riches increase, let thy mind hold pace
with them; and think it not enough to be
Liberal but* Munificent.

— SIR THOMAS BROWNE

---

310. murk-y mûrk'-ĭ [*mirce* (Anglo-Saxon), "dark"] — Gloomy; dark.

The *murky* night and the lurid glare of the lights gave the amusement park a depressing rather than a gay atmosphere.

Related Forms: murk (darkness), murkily, murkiness

Synonyms: dismal, fuliginous, tenebrous; dim, cheerless; hazy

Antonyms: clear, bright, resplendent, lustrous, luminous, fulgent, coruscating, glowing

Phrases: a *dark* (cheerless) prospect; a *dark* (secret) motive; the Dark Ages

311. mys-tique mĭ-stēk' [*mystikos* (Greek), "an initiate into the mysteries"] — A distinctive air or character of mystery and mystical power surrounding a person, or pursuit.

The *mystique* of John F. Kennedy, with its combination of youth and dynamic forward-looking purpose, strongly appealed to young people.

Synonyms: aura, emanation (a subtle radiation proceeding from a person or thing), charisma (the spiritual power of personal qualities that captivates large numbers of people)

312. na-ïve nä-ēv' [*naïf* (French), "native," "innate"] — Simple or unaffected in manner, usually suggesting a person with little worldly knowledge; lacking in sophistication.

Only a *naïve* person like Tom could be induced to invest his savings in such a fantastic scheme.

Related Forms: naïf, naïveté (pronounce the final e like *a* as in *way*), naïvely

Synonyms: unsophisticated, ingenuous, guileless, artless, unaffected, unsuspecting

Antonyms: sophisticated, affected, guileful, artful, cunning

313. **neb-u-lous** nĕb'-ū-lŭs [*nebulosus* (Latin), "misty," "cloudy"] — Cloudy; hazy or vague.

The administrator said that he would like to present the faculty with a well-formulated plan rather than a *nebulous* one.

Related Forms: nebulously, nebulousness, nebular, nebula (a faintly bright formation of clouds appearing in the heavens on a clear night)

Synonyms: misty, shadowy, obscure, confused, indefinite, indistinct

Antonyms: clear, distinct, comprehensible, certain, luminous

314. **ne-far-i-ous** nĕ-fâr'-ĭ-ŭs [*nefas* (Latin), "crime," "wrong"; from *ne*, "not" + *fas*, "divine law"] — Grossly wicked.

The newspaper exposed the *nefarious* operations of the corrupt politicians who were seeking to control the city government.

Related Forms: nefariously, nefariousness

Synonyms: heinous, flagitious, impious, infamous, iniquitous, detestable, criminal, execrable, abominable

Antonyms: good, virtuous, exemplary, innocent, honest

315. **ne-o-phyte** nē'-ĕ-fīt [*neo* (Greek), "new" + *phytos* "planted"] — A beginner.

Considering that Phil is only a *neophyte* in his profession, his progress in mastering some highly complicated technical procedures in so short a time has been phenomenal.

Related Form: neophytic

Synonyms: novice, tyro, apprentice

Antonyms: veteran, expert, adept, connoisseur

Phrases: to be green (a greenhorn) at (something)
a rooky (slang) "a recruit"
a skilled hand

316. noc-tur-nal nŏk-tûr′-năl [*nox, noctis* (Latin), "night"]
— Belonging to, or occurring in, the night.

The condition of my cat after he returns each morning from his *nocturnal* wanderings can only be described as disheveled.

Related Forms: nocturnally, nocturne (a composition of a pensive, melancholy character)

Synonym: nightly

Antonyms: diurnal (pertaining to the day), daily

317. noi-some noi′-sŭm [variant of *annoy* + *some*] — Unwholesome or harmful; foul-smelling.

The poor of Elizabethan London lived in *noisome* surroundings of open sewers and squalid dwellings.

Related Forms: noisomeness

Synonyms: noxious, disgusting, malodorous, putrid, offensive, fetid, mephitic, deleterious

Antonyms: salubrious, healthful; beneficial

Phrase: a noisome odor

Note: Do not confuse noisome with noisy, "making noise."

318. nom-i-nal nŏm′-ĭ-năl [*nomen, nominis* (Latin), "name"]
— Existing in name only; hence, so unimportant as to be unworthy of the name.

In Italy the President is only the *nominal* head of the state; actually the Prime Minister directs the government.

Related Form: nominally

Antonyms: real, actual

319. non-cha-lance nŏn′-shȧ-läns [*non*, "not" + *calere* (Latin), "to be warm"] — Indifference; gay or cool unconcern.

Though he was deeply concerned, he tried to hide his real feelings behind an air of *nonchalance*.

Related Forms: nonchalant, nonchalantly

Synonyms: casualness; unruffled, insouciant, blasé, lackadaisical

Antonyms: concerned, agitated, perturbed, ruffled

320. nov-ice nŏv′-ĭs [*novus* (Latin), "new"]

1. A beginner.

Nero, the emperor who supposedly fiddled while Rome burned, was a *novice* in the art of cruelty compared with Adolf Hitler, who practiced genocide.

Related Forms: novitiate or noviciate (the state of being a novice; the period of apprenticeship; the quarters set aside for novices)

Synonyms: neophyte, probationer, tyro, catechumen (a beginner in receiving religious instruction), learner, newcomer, apprentice

Antonyms: expert, adept, master

2. A candidate for a religious order who is on probation in a religious house.

The *novice* found his first days in the monastery lonely, but gradually he came to like the quiet and contemplative life it offered.

321. nox-ious nŏk′-shŭs [*noxius* (Latin), "harmful"; from *nocere*, "to hurt"] — Harmful to morals or health; destructive.

Some control is necessary to prevent the *noxious* waste products of industry from poisoning our air and water.

Related Form: noxiousness

Synonyms: baneful, pestiferous, corrupting, pernicious; noisome

Antonyms: beneficial, salubrious, salutary

322. ob-du-rate ŏb'-dŭ-rĭt [*ob* (Latin), "against" + *durus* "hard"] — Unyielding to persuasion; hard-hearted; persistently unrepentant.

Despite our persistent pleas to have him change his mind, he remained as *obdurate* in his decision as ever.

Related Forms: obduracy, obdurateness

Synonyms: inflexible, firm, intransigent, tenacious, obstinate, unbending, dogged, callous, impenitent

Antonyms: yielding, submissive, compliant; insensitive; penitent

Phrase: a stand-patter

323. o-bese ô-bēs' [*obesus* (Latin), "stout"] — Very fat.

Falstaff, in Shakespeare's *Henry IV*, is represented on the stage as an *obese* clown who is so fat that he "lards" the earth he walks on.

Related Forms: obesely, obeseness, obesity

Synonyms: stout, corpulent, fleshy, portly, adipose, rotund, beefy, pudgy, paunchy, burly

Antonyms: thin, emaciated, lean, haggard, gaunt

324. ob-lit-er-ate ŏb-lĭt'-ēr-āt [*ob* (Latin), "over" + *littera*, "letter"] — To efface or destroy completely.

Unless the great nations agree to control the spread of nuclear weapons, mankind will be *obliterated*.

Related Form: obliteration

Synonyms: blot out, expunge, erase, cancel, raze

Antonyms: perpetuate, memorialize

325. ob-lo-quy ŏb′-lō-kwĭ [*ob* (Latin), "against" + *loqui*, "to speak"]

1. Reproachful, abusive speech.

> The prosecutor for the state heaped *obloquy* upon the alleged spy for attempting to betray his country to the enemy.

2. The state or condition of being in disgrace.

> The colonel, who had recently had the esteem of his men, felt keenly the *obloquy* that followed the court-martial.

Synonyms: censure, invective, opprobrium, reprehension, dishonor, shame, disgrace, infamy, ignominy

Antonyms: eulogy, encomium, panegyric, praise, acclaim, commendation, honor, renown, glory, credit

EXERCISES

I. Words in Context

One-Word Omissions

In each of the following sentences substitute for the blank an appropriate word selected from Words 306-325 (or their derivatives) of the Basic Vocabulary List.

1. Commenting on the vast diversity of human nature, W. Somerset Maugham said, "How _____ are the elements that go to make up a human being!"

2. Whether civilization could survive another world war is still a _____ question.

3. Many a small town feels deeply grateful to Andrew Carnegie for his _____ gift of a free public library.

4. Friar Tuck, despite his clerical habit, was engaged in a very _____ activity; he was roasting a haunch of venison for the evening meal of Robin's Merry Men.

5. While you are getting your training in our business, your salary will be merely _____.

6. As a layman, I have only a very _____ idea of Einstein's theory of relativity.

II. Words Out of Context

In each group below select the word or expression that most clearly expresses the meaning of the word at the left.

1. **mystique**   (*a*) puzzle   (*b*) aura   (*c*) problem   (*d*) mystery

2. **neophyte**   (*a*) newcomer   (*b*) professional   (*c*) nocturnal animal   (*d*) apprentice

3. **noisome**   (*a*) foul-smelling   (*b*) annoying   (*c*) rowdy   (*d*) chaotic

4. **nonchalance**   (*a*) heterogeneity   (*b*) reluctance   (*c*) cool unconcern   (*d*) discord

5. **noxious**   (*a*) unearthly   (*b*) nightly   (*c*) treacherous   (*d*) injurious

6. **obdurate**   (*a*) stubborn   (*b*) objectionable   (*c*) eternal   (*d*) hostile

7. **nefarious**   (*a*) virtuous   (*b*) distant   (*c*) grossly wicked   (*d*) diversified

8. **obliterate**   (*a*) forget   (*b*) expunge   (*c*) spread   (*d*) interpose objection

9. **murky**   (*a*) blunt   (*b*) filthy   (*c*) dark   (*d*) humid

10. **nebulous**   (*a*) doubtful   (*b*) decisive   (*c*) ethereal   (*d*) hazy

III. Synonyms and Antonyms

Give two synonyms and one antonym for each of the following words.

mundane	obese	nefarious	nonchalant
murky	naïve	obdurate	noxious

WORD BUILDING

I. PREFIX

The Latin prefix **ob**, "before" "against" "completely," is the source of many English words including *obliterate* and *obloquy*, studied in this lesson.

obstruct — to bar passage against

obstacle (literally, *ob*, "against" + *stare*, "to stand") — something that stands in the way

II. ROOTS

A. The Greek root **neos**, "new" "recent" and its related Latin root **novus**, "new," are found in many English words including *neophyte* and *novice*, studied in this lesson.

novelty — newness

neo-facism — a new recent brand of fascism

B. The Latin root **littera**, "letter" is found in many English words including *obliterate*, studied in this lesson

illiterate — unable to read

literal — following the exact letter (or meaning)

EXERCISES

I. Word-Building Activities

1. *Define in the light of its origin each of the following words.*

   innovate   novitiate   Neo-Latin   neologism
   Neo-Darwinism

2. *Indicate the part which the prefix* **ob** *plays in the meaning of the following words.*

   obtrude   obsession   offer   (ob + ferre)   obloquy

3. A literal translation is one that   (*a*) translates the words of the original freely   (*b*) was erased originally by the author   (*c*) exactly represents the given words in the original

II. Fun With Words

A. What Time Is It?

Match the word in Column A with the appropriate period of time the word denotes in Column B.

A	B
1. **millennium**	(*a*) a period of ten years
2. **centenary**	(*b*) twenty years
3. **perennial**	(*c*) occurring at the same time
	(*d*) occurring in an instant
4. **aeon**	(*e*) 100th anniversary
5. **sesquicentennial**	(*f*) between 70 and 80 years old
6. **decade**	(*g*) 150th anniversary
	(*h*) perpetual; enduring
7. **score**	(*i*) an indefinitely long period of time
8. **septuagenarian**	(*j*) a period of a thousand years
9. **simultaneous**	
10. **instantaneous**	

B. Vogue Words

The vogue word *mystique* appears in the Basic Word List in this lesson. Now try to define the following vogue words.

1. **polarization**
2. **proliferation**
3. **charisma**
4. **neurosis**
5. **complex** (*noun*)
6. **escalation**

III. For the Ambitious Student

Define each of the following words, give its etymology, and use each in a short sentence.

1. **legate**
2. **lesion**
3. **libretto**
4. **limpid**
5. **litigation**
6. **logrolling**
7. **lout**
8. **macabre**
9. **mainstay**
10. **malapropism**

LESSON TWENTY-TWO

326. obsequious	338. ostracize
327. obsolete	339. panacea
328. obviate	340. pandemonium
329. odium	341. paradox
330. ominous	342. paragon
331. omniscient	343. paraphrase
332. opportunist	344. parsimonious
333. opprobrium	345. pastoral
334. opulence	346. pejorative
335. orthodox	347. penury
336. ostensible	348. peremptory
337. ostentation	349. perfunctory

350. pernicious

326. ob-se-qui-ous ŏb-sē′-kwĭ-ŭs [*ob* (Latin), "toward" + *sequi*, "to follow"] — Excessively or slavishly submissive; overly willing to obey.

The *obsequious* person will seek to ingratiate himself by patterning his behavior solely on what he thinks will please others.

Related Forms: obsequiously, obsequiousness

Synonyms: sycophantic, cringing, fawning, truckling, servile, meek, compliant, ingratiating

Antonyms: independent, condescending, proud, overbearing, arrogant, haughty, blustering, swaggering, supercilious

Phrase: to eat crow (to suffer humiliation)

327. ob-so-lete ŏb′-sṡ-lēt [*obsolescere* (Latin), "to wear out gradually," "to fall into disuse"] — No longer in use.

At one time the term "free trade" which means "unrestricted trade between countries," had a meaning, now *obsolete*, of "smuggling."

Related Forms: obsoleteness, obsolescent, obsolescence

Synonyms: unfashionable, out-of-date, discarded, old-fashioned, outworn, ancient, antiquated, archaic (when applied to language)

Antonyms: novel, fresh, new, fashionable; neologism (a newly coined word or phrase)

328. ob-vi-ate ŏb'-vĭ-āt [ob (Latin), "against" + via, "way"]
— To prevent or eliminate disadvantages or difficulties by anticipatory action; to render unnecessary.

Concentrating on your school work during the year will *obviate* the necessity to "cram" when exam time comes along.

Related Form: obviation

Synonyms: avert, preclude, anticipate

THAT WORD
Trivial

In former times it was a common practice for neighbors to meet at the crossroads to discuss ordinary things, to chat, gossip, etc. From this custom is derived our words trivial [tres (Latin) "three" + via "road," *the junction at which three roads converged and served as a station for small (trivial) talk*] *and* trivia, *meaning "inconsequential or inessential things."*

---

329. o-di-um ō'-dĭ-ŭm [odium (Latin), "hatred," perhaps originally derived from odor, "smell"] — The state or quality of being hated; the disgrace attached to something hated or reproachful.

Odium, not esteem, will be the reward of a person who advances himself at the expense of others.

Related Forms: odious, odiously, odiousness

Synonyms: abhorrence, opprobrium (see page 371), discredit, ignominy (see page 302), detestation, reproach, disgust, infamy, repugnance

Antonyms: eulogy, panegyric, flattery, commendation

There is no odor so bad as that
which arises from goodness tainted.

— THOREAU

---

330. om-i-nous ŏm'-ĭ-nŭs [*omen* (Latin), "a foreboding" +
osus, "full of"] — Pertaining to an evil omen; foreshadowing evil.

The *omnious* silence that greeted the proposal presented by one
of the member nations in the UN foreshadowed its eventual
defeat.

Related Forms: ominously, ominousness

Synonyms: threatening, sinister, portentous (*noun:* portent),
inauspicious, precursor, unpropitious, foreboding (*verb:*
bode)

Phrases: a bird of ill omen; of good omen

Note: The words <u>omen</u> and <u>portent</u> originally denoted something beneficial <u>or</u>
evil. However, the adjectives <u>ominous</u> and <u>portentous</u> in modern usage
connote evil or an unfortunate future event.

331. om-nis-cient ŏm-nĭsh'-ĕnt [*omnis* (Latin), "all" + *sciens, scientis,* "knowing"] — Having unlimited knowledge.

Kate is such a "know-it-all" that there are times when I think
she believes herself to be *omniscient.*

Related Forms: omniscience, omnisciently

Other **omni** words: omnipresent, omnifarious (of all kinds),
omnipotent (all powerful), omnivorous (eating all kinds of
foods indiscriminately)

332. op-por-tu-nist ŏp-ŏr-tū'-nĭst [*ob* (Latin), "opposite" +
portus "harbor"] — One who takes advantage of circumstances to promote his own interest regardless of his
stated principles or party loyalty, etc.; one who defers
his action for a time best suitable for his advantage.

Did the Senator change his political party because of sincere conviction, or is he simply behaving like an *opportunist* to join the winning side?

Related Forms: opportune, opportunism, opportunity

Synonyms: compromising, convenient, propitious, seasonable, timely, fitting, expedient

Antonyms: unseasonable, untimely, inexpedient, unpropitious

Phrases: a time-server; a well-timed thrust; seize the opportunity; a temporary expedient; in the nick of time

---

Principle is ever my motto; not expediency.

— DISRAELI

---

333. op-pro-bri-um ŏ-prō'-brĭ-ŭm [*ob* (Latin), "against" + *probrum*, "disgraceful act"] — Disgrace or shame as a result of evil actions; reproach mixed with contempt; reproachful and contemptuous language.

The obscenity of his language and the rudeness of his behavior brought down upon Bob the *opprobrium* of the entire community.

Related Forms: opprobrious, opprobriously

Synonyms: infamy, obloquy, discredit, contumely (*adj.* contumelious), ignominy (*adj.* ignominious), disrepute

Antonyms: commendation, encomium, flattery, eulogy

Phrase: under a cloud

334. op-u-lence ŏp'-ŭ-lĕns [*ops, opis,* (Latin), "riches," "power"] — Wealth, abundance.

The beautiful setting, the magnificent gowns and jewels of the women, the wonderful food, all combined to make a party which was distinguished for its *opulence*.

Related Form: opulent

Synonyms: affluence, luxury, profusion

Antonyms: scantiness, poverty, impecuniosity, indigence, destitution

335. or-tho-dox ôr'-thŏ-dŏks [*orthos* (Greek), "correct" + *doxa*, "position" "opinion"] — Conforming to an established tradition or doctrine.

Tomlinson invariably took the *orthodox* view of a subject, preferring to avoid the untested or unconventional line of thinking.

Related Form: orthodoxy

Synonyms: conventional, traditional, conformist

Antonyms: heterodox, nonconformist, heretical (See page 298 for an analysis of the word *heresy*.)

Phrase: the Establishment (the existing power structure in society)

Note: In the religious denotation, an orthodox person is one who adheres strictly to the doctrine and principle of the ruling church authorities.

336. os-ten-si-ble ŏs-tĕn'-sĭ-b'l [*ostensus* (Latin), "displayed" + *ible*] — Outwardly appearing; professed (as opposed to real).

John's *ostensible* cheerfulness did not deceive his parents to whom it was obvious that his gaiety was forced.

Synonyms: apparent, pretended, manifest

337. os-ten-ta-tion ŏs-tĕn-tā'-shŭn [*ob* (Latin), "toward" + *tendere*, "to stretch"] — Unnecessary, excessive, or pretentious display.

Whoever wishes to attain an English style, familiar but not coarse, and elegant but not *ostentatious*, must give his days and nights to Addison.* — SAMUEL JOHNSON

* Joseph Addison was a great 18th century essayist. His writings deal with the need for reason and moderation.

Related Forms: ostentatious, ostentatiously, ostentatiousness

Synonyms: show, parade, pomp, pomposity, garishness, vanity, vainglory, pretentiousness, grandeur, splendor, ornateness

Antonyms: simplicity, unpretentiousness, modesty, reserve

338. os-tra-cize ŏs'-tră-sīz [*ostrakon* (Greek), "a tablet used in voting"] — To exclude from public or private favor and privileges.

In some societies any deviation from accepted patterns of behavior can cause one to be *ostracized.*

Related Form: ostracism

Synonyms: banish (*noun:* banishment), bar, exile, outlaw, proscribe, blacklist, blackball; a pariah

Note: Among the ancient Greeks in Athens and other cities, it was the practice to banish from the country for a period of from five to ten years, without trial, any person who was considered politically dangerous to the state. The victim did not necessarily suffer disgrace on that account. This was done by voting on ostrakons or tiles or potsherds, pieces of broken crockery or earthenware which lay scattered about the marketplace. From this voting medium we get our present English word ostracize, meaning, to exclude from favor or from ordinary social intercourse by general consent. Our word oyster is derived from the same source as os (as in ostracism) meaning bone or shell.

339. pan-a-ce-a păn-ȧ-sē'-ȧ [*pan* (Greek), "all" + *akos,* "remedy"] — A remedy for all ills.

A century ago, philosophers as well as political economists regarded democracy as a *panacea* for all the then current political ills.

Synonyms: cure-all, nostrum

340. pan-de-mo-ni-um păn-dĕ-mō'-nĭ-ŭm [*pan* (Greek), "all" + *daimon,* "a demon"] — A wild uproar or general disorder.

Although *pandemonium* could have been expected when thousands of young people gathered at a music festival, everyone was pleasant and well-behaved.

Synonyms: confusion, chaos

Antonyms: tranquillity, calm, order

Note: Pandemonium was the name for the abode of all the demons. It was also the name for the palace of Satan or the lower regions. Then it came to mean a place like Pandemonium; an uproar like that of the lower regions; uproar in general.

341. par-a-dox păr'-à-dŏks [*para* (Greek), "beside," "contrary to" + *doxa,* "opinion," from *dokein,* "to think"] — A self-contradictory statement; a statement or a person that is seemingly contradictory or inconsistent; something that appears to be absurd and yet may be true.

It is one of *life's* paradoxes that a person may be a complete rogue, but if he performs his misdeeds with style he will be admired.

Related Forms: paradoxical, paradoxically

Synonyms: self-contradiction, anomaly

"Life is too important a matter to be taken seriously."
"It is always a silly thing to give advice, but to give good advice is absolutely fatal."
"One's real life is so often the life that one does not lead."

— OSCAR WILDE

---

342. par-a-gon păr'-à-gŏn păr'-à-gŭn [probably from *parakonan* (Greek), "to rub against a whetstone"; from *para,* "against" + *akone* (Greek), "whetstone." In other words, philologically speaking, a *paragon* is one who will stand up when tried by a touchstone or a standard of comparison.] — A model of excellence or perfection.

What a piece of work is a man! how noble in reason! how infinite in faculty! in form and moving how express and admirable! in action how like an angel! in apprehension how like a God! the beauty of the world! the *paragon* of animals.

— SHAKESPEARE, *Hamlet*

374

Synonyms: model, exemplar (*verb:* exemplify), pattern

343. par-a-phrase păr'-ȧ-frāz [*paraphrazein* (Greek), "to say the same thing in other words"; from *para,* "beside" + *phrazein,* "to speak"] — A rendering of a text or passage usually given in another form for clearness.

The Anglo-Saxon monk Caedmon wrote a *paraphrase* of the prose parts of the Bible in the form of poetry.

Related Form: paraphrastic

Synonyms: version, rewording, restatement, free rendering

344. par-si-mo-ni-ous pär-sĭ-mō'-nĭ-ŭs [*parcere, parsum* (Latin), "save"] — Excessively frugal or stingy.

One of the richest men in the world is said to be so *parsimonious* that he installed a coin-fed telephone in his home for the use of his guests.

Related Forms: parsimony, parsimoniously

Synonyms: avaricious, miserly, niggardly (*noun:* niggardliness), thrifty, close (*colloquial*), penurious, tight-fisted, illiberal, sparing, grasping. *Verbs:* stint, scrimp, skimp (*colloq.*)

Antonyms: lavish, generous, magnanimous, bountiful, extravagant, prodigal; splurge

---

The love of money is the root of all evil.

— BIBLE

---

345. pas-to-ral păs'-tö-răl [*pastor* (Latin), "a shepherd"; from *pascere,* "to feed."]

1. Pertaining to rural life.

Robert Burns is famous for his *pastoral* poems, the most famous of them being "The Cotter's Saturday Night," which describes Scottish peasant life.

2. Relating to a minister and his duties.

The Reverend Thomas Peters devotes many hours during the week to such *pastoral* duties as visiting sick parishoners and troubled families.

Related Forms: pastorally, pastor, pastorate

Synonyms: bucolic, rustic, idyllic, Arcadian

Antonyms: metropolitan, urban

Note: A pastorelle is a piece of music suggestive of country life. Figuratively speaking, a pastor is both a shepherd and one who takes spiritual care (like a shepherd his flock) of people in his parish.

346. pe-jo-ra-tive pē'-jŏ-rā-tĭv   pĭ-jôr'-à-tĭv   pĭ-jŏr'-à-tĭv [*pejoratus* (Latin), "having been made worse"] — Having a depreciating sense or effect.

The dictionary definition of "opportunist" shows it to be a word of definitely *pejorative* quality.

Related Form: pejoration

Synonyms: disparaging, deprecatory

Note: Some words with pejorative connotations: obsequious for humble; pedantic for scholarly; parsimonious for frugal.

347. pen-u-ry pĕn'-û-rĭ [*penuria* (Latin), "want"] — Extreme poverty; lacking in means or resources.

New sources of food, and better methods of production must be developed if the population explosion is not to result in large numbers of people living in *penury*.

Related Forms: penurious, penuriousness

Synonyms: destitution, scarcity, dearth, privation, pauperism, indigence, need; niggardly

Antonyms: opulence; wealth; plethora

Note: The adjective penurious has several meanings or connotations. Basically, it denotes utter want, but it is often used to denote "extreme stinginess," "miserliness"; "poorly supplied"; "lacking in resources." In other words it has a pejorative meaning.

348. per-emp-to-ry pĕr-ĕmp′-tō-rĭ pĕr′-ĕmp-tō-rĭ [*perempere* (Latin), "to take away entirely"; from *per*, "thoroughly," "very" + *emere, emptus*, "take," "buy"] — Positive in expressing an opinion; leaving no opportunity for refusal or denial, as a *peremptory* demand.

The foreman learned that he could get more cooperation from workers by making polite requests instead of issuing *peremptory* orders.

Related Forms: peremptorily, peremptoriness

Synonyms: positive, imperative, final, incontrovertible, stubborn, imperious (dictatorial), decisive, arbitrary

Antonyms: mild, tentative, bland, indecisive

Note: In law, a peremptory edict or writ is one that is decisive and excludes debate. A peremptory challenge is a formal objection raised by either side in a legal contest as to the service of a particular juror. The qualification peremptory indicates that the protestant need not show cause for his objection.

349. per-func-to-ry pĕr-fŭngk′-tō-rĭ [*perfunctorius* (Latin), "carelessly done;" from *per*, "fully" + *fungi, functus*, "perform," that is to say, "to get done with it"] — Done half-heartedly or mechanically merely to comply with the letter of duty.

Because math was far from my favorite subject, I did my assignments in a *perfunctory* fashion and had to repeat the course.

Related Forms: perfunctorily, perfunctoriness

Synonyms: automatic, indifferent, superficial, mechanical, routine, slack, cursory

Antonyms: zealous, meticulous, vigilant, observant, painstaking

350. per-ni-cious pĕr-nĭsh′-ŭs [*per* (Latin), "thoroughly" + *nex, necis*, "death"] — Highly injurious; evil or wicked.

Despite a great deal of evidence pointing to the *pernicious* effects of smoking cigarettes, many people refuse to give up the habit.

Related Forms: perniciously, perniciousness

Synonyms: harmful, destructive, deleterious, malicious, ruinous, noxious, baneful, deadly

Antonyms: wholesome, beneficial, salubrious, salutary, beneficient; innocuous

EXERCISES

I. Words Out of Context

In each group below, select the word or expression that most clearly expresses the meaning of the word at the left.

1. **ostensible** (*a*) garish (*b*) apparent (*c*) persistent (*d*) irrefutable

2. **pejorative** (*a*) depreciative (*b*) execrable (*c*) swearing falsely (*d*) optional

3. **obsequious** (*a*) discreditable (*b*) linked (*c*) timorous (*d*) servile

4. **opportune** (*a*) occasional (*b*) portentous (*c*) expedient (*d*) eventful

5. **opprobrium** (*a*) disgrace (*b*) oppression (*c*) timeliness (*d*) protest

II. Words in Context

One-Word Omissions

In each of the following sentences substitute for the blank an appropriate word selected from Words 326-350 (or their derivatives) of the Basic Vocabulary List.

1. A _____ of Benjamin Franklin's witty comment that "Fish and visitors smell after three days," could be the rather prosaic, "Visitors should not outstay their welcome."

2. The Scriptural aphorism "From him that hath not shall be taken away even that which he hath" is a good example of a(n) _____."

3. I think that a violent thunderstorm is approaching; that black cloud on the horizon looks _____.

4. When our team finally made the first touchdown of the game, _____ broke loose among our rooters.

5. Only a quack would claim to have discovered a _____ for all the ills that men are heir to.

6. The Athenians frequently _____d a statesman who had become so popular that they feared he might make himself dictator of their commonwealth.

7. The nouveaux-riches are often given to _____ whereas many old established families of wealth are unpretentious in speech and manner.

8. You talk like Sir Oracle! Do you really believe yourself to be _____?

9. My uncle is so _____ that, no matter how cold the weather is, he never starts his furnace fire before November 15.

10. Association with unprincipled persons sometimes has a _____ effect upon a weak character.

III. Synonyms and Antonyms

In each group below select the two words that are either (a) synonyms or (b) antonyms.

1. (a) arrogant (b) momentous (c) truckling
   (d) timely

2. (a) overbearing (b) archaic (c) ignominious
   (d) antiquated

3. (a) bestow (b) propitiate (c) presage (d) betoken

4. (a) contumely (b) indigence (c) retrogression
   (d) encomium

5. (a) orthodox (b) paradoxical (c) pompous
   (d) modest

6. (a) lurch (b) scrimp (c) disparage (d) splurge

WORD BUILDING

I. PREFIX

The Latin prefix **per** "through" "fully" "throughout" is a common source element in many English words including *pernicious, peremptory,* and *perfunctory* studied in this lesson.

> *pervade* — to spread throughout
>
> *perspicuous* — to understand fully

II. ROOTS

A. The Latin root **via,** "way," "road" is a source element in *obviate,* studied in this lesson.

> *impervious* — not affording a passage or way through
>
> *deviate* — to change direction

B. The Greek root **ortho,** "right" is found in the word *orthodox,* studied in this lesson.

> *orthodontia* — a branch of dentistry dealing with correcting irregularity in teeth formation
>
> *orthography* — the correct spelling of words

C. The Latin root **sequ-, secut-** "follow" is the source of many English words including *obsequious,* studied in this lesson.

> *subsequent* — following in point of time
>
> *execute* — to follow out

D. The Greek root **pan,** "all," "universal" is the source of *pandemonium* and *panacea.*

> *Pan-American* — pertaining to all Americans
>
> *pandemic* — epidemic over a wide area

E. The Greek source element **para,** "beside," "contrary to," "against" appears in *paraphrase, paradox,* and *paragon,* studied in this lesson.

parasite (literally, eating beside another) — a person who lives at another's expense

F. The Latin root **sciens,** "know" is the source of many English words including *omniscient,* studied in this lesson.

prescient — foreseeing

EXERCISES

Words in Context

To Believe or Not to Believe

Complete the following sentences by selecting the letter item which best completes the statement.

1. A system of belief or formula of belief is a

    (*a*) credo (*b*) credential (*c*) credulity (*d*) denomination

2. A person who is easily imposed upon or easily deceived into believing what he is told is a(n)

    (*a*) charlatan (*b*) optimist (*c*) gull (*d*) ingenue

3. To give *credence* to a statement is to

    (*a*) doubt it (*b*) believe it (*c*) reserve decision on it (*d*) criticize it

4. A *creditable* performance

    (*a*) merits belief (*b*) is true to life
    (*c*) worthy of pay (*d*) is praiseworthy

5. A person who believes that man can never know the nature of God is a(n)

    (*a*) skeptic (*b*) infidel (*c*) agnostic (*d*) atheist

LESSON TWENTY-THREE

351. perspicacious	363. precursor
352. pertinacity	364. predatory
353. pertinent	365. prelude
354. pique	366. prerogative
355. plagiarism	367. prevaricate
356. platitude	368. procrastinate
357. plebeian	369. prolific
358. plethora	370. prolix
359. posthumous	371. propensity
360. precarious	372. propitiate
361. preclude	373. protuberant
362. precocious	374. prowess
	375. pseudonym

351. per-spi-ca-cious pûr-spĭ-kā'-shŭs [*per* (Latin), "through" + *spicere*, "to see"] — Having a keen and penetrating mind; sharp-sighted.

An incisive mind and a keen wit made Benjamin Franklin a *perspicacious* and successful diplomat.

Related Forms: perspicaciously, perspicacity

Synonyms: acute, astute, insightful, sagacious (*noun:* sagacity), shrewd, discerning (*noun:* discernment), penetrating

Antonyms: dull, obtuse

352. per-ti-nac-i-ty pûr-tĭ-năs'-ĭ-tĭ [*per* (Latin), "completely" + *tenax*, "tenacious"] — The state or quality of clinging doggedly to a purpose or an opinion.

The many opportunities offered by the United States allowed the *pertinacity* of many of the immigrants of the early 20th century to be rewarded by success.

Related Forms: pertinacious, pertinaciously, pertinaciousness

Synonyms: tenacity, obduracy, perseverance, obstinacy, inflexibility, doggedness, persistency, intractability, steadfastness

Antonyms: tractableness, pliability, flexibility, complaisance

353. per-ti-nent pûr'-tĭ-nĕnt [*per* (Latin), "through" + *te-nere*, "to hold"] — Fitting or appropriate; pertaining to the matter in hand.

This brochure gives you all the facts *pertinent* to the operation of this machine.

Related Forms: pertinence, pertinency; pertain (*verb*)

Synonyms: relevant (directly bearing on the project), germane; appertaining to, relative, apposite, apt, touching (on)

Antonyms: unrelated, inappropriate, irrelevant, far-fetched, extraneous, inapplicable

Phrases: *pertinent* details, an *apt* reply
    a point *germane* to the question
    a propos, apropos of, as regards
    in re (in the matter of)

Note: Do not confuse **pertinent** with **impertinent** or **pert,** "insolent," "saucy," "bold."

354. pique (*noun* and *verb*) pēk [*piquer* (French), "to sting"]

1. To react with sharp resentment or wounded pride.

Piqued because he was assigned a corner seat on the dais, the prominent actor strode off the platform in a huff.

Synonyms: nettle, vex, irritate, sting, annoy; resentment, vexation, umbrage

Antonyms: pleased, delighted

2. To excite curiosity or interest.

The painting *piqued* my curiosity so much that I lingered nearly an hour before it to figure out what it was supposed to represent.

Synonyms: arouse, provoke, stir, stimulate

3. To value oneself highly or proudly; to please oneself.

He *piqued* himself on his ability to act.

Related Forms: piquant (agreeably sharp and stimulating, as piquant wit); racy

Phrases: piqued at a slight; take umbrage at; bridle (at); to draw up the head in scorn; get on one's high horse; puffed up (like a peacock)

355. pla-gi-a-rism plā′-jĭ-à-rĭz′m [*plagiarius* (Latin), "kidnaper"] — Adopting and reproducing without acknowledgement as one's own the writings or ideas of another.

Although the writer admitted that passages in his story are similar to several in Hemingway he denied the charge of deliberate *plagiarism*.

Related Forms: plagiarize, plagiarist, plagiarizer, plagiary

Synonyms: appropriation, theft, piracy

356. plat-i-tude plăt′-ĭ-tūd [*plat* (French), "flat" + *tude* (suffix making adjectives into nouns)] — A dull and commonplace remark solemnly expressed.

The speaker was an unoriginal and uncreative thinker who delivered his *platitudes* as if they were the wit and wisdom of the ages.

Related Forms: platitudinize, platitudinous, platitudinarian

Synonyms: truism, bromide (*adj.* bromidic), flatness, triteness, insipidity, banality (*adj:* banal)

Antonyms: originality, verve, piquancy

357. ple-be-ian plĕ-bē′-yăn [*plebs* (Latin), "the common people"] — Pertaining to the common people; hence, common or vulgar.

Although he was a snob and did his best to be taken for an aristocrat, Barry betrayed his *plebeian* origins by his habit of chewing on a toothpick.

Related Form: plebeianism

Synonyms: popular, undistinguished, low-born, ill-bred, proletarian

Antonyms: patrician, aristocratic, distinguished

358. pleth-o-ra plĕth'-ô-rȧ [*plethore* (Greek), "fulness"] — The state of being full to excess.

Sated by a *plethora* of food and drink, the party-goers sat around in a state of somnolence.

Related Form: plethoric

Synonyms: oversatiety, overabundance, turgidness, inflation, bloat, superabundance, bombast

Antonyms: scarcity, conciseness, terseness, succinctness

359. post-hu-mous pŏs'-tû-mŭs [*postumus* (Latin), "late born"] — Born after the father's death; in general, occurring after a person's death.

A *posthumous* award of a Medal of Honor was presented to the widow of the brave man.

Related Form: posthumously

360. pre-car-i-ous prĕ-kâr'-ĭ-ŭs [*prex, precis* (Latin), "obtained by prayer or begging"] — Dependent on circumstances or chances that are outside one's control; hence, very uncertain, risky, dangerous or insecure.

The secretary had to resign his position because of his persistent *precarious* health.

Related Forms: precariously, precariousness

Synonyms: unsettled, hazardous, perilous

Antonyms: secure, stable, settled, certain, fixed

Phrase: a precarious livelihood

361. pre-clude prĕ-klōōd' [*prae* (Latin), "before" + *claudere*, "to shut"] — To prevent or render ineffectual or impossible by taking necessary steps beforehand.

John tried to *preclude* any chance of failure on his finals by cramming for seven hours the night before the examination.

Related Forms: preclusion, preclusive

Synonyms: obviate, forestall, debar, hinder, frustrate, avert, thwart, foil, balk, impede

Antonyms: foster, abet, incite, cause, engender

362. **pre-co-cious** prĕ-kō'-shŭs [*prae* (Latin), "before" + *coquere*, "to cook"; hence, prematurely cooked or ripe"] — Of remarkably early mental development.

A psychologist recently observed that too often the pert child is unnecessarily excused as a *precocious* one.

Related Forms: precociously, precociousness, precocity

Synonyms: premature, forward

Antonyms: backward, retarded, obtuse

363. **pre-cur-sor** prĕ-kûr'-sẽr [*prae* (Latin), "before" + *currere*, "to run"] — A person or thing that goes before to indicate what is to follow.

Corruption and cynicism were *precursors* of the fall of the Roman Empire.

Related Form: precursory

Synonyms: harbinger, forerunner, herald, predecessor, messenger, premonitory

364. **pred-a-to-ry** prĕd'-ȧ-tō-rĭ prĕd'-ȧ-tẽr-ĭ [*praeda* (Latin), "prey," "booty"] — Characterized by plundering.

Some wars, the anthropologist declared, are but a survival of the *predatory* habits of primitive tribesmen.

Related Forms: predator (*noun:* one who plunders); predatorily, predatoriness, predacious (*variant spelling:* predaceous)

Synonyms: plaguing, preying, despoiling, depredating, pillaging

365. pre-lude prēl′ūd prĕ′-lūd [*praeludere* (Latin), from *prae*, "before" + *ludere*, "to play"]

1. Something done, written, or said to prepare the way for a more important matter.

   A series of firm notes exchanged between the two countries was the *prelude* to a declaration of war.

2. In music, a movement introducing the theme; a piece, especially an organ solo, played at the beginning of a service.

   We got to the wedding just in time: as the taxi drew up at the church the organist was playing the *prelude*.

Related Forms: prelusive, prelusion, prelusory

Synonyms: overture, preface, introduction, preamble, prologue, preliminary

Antonyms: postlude, epilogue

366. pre-rog-a-tive prĕ-rŏg′-ȧ-tĭv [*prae* (Latin), "before" + *rogare*, "to demand"] — A privilege, an advantage, or power assumed as of right or inherent in an office or rank.

The woman's *prerogative* of getting a seat in a crowded bus is gradually disappearing in this age of the equality of the sexes.

Synonyms: privilege, right, exemption, immunity, license

367. pre-var-i-cate prĕ-văr′-ĭ-kāt [*prae* (Latin), "before" + *varicare*, "to straddle"] — To evade the truth by quibbling or misrepresentation.

The witness on the stand tried to wiggle out of an uncomfortable admission by *prevaricating* instead of giving a direct answer to the question.

Related Forms: prevarication, prevaricator

Synonyms: equivocate, quibble

Note: In Roman times, the **prevaricator** was a prosecuting attorney who presented his case in court so half-heartedly that the defendant was acquitted. By derivation, the Roman prevaricator was one who straddled, that is, had one foot on each side of the case. Thus, in modern use, one is said to prevaricate when one equivocates, or says "yes" and "no" with the intention to deceive or to avoid telling the truth.

Phrase: talking through both sides of the mouth

368. pro-cras-ti-nate prŏ-krăs′tĭ-nāt [*pro* (Latin), "forward" + *crastinus*, "of tomorrow"] — To put off habitually from day to day.

Bill *procrastinated* so long in filing his college application that, when he finally sent it, the authorities would not accept it.

Related Forms: procrastination, procrastinator

Synonyms: defer, postpone, delay, protract, temporize, table, vacillate, dawdle

Antonym: anticipate

Phrase: to be dilatory

Procrastination is the thief of time.

— YOUNG

---

369. pro-lif-ic prŏ-lĭf′-ĭk [*proles* (Latin), "offspring" + *facere*, "to make"]

1. Producing young or fruit abundantly.

   The heavy spring rainfall has made our fruit trees unusually *prolific*.

2. Highly productive of ideas or creative work.

   Dumas was a *prolific* writer, having produced more than fifty novels.

Related Form: prolifically

Synonyms: fertile, voluminous, fruitful, fecund, teeming, inventive

Antonyms: barren, sterile, unfruitful

370. pro-lix prō'-lĭks prō-lĭks' [*pro* (Latin), "forth" + *liquere* (*lixus*), "flow"] — Using more words in speaking or writing than necessary; long drawn out.

A perspicacious person is able to present his ideas clearly and succinctly without the need to be *prolix*.

Related Forms: prolixity, prolixness

Synonyms: verbose (*noun:* verbosity), profuse, diffuse, wordy, copious, discursive, bombastic, tautological; tedious, long-winded

Antonyms: concise, laconic, trenchant, succinct, compressed, epigramatic, to the point

371. pro-pen-si-ty prō-pĕn'-sĭ-tĭ [*pro* (Latin), "forward" + *pensus*, "hang"] — Natural or habitual inclination or bent.

Having returned from a visit to England, George showed a marked *propensity* for everything English, including an Oxford accent.

Synonyms: tendency, disposition bias

372. pro-pi-ti-ate prŏ-pĭsh'-ĭ-āt [*propitius* (Latin), "favorable"] — To obtain the good will or grace of a person; to quiet or pacify.

Nothing save complete and abject surrender to his exorbitant demands would *propitiate* the aggressor.

Related Forms: propitiation, propitiatory, propitiative

Synonyms: appease, placate, allay, conciliate, mollify

Antonyms: antagonize, alienate

373. pro-tu-ber-ant prŏ-tū'-bēr-ănt [*pro* (Latin), "forward" + *tuber*, "a swelling"] — Bulging or swelling out.

Cyrano de Bergerac by Edmond Rostand was written about a man with a very *protuberant* nose.

Related Forms: protuberantly, protuberance, protuberate, protuberation

Synonyms: prominent, projecting, bulbous, tumid, tuberous

Antonyms: receding, recessive

374. prow-ess prou'-ĕs prou'-ĭs [*proèce* (Old French), "valor"; from *prou*, "valiant"]

1. Remarkable bravery or skill, usually a combination of both, in a military sense.

   The bravery and skill of Alexander the Great of Macedon has made his name almost synonymous with *prowess*.

2. Outstanding ability or skill.

   The athlete who displayed the greatest *prowess* in throwing the discus won honors for his country at the Olympic Games.

Synonyms: daring, courage, valor, gallantry, intrepidity, mettle, pluck

Antonyms: cowardice, timidity, pusillanimity

375. pseu-do-nym sū'-dô-nĭm psū'-dô-nĭm [*pseudonyme* (French); from *pseudonymos* (Greek); from *pseudes*, "false" + *onyma, onama*, "name"]—An assumed name.

Kathie Butler would occasionally sign herself "Kathleen Evangeline B." but she really preferred the *pseudonym* of "Parsley J. York."

Related Form: pseudonymous

Synonyms: pen name, nom de plume, alias, cryptonym

Note: Pseudo is a common English prefix, from the Greek pseudes, meaning false.

EXERCISES

Words in Context

A. Words in Phrases

Select the one of the four suggested words or phrases which most clearly expresses the meaning of the italicized word in each phrase below:

1. a *posthumous* award is (a) belated (b) unwarranted (c) occurring after death (d) meritorious

2. a *precarious* situation is (a) perilous (b) anticipated (c) unalterable (d) complicated

3. a *predatory* group (a) plundering (b) precocious (c) aggressive (d) well-knit

4. showed extraordinary *prowess* (a) insight (b) potentiality (c) timidity (d) valor

5. a *prolific* writer (a) discursive (b) boring (c) voluminous (d) highly imaginative

B. One-Word Omissions

In each of the following sentences substitute for the blank an appropriate word from Words 351-375 (including derivatives).

1. Judge Whiffledinger's speech was just one long series of _____ without a single grain of originality to enliven it.

2. Poe once accused Longfellow of _____, asserting that the latter had stolen certain of his lines from Poe's "The Raven."

3. "Your lengthy but uninspired composition," commented the professor, "suffers from a _____ of words and a dearth of ideas."

4. I fear my tastes are somewhat _____; I actually prefer good plain food to caviar.

5. "Just for openers," said my father as a _____ to his scolding, "we will dispense with your allowance."

WORD BUILDING

I. PREFIXES

A. The Latin prefix **pre-**, from **prae-**, "before," is the source of many English words, including *preclude, precocious, precursor, prelude, prerogative,* and *prevaricate,* studied in this lesson.

predict — to tell ahead of time; hence, to prophesy

prejudge — to judge beforehand

B. The Latin prefix **pro-**, "before" "forward" "forth," is found in many English words including *prolix, propensity,* and *protuberant,* studied in this lesson.

propel — to drive forward

II. ROOT

The Latin root **ludere, lusus,** "play," appears in *prelude,* studied in this lesson.

collude (literally, "to play with") — to conspire

illusion (literally, "to play upon") — state of being deceived by false show

For an analysis of **per** (see page 322); **spicere** (see page 154); **currere** (see page 176); **facere** (see page 222); and **onyma** (see page 306).

EXERCISES

I. Word Building Activities

1. *Define the following words in the light of their origin.*

   pervade   pellucid   perfidious   perspective   recur
   discursive   factotum

2. Give two English words which are derived in part from:

   prae, para, per, facere, onyma, spicere, ludere.

II. Word Analysis and Word Building

1. An 18th-century Anglican bishop named William War-
   burton once said: "*Orthodoxy* is my *doxy*, and *heterodoxy*
   is another man's *doxy*." What did the brilliant bishop
   mean by this? Explain, by definition or otherwise, the
   meaning of *orthodoxy* and *heterodoxy*.

2. Distinguish among *paraphrase, version, translation, edition, concordance.* Can you name a famous paraphrase of
   the Bible? A famous translation? A famous version? Of
   what value is a concordance to Shakespeare or the Bible?

3. Why may ticket-scalpers be said, literally, to "pre-empt"
   the best seats at popular entertainments?

4. *Caveat emptor* is an old legal Latin maxim. "Let the purchaser beware." This tells us (*a*) that the seller is dishonest (*b*) that the buyer is being imposed upon (*c*)
   that we buy at our own risk.

III. A Dictionary Project: Foreign Words and Phrases

Most dictionaries define common foreign words and phrases
either in a special section in the appendix or in the main body
of the word entry. The unabridged section of *The Random
House Dictionary of the English Language* has, in fact, four
such separate concise dictionaries, French, English, Italian, and
German, with Latin words and phrases defined and explained
as main entries in the dictionary.

*What do the following Latin phrases which are commonly
used in English mean?*

1.	ipse dixit	6.	ex post facto
2.	quid pro quo	7.	in memoriam
3.	alter ego	8.	ipso facto
4.	dramatis personae	9.	ad infinitum
5.	e pluribus unum	10.	status quo

LESSON TWENTY-FOUR

376. puerile	388. recant
377. pugnacious	389. recondite
378. punctilious	390. redoubtable
379. pungent	391. refractory
380. pusillanimous	392. relegate
381. quell	393. remorse
382. querulous	394. remuneration
383. rabble	395. renegade
384. raconteur	396. reprisal
385. rancor	397. respite
386. raze	398. reticent
387. recalcitrant	399. retribution
	400. ribald

---

376. pu-er-ile pū'-ēr-ĭl [*puer* (Latin), "child," "boy"] —
Characteristic of a child; childishly foolish, trivial.

The class was bored by the *puerile* remarks of the speaker at
the assembly who was obviously talking down to them.

Related Form: puerility

Synonyms: childish, juvenile, silly, inane

Antonyms: mature, adult

377. pug-na-cious pŭg-nā'-shŭs [*pugnare* (Latin), "to fight"]
— Inclined to fight; quarrelsome.

John Keats, the poet, was a *pugnacious* little fellow at school,
quick to use his fists at the slightest provocation.

Related Forms: pugnacity, pugnaciousness

Synonyms: bellicose, disputatious, contentious, argumentative,
combative

Antonyms: pacific, peace-loving

Phrase: in the thick of the fray

Historical Note: The Roman Marcus Cato had such great hatred and fear of Rome's rival Carthage that he concluded every speech, letter, and conversation with the words <u>Delenda est Carthago</u> — "Carthage must be destroyed."

378. punc·til·i·ous pŭngk-tĭl′-ĭ-ŭs   pŭngk-tĭl′-yŭs   [*puntilloso* (Spanish), from *puntillo,* "a small point;" from *punctum* (Latin), "a point"] — Scrupulously exact or attentive to the nice points of manners, dress, procedures, etc.

As chairman of our club, John is *punctilious* in observing parliamentary procedure to all the fine points indicated in the manual by Wines and Card.

Related Forms: punctiliously, punctiliousness, punctilio

Synonyms: scrupulous, precise, meticulous, correct, overnice, fastidious, demanding, rigid

Antonyms: careless, negligent, slipshod

379. pun·gent pŭn′-jĕnt   [*pungere* (Latin), "to puncture"]

1. Said of anything that causes a sharp sensation, as of smell or taste.

   The *pungent* odor of pickles and spices which filled the delicatessen whetted our appetites and made us order more than we really wanted.

2. Said of words that are sharp or piercing; mentally stimulating.

   Chief Justice Oliver Wendell Holmes was famous for his *pungent* comments on human affairs as well as on law.

Related Forms: pungently, pungency

Synonyms: tart, piquant, biting, piercing, poignant, sharp, caustic, incisive, acrid, tangy, nippy, racy

Antonyms: insipid, vapid, tasteless, unsavory, flat

380. pu·sil·lan·i·mous pū-sĭ-lăn′-ĭ-mŭs   [*pusillus* (Latin,) "very little + *animus,* "the mind"] — Lacking in courage; cowardly or mean-spirited.

A nasty fellow at best, the sycophant was obsequious to his superiors, arrogant to his inferiors, and *pusillanimous* when challenged.

Related Forms: pusillanimously, pusillanimity

Synonyms: craven, timorous, recreant, faint-hearted, dastard, poltroon, lily-livered; base

Antonyms: courageous, daring, intrepid, venturesome, noble, rash, valorous, brave, heroic, spirited

---

It is easy to be brave from a safe distance.

— AESOP

---

381. quell kwĕl [*cwellan* (Anglo-Saxon), "to kill"] — To put down, as a riot; to pacify or soothe.

One of the skills which a veteran police officer usually has is knowing how to *quell* public disturbances or riots.

Synonyms: subdue, quash, overpower, overcome, crush, suppress, quiet, calm

382. quer-u-lous kwĕr'-ū-lŭs   kwĕr'-ōō-lŭs [*queri* (Latin), "to complain"]

1. Given to habitual complaining or fault-finding.

   Querulous by nature, the tenant seldom met her landlord without voicing a complaint of one kind or another.

2. Sounding as though complaining.

   The tone of her *querulous* whining voice was highly irritating.

Related Forms: querulously, querulousness

Synonyms: fretful, petulant, plaintive, whining; discontented, peevish; caviling, captious, carping, hypercritical

Antonyms: affable, good-natured, complaisant, agreeable

Phrase: a querulous tone

383. rab·ble răb'-'l [Origin uncertain] — A noisy disorderly crowd; the mob, the common people.

The authoritarian condemned the crowd as *rabble* and refused to listen to their requests.

Synonyms: hoi polloi, throng, crowd, populace, the multitude, the masses, proletariat, *canaille*

Phrases: a rabble rouser (one who stirs up the people); the common herd; the dregs of society

---

The mob has many heads but no brains.

— FULLER

---

384. rac·on·teur răk-ŏn-tûr' [*raconteur* (French), "a storyteller"] — A person who is skilled in telling stories or anecdotes.

It was not a very funny joke, but Jim was such a good *raconteur* that everyone roared with laughter.

385. ran·cor răng'-kĕr [*rancere* (Latin), "to be sour"] — Intense ill will or malice.

The *rancor* displayed by the debaters made an objective discussion of the issues impossible.

Related Forms: rancorous, rancorousness

Synonyms: spite, malignity, malevolence, vindictiveness, ill-humor, enmity, antagonism

Antonyms: amity, good will, benignity, amenity, complaisance

386. raze rāz [*radere, rasum* (Latin), "scrape"] — To level to the ground; to blot out or destroy.

The bomb had *razed* every building in the city within a radius of five miles; only heaps of rubble remained.

Synonyms: efface, obliterate, demolish, ruin, erase, devastate

Antonyms: rear, raise, erect, construct, build, establish

387. re-cal-ci-trant rĕ-kăl′-sĭ-trănt [re (Latin), "back" + *calx*, "a heel"] — Stubbornly hostile or insubordinate.

A *recalcitrant* handful of Senators, impervious even to rational arguments of their colleagues, have often effectively blocked legislation favored by the majority.

Related Forms: recalcitrance, recalcitrancy

Synonyms: resistant, refractory, fractious, headstrong, contumacious (scornful of lawful authority), intransigent

Antonyms: obsequious, amenable, submissive, compliant

388. re-cant rĕ-kănt′ [re (Latin), "back" + *cantare*, "to sing"] — To withdraw publicly an opinion previously held or avowed.

Although threatened with imprisonment for his open espousal of democratic ideals, the opponent of totalitarian tyranny refused to *recant*.

Related Form: recantation

Synonyms: renounce, abjure, rescind, repudiate, disown, disavow, forswear, disclaim, retract

Antonyms: avow, aver, affirm, announce, asseverate, avouch, acknowledge, declare

389. rec-on-dite rĕk′-ŏn-dīt rĭ′-kŏn-dĭt [re (Latin), "again" + *condere* "to hide"] — Beyond ordinary knowledge and understanding; dealing in profound or obscure matters.

The philosophical lecture was too *recondite* for the young audience, most of whom could not understand the speaker's abstruse references.

Related Form: reconditeness

Synonyms: obscure, occult, esoteric

Antonyms: simple, uncomplicated, simplistic (oversimplified), clear

Phrase: recondite facts

390. re-doubt-a-ble rĕ-dout′-à-b′l [re (Latin), "again" + *dubitare*, "to doubt," "to fear"] — Arousing dread or fear.

The incumbent Senator, realizing that he was faced with a *redoubtable* opponent to his reelection, decided to campaign in every small town in the state.

Related Forms: redoubtably, redoubtableness

Synonyms: petrifying, formidable, doughty, frightful, dreadful, fearful, menacing, alarming, terrifying, terrible; terror-stricken

Antonyms: feeble, weak, powerless, helpless, harmless

391. re-frac-to-ry rĕ-frăk′-tô-rĭ [re (Latin), "back" + *frangere*, "to break"] — Stubbornly refusing to comply with another's wishes; resisting ordinary methods of treatment (as a refractory disease).

Since reason had failed to convince the *refractory* boy that he had to comply with the rules, the principal decided to expel him.

Related Forms: refractorily, refractoriness

Synonyms: obstinate, stubborn, obdurate, mulish, recalcitrant, contumacious, perverse, intractable, ungovernable, rebellious, disobedient, unruly

Antonyms: pliable, obedient, conciliatory, docile, amenable, tractable

392. rel-e-gate rĕl′-ê-gāt [re (Latin), "back" + *legare*, "to send as an ambassador."]

1. To remove to a less prominent or desirable position.

   In view of the clamorous opposition on the floor of the House, the bill was *relegated* to the legislative committee for reconsideration.

2. To assign to a particular class or group.

   Historians have *relegated* Marco Polo's tales to the realm of fiction rather than to history.

Related Form: relegation

Synonyms: consign, reassign, commit, refer, delegate, deputize

393. **re-morse** rė-môrs′ [re (Latin), "back" + *morsus* "bitten"] — Keen self-reproach for wrong doing; penitent regret.

Pangs of *remorse* will do little to undo a wrong done, or an unkindness committed.

Related Forms: remorseful, remorseless (*synonyms:* merciless, pitiless, hardhearted, unconscionable)

Synonyms: anguish, compunction, contrition, conscience-stricken, qualms

Antonyms: impenitence, obduracy

Phrase: twinges of conscience

Remorse is memory awake.

— EMILY DICKINSON

---

394. **re-mu-ner-a-tion** rė-mū-nēr-ā′-shŭn [re (Latin), "back" + *munerare*, "to reward"; from *munus*, "a gift," "an office"] — Recompense or reward for services rendered.

Many of our most prominent industrialists and scientists have served their country on numerous occasions without *remuneration.*

Related Forms: remunerate, remunerative

Synonyms: pay, compensation, consideration, emolument, profit, requital

Phrase: remunerative work

395. **ren-e-gade** rĕn′-ĕ-gād [re (Latin), "again" + *negare,* "to deny"] — One who deserts one's party or cause for another.

Many respected officials of totalitarian governments have been termed *renegades* when they speak out in favor of more democratic methods.

Related Form: renege (rĕ-nĭg′, rĕ-nēg′) "to desert one's party, faith, or cause;" "to go back on one's word"

Synonyms: turncoat, apostate

396. re-pris-al rĕ-prīz′-ăl [*reprehendere* (Latin), "to take back"] — The act of using force in seizing the property of, or inflicting loss or damage on, another nation to redress an injury; retaliation for damages or losses sustained; an injury done, especially in war, against an opponent, in return for an injury received.

Soviet Russia expelled two of our attaches in the foreign office in Moscow in *reprisal* for our expulsion of two of their aides in Washington.

Synonyms: retaliation, redress, reparation, revenge

397. res-pite rĕs′-pĭt [*re* (Latin), "back" + *specere*, "to look"]

1. A temporary postponement or cessation of work or pain.

A *respite* from labor in the form of a vacation has a salutary effect on a worker.

2. In law, a temporary delay in the execution of a sentence.

The judge granted the condemned man a *respite* of thirty days, pending a review of the case by another judge.

Synonyms: delay, postponement, reprieve, pause, stay, surcease

Note: <u>Respite</u> can also be used as a verb meaning "to relieve temporarily from something trying or distressing."

398. ret-i-cent rĕt′-ĭ-sĕnt [*re* (Latin), "again" + *tacere*, "to be silent"] — Habitually silent.

No one listens to Peter who is as talkative as a parrot, but when Matthew, who is usually *reticent*, speaks out, he is listened to with respect.

Related Form: reticence

Synonyms: uncommunicative, taciturn, reserved (in speech), laconic

Antonyms: garrulous, loquacious, talkative, voluble

Let a fool hold his tongue and he will pass for a sage.

— PUBLILIUS

---

399. re-tri-bu-tion rĕt-rĭ-bū′-shŭn [*re* (Latin), "back" + *tribuere*, "to pay"] — The giving or receiving of just payment, especially of punishment; that which is given or exacted, specifically punishment.

The preacher declared that, as night follows day, *retribution* follows sin; no sinner can escape the punishment.

Related Forms: retributive, retributory

Synonyms: requital, repayment, recompense, nemesis

Phrase: retributive justice

400. rib-ald rĭb′-ăld [*ribault* (Old French), "a ruffian"] — Indecent or offensive in language; profane; one who is *ribald*.

Although many of Chaucer's stories are today considered *ribald*, they were not thought to be coarse at the time he wrote.

Related Forms: ribaldry, ribaldish

Synonyms: scurrilous, low, uproarious, obscene, licentious, salacious

Antonyms: modest, pure, restrained, decent, refined, decorous

EXERCISES

I. Words Out of Context

In each group below, select the word or expression that most clearly expresses the meaning of the word at the left.

1. **pungent**   (*a*) hostile (*b*) offensive (*c*) acrid (*d*) witty

2. **raze**   (*a*) object (*b*) rear (*c*) elevate (*d*) demolish

3. **recant**   (*a*) disavow (*b*) repeat (*c*) summarize (*d*) sing again

4. **pugnacious**   (*a*) conspicuous (*b*) bellicose (*c*) ill-mannered (*d*) foul-smelling

5. **refractory**   (*a*) quarrelsome (*b*) garrulous (*c*) unamenable (*d*) fragile

II. Words in Context

A. One-Word Omissions

In each of the following sentences substitute for the blank an appropriate word (including derivatives) from the Basic Vocabulary List for this lesson (Words 375-400).

1. In the heyday of the British Empire, it was said that many colonial officials were so _____ about the conventions that they would dress for dinner even when they were alone in remote jungle or desert outposts.

2. The police were called out to _____ the riot.

3. The behavior of grown men who join organizations in order to wear fancy fezzes and garish sashes seem to me very _____.

4. A good _____ whose stories are really witty, is an asset to any party.

5. No _____ breed of men could have endured the hardships which our pioneer forefathers had to undergo.

B. Words in Phrases

Select one of the four suggested words or phrases which most nearly defines the italicized word in each phrase.

1. a *querulous* temperament (*a*) curious (*b*) full of complaints (*c*) unstable (*d*) refractory

2. a *ribald* remark (*a*) rude (*b*) poignant (*c*) witty (*d*) coarsely mocking

3. regarded as a *renegade* (*a*) denial (*b*) retraction (*c*) turncoat (*d*) backward step

4. a *redoubtable* enemy (*a*) formidable (*b*) vacillating (*c*) routed (*d*) canny

III. Analogies

Complete the following analogies.

1. assiduous : beaver = (*a*) frigid : wolf (*b*) fleet : greyhound (*c*) abstemious : camel (*d*) shrewd : bear

2. slake : thirst = (*a*) submit : defeat (*b*) reject : demand (*c*) tranquilize : excitement (*d*) admonish : aggressor

3. spice : aroma = (*a*) cinnamon : piquant (*b*) perfume : scent (*c*) swamp : bog (*d*) parsley : garden

4. simmer : boil = (*a*) challenge : audacity (*b*) abomination : abhorrence (*c*) rage : temper (*d*) disagreement : altercation

5. momentous : paltry = (*a*) present : inconsequential (*b*) miniature : gigantic (*c*) critical : significant (*d*) major : minor

WORD BUILDING

I. PREFIX

The Latin prefix **re,** "back" "again" is a source element of many English words including *recalcitrant, recant, redoubtable, remorse,* etc.

reprint — print again

revert — turn back

II. ROOTS

A. The Latin root **punct-, pung-,** "to sting" appears in *pungent* in this week's lesson.

puncture — to pierce

B. The Latin root **cant** from *cantare,* "to sing" is the source of many English words, including *recant* studied in this week's lesson.

cantata — a musical composition sung but not acted

C. The word *refractory* studied in this week's lesson contains the Latin root **frang-, fract,** "break or bend."

fracture — a break

See the analyses of **animus** "mind" on page 350 and of **specere,** on page 154.

EXERCISES

Etymology Mastery Test

1. *Define, give the etymology, and use in a short sentence each of the following words.*

cantor descant enchant canto cant

2. *Define the following words in the light of their origin.*

poignant pungent punt expunge compunction punctilious

3. *Show how the Latin prefix* **re,** *"again" "back," alters the meaning of the following words.*

reactionary reread rebate redress revert remunerate retribution

LESSON TWENTY-FIVE

401. ruminate	413. secular
402. sacrilegious	414. sedate
403. sagacity	415. sedulous
404. salient	416. senile
405. salubrious	417. sinecure
406. sanction	418. sinister
407. sanguine	419. specious
408. sardonic	420. sporadic
409. sartorial	421. stentorian
410. saturnine	422. stigmatize
411. scourge	423. strident
412. scrutinize	424. succulent

425. supercilious

401. ru-min-ate rōō'-mĭ-nāt [*rumen* (Latin), "the throat"]
— To ponder over; meditate on.

The sematicist spent many hours checking reference books and *ruminating* over the correct usage of various words.

Related Forms: ruminant, ruminative, rumination

Synonyms: cogitate, muse, reflect, deliberate, consider

Note: A <u>ruminant</u> is the general name given to a division of hoofed mammals that chew the cud, including cows, deer, camels, oxen, sheep, etc. In a special sense, the word <u>ruminate,</u> referring to these animals, means "to chew the cud as ruminants do."

402. sac-ri-le-gious săk-rĭ-lē'-jŭs   săk-rĭ-lĭj'-ŭs [*sacrilegus* (Latin), "stealing sacred things"; from *sacer*, "holy" + *legere*, "to gather or pick up"] — Treating holy matters irreverently.

In Puritan Boston it was considered *sacrilegious* to read any book other than the Bible on Sunday.

Related Forms: sacrilege, sacrilegiously, sacrilegiousness

Synonyms: profane, unholy, blasphemous, impious, ungodly, irreligious, unhallowed, unsanctified, irreverent

Antonyms: religious, sacred, holy, godly, pious, devout, reverent, consecrated

403. sa-gac-i-ty sȧ-găs'-ĭ-tĭ [*sagax, sagacis* (Latin), "having keen senses," "acute," "clever"] — Sharpness or quickness of sense perception, keenness of discernment; soundness of judgment.

As the representative in England of the American colonies, Benjamin Franklin displayed great *sagacity* in avoiding all the pitfalls prepared for him by English statesmen.

Related Forms: sagacious, sagaciously, sage

Synonyms: perspicacity, astuteness, acuteness, shrewdness, wisdom, sapience, penetration

Antonyms: obtuseness, dullness, stupidity

404. sa-li-ent sā'-lĭ-ĕnt (*adjective* and *noun*) [*saliens* (Latin); from *salire*, "to leap"]

1. (*adj.*) Moving by leaps and bounds; projecting outwardly; prominent or conspicuous.

   The pointed arch is a *salient* feature of Gothic architecture.

2. (*noun*) An outwardly projecting part of a military position or line.

   Our capture of the enemy's *salient* made victory certain.

Related Forms: salience, saliency, (*verb*, sally "rush forth")

Synonyms: prominent, outstanding, noticeable, striking, arresting, jutting, protuberant

Antonyms: obscure, inconspicuous, receding, recessed

Phrases: a salient quality
a salient position
a salient point

405. sa-lu-bri-ous să-lū'-brĭ-ŭs [*salus* (Latin), "health"] — Contributing to well-being, especially physical; invigorating, as *salubrious* climate.

Golf is *salubrious* exercise, especially for people over forty years of age.

Related Forms: salubriously, salubriousness, salubrity (*verb:* salubrify)

Synonyms: salutary, beneficial, healthful, wholesome

Antonyms: deleterious, unhealthful, noxious, harmful, baneful

406. sanc-tion (*noun* and *verb*) săngk'-shŭn [*sanctus* (Latin), "sacred," "rendered sacred"] — To authorize or approve; authoritative approval.

Congress refused to *sanction* certain foreign policy measures advocated by the President.

Synonyms: ratify (solemnly), confirm, countenance, endorse

Antonyms: veto, discountenance, disavow, forbid

Note 1: Do not confuse <u>sanction</u> with <u>sanctity</u> "holiness, godliness."

Note 2: In international law, <u>sanctions</u> refer to actions by one or more states designed to compel another state to comply with stated legal obligations.

407. san-guine săng'-gwĭn [*sanguis, sanguinis* (Latin), "blood"] — Blood-red in color; of a hopeful disposition.

Tom was a big, ruddy, blond fellow, as *sanguine* of disposition as he was of complexion, always certain that everything would turn out for the best.

Related Forms: sanguineness, sanguinary (bloody), sanguineous

Synonyms: ruddy, optimistic, ardent, confident (as, "sanguine of success"), buoyant, blood-thirsty

Antonyms: pale, pessimistic, despondent, despairing

Phrase: sanguine prospects

408. sar-don-ic sär-dŏn'-ĭk [*sardonique* (French); from *sardanios* (Greek)] — Showing mockery, or sneering bitterly (usually refers to laughter or humor).

The policeman's face wore a *sardonic* smile as he asked me where the fire was.

Related Form: sardonically

Synonyms: disdainful, sarcastic, derisive, mocking, scornful

Antonyms: benign, respectful, deferential, panegyrical

409. sar-to-ri-al sär-tô'rĭ-ȧl [*sartor* (Latin), "a tailor"] — Pertaining to a tailor or his work; pertaining to men's clothes.

Messrs. Lewis and Devenaugh, Tailors to His Majesty, were responsible for the fine *sartorial* effect presented by the King at all times.

Related Form: sartorially

410. sat-ur-nine săt'-ēr-nīn [Saturn, the planet which is supposed by astrologers to predispose toward gloom those born under its influence] — Of a dull or gloomy temperament.

His many misfortunes transformed Henry from a genial, thoroughly likable fellow to a querulous and *saturnine* man.

Synonyms: melancholy, phlegmatic, lugubrious, dour, glum, morose, surly, grave

Antonyms: volatile, swift, inconstant, affable, genial, mercurial, gay, light-hearted

Note: The influence of the planet Mercury was believed by astrologers to make those born under its ascendancy <u>mercurial</u>, that is, light-hearted, gay, and somewhat inconstant or fickle.

411. scourge skûrj (*verb* and *noun*) [*excoriare* (Latin), literally "to strip off the hide"; from *ex* "off" + *corium*, "hide"] — To inflict severe punishment or cause great suffering or misfortune; whip severely; to torment.

In the middle ages the bubonic plague was one of mankind's greatest *scourges*.

Synonyms: afflict, torment, flog, lash, punish severely; pestilence, tribulation; calamitous

Phrase: the scourge of war

412. scru-ti-nize skroo'-tĭ-nīz [*scrutare* (Latin), "search into closely"] — To examine closely or critically.

I reread my composition carefully, *scrutinizing* it for possible errors I might have overlooked in writing it.

Related Form: scrutiny (noun)

Synonyms: inspection, critique, investigation, probe, inquiry, check-up; scan

Phrase: critical examination

413. sec-u-lar sĕk'-ū-lẽr [*saeculum* (Latin), "the world"] — Pertaining to the world or temporary earthly things as distinguished from things of the spirit; hence, not under church control; concerned with worldly matters.

Pupils were permitted one afternoon a week off from their *secular* studies in order to receive religious instruction.

Related Form: secularism (sectional hatred or prejudice)

Synonyms: profane, temporal (meaning, "earthly or short-lived"), ephemeral, mundane, worldly; a layman

Antonyms: sacred, ecclesiastical, religious

414. se-date sê-dāt' [*sedatus* (Latin), "calm"]—Composed; undisturbed by excitement.

The calm, *sedate* manner of the witness was in sharp contrast to the histrionic rantings of the prosecuting attorney.

Related Forms: sedateness, sedative (soothing, having a calming effect)

Synonyms: sober, serene, dignified, calm, collected, demure, equable, staid, imperturbable, settled, poised

410

Antonyms: ruffled, frivolous, upset

Phrases: sedate behavior

calm and collected under stress

415. sed-u-lous sĕd′-ū-lŭs [*sedulus* (Latin), "careful"] —
Steady in attention and industry.

Willingness to give *sedulous* attention to every detail is one of
the characteristics of a dedicated scientist.

Related Form: sedulousness

Synonyms: diligent, painstaking, assiduous, industrious, persevering, unremitting, persistent

Antonyms: indolent, slothful, idle, procrastinating, desultory

416. se-nile sē′-nīl sē′-nĭl [*senilis* (Latin), "an old man"]
— Pertaining to, or characteristic of, old age; showing the
weaknesses of old age.

"I may be superannuated, but I certainly am not *senile,*" remarked the teacher at his retirement dinner.

Related Form: senility

Synonyms: aged, decrepit, doddering, infirm

Antonyms: youthful, adolescent, juvenile

417. si-ne-cure sī′-nĕ-kūr sĭn′-ĕ-kūr [*sine* (Latin), "without" + *cura*, "care," "cure (of souls)"] — Employment
or an office of value requiring little or no responsibility
or labor.

Mr. Gray's job appears to be a *sinecure;* he is even able to get
away every afternoon for a game of golf.

Related Forms: sinecural, sinecurism

418. sin-is-ter sĭn′-ĭs-tĕr [*sinister* (Latin), "left; the left
hand"] — Evil, wicked, base; foreshadowing misfortune.

The German student of the late nineteenth century admired the
sinister appearance of a face scarred by the results of many
duels.

Related Forms: sinistrous, sinisterly

Synonyms: ill-omened, ominous, inauspicious, sinful, corrupt, disastrous, dishonest, portentous, malevolent, malignant

Antonyms: virtuous, favorable

Phrases: a sinister leer (a look of lurking malevolence); a sinister beginning; a sinister influence

Note: It is interesting to note that sinister, in Roman social life, meant lucky. The Romans faced south when casting fortunes so that the left side was to the East, or the lucky side. According to the Greek custom, the sinister or left side was the unlucky side. The meaning of sinister as the "left side" is archaic. In heraldry, the sinistral side is the side of the shield toward the left of the bearer, that is, on the right side (dextral) of the observer.

419. spe-cious spē'-shŭs [*species* (Latin), "kind," "appearance"] — Superficially attractive, just, or correct, but in reality quite the opposite.

To defend the use of marijuana by saying that it is no worse than alcohol is a *specious* argument at best.

Related Forms: speciously, speciousness

Synonyms: fair-seeming, plausible, ostensible, feasible, apparent, credible, faulty

Antonyms: genuine, sound, valid, real, implausible, unlikely

Phrases: specious reasoning, a plausible excuse, surface appearance

Note: Spurious, often confused with specious in use, means "not genuine or authentic," counterfeit; specious implies deceit or hypocrisy.

420. spo-rad-ic spō-răd'-ĭk [*sporadikos* (Greek), "scattered"] — Occurring in scattered single cases; here and there; happening at irregular intervals in time.

There were *sporadic* incidents of violence, but for the most part the riot was over.

Related Form: sporadically

Synonyms: occasional, unconnected, separate, periodic, dispersed, widely spaced

Antonyms: chronic, continuous, unremitting, without respite; bunched, serried, conglomerative

Phrases: sporadic occurrences, isolated cases

421. sten-to-ri-an stĕn-tō′-rĭ-ăn [*Stentor* (Greek) — See story below.] — Exceedingly loud; capable of very loud utterance.

From the loud speaker in the convention hall a *stentorian* voice made the announcements to the assembled delegates.

Synonyms: resonant, vociferous, clangorous

Antonyms: low, faint, subdued, dim, barely audible

Phrases: *sotto voce*, "in a low tone so as not to be overheard," *pianissimo* (musical term), "very softly"

Note: The word stentorian comes from Stentor, the name of a famous Greek herald. So powerful was Stentor's voice, which according to Homer was louder than the combined voices of fifty men of normal vocal powers, that the Greek leaders in the Trojan war used Stentor as a one-man broadcasting system to relay their messages to their besieged enemies behind the walls of Troy. Perhaps the two most famous messages thus relayed by Stentor were Achilles' challenge to Hector and the announcement that the Greeks were about to present to their doughty enemies the remarkable gift of a huge wooden horse.

422. stig-ma-tize stĭg′-mà-tīz [*stigma* (Greek and Latin), "a brand or the mark of a pointed instrument" (See below for the story behind the word.)] — To mark with a stigma, a reproach, or disgrace; to brand or blemish.

Stigmatized by his fellow-countrymen as a traitor, Benedict Arnold spent his last years as an exile in England.

Related Forms: stigma, stigmatic, stigmatization

Synonyms: brand, mark (with the stamp of infamy), denounce

Note: The Greeks and the Romans used to brand their slaves by applying to their foreheads a red-hot iron marked with certain letters and then rubbing coloring matter into the wounds. A slave thus branded was called a stigmatic, from the word stigma meaning "a brand."

The term stigmata (plural of stigma) is used to designate the impressions of marks on the body of Christ made by the Crown of Thorns and the nails driven through His hands and feet. Devout Catholics believe that replicas of such marks have (by divine favor) appeared miraculously on the bodies of certain men and women, among them St. Francis of Assisi, on whose body the marks, or stigmata, are said to have been impressed by a seraph with six wings.

423. stri-dent strī'-děnt [*stridens* (Latin), "to make a grating noise"] — Harsh-sounding; making a creaking sound.

Flora is a beautiful girl, but her voice, *strident* as a crow's, mars her image.

Related Forms: stridently, stridence, stridency

Synonyms: shrill, grating

Antonyms: soft, euphonious, mellifluous

424. suc-cu-lent sŭk'-kṳ-lĕnt [*succus* (Latin), "juice"] — Juicy; hence, figuratively, full of life and interest.

The *succulent* Malaga grape is much favored by vintners because of its copious yield of juice.

Related Forms: succulently, succulentness, succulence, succulency

Synonyms: sappy, sapid, interesting

Antonyms: dry, desiccated, lifeless, uninteresting, vapid

425. su-per-cil-i-ous sū-pēr-sĭl'-ĭ-ŭs [*supercilium* (Latin), "with raised eyebrows"; from *super*, "over," "up" + *cilium*, "an eyelid"] — Proudly contemptuous.

The *supercilious* attitude used by Henry in any difference of opinion seemed to imply that anyone who didn't agree with him was an idiot.

Related Forms: superciliously, superciliousness

Synonyms: arrogant, scornful, haughty, disdainful, insolent, overbearing, superior

Antonyms: humble, modest, meek, servile, obsequious

EXERCISES

I. Words in Context

A. One-Word Omissions

In each of the following sentences substitute for the blank an appropriate word from Words 401-425 on the Basic Vocabulary List.

1. The press would have us believe that the _____ features of today's young people consist of long hair and drug usage.

2. Train announcers usually have _____ voices.

3. Beau Brummel was renowned for his _____ elegance.

4. The thin, dry air of the Colorado mountains is considered _____ for patients with diseases of the lungs.

5. This lazy fellow will accept no job that is not a _____.

B. Words in Phrases of Sentences

Select the letter preceding the item which most clearly defines the word in italics.

1. John spent his time in *rumination*. This means that John was
   (*a*) postponing what he had to do (*b*) meditating
   (*c*) spreading rumors

2. A *sinister* smile is one that is
   (*a*) wicked (*b*) half-hearted (*c*) broad

3. A *supercilious* attitude is
   (*a*) highly critical (*b*) haughty (*c*) hypocritical

4. A *succulent* bit of gossip is
   (*a*) underhanded (*b*) derogatory (*c*) interesting

5. Fred was *stigmatized* for his behavior. This means that he was
   (*a*) lauded (*b*) denounced (*c*) chastised

II. Words Out of Context

In each group below, select the word or expression that most clearly expresses the meaning of the word at the left.

1. **sedate**
   (*a*) industrious (*b*) composed
   (*c*) ruffled (*d*) equitable

2. **scrutinize**
   (*a*) examine closely (*b*) regard scornfully (*c*) criticize acutely (*d*) brand

3. **sanction**
   (*a*) devoutness (*b*) disapprobation
   (*c*) approval (*d*) place of refuge

4. **sanguine**
   (*a*) bloody (*b*) unaggressive
   (*c*) reverent (*d*) optimistic

5. **sardonic**
   (*a*) sneering (*b*) loud-voiced
   (*c*) captious (*d*) sacrilegious

6. **saturnine**
   (*a*) witty (*b*) self-confident·
   (*c*) highly satisfied (*d*) of gloomy temperament

7. **scourge**
   (*a*) great affliction (*b*) cleanser
   (*c*) reprimand (*d*) scowl

8. **secular**
   (*a*) eternal (*b*) desiccated
   (*c*) mundane (*d*) religious

9. **sedulous**
   (*a*) secretive (*b*) diligent
   (*c*) soothing (*d*) treacherous

10. **sporadic**
    (*a*) at scattered intervals (*b*) embryonic (*c*) unremitting (*d*) arrogant

III. Syllabication and Pronunciation

Syllabicate and indicate by a stress and diacritical mark the correct pronunciation of each of the following words.

1. **sacrilegious**   3. **scourge**   5. **sinecure**
2. **sanguine**   4. **senile**   6. **specious**

WORD BUILDING

I. PREFIX

The Latin prefix **super,** "above," "over" is a source element in many English words, including *supercilious,* studied in this lesson.

superabundant — more than abundant

superpose — to place or lay above something

II. ROOTS

A. The Latin root **sacer,** "sacred," "accursed" is the source of many English words including *sanction, sacrilegious,* studied in this lesson. Other words from this root are *sacrosanct* (most sacred or inviolable), *sacrament* (a holy rite), *desecrate* (to profane), *sacrifice* (literally, "to make sacred; hence, to give up something cherished for something thought more desirable), *sacristan* (one who is in charge of a church).

B. The Latin root **cura,** "care," "cure" is the source of *sinecure* studied in this lesson.

curate (literally, "one who is in charge of the cure of souls") — a priest

curative — relative to a cure

EXERCISES

I. Etymology Mastery Test

1. *Define each of the following words in the light of its derivation.*

   ruminate   sagacity   salubrious   sanguine   sardonic

2. Give, define, and indicate the etymology of three words containing the prefix *super.*

II. Word Analysis and Development

1. *Give three English words for each of the following roots.*
   leg frang lev sacer sagax salire

2. In ancient Rome an official who governed a province was called a *legate*. Explain the origin of this title. Why is the "legate of the Pope" so called? What is meant by the expression "a foreign legation"?

3. Using your knowledge of physics, define "refraction of light" in terms of the origin of the word "refraction." What is a "refractory ore"? What kind of diseases do doctors call "refractory"?

4. *Tell the interesting story behind each of the following words.*

   forum rostrum pulpit circus

5. If you were admitted to the "inner sanctum" of an organization, would that status entitle you to (*a*) know its history (*b*) be its "high priest" (*c*) know all its secrets?

6. The sentence "The ties of consanguinity are strong" means (*a*) Birds of a feather flock together. (*b*) Blood is thicker than water. (*c*) A man is known by the company he keeps. (*d*) Like father, like son.

7. A famous book by Thomas Carlyle bears the title *Sartor Resartus*. What is the meaning of this title?

8. (*a*) *From the following list, select words that are synonymous with "decorous."*

composed	unruffled	balmy
composite	wholesome	decent
deceptive	curt	gaudy

   (*b*) *From the following list, select the words that are synonyms for "decorated."*

embellished	decked	decoyed	dismayed
arraigned	ornamental	beautified	arrayed

LESSON TWENTY-SIX

426. surmise	438. unremitting
427. surreptitious	439. urban
428. taciturn	440. vacillate
429. tangible	441. vagary
430. temerity	442. venerable
431. tentative	443. verbatim
432. terse	444. verbose
433. trenchant	445. vicissitude
434. trite	446. vindictive
435. truculent	447. virulent
436. turgid	448. vitiate
437. ubiquitous	449. wrath

450. zeal

426. sur-mise (*noun* and *verb*) sŭr-mīz' [*super* (*Latin*), "on" + *mittere, missus,* "to put"] — To guess; an idea or inference based more on a guess than on sufficient evidence.

I do not know definitely what Sid's reaction to the proposal was, but judging from the expression on his face I can *surmise* that he must have been very unhappy about it.

Synonyms: conjecture, presume, divine; supposition

Antonym: certitude

Phrases: a matter of conjecture, a random guess, hazard a guess

---

Columbus found a world, and had no chart,
Save one that faith deciphered in the skies;
To trust the soul's invincible surmise.
Was all his science and his art.
— SANTAYANA

---

427. sur-rep-ti-tious sŭr-ĕp-tĭsh'-ŭs [*sub* (Latin), "under" + *rapere*, "to snatch"] — Done in a stealthy, unauthorized, or underhanded manner, introduced secretly or fraudulently.

"In order to lose weight," said the doctor, "you must give up those *surreptitious* midnight forays into the refrigerator."

Related Forms: surreptitiously, surreptitiousness

Synonyms: furtive, secret, clandestine, covert

Antonyms: open, aboveboard, straightforward, forthright, undisguised, overt

428. tac-i-turn tăs'-ĭ-tûrn [*tacitus* (Latin), "silent"] — Not given to conversation; customarily silent.

The Biblical injunction "Let your communications be as Yea and Nay" was observed by Whittier's *taciturn* Quaker father.

Related Forms: taciturnly, taciturnity, tacit (implied, not expressed)

Synonyms: reserved, reticent, laconic, close-mouthed, uncommunicative

Antonyms: loquacious, garrulous, talkative, voluble, unreserved, communicative

Phrase: a tacit agreement

429. tan-gi-ble tăn'-jĭ-b'l [*tangere, tactus* (Latin), "touch"] — Perceptible to the touch, capable of being touched; hence, real.

New methods of farming and better equipment had the *tangible* result of an increased yield of wheat for each acre of land.

Related Forms: tangibly, tangibleness, tangibility

Synonyms: palpable, substantial, perceptible, concrete, discernible, material, actual

Antonyms: intangible, imperceptible, nebulous, imaginary, unsubstantial, impalpable, visionary, tenuous (of slight significance; unsubstantial)

420

Phrase: tangible evidence

430. te-mer-i-ty tĕ-mĕr′-ĭ-tĭ [*temere* (Latin), "rashly"] —Rash contempt of danger or other serious consequences; reckless boldness.

Bob is pugnacious enough to have the *temerity* to fight a mountain lion if one crossed his path.

Related Forms: temerarious, temerariously

Synonyms: foolhardiness, nerve, cheek, gall, boldness, audacity, effrontery, recklessness, venturesomeness

Antonyms: caution, prudence, circumspection, wariness

Note: Do not confuse timorous, "fearful" with temerarious, "recklessly bold."

431. ten-ta-tive tĕn′-tà-tĭv [*tentare* (Latin), "to try"] — In the nature of an experiment or trial; made provisional upon unpredictable future events.

Our plans for the picnic tomorrow are merely *tentative;* if the weather is inclement, we shall call the affair off.

Related Form: tentatively

Synonyms: temporary, experimental, empirical (depending only on experience or observation)

Antonyms: final, definite, settled, certain

432. terse tûrs [*tergere, tersus* (Latin), "to clean"] — Concise, brief, and meaningful.

To the question, "Are you prepared to surrender?" Winston Churchill made the *terse* answer, "Not a speck of British soil!"

Related Forms: tersely, terseness

Synonyms: succinct, pithy, sententious, pointed

Antonyms: verbose, tautological, redundant, circumlocutory (synonymous with the slang expression "beating around the bush"), prolix, diffuse

Phrases: a *terse* style of writing; a *terse* phrase

433. **trench-ant** trĕn'-chȧnt [*trenchant* (Old French), "cutting"] — Having a sharp edge (physically); hence, cutting, biting, keen (figuratively).

Dorothy Parker, a noted wit, once denigrated the performance of an actress by the *trenchant* comment, "She ran the whole gamut of emotion from A to B."

Related Forms: trenchant, trenchantly

Synonyms: keen, biting (each with figurative as well as literal meaning), incisive, clear-cut, caustic

Antonyms: dull, obtuse, blunt, blurred

434. **trite** trīt [*tritus* (Latin), "rub," "worn out"] — Lacking freshness or novelty.

The author of the biography of Emily Dickinson did a good job of his research, but his presentation of his material is both *trite* and unimaginative.

Related Forms: tritely, triteness

Synonyms: stale, hackneyed, banal, commonplace, cliché, vapid, stereotyped

Antonyms: fresh, original, novel, vivid, piquant

Note: Webster's Student Dictionary makes the following distinction: "Trite implies especially lack of novelty or interest; that is hackneyed which is worn out, as it were, by constant use; banal suggests the vapid or the commonplace."

435. **truc-u-lent** trŭk'-ụ-lĕnt [*truculentus* (Latin), "savage"] — Fierce and cruel; savagely harsh.

"Negotiations will be suspended until such time as both parties agree to abandon their *truculent* attitude and listen to reason," said the arbitrator.

Synonyms: ferocious (*noun:* ferocity), ruthless, rapacious, savage, haughtily defiant

Antonyms: mild-mannered, mild, tame, tender, kindly, gentle, benign

422

436. tur-gid tûr'-jĭd [*turgidus* (Latin), "swollen"] — Distended abnormally.

The politician's speech was full of catch-words, devoid of meaning and *turgid* to an extreme.

Related Forms: turgidly, turgidity, turgidness

Synonyms: swollen, inflated, tumid, pompous, bombastic

Antonyms: deflated, pithy, concise, terse

437. u-biq-ui-tous û-bĭk'-wĭ-tŭs [*ubi* (Latin), "where" + *quietis*, "you seek"] — Everywhere present; existing everywhere at one and the same time.

One almost gets the impression that Peter is *ubiquitous;* if there's a social gathering, there is Peter.

Related Forms: ubiquity, ubiquitousness

Synonym: omnipresent

438. un-re-mit-ting ŭn-rē-mĭt'-ĭng [negative of "remitting"; from *re*, "again" + *mittere* (Latin), "to send"] — Not slackening or relaxing.

It took several months of *unremitting* toil to repair the damage caused by the hurricane.

Related Forms: unremittingly, unremittingness

Synonyms: incessant, continuous, constant, perpetual, persevering

Antonyms: periodic, inconstant, sporadic, intermittent

439. ur-ban ûr'-băn [*urbs* (Latin), "city or town"] — Of a city or town.

An *urban* existence has its attractions for those who love the life, conveniences, and movement of a large city.

Synonyms: city-like, metropolitan, megalopolis (an urban region consisting of several large adjoining cities and suburbs)

Antonyms: rural, bucolic, pastoral

Note: Do not confuse ûrbān with ur-bane (ur-ban') meaning "suave, extremely sophisticated, smooth, sleek."

440. vac-il-late văs'-ĭ-lāt' [*vacillare, vacillatus* (Latin), "move first one way and then another; as in staggering or reeling"] — To veer or swerve continually from one opinion or course to another.

We are on the horns of a dilemma; neither course of action seems good, yet if we *vacillate* any longer, the time for action will have passed.

Related Forms: vacillation, vacillatory, vacillatingly

Synonyms: hesitate, waver, oscillate, falter, fluctuate; irresolute; inconstancy

Antonyms: adhere, persist, stick, persevere, constant (*noun:* constancy)

441. va-ga-ry vȧ-gā'-rĭ [*vagari* (Latin), "to wander off"] — A casual or extravagant idea or notion.

The decision to drop out of school and hitch-hike around the country is too important to be dismissed as a mere adolescent *vagary.*

Related Forms: vagarious, vagariously

Synonyms: caprice, freak, whim, whimsey, crotchet

Phrase: a maggot (an odd fancy) in the brain

442. ven-er-able věn'-ēr-ȧ-b'l [*venerari* (Latin), "to honor"] — Worthy of reverence; rendered sacred by historic or other association.

Although he had retired from public life many years before, the *venerable* statesman was frequently consulted in matters of importance.

Related Forms: venerate (*verb:* meaning "to hold in high respect"); veneration, venerability

Synonyms: revered, honorable, estimable, august, respected, reverence

Antonyms: scorned; downgrade, dishonor

Venerable men! You have come down to us from a former generation. Heaven has bounteously lengthened out your lives, that you might behold this joyous day.

— DANIEL WEBSTER, *Address on Laying the Cornerstone of the Bunker Hill Monument, 1825*

---

443. ver-ba-tim vĕr-bā'-tĭm [*verbum* (Latin), "word"] — Word for word; literally.

The speech by the President was of sufficient importance for it to be printed *verbatim* by all the major newspapers of the country.

Antonyms: paraphrase; figuratively

Phrases: repeated it *verbatim*, a *verbatim* account

444. ver-bose vêr-bōs' [*verbum* (Latin), "word"] — Wordy, characterized by a superfluity of words.

Polonius, a *verbose* character in Shakespeare's *Hamlet*, contributes considerable humor to the play by using a dozen words where one would do.

Related Forms: verbosity, verboseness

Synonyms: verbiage (wordiness); prolix, long-winded, garrulous (talkative), circumlocutory, tautological, diffuse (the opposite of concise)

Antonyms: laconic, terse, pithy, succinct, concise

445. vi·cis·si·tude vĭ-sĭs'-ĭ-tūd [*vicisitudo* (Latin), "a change"] — A sudden change from one condition to another, usually unexpected.

"As I look back on my life," said the venerable sage, "I realize that many of its *vicissitudes* could be dealt with by means of the simple phrase 'And this too shall pass.' "

Synonyms: mutation, mutability, alternation, ups and downs.

446. vin·dic·tive vĭn-dĭk'-tĭv [*vindicta* (Latin), "revenge"] — Prompted by, or inclined to seek, revenge.

Lincoln was by no means a *vindictive* man; on the contrary, he overlooked or forgot the injuries done him.

Related Forms: vindictively, vindictiveness

Synonyms: vengeful, revengeful, implacable

Antonyms: forgiving, magnanimous

Note: Do not confuse vindictive with vindicate "to clear from a charge or suspicion"; "to justify," as "later events vindicated his original claims."

447. vir·u·lent vĭr'-ōō-lĕnt [*virulentus* (Latin), from *virus*, "poison"] — Bitterly malicious or venomous.

Aaron Burr's *virulent* hatred of Alexander Hamilton resulted in the duel that proved fatal for Hamilton.

Related Forms: virulence, virulently, virulency

Synonyms: acrimonious; poisonous, toxic, malignant, noxious, baneful, hostile, bitter

Antonyms: benignant, benign, gentle, innocuous

Phrase: a virulent (malignant) disease

Note: Do not confuse virulent with virile, "of a manlike or manly nature."

448. vit·i·ate vĭsh'-ĭ-āt [*vitiare, vitiatus* (Latin), "injure," from *vitium*, "a fault"] — To render ineffective or destroy the validity of an object.

The judge would have been glad to grant an adjournment had not the truculence of the attorney's behavior *vitiated* his otherwise perfectly rational argument.

426

Related Form: vitiation

Synonyms: mar, invalidate, negate, nullify, corrupt, contaminate, pervert, devitalize

Antonyms: validate, vitalize, energize, engender

449. wrath răth [*wrath* (Anglo-Saxon, "anger")] — Intense anger.

My father's *wrath* will know no bounds when he sees the damage I have done to his car.

Related Forms: wrathful, wrathfulness

Synonyms: rage, fury, resentment, indignation

Antonyms: calm, serene, placid, tranquil

A soft answer turneth away wrath.

— THE BIBLE

---

450. zeal zēl [*zelos* (Greek), "great earnestness"] — Ardor for a person, cause, or object; eager desire or endeavor.

To apply oneself to a task with *zeal* is to see a task well done.

Related Forms: zealousness, zealot (one who displays excessive zeal), zealously

Synonyms: diligence, earnestness, intensity, enthusiasm

Antonyms: apathy, indifference, nonchalance; lackadaisical

EXERCISES

I. Words Out of Context

In each group below select the word or expression that most clearly expresses the meaning of the word at the left.

1. verbatim   (*a*) prolixity (*b*) word for word
                (*c*) verbosity (*d*) wit

2. surmise   (*a*) conjecture   (*b*) conquest
                       (*c*) vulnerability   (*d*) perception

3. surreptitious   (*a*) narrow-minded   (*b*) treacherous
                       (*c*) of ill repute   (*d*) clandestine

4. temerity   (*a*) rash boldness   (*b*) fearfulness
                       (*c*) circumspection   (*d*) awe

5. vagary   (*a*) wandering   (*b*) idea   (*c*) caprice
                       (*d*) practical joke

II. Words in Context

One-Word Omissions

In each of the following sentences substitute for the blank an appropriate word from Words 426-450 (including derivatives) from the Basic Vocabulary List.

1. No one could deny that one of the factors involved in saving the tract of forest land for use as a national park was the _____ argument of the conservationists.

2. Until the facts are studied further, any attempts to deal with the problems of today's cities can be only _____.

3. We must give the city council some _____ evidence of the success of our program before they will allot us any more money.

4. The disease germs of cholera are highly _____.

5. I do not love the country in winter. From November to April I prefer a(n) _____ life.

III. Relative Forms

Give a noun form for each of the following adjectives.

     1. vitiate   4. taciturn
     2. turgid   5. trite
     3. trenchant   6. surreptitious

WORD BUILDING

I. PREFIX

The Latin prefix **sub-**, "under" is a source element in many English words, including *surreptitious*.

> *submerge* — to put under or plunge into water
> *subjacent* — lying under

II. ROOT

The Latin root **tang- tact-** is a source of *tangible* studied in this lesson.

> *tactile* — pertaining to the sense of touch
> *tangent* — touching

EXERCISES

I. Word Building Activities

1. *Define and illustrate the part the prefix* **sub** *plays in the meaning of each of the following words.*

   subconscious subjugate subterfuge subversion subscribe

2. *Define the following words in the light of their Latin root.*

   tact attain contingent contiguous contagion

II. Fun With Words

The Story Behind the Phrase

Certain phrases have become part of idiomatic expression in our language because they were originally used in connection with notable exploits or stories of universal interest. Consider, as an example, the phrase "his Achilles' heel." This phrase recalls the incident in Homer's *Iliad* in which Achilles' mother, in obedience to the prophecy that if she submerged her son in the waters of the Styx he would be rendered invulnerable against death by the hands of his enemies. Accordingly, holding the baby by the heel she submerged him into the Styx, but she did not realize that he would not be invulnerable at the heel since this part of his body did not receive the anti-death treatment. Thus the only way Achilles could be wounded mortally was by a decisive blow at his heel. Paris successfully wounded him by an arrow shot in the heel. The expression "Achilles' heel" is a current expression meaning a person's vulnerable spot.

A. Historical Allusions

Under Column A you will find an expression with a long-standing legend or history and is often employed to describe a human trait or a human condition. Under Column B is a list of proper names to each of which may be traced the link to the expression in A. (a) Give the meaning of each phrase in A and recount the story behind it. (b) Match each phrase in A with the appropriate name in B that is the central character in the story.

A	B
1. the kiss of death	(a) Satan
2. the Midas touch	(b) Judas
3. forbidden fruit	(c) Mona Lisa
4. the Gioconda smile	(d) A king of ancient times

B. Word Ancestors

Below, you will find a list of words each of which is now used in ordinary speech. Give (a) the meaning of each word, (b) the name of the person from which each is derived and tell the story behind the word.

boycott	mausoleum
epicure	macadam
dunce	galvanize
martinet	lynch
guillotine	protean

FINAL TEST

Words Out of Context

A. Meanings

In each group below, select the word or expression that most clearly expresses the meaning of the word at the left.

1. **adamant**   (*a*) resilient   (*b*) audacious (*c*) execrable   (*d*) obdurate

2. **badger**   (*a*) baffle   (*b*) banter (*c*) harass   (*d*) backlash

3. **chauvinist**   (*a*) zealous partisan   (*b*) mountebank (*c*) philanthropist   (*d*) activist

4. **diffident**   (*a*) dissident   (*b*) antagonistic (*c*) distraught   (*d*) reserved

5. **emulate**   (*a*) feign   (*b*) elicit   (*c*) disparage (*d*) try to equal or excel

6. **furtive**   (*a*) clandestine   (*b*) seditious (*c*) esoteric   (*d*) modest

7. **garish**   (*a*) peevish   (*b*) fatuous (*c*) excessively showy   (*d*) maudlin

8. **judicious**   (*a*) unbiased   (*b*) discreet (*c*) equitable   (*d*) pertaining to law

9. **lurid**   (*a*) sensationally vivid   (*b*) attractive (*c*) obscene   (*d*) propitious

10. **murky**   (*a*) muddy   (*b*) impertinent (*c*) dark   (*d*) dull

11. **nebulous**   (*a*) ethereal   (*b*) fetid   (*c*) stellar (*d*) hazy

12. **opportune**   (*a*) mercenary   (*b*) expedient (*c*) nefarious   (*d*) relevant

13. **pejorative**   (*a*) rescinding   (*b*) paradoxical (*c*) peremptory   (*d*) depreciative

14. **quixotic** (*a*) curious (*b*) ludicrous
(*c*) incongruous
(*d*) extravagantly impracticable

15. **rancor** (*a*) foul smell (*b*) bitter ill-will
(*c*) stridency (*d*) pique

B. Synonyms and Antonyms

*In each group below select the two words that are either
(a) synonyms or (b) antonyms.*

1. (*a*) incipient (*b*) acerb (*c*) embryonic (*d*) motley

2. (*a*) euphony (*b*) eulogy (*c*) cacophony (*d*) dearth

3. (*a*) deleterious (*b*) baleful (*c*) lugubrious
(*d*) baneful

4. (*a*) effrontery (*b*) dereliction (*c*) magnanimity
(*d*) avarice

5. (*a*) escalate (*b*) fluctuate (*c*) coruscate
(*d*) augment

C. Analogies

Complete the following analogies.

1. gregarious : introvert = (*a*) ivory tower : hermit
(*b*) unsociable : extrovert (*c*) vacillating : convert
(*d*) independent : nomad

2. campaign : fiasco = (*a*) investment : bankruptcy
(*b*) climax : tragedy (*c*) virtuoso : pejorative
(*d*) perplexity : dilemma

3. feign : fain = (*a*) pretend : subtend (*b*) reign : rain
(*c*) deceive : perceive (*d*) grate : great

4. emulate : exemplary = (*a*) imitate : inimitable
(*b*) expunge : deleterious (*c*) disdain : wicked
(*d*) eschew : digestible

5. cliché : banal = (*a*) bon mot : witty (*b*) maxim :
platitudinous (*c*) proverb : instructive
(*d*) precept : epigrammatical

BASIC WORD LIST

The following tabulation contains all of the words in the Basic Word List (printed here in *italics*). In addition, most of the supplementary words introduced in connection with the discussion and exercises are listed. The numbers refer to the pages on which the words will be found. The *italicized numbers* indicate the pages on which the basic words are discussed in detail.

436

gingerly, 145
gluttonous, 3, 74
gnostic, 24
goad, 1
gourmand, 249
gourmet, 249
gracious, 167, 189
grave, 32
gravitate, 32
greed, 92, 186
gregarious, 285
grievous, 32
grimace, 286
gross 230
groveling, 2
Grundyism, 190
guile, 228
guileless, 117
guilty, 185
gull, 228

hackneyed, 94, 286, 422
haggard, 287
harangue 294
harbinger, 285
harmony, 41, 43, 112
harrow, 93, 295
harry, 93
haughty, 2, 114, 296
hauteur 296
headlong, 145
headstrong, 19, 227, 296
hedonist, 74
heedless, 145
heighten, 1, 22, 41, 76
heinous, 280, 297
herculean, 297
heresiarch, 298
heresy, 298
hermit, 74
hiatus, 298
hibernate, 299
hidebound, 112
hideous, 160
highfalutin, 114
high-handed, 60
hilarious, 299
histrionic, 299
histrionics, 300
hoax, 300
Hobson's Choice, 214
holocaust, 140
homely, 160
honorarium, 232
hoodwink, 228, 300
hoot, 21
horns of dilemma, 215
hubbub, 146
hue, 300
hue and cry, 146, 301
humane, 95, 147
humanitarian, 130
humble, 114, 213
humbug, 132
hybrid, 301

hyperbole, 301
hypercritical, 130, 306

icon, 229
iconoclast, 38, 230
idealistic, 188
idiosyncrasy, 302
idolize, 186
ignominy, 302
illicit, 231, 303
illiterate, 366
illusion, 392
immaculate, 310
immodest, 209
immutable, 310
impasse, 189, 311
impeccable, 311
impecunious, 211
impediment, 94, 312
impedimenta, 312
impel, 148
impenitent, 167
imperious, 60, 227, 377
impervious, 18, 312
implacable 312
implicate, 238
impostor, 132
imposture, 228
imprudent, 145, 209
impugn, 6, 163, 182, 313
impunity, 313
inane, 313
inarticulate, 306, 314
in camera, 286
incarcerate, 314
incendiary, 315
incense, 315
incipient, 139, 315
incognito, 315
incompatibility, 5, 44
incongruous, 316
incriminate, 6
inculpate, 6
incumbent, 316
indictment, 15, 33, 163
indigenous, 222, 233, 255
indigent, 211, 255, 317
indiscreet, 145, 317
indoctrinate, 239
indolent, 75, 163, 175
indomitable, 317
inductive reasoning, 325
indulgent, 3, 78
indurate, 115
ineducable, 227
inelastic, 306
inept, 166, 213
inert, 75, 229, 324
inexorable, 18, 147, 324
inference, 166, 325
infidel, 24
ingenious, 326
ingenuous, 117, 326
ingratiate, 326
ink, 131, 140

inordinate, 326
inscrutable, 327
insidious, 327
insipid, 94, 328
interject, 12
interrogate, 222
intervene, 155
intractable, 129, 227
intramural, 336
intransigent, 227
intrepid, 328
intrinsic, 329
introspective, 336
introverted, 269
inured, 115
inveigh, 329
inveigle, 115, 329
inveterate, 330
irascible, 75, 330
irony, 331
ivory tower, 286

jabberwocky, 126
jaunty, 332
jeer, 332
jejune, 94
jeopardize, 333
jet, 12
jetty, 12
jingoism, 132
jocund, 181, 189
jollity, 181
jostle, 333
judicial, 339
judicious, 145, 339
junto, 182

know-how, 165
knowledgeable, 165

laborious, 60
laconic, 340
languid, 40, 75
latent, 340
laud, 20, 216
laudable, 185, 341
laudatory, 130, 211, 216
leaflet, 113
lecturn, 142
leer, 412
lethargy, 57, 214, 229, 341
lethean, 341
levity, 48, 341
liable, 59
liberal, 227
liberality, 92, 112
light-hearted, 189
likely, 59
linsey-woolsey, 127
literal, 366
loan word, 142
loathing, 3, 55, 92
loquacious, 342
lucrative, 342
lucre, 342

437

perverse, 129
peruse, 161
pervade, 380
petulant, 129
pew, 142
phlegmatic, 229
phobia, 281
pianissimo, 413
pietistic, 23
pilfer, 232
pinched, 231
pinnacle, 184
pious, 23
pique, 383
piquant, 94, 384
pitiless, 147
placate, 57, 177
placid, 177
plagiarism, 384
plaintiff, 15
platitude, 147, 384
plebeian, 384
plethora, 385
pliable, 19
plight, 214
plump, 231
poise, 58, 216
polytheism, 33
pompous, 114
ponder, 161
portent, 370
portmanteau, 127
posthumous, 385
potent, 148, 229
potential, 340
practicable, 271
precipitate, 145
predicament, 33, 214
predilection, 93
pre-eminent, 166
premonition, 58
prerogative, 222
prescient, 380
presentiment, 58
presumptuous, 77, 114, 230
pretentious, 114
priggish, 209
prim, 209
precarious, 385
preclude, 385
precocious, 198, 386
precursor, 176, 386
predatory, 386
prelude, 387
prerogative, 387
prevaricate, 387
proclivity, 20, 56; 59, 93
procrastinate, 214, 388
prodigal, 92, 140
profuse, 182
prognosis, 33, 176
prognosticate, 176
prolific, 229, 388
prolix, 389
propel, 392

propensity, 20, 56, 389
propitiate, 57, 389
propriety, 77
proscribe, 55
prospect, 154
protest, 210
protracted, 187
protuberant, 389
provincial, 130
prowess, 390
prudish, 209
pseudo, 390
pseudonym, 390
psychotherapy, 65
puerile, 394
pugnacious, 22, 95, 129, 394
punctilious, 190, 210, 395
pundit, 165
pungent, 131, 395
puritan, 74
purloin, 232
purse-proud, 296
pusillanimous, 395

quack, 132
qualm, 58
quandary, 216
quell, 396
querulous, 396
quibble, 144, 270
quiescent, 229
quirk, 129

rabble, 129, 397
rabble rouser, 208, 397
raconteur, 397
rag-tag, 129
rancor, 95, 397
rank, 280
rapacious, 93, 186
rapport, 43
rapprochement, 43
raw-boned, 231
raze, 397
rebate, 1
recalcitrant, 190, 398
recant, 398
recede, 1, 2
recessive, 1
recipe, 139
recipient, 139
reckless, 76, 145
recluse, 74
recondite, 4, 251, 398
reconnaissance, 176
recur, 176
recusant, 298
redolence, 73, 163
redoubtable, 399
refractory, 399
refute, 182
relegate, 399
relentless, 18, 147
relevant, 148, 383
remonstrate, 210

remorse, 166, 167, 400
remuneration, 232, 400
renegade, 57, 400
renege, 401
repentant, 166
reprieve, 15
reprisal, 401
reproach, 20
reprove, 20, 130
repugnant, 3, 92
repulsive, 160
resilient, 221
respite, 299, 401
reticent, 401
retiring, 22, 213
retribution, 402
retrospect, 154
revert, 405
ribald, 402
riffraff, 129
rigorous, 78
ringleader, 208
ruminant, 406
ruminate, 406
rural, 41, 113, 114
rustic, 40

saccharine, 131
sacrament, 260, 417
sacrilegious, 406
sacristan, 261, 417
sacrosanct, 417
sagacity, 407
salient, 221, 407
sallow, 114
sally, 221, 407
salubrious, 408
salutary, 75, 207
sanction, 182, 210, 408
sanctions, 408
sanctity, 408
sanguine, 408
sanguinary, 408
sarcastic, 6, 131, 188
sardonic, 409
sartorial, 409
saturnine, 181, 409
schism, 42
scorn, 21, 167
scourge, 409
scruple, 208
scrutinize, 161, 410
scurrility, 167
Scylla, 215
secular, 38, 410
secularism, 410
sedate, 209, 410
sedative, 84, 410
sedentary, 84
sediment, 84
seduce, 330
sedulous, 75, 84, 411
segregate, 238
self-indulgent, 3, 74
self-opinionated, 227

440